New Music at Darmstadt

New Music at Darmstadt explores the rise and fall of the so-called 'Darmstadt School', through a wealth of primary sources and analytical commentary. Martin Iddon's book examines the creation of the Darmstadt New Music Courses and the slow development and subsequent collapse of the idea of the Darmstadt School, showing how participants in the West German new music scene, including Herbert Eimert and a range of journalistic commentators, created an image of a coherent entity, despite the very diverse range of compositional practices on display at the courses. The book also explores the collapse of the seeming collegiality of the Darmstadt composers, which crystallised around the arrival there in 1958 of the most famous, and notorious, of all post-war composers, John Cage, an event that, Carl Dahlhaus opined, 'swept across the European avant-garde like a natural disaster'.

MARTIN IDDON is Associate Professor of Music at the University of Leeds. He previously lectured at University College Cork and Lancaster University, and studied composition and musicology at the universities of Durham and Cambridge. His musicological research largely focusses on post-war music in Germany and the United States of America, and has been published in numerous leading journals, including *Musical Quarterly*, *twentieth-century music*, and *Contemporary Music Review*. His music has been performed in Europe, North America, and Australasia, and has been featured on BBC Radio 3, Radio New Zealand, and the Österreichischer Rundfunk.

Music Since 1900

GENERAL EDITOR Arnold Whittall

This series – formerly *Music in the Twentieth Century* – offers a wide perspective on music and musical life since the end of the nineteenth century. Books included range from historical and biographical studies concentrating particularly on the context and circumstances in which composers were writing, to analytical and critical studies concerned with the nature of musical language and questions of compositional process. The importance given to context will also be reflected in studies dealing with, for example, the patronage, publishing, and promotion of new music, and in accounts of the musical life of particular countries.

Titles in the series

Jonathan Cross
The Stravinsky Legacy

Michael Nyman
Experimental Music: Cage and Beyond

Jennifer Doctor
The BBC and Ultra-Modern Music, 1922–1936

Robert Adlington
The Music of Harrison Birtwistle

Keith Potter
Four Musical Minimalists: La Monte Young, Terry Riley, Steve Reich, Philip Glass

Carlo Caballero
Fauré and French Musical Aesthetics

Peter Burt
The Music of Toru Takemitsu

David Clarke
The Music and Thought of Michael Tippett: Modern Times and Metaphysics

M. J. Grant
Serial Music, Serial Aesthetics: Compositional Theory in Post-War Europe

Philip Rupprecht
Britten's Musical Language

Mark Carroll
Music and Ideology in Cold War Europe

Adrian Thomas
Polish Music since Szymanowski

J. P. E. Harper-Scott
Edward Elgar, Modernist

Yayoi Uno Everett
The Music of Louis Andriessen

Ethan Haimo
Schoenberg's Transformation of Musical Language

Rachel Beckles Willson
Ligeti, Kurtág, and Hungarian Music during the Cold War

Michael Cherlin
Schoenberg's Musical Imagination

Joseph N. Straus
Twelve-Tone Music in America

David Metzer
Musical Modernism at the Turn of the Twenty-First Century

Edward Campbell
Boulez, Music and Philosophy

Jonathan Goldman
The Musical Language of Pierre Boulez: Writings and Compositions

Pieter C. van den Toorn and John McGinness
Stravinsky and the Russian Period: Sound and Legacy of a Musical Idiom

David Beard
Harrison Birtwistle's Operas and Music Theatre

Heather Wiebe
Britten's Unquiet Pasts: Sound and Memory in Postwar Reconstruction

Beate Kutschke and Barley Norton
Music and Protest in 1968

Graham Griffiths
Stravinsky's Piano: Genesis of a Musical Language

Martin Iddon
John Cage and David Tudor: Correspondence on Interpretation and Performance

Martin Iddon
New Music at Darmstadt: Nono, Stockhausen, Cage, and Boulez

New Music at Darmstadt

Nono, Stockhausen, Cage, and Boulez

Martin Iddon

CAMBRIDGE
UNIVERSITY PRESS

University Printing House, Cambridge CB2 8BS, United Kingdom

Published in the United States of America by Cambridge University Press, New York

Cambridge University Press is part of the University of Cambridge.

It furthers the University's mission by disseminating knowledge in the pursuit of education, learning and research at the highest international levels of excellence.

www.cambridge.org
Information on this title: www.cambridge.org/9781107033290

© Martin Iddon 2013

This publication is in copyright. Subject to statutory exception and to the provisions of relevant collective licensing agreements, no reproduction of any part may take place without the written permission of Cambridge University Press.

First published 2013

A catalogue record for this publication is available from the British Library

Library of Congress Cataloguing in Publication data
Iddon, Martin, 1975–
New music at Darmstadt : Nono, Stockhausen, Cage, and Boulez / Martin Iddon.
    p. cm. – (Music since 1900)
Includes bibliographical references and index.
ISBN 978-1-107-03329-0
1. Music – Germany – Darmstadt – 20th century – History and criticism.   2. Nono, Luigi – Criticism and interpretation.   3. Stockhausen, Karlheinz, 1928–2007 – Criticism and interpretation.   4. Cage, John – Criticism and interpretation.   5. Boulez, Pierre, 1925 – Criticism and interpretation   I. Title.
ML275.8.D35I43   2013
780.943′41670904–dc23   2012034204

ISBN 978-1-107-03329-0 Hardback

Cambridge University Press has no responsibility for the persistence or accuracy of URLs for external or third-party internet websites referred to in this publication, and does not guarantee that any content on such websites is, or will remain, accurate or appropriate.

Contents

List of musical examples   *page* viii
List of figures   ix
List of tables   x
Preface   xi
Chronology of major events at Darmstadt, 1949–61   xv
List of abbreviations   xxiii

Introduction: Music after catastrophe   1

Part I   The accidental serialists   33

1   Arrivals   35

2   Schools   110

     Excursus: October 1954, Donaueschingen and Cologne   156

Part II Chance encounters   165

3   Precursors   167

4   The Cage shock   196

5   In Cage's wake   229

     Conclusion: A stranger in paradise?   300

Bibliography   304
Index   324

Musical examples

1.1 Luigi Nono, *Variazioni canoniche*, bb. 153–64   *page* 41
1.2 Luigi Nono, *Polifonica–Monodia–Ritmica*, bb. 63–72   46
1.3 Heptachords in Karel Goeyvaerts, Sonata for Two Pianos, second movement   54
1.4 Disposition of heptachords in Karel Goeyvaerts, Sonata for Two Pianos, second movement   54
1.5 Pitch values in Karel Goeyvaerts, Sonata for Two Pianos, second movement   55
1.6 Karel Goeyvaerts, Sonata for Two Pianos, second movement, bb. 1–8   56
1.7 Source melodic line in Luigi Nono, 'Tarde'   78
1.8 Luigi Nono, 'Tarde', bb. 1–5   78
1.9 Dispersal of pitches from underlying skeleton in Karlheinz Stockhausen, Klavierstück III   105
2.1 Bruno Maderna, *Quartetto per archi in due tempi*, bb. 1–10   121
2.2 Pitch and rhythm series of Anton Webern, Variations, op. 30   142
2.3 Nono's mirror of rhythmic elements in Anton Webern, Variations, op. 30   142

Figures

1.1 Rhythmic 'series' of Luigi Nono, *Variazioni canoniche*   page 40
1.2 Rhythmic permutations in Luigi Nono, *Polifonica–Monodia–Ritmica*   45
1.3 Synthetic number values in Karel Goeyvaerts, Sonata for Two Pianos, second movement   55
1.4 Blumröder's table of pitch 'crossings' in the first part of Karlheinz Stockhausen, *Kreuzspiel*   74
1.5 Blumröder's table of octave dispositions in the first part of Karlheinz Stockhausen, *Kreuzspiel*   75
1.6 Blumröder's table of rhythm distribution by pitch class in the first part of Karlheinz Stockhausen, *Kreuzspiel*   75
1.7 Transformation of interval to duration in Luigi Nono, 'Tarde'   77
1.8 Derivation of rhythmic line from intervallic content in Luigi Nono, 'Tarde'   77
1.9 Blumröder's table of pitch distribution and proportions in Karlheinz Stockhausen, Klavierstück III   105

Tables

1.1 Sketch formal outline of Karel Goeyvaerts, Sonata for Two Pianos, second movement *page* 55
1.2 Core permutations in Luigi Nono, 'Tarde' 76
1.3 Displacement array in Bruno Maderna, *Musica su due dimensioni* 79
1.4 Serial arrays 1–4 in Bruno Maderna, *Musica su due dimensioni* 80
2.1 Magic square for Bruno Maderna, *Quartetto per archi in due tempi* 122
2.2 Row dispersal in Bruno Maderna, *Quartetto per archi in due tempi*, first movement 123

Preface

This volume is a study of the reception of new music, principally that which has been described as total (or, better, multiple) serialism, at Darmstadt from the foundation of the new music courses in that city through to the death of its first director, Wolfgang Steinecke, in 1961, following too the breakdown of perceptions of the centrality of serialism at Darmstadt after the visit of John Cage to the courses in 1958.

The volume opens with a lengthy introduction, which seeks to explain the very particular social and historical climate in which it was possible for the Darmstadt New Music Courses to come into being at all and, vitally, aims to give some flavour of the ways in which Steinecke operated (and, arguably, had to operate). Since these economic and political concerns cease to represent a major factor in the continuation of the courses from this point onwards, coverage of such issues is confined to the Introduction. Especially in these early years, the contingencies of pre-currency-reform – and, perforce, pre-*Wirtschaftswunder* – West Germany are to the fore: this introduction also shows the courses move from a situation which was, broadly, hand-to-mouth to one in which they had become, for the most part, financially stable on a continuing basis.

The central two large parts of the volume overlap: the first examines the history of the new music courses from the perspective of the development of serial trends, broadly conceived, until 1957; the second looks at the arrival of John Cage on the European scene, beginning with Wolfgang Rebner's lecture on American music at the 1954 courses, and leading up to the end of the first era of the Darmstadt courses in 1961. This is, then, the period often thought of as the 'golden age' of Darmstadt, the era of the 'Darmstadt School' and of Boulez, Maderna, Nono, and Stockhausen at the head of the courses. The characterisation is not wholly without foundation but, as I hope this volume will show, the situation at Darmstadt was certainly much more complex and fluid.

I seek, then, to achieve several, relatively modest ends. First, I aim to suggest that the idea that the name Darmstadt should be held to stand for a 'citadel of the avant-garde', as Brigitte Schiffer would later have it,[1] under the sign of multiple serialism, is one which requires more attention. Part I of

---

[1] Brigitte Schiffer, 'The Citadel of the Avant-Garde', *World of Music*, vol. 11, no. 3 (1969), 32–43.

this volume endeavours to show that, on the one hand, what composers were actually doing in compositional terms across the 1950s can only occasionally be viewed as being part of a generalised, or generalisable, trajectory and that, although pre-compositional planning played its part, multiple serialism was almost certainly not a single thing and was, in any case, not characterised by the almost literal transcription of numerical conceits. On the other hand, Part I suggests that the idea of unity amongst a small group of composers (often regarded as a 'sect' or a 'cult' at the time) was the product of a particular press reception, encouraged by, not least, Herbert Eimert. This last aspect of the enquiry in Part I contains the proposition that Eimert used the young Darmstadt composers as symbolic tokens in a dispute which tacitly developed between him and Theodor W. Adorno regarding the 'proper' course of new music after the end of World War II, a debate which bifurcated into a second dispute between Adorno and the critic Heinz-Klaus Metzger regarding the ethical dimensions of post-war music (and questions of what Adorno may actually have known of it). Finally, as a consequence of the above, Part I aims to demonstrate that, on the level of prominence and institutional authority, the earliest point at which one can speak of a 'Darmstadt School' is 1955; the latest is 1957, the year before Cage's arrival, which has been held to represent the symbolic end of that notion. In a sense, by 1958, there was no serial orthodoxy to vanquish, only the discourse which surrounded it.

Second, in Part II, I endeavour to show that, while the perception that it was Cage, in part at least, who brought an end to the idea of the 'Darmstadt School' is at root correct, Cage's presence at Darmstadt operated in a way not wholly dissimilar to the ways in which Boulez, Nono, and Stockhausen (particularly, though not exclusively) were construed. This is to say that, ultimately, it was not Cage's music that was at stake – even if dividing lines were drawn according to whether one thought that one had to improvise in order to perform Cage's music – but rather Cage's words: these were used to construct a particular image of Cage, a totem, which often had little to do with how Cage presented himself and much more to do with local musico-political issues. If it was Eimert who was most obviously (if probably inadvertently) responsible for the foundation of the idea which led to the creation of the 'Darmstadt School', it was Cage's primary translator into German, Heinz-Klaus Metzger, who turned Cage into a class fighter. Indeed, Metzger was at the heart of much of the Darmstadt debate around Cage, translating and/or delivering lectures by Boulez and Stockhausen, too, in the second half of the 1950s, as well as having polemicised against Adorno earlier. Finally, I propose that the effects of Cage's visit might be fruitfully understood utilising a principally sociological framework, viewing

Preface

him as operating like a 'stranger' in the sense in which Zygmunt Bauman uses the word.[2]

While we were co-editing an issue of *Contemporary Music Review* devoted to the Darmstadt New Music Courses, Paul Attinello hit upon the propitious title for that volume, *Other Darmstadts*. In the writing of this rather more substantial contribution to the scholarship surrounding the Darmstadt New Music Courses, it has become clear to me that, in a sense, any narrative that seeks to tell a story of new music in Darmstadt is necessarily a story of a certain 'other Darmstadt'. Even in a volume on the scale of the present one, which is ostensibly a history of Darmstadt's 'golden age' in the 1950s, I am aware that the tale that is told here is parlously partial. The voices of performers, with the notable exception of the pianist David Tudor, are largely absent. Likewise, though I stress that the idea of a Darmstadt dominated by serialism of various hues throughout the 1950s is erroneous, I nevertheless concentrate on the ways in which the composers who became known as the 'Darmstadt School' came to prominence on that stage. This is, to be sure, at the expense of composers from outside Western Europe and North America; there remains much to be said regarding the position of composers from Eastern Europe, South America, and Asia at Darmstadt. My account, too, is 'under the surface' the story of Darmstadt under its first director, Wolfgang Steinecke. The matters discussed here, as I hint at various points, continued to be of significance at Darmstadt during the tenure of its second director, Ernst Thomas, and a comprehensive account of the Thomas era remains to be written. I hope that, as well as achieving the aims it sets itself, the volume may also spur others to think that there is, still, more to be written on the subject of Darmstadt.

In the writing of a volume of this length, inevitably one owes thanks to a great many people, for a great many things: Roger Parker, almost certainly without realising it, set me off on the path to investigate Darmstadt, now more than a decade ago; Georgina Born, John Butt, and Ian Cross all offered invaluable advice on my doctoral thesis, which concentrated on the new music courses in the 1970s; the Deutscher Akademischer Austauschdienst funded my initial trips to the Internationales Musikinstitut Darmstadt during my doctoral studies; more latterly, the British Academy and the Arts and Humanities Research Council supported the research by providing generous funding which allowed the initial archival research to be undertaken and a year's sabbatical to be taken for the writing of the present volume; Arnold Whittall and Vicki Cooper have offered extremely useful help and advice throughout the process of developing the volume for

---

[2] See Zygmunt Bauman, *Postmodernity and its Discontents* (Cambridge: Polity, 1997), 17–34.

Cambridge University Press, as did the anonymous reviewers of earlier drafts of the text which appears here; former colleagues at Lancaster and current colleagues at Leeds have been generous in their support during periods of research leave devoted to this project; Jeanette Casey, D. J. Hoek, Jürgen Krebber, Nancy Perloff, and Mark Zelesky have between them made visits to the various archives drawn on in this study as pleasurable as they were fruitful; I am grateful to the Internationales Musikinstitut Darmstadt for permission to quote from correspondence held there, as well as to the John Cage Trust, the heirs of Luigi Nono, the David Tudor Trust, and Pierre Boulez for permission to quote from their correspondence, as well as to Christoph von Blumröder for permission to make use of his analytical examples in respect of Stockhausen's *Kreuzspiel* and Klavierstück III; Pierre Boulez, Gottfried Michael Koenig, Helmut Lachenmann, Wilhelm Schlüter, and Otto Tomek consented to be interviewed for this project and, though their verbatim words do not appear in the text, numerous insights they gave inform what is presented here in significant ways; I owe a debt of thanks to Dan Wilson for his help in setting many of the examples within the volume; I have benefited immeasurably from discussions with colleagues working on subjects related to my own, not least Paul Attinello, Markus Bandur, Amy C. Beal, Gianmario Borio, Geoff Chew, Jan Christaens, Mark Delaere, Jenny Doctor, Christopher Fox, Björn Heile, Rainer Nonnenmann, Irna Priore, Christopher Shultis, and Marcus Zagorski. Trevor Bača, Mark Barden, John Fallas, Fabrice Fitch, Lois Fitch, Adam Greig, Roddy Hawkins, Eleri Pound, Ian H. Power, Antti Saario, Mic Spencer, Ed Venn, and Fredrik Wallberg have all had to endure more conversations than is in any way reasonable regarding Darmstadt over many years: as well as earning my gratitude for their forbearance and friendship, they have, perhaps unwittingly, contributed to the thought presented in the current volume; across the course of writing, I have benefited immensely from the advice and support of Ian Pace, who has pointed me in the direction of a wide variety of archival sources that I would not otherwise have encountered: no less valuable than the sharing of resources has been the sharing of ideas, however, and for many long discussions, I am hugely grateful; last, but in no sense least, I owe a huge debt of thanks, first, to my parents, without whom this work would not have been started, and, second, to my wife Kate, without whom it would certainly not have been finished: it is dedicated to all three, with love.

Chronology of major events at Darmstadt, 1949–61

This chronology highlights only those events which are of direct relevance to the present volume. More comprehensive chronologies of events at the Darmstadt New Music Courses may be found in Gianmario Borio and Hermann Danuser (eds.), *Im Zenit der Moderne* (Freiburg im Breisgau: Rombach, 1997), vol. III, 513–638; Markus Grassl and Reinhard Kapp (eds.), *Darmstadt-Gespräche* (Vienna: Böhlau, 1996), 271–339; and Antonio Trudu, *La 'scuola' di Darmstadt* (Milan: Unicopli, 1992), 349–71.

1949
9 July performance: Bruno Maderna, Fantasia for two pianos (Carl Seeman, Peter Stadlen)

1950
26 August performance: Bruno Maderna, *Composizione II* for chamber orchestra (Darmstadt Landestheater Orchestra, dir. Hermann Scherchen)
27 August performance: Luigi Nono, *Variazioni canoniche sulla serie dell'op. 41 di Arnold Schoenberg* (Darmstadt Landestheater Orchestra, dir. Hermann Scherchen)

1951
Course: Theodor W. Adorno, 'Working Group for Free Composition'
26 June lecture: Antoine Goléa, 'Die Situation der Neuen Musik in Frankreich' (included recording of Oliver Messiaen, *Mode de valeurs et d'intensités*)
2 July performance: Arnold Schoenberg, 'Der Tanz um das goldene Kalb', from *Moses und Aron* (Ruth Wilke (sop.), Petra Boser (alt.), Franz Köth and Heinz Janssen (ten.), Willibald Vohla (bar.); choir of the Darmstadt Landestheater with assistance from the Darmstadt Music Society; Darmstadt Landestheater Orchestra, dir. Hermann Scherchen)
4 July lecture: Theodor W. Adorno, 'Anton Webern'
8 July performance: Karel Goeyvaerts, *Music for Violin, Contralto, and Piano* (Werner Neuhaus (vln), Erika Bollweg (alt.), Heribert Esser (pno)
9 July lecture: Robert Beyer, 'Musik und Technik'

Lecture:	Werner Meyer-Eppler, 'Möglichkeiten der elektronischen Klangerzeugung'
10 July lecture:	Pierre Schaeffer, 'La musique concrète'
Performance:	Pierre Henry and Pierre Schaeffer, *Symphonie pour un homme seul*
	Pierre Henry and Pierre Schaeffer, *Orphée 51*
Performance:	Luigi Nono, *Polifonica–Monodia–Ritmica* (Darmstadt Landestheater Orchestra, dir. Hermann Scherchen)

1952

19 July performance:	Pierre Boulez, Second Piano Sonata (Yvonne Loriod)
20 July performance:	Karel Goeyvaerts, Second Violin Concerto (André Gertler (vln), Darmstadt Landestheater Orchestra, dir. Hermann Scherchen)
21 July lectures:	Herbert Eimert, 'Probleme der elektronischen Musik'
	Werner Meyer-Eppler, 'Vorführung von Klangmodellen'
	Antoine Goléa, 'Einführung in die Musique concrète'
	Pierre Boulez, 'Commentary on the Following Pieces':
Performance:	Pierre Henry, *Antiphonie*
	Pierre Boulez, *Deux études concrète*s
	Olivier Messiaen, *Timbres-durées*
	Pierre Schaeffer, *Maskerage*
Performance:	Camillo Togni, *Omaggio a Bach* (Gerd Kämper and Camillo Togni (pno))
	Jacques Wildberger, Quartet (Hans Mertens (flt.), Sigmar Rosokowsky (clt), Kurt Christian Stier (vln), Werner Huth (vcl.))
	Karlheinz Stockhausen, *Kreuzspiel* (Romolo Grano (ob.), Friedrich Wildgans (bs clt), Irmela Sand (pno), Hans Roßmann, Bruno Maderna, Willy Trupfheller, Paul Geppert (perc.), dir. Karlheinz Stockhausen)
	Bruno Maderna, *Musica su due dimensioni* (Severino Gazzelloni (flt.), Romolo Grano (perc.))
	Luigi Nono, *España en el corazón* (Gabrille Dumaine (sop.), Hans Hildenbrandt (bar.); faculty members and students of the Darmstadt New Music Courses, as well as members of the Darmstadt

Chronology of major events at Darmstadt, 1949–61   xvii

	Landestheater Orchestra, dir. Bruno Maderna)
1953	
23 July performance:	Anton Webern, Six Bagatelles, op. 9 (Cologne String Quartet: Wolfgang Marschner (vln 1), Günther Krone (vln 2), Ernst Sandfort (vla), Maurits Frank (vcl.))
	Anton Webern, Three Short Pieces, op. 11 (Maurits Frank (vcl.), Else Stock (pno))
	Anton Webern, Three Lieder, op. 23 (Ilona Steingruber (sop.), Else Stock (pno))
	Anton Webern, Four Pieces, op. 7 (Rudolf Kolisch (vln), Allan Willman (pno))
	Anton Webern, Five Movements, op. 5 (Cologne String Quartet)
	With introductory texts from Herbert Eimert, Luigi Nono, Karlheinz Stockhausen, Karel Goeyvaerts (*in absentia*), and Pierre Boulez (*in absentia*)
24 July discussion:	Antoine Goléa (moderator), Hermann Heiß, Bruno Maderna, and Olivier Messiaen, 'Positionen und Möglichkeiten der Neuen Musik heute'
	Including recording of Pierre Boulez, *Polyphonie X*; Karlheinz Stockhausen, *Kontra-Punkte*; Luigi Nono, *Y su sangre ya viene cantando*
28 July lecture:	Werner Meyer-Eppler, 'Die akustischen Grundlagen der elektronischen Musik'
Lecture:	Herbert Eimert, 'Die kompositorischen Grundlagen der elektronischen Musik'
30 July performance:	Bruno Maderna, *Quattro lettere* (Ilona Steingruber (sop.), Heinz Rehfuß (bass), faculty members and students of the Darmstadt New Music Courses, as well as members of the Darmstadt Landestheater Orchestra, dir. Bruno Maderna)
1954	
Course:	Bruno Maderna and Giselher Klebe, 'International Working Group of Young Composers'
13 August lecture:	Edward Wolfgang Rebner, 'Amerikanische Experimentalmusik (mit musikalischen Beispielen von Charles Ives, Edgard Varèse, Henry Cowell, John Cage u.a.)'
17 August performance:	Pierre Boulez, Second Piano Sonata, first movement (Yvonne Loriod)

18 August performance:	Henri Pousseur, *Trois chants sacrés* (Jeanne Aldridge (sop.), Hans Otto Spingel (vln), Clemens Graf (vla), Wolfgang Erpenbeck (vcl.))
21 August performance:	Michel Fano, Sonata I (Astrid and Hansotto Schmidt Neuhaus (pno))
	Karlheinz Stockhausen, Klavierstücke I–V (Marcelle Mercenier (pno))
22 August performance:	Bruno Maderna, Flute Concerto (Severino Gazzelloni (flt.), Symphony Orchestra of the Hessischer Rundfunk, dir. Ernest Bour)
25 August performance:	Luigi Nono, *La Victoire de Guernica* (Symphony Orchestra and Choir of the Hessischer Rundfunk, dir. Hermann Scherchen)

1955

Course:	Pierre Boulez, Hans Werner Henze, and Bruno Maderna, 'International Working Group of Young Composers'
30 May performance:	Luigi Nono, *Incontri* (Symphony Orchestra of the Südwestfunk, Baden-Baden, dir. Hans Rosbaud)
1 June performance:	Bruno Maderna, *Quartetto per archi in due tempi* (Drolc Quartet)
	Karlheinz Stockhausen, Klavierstücke V–VIII (Marcelle Mercenier (pno))
2 June lecture:	Pierre Boulez, 'Claude Debussy et Anton Webern'
Performance:	Pierre Boulez, *Structures*, book 1 (Yvonne Loriod and Hans Alexander Kaul (pno))

1956

Courses:	Pierre Boulez, 'Working Group on Composition and Analysis'
	Bruno Maderna, 'Working Group on Conducting and Realisation'
	David Tudor, 'Working Group on Pianistic Realisation'
12 July performance:	Stefan Wolpe, Passacaglia (David Tudor (pno))
Performance:	Luigi Nono, *Canti per 13* (Symphony Orchestra of the Hessischer Rundfunk, dir. Otto Mazerath)
15 July performance:	Pierre Boulez, Flute Sonatine (Severino Gazzelloni (flt.), David Tudor (pno))
18 July performance:	Karlheinz Stockhausen, Klavierstücke V–VIII (David Tudor (pno))
	Bruno Maderna, *Quartetto per archi in due tempi* (Quatuor Parrenin)
	Pierre Boulez, *Le Marteau sans maître* (Beate Klostermann (alt.), Karl Heinz Ulrich (alt. flt.),

Chronology of major events at Darmstadt, 1949–61

	Clemens Graf (vla), Karl Heinz Böttner (gtr), Christoph Caskel (vibr.) Hans Erman (xylorimba), Peter Michels (perc.))
19 July lecture:	Stefan Wolpe, 'Über neue – und nicht so neue – Musik in Amerika' (with assistance from David Tudor)
Performance:	Karlheinz Stockhausen, *Gesang der Jünglinge*

1957

Courses:	Henri Pousseur, 'Anton Weberns Gesamtwerk'
	Luigi Nono, 'Schoenbergs Kompositionstechnik'
	Karlheinz Stockhausen, 'Analyse neuer Werke'
18 July performance:	Pierre Boulez, Flute Sonatine (Severino Gazzelloni (flt.), Aloys Kontarsky (pno))
19 July lecture:	Theodor W. Adorno, 'Kriterien der neuen Musik I'
20 July lecture:	Theodor W. Adorno, 'Kriterien der neuen Musik II'
22 July lecture:	Karlheinz Stockhausen, 'Der neue Instrumentalstil'
Performance:	Karlheinz Stockhausen, *Zeitmasse* (Wind Quintet of the Kölner Rundfunk Symphony Orchestra: Hans-Jürgen Möhring (flt.), Wilhelm Meyer (ob.), Richard Hartung (cor anglais), Paul Blöcher (clt), Karl Weiß (bsn))
23 July lecture:	Luigi Nono, 'Die Entwicklung der Reihentechnik'
24 July lecture:	Pierre Boulez, 'Alea' (translated into German and read by Heinz-Klaus Metzger)
25 July lecture:	Karlheinz Stockhausen, 'Musik und Sprache'
26 July lecture:	Theodor W. Adorno, 'Kriterien der neuen Musik III'
27 July lecture:	Theodor W. Adorno, 'Kriterien der neuen Musik IV'
Performance:	Earle Brown, *Music for Cello and Piano* (Werner Taube (vcl.), Alfons Kontarsky (pno))
28 July performance:	Karlheinz Stockhausen, Klavierstück XI (Paul Jacobs (pno))

1958

Courses:	John Cage, 'Composition as Process'
	Bruno Maderna, 'Der neue Instrumentalstil'
3 September performance:	John Cage, *Music for Two Pianos*
	Earle Brown, *Four Systems*
	Morton Feldman, *Two Pianos*
	John Cage, *Variations I*
	Christian Wolff, *Duo for Pianists I*
	John Cage, *Winter Music*
	Christian Wolff, *Duo for Pianists II* (John Cage and David Tudor (pno))

4 September lecture:	Karlheinz Stockhausen, 'Musik im Raum'
6 September lecture:	John Cage, 'Changes', including performance of John Cage, *Music of Changes* (David Tudor (pno))
Performance:	Karlheinz Stockhausen, *Kontra-Punkte* (Domaine Musical, dir. Bruno Maderna)
7 September performance:	Luigi Nono, *Cori di Didone* (Kölner Rundfunk Choir, dir. Bernhard Zimmermann)
8 September lecture:	John Cage, 'Indeterminacy', including performances of Karlheinz Stockhausen, Klavierstück XI, and John Cage, *Variations I* (David Tudor (pno))
9 September lecture:	John Cage, 'Communication', including performances of Bo Nilsson, *Quantitäten*, and Christian Wolff, *For Prepared Piano* (David Tudor (pno))
Performance:	Pierre Boulez, *Le Soleil des eaux* (Symphony Orchestra and Choir of the Hessischer Rundfunk, dir. Ernest Bour)
11 September performance:	Earle Brown, *Pentathis* (David Tudor (pno), Domaine Musical, dir. Bruno Maderna)
12 September performance:	Luigi Nono, *Composizione per orchestra n. 1* (Darmstadt Landestheater Orchestra, dir. Hans Zanotelli)

1959

Pre-courses:	Luigi Nono and Karlheinz Stockhausen, composition
Main courses:	Luigi Nono and Karlheinz Stockhausen, composition
25 August performance:	Karlheinz Stockhausen, Klavierstück VI (David Tudor (pno))
	Pierre Boulez, First Piano Sonata (David Tudor (pno))
	Karlheinz Stockhausen, *Zyklus* (Christoph Caskel (perc.))
26 August lecture:	Karlheinz Stockhausen, 'Musik und Graphik I'
27 August lecture:	Karlheinz Stockhausen, 'Musik und Graphik II', including performance of Karlheinz Stockhausen, *Zyklus* (Christoph Caskel (perc.))
28 August lecture:	Karlheinz Stockhausen, 'Musik und Graphik III', including performance of Cornelius Cardew, *February Piece I* (Cornelius Cardew (pno)), and recording of John Cage, *Concert for Piano and Orchestra*
29 August lecture:	Karlheinz Stockhausen 'Musik und Graphik IV', including performances of Sylvano Bussotti, *Five*

Chronology of major events at Darmstadt, 1949–61

	Piano Pieces for David Tudor, Nos. 2, 3, and 5 (David Tudor (pno)) and Mauricio Kagel, *Transición II* (David Tudor (pno), Christoph Caskel (perc.), and Mauricio Kagel (sound engineer))
30 August lecture:	Pierre Boulez, 'Kommentar zur 3. Klaviersonate', including performance of Pierre Boulez, Third Piano Sonata (Pierre Boulez (pno))
31 August lecture:	Karlheinz Stockhausen, 'Musik und Graphik V', including performance of Mauricio Kagel, *Transición II* (David Tudor (pno), Christoph Caskel (perc.), and Mauricio Kagel (sound engineer))
1 September lecture:	Luigi Nono, 'Geschichte und Gegenwart in der Musik von heute', including performance of Earle Brown, *Hodograph I* (Severino Gazzelloni (flt.), David Tudor (pno, celesta), Christoph Caskel (orchestral bells, marimba)
2 September performance:	Bruno Maderna, Piano Concerto
	Luigi Nono, *Composizione per orchestra n. 2: Diario polacco '58* (David Tudor (pno), Symphony Orchestra of the Hessischer Rundfunk, dir. Bruno Maderna)
3 September performance:	Pierre Boulez, Flute Sonatine (Rainer Schuelein (flt.), Aloys Kontarsky (pno))
	Pierre Boulez, First Piano Sonata (Harald Bojé (pno))
	Pierre Boulez, First Piano Sonata (Erika Haase (pno))
	Karlheinz Stockhausen, *Zyklus* (Heinz Haedler (perc.))
	Karlheinz Stockhausen, *Zyklus* (Toni Roeder (perc.))
Performance:	Karlheinz Stockhausen, *Kreuzspiel* (Alfred Schweinfurter (ob.), Wolfgang Marx (bs clt), David Tudor (pno), Christoph Caskel, Heinz Haedler, Manfred Wehner (perc.), dir. Karlheinz Stockhausen)
	Cornelius Cardew, *Two Books of Study for Pianists* (Cornelius Cardew, Richard Rodney Bennett (pno))
4 September performance:	Mauricio Kagel, *Transición II*
	John Cage, *Aria* with *Fontana Mix*
	Bruno Maderna, *Musica su due dimensioni* (Cathy Berberian (mezz. sop.), Severino Gazzelloni (flt.),

David Tudor (pno), Christoph Caskel (perc.), Mauricio Kagel (sound engineer))

1960

7 July lecture:	Luigi Nono, 'Text–Musik–Gesang I', with recording of Arnold Schoenberg, *A Survivor from Warsaw*
8 July lecture:	Luigi Nono, 'Text–Musik–Gesang II', with recordings of Luigi Nono, *La terra e la compagna* and *Cori di Didone*
10 July performance:	Pierre Boulez, *Pli selon pli* (Eva Maria Rogner (sop.), Orchestra of the Südwestfunk, dir. Pierre Boulez)
13 July lecture:	Karlheinz Stockhausen, 'Vieldeutige Form', presented by, and with a commentary from, Heinz-Klaus Metzger

1961

4 September lecture:	Theodor W. Adorno, 'Vers une musique informelle I'
5 September lecture:	Theodor W. Adorno, 'Vers une musique informelle II'

Abbreviations

ALN Archivio Luigi Nono, Venice, Italy
GRI Getty Research Institute, Los Angeles, CA
IMD Internationales Musikinstitut Darmstadt
JCC John Cage Collection, Northwestern University, Evanston, IL
JCP John Cage Papers, Wesleyan University, Middletown, CT
SAD Stadtarchiv Darmstadt

Introduction

Music after catastrophe

Wolfgang Steinecke and Ludwig Metzger

The idea that music might form a counterpoint to aerial bombardment seems, perhaps, an idea that one might attach to conflicts after 1945, at its most obvious in the famous images of a devastating helicopter attack over a Vietnamese beach to the accompaniment of the 'Ride of the Valkyries' in Francis Ford Coppola's *Apocalypse Now* (1979). Yet, as Lepenies puts it, '[t]he music of Richard Strauss remained, in a curious way, a basso continuo to the ongoing work of the destruction of German cities.'[1] It was a particular Strauss, too: that of the nostalgic retreat into the Viennese past, as in *Der Rosenkavalier*. As one survivor recalled, on the evening before the air strike that would almost wholly destroy the city of Darmstadt, he 'listened to some songs on the radio from the sensuous world of the rococo, portrayed in Strauss's magical music'.[2] Similarly, on the night of the bombing raid which devastated Dresden, in a signal to the German fighter pilots who were already in the air to defend against an Allied air raid on an as yet unknown German city, the ground station broadcast waltzes from *Rosenkavalier*. The crew members, well educated in German culture, presumed that this meant the bombing raid was to take place over Vienna, the city of *Rosenkavalier*. By the time they realised that it was the city of *Rosenkavalier*'s première, Dresden, which was at risk, there was little hope of their turning back in time to help prevent the flattening of the city.[3]

The raid on Darmstadt, on the night between 11 and 12 September 1944, remembered locally as the 'Brandnacht', left the city in ruins. From the German perspective, Darmstadt had not been regarded as being at particular risk. Nevertheless, the presence of a major factory of the chemical and pharmaceutical giant Merck and the local technical university, which had trained experts in rocket technology who had worked on the V2 ballistic missile, meant that Darmstadt was listed in the British Ministry of Economic Warfare's *Guide to the Economic Importance of German Towns and Cities*. In

---

[1] Wolf Lepenies, *The Seduction of Culture in German History* (Princeton University Press, 2006), 2.
[2] W. G. Sebald, *Luftkrieg und Literatur* (Frankfurt: Fischer, 2005 [2001]), 49. An English translation of this volume is published as *The Natural History of Destruction*, tr. Anthea Bell (New York: Random House, 2003 [2001]).
[3] Lepenies, *The Seduction of Culture*, 1–2.

line with the British campaign of 'moral bombing', however, it was not the Merck site, north of the city, which was attacked, but rather the city itself: Darmstadt was practically razed to the ground in the space of a strike which took less than half an hour, as the Royal Air Force tested the strategy which would, in February 1945, have equally ruinous consequences for Dresden.[4]

On the night of the bombing itself, between eleven and twelve thousand people were killed, while seventy thousand were left homeless; 78 per cent of the city centre and 52.4 per cent of the whole municipal area was destroyed. Amongst the buildings obliterated was the family home of Darmstadt's first post-war mayor, Ludwig Metzger, and the building in which the Darmstadt composer Hermann Heiß, who would lead composition courses at the first Darmstadt Ferienkurse, lived.[5] It was estimated that the number of inhabitants of the city plummeted to roughly 51,000 after the bombing, from a total of 115,000 before the start of the war. The first accurate post-war figures number the citizens of Darmstadt, as at October 1946, at 78,000.[6] The Prince of Hesse saw the devastation from his estate some fifteen kilometres away: 'The flare grew and grew until the whole southern sky burned red and yellow.'[7] Unsurprisingly, Darmstadt's cultural institutions were similarly obliterated: in principle no official venue for the presentation of artistic work remained, although the city's cultural life was preserved in limited ways through performances in the few church buildings which survived.

A visiting British scientist, D. A. Spencer, described the devastation in evocative terms in his diary as he passed through the city in the summer of 1945: 'Darmstadt is a city of the dead – literally and figuratively. Not a soul in its alleyways between red rubble that were once streets. Long vistas of gaunt ruins – most only shoulder high. And overpowering silence everywhere.'[8] The German author Erich Kästner, whose work had been burned as a part of 1933's 'cleansing' by fire and who had been effectively banned from any public criticism of the Reich by the Reichsschrifttumskammer (Reich Chamber of Literature), visited Darmstadt too, in April 1946:

> To all intents and purposes, Darmstadt no longer exists. It was flattened in a twenty-minute attack [. . .] Today the streets have been swept clean, 'scrupulously' clean, one might think. The blasted city lies there like an empty

---

[4] Elke Gerberding, *Darmstädter Kulturpolitik in der Nachkriegszeit 1945–1949* (Darmstadt: Justus von Liebig, 1996), 17.
[5] See Susanne Király, *Ludwig Metzger: Politiker aus christliche Verantwortung* (Darmstadt: Hessische Historische Kommission Darmstadt and Historische Kommission für Hessen, 2004), 155, and Herbert Henck, *Hermann Heiß: Nachträge einer Biografie* (Deinstadt: Kompost, 2009), 387.
[6] Gerberding, *Darmstädter Kulturpolitik*, 17–19. See also Király, *Ludwig Metzger*, 155.
[7] Quoted in Sebald, *Luftkrieg und Literatur*, 30.
[8] D. A. Spencer, quoted in Douglas Botting, *In the Ruins of the Reich* (London: Methuen, 2005 [1985]), 158.

Introduction: music after catastrophe

jewellery case. The tram goes from one end of the city to another as if across a well-raked graveyard [...] The wreck of Darmstadt was the destination of a journey the purpose of which was to establish just how alive a dead city can be. The state theatre has organised two days of premieres in the former orangery [...] It may be asserted, without exaggeration, that until now no other city, even one ten or twenty times larger, and no other performance company, even if one were confidently to name many more and many better-known ones, has come up with such an interesting and rich programme.[9]

Darmstadt's rebuilding of its cultural life in the immediate post-war era was striking even at the time, in a world where returning émigrés, like Theodor Adorno, would be astonished by the feverish excitement amongst young Germans for all things cultural and spiritual.[10] Two examples cited by Lepenies give the impression well enough. A letter from Adorno to Thomas Mann, dated 28 December 1949, shows him 'overwhelmed by the passion and seriousness of his students'. These same students refused to take a break in their class because they had not yet fully understood Kant's transcendental dialectics (either that, they demanded, or the class must continue into the vacation: 'How could they relax without having finished Hegel's *Phenomenology of the Spirit*?'). In 1946, Karl Jaspers had described a similar situation to Hannah Arendt: 'We recently heard a superb report on the "idea" in Plato and Hegel, totally abstract, followed by a discussion that was as alive and intense as if we were dealing with the most current of problems.'[11]

Although, in the case of music at least, Adorno was hardly as optimistic about the new Germany as Jaspers (or that utopian vision described in Friedrich Meinecke's *The German Catastrophe*), across Germany there was seemingly a hunger for new thinking and new art. As Gerberding observes, the cultural situation of post-war Germany is best regarded as developing in the way it did 'not *despite* but *precisely because* the circumstances were difficult'.[12] Certainly, few German politicians, in Hesse not least, were not readying themselves to take up the challenge that Lepenies argues faced them: 'To survive the rupture of civilization it had inflicted upon Europe, Germany would have to give up the most German of all ideologies: the illusion that culture can compensate for politics.' As he says, 'this process took a long time'.[13] One of the principal aims, indeed, of the American Information Control Division (ICD) was precisely to demonstrate the fallacy of an assumed superiority of German *Kultur*, even if the Americans did not seem to consider too deeply the long-held division in

---

[9] Erich Kästner in the *Neue Zeitung*, for which he was culture editor, on 5 April 1946. Quoted in Gerberding, *Darmstädter Kulturpolitik*, 7.
[10] Lepenies, *The Seduction of Culture*, 134.   [11] Ibid., 135.
[12] Gerberding, *Darmstädter Kulturpolitik*, 7.   [13] Lepenies, *The Seduction of Culture*, 47–8.

German thought and life between the high products of *Kultur* and their almost absolute separation from the everyday products of *Zivilisation*. As Monod describes John Bitter, employed by the ICD in Berlin:

> His job was to serve as a kind of sentinel watching over the birth of artistic freedom. As a music officer, Bitter was to ensure that no works endorsing fascist or militarist ideals were performed, that compositions suppressed in the Third Reich (such as Mendelssohn's) were restored to the concert hall, that artists celebrated by the Nazis were blocked from further performances, that the influence of the state in the cultural sector was minimized, and that German audiences were taught that the music of other nations and cultures was as valid and worthy as their own.[14]

Regardless of what the desires of the Americans may have been, Darmstadt was not unusual in looking to culture to rectify political failings. Moreover, the American sentinels were hardly all-seeing. In terms of the immediate thirst for culture, though, the state of Hesse, and Darmstadt in particular, seemed to represent an extreme case, as Kästner suggested. Indeed, the very particular difficulties of administering the city of Darmstadt had profound significance for what developed there.

The state of Hesse itself was (and remains) for the most part a geographical invention of the post-war American military government, following consultations with German civil servants, academics, and émigrés, made up of the larger portion of the former Prussian province of Hesse-Nassau, which encompassed Wiesbaden, Frankfurt, and territory as far north as Kassel and much of the Duchy of Hesse, including the city of Darmstadt itself as well as further territories north of Frankfurt. That portion of the Duchy of Hesse west of the Rhine, including the city of Mainz, was administered by the French occupation forces and became part of Rhineland-Palatinate.[15]

The situation in Hesse was, certainly, seemingly parlous for the arts. In contrast to Württemberg-Baden, which budgeted DM 2 million for its theatre in 1948–9, and Bavaria, which put forward DM 2.5 million, Hesse provided only the comparatively small sum of DM 400,000.[16] Hesse was particularly unfortunate in the way in which the division of the territories which made up the new state had gone. It found itself in possession of not one but three Landestheater, as well as a municipal theatre in Giessen, which was keen to come under central state control. In the event, quite the reverse

---

[14] David Monod, *Settling Scores: German Music, Denazification, and the Americans, 1945–1953* (Chapel Hill, NC: University of North Carolina Press, 2005), 13.
[15] See Michael R. Hayse, *Recasting West German Elites: Higher Civil Servants, Business Leaders and Physicians in Hesse between Nazism and Democracy, 1945–1955* (New York: Berghahn, 2003), 7.
[16] See Monod, *Settling Scores*, 189.

Introduction: music after catastrophe

occurred, as the state of Hesse released the administration of the theatres in both Kassel and Darmstadt to the municipal authorities.[17] This move limited the liability of the state with regard to the costs of the theatres, but meant that the influence of central Hessian government was similarly limited. For the most part, in the immediate post-war period at least, Hesse's influence on the running of the arts in Darmstadt (and Kassel) was reduced to acting as a negotiator between the artistic directors, the cities, and the unions. The cultural life of the city of Darmstadt was, so far as Hesse was concerned, largely a matter for the city itself. It is in this context that many of the new initiatives of the early post-war years, not least the foundation of the Darmstadt New Music Courses, must be read. It also lends an additional significance to the words of Julius Reiber, Darmstadt's then deputy mayor, in the *Darmstädter Echo* of 16 January 1946:

> In view of the destroyed city it was stated on many sides that only the procurement of space to build, only the clearance of the rubble, and only the rebuilding were the pressing problems and that, in the current state of emergency, the theatre, the technical university, the schools, in fact all spiritual, artistic, and cultural needs were secondary and irrelevant [. . .] It will take us many years to rebuild houses, but we cannot leave people for that length of time without sustenance for the spirit and its cultural needs.[18]

In view of the relative autonomy under which Darmstadt found itself able to operate, such attitudes were ones on which the city was able to capitalise. The significance of them should certainly not be underestimated, given that Reiber wrote this in the middle of the so-called 'hunger winter' of 1946–7, in which it seemed that the German economy was already trapped in a vicious (and, as Jarausch puts it, 'deadly') cycle.[19] Hesse was, too, critically short of supplies even in comparison with the other German Länder:

> In the Western zones of Germany the maximum daily ration for normal consumers was supposed to be 1,550 calories. In practice it was never as much as this and varied from 804 calories in Hesse to 1,150 calories in the Rhineland. In the British zone the basic ration was 1,048 calories for more than a year after the war. By comparison civilians in Britain got 2,800 calories, German farmers 3,000, and American GIs 4,200 – the highest calorie intake of any human beings in Europe.[20]

---

[17] Ibid., 106.
[18] Julius Reiber, *Darmstädter Echo*, 16 January 1946, quoted in Judith S. Ulmer, *Geschichte des Georg-Büchner-Preises: Soziologie eines Rituals* (Berlin: Walter de Gruyter, 2006), 94.
[19] Konrad H. Jarausch, *After Hitler: Recivilizing Germans, 1945–1995* (Oxford University Press, 2006), 82.
[20] Botting, *In the Ruins of the Reich*, 168.

In making decisions that balanced the hunger for culture and very real and present hunger for the basic necessities of life, it was the precise people involved who made it possible for the situation to develop in the way in which it did. Central to this were two figures: Darmstadt's first post-war mayor, Ludwig Metzger, and its first post-war head of culture, Wolfgang Steinecke.

Ludwig Metzger had been an active figure in Darmstadt's political life before the war, predominantly as a lawyer. His political sympathies, too, were eminently clear or, at least, it was certain that he was interested in the carrying-out of the law, even where that might place him into conflict with the National Socialists. In 1935, for instance, Metzger represented four men in a treason case, arguing that the informant from the Sturmabteilung (SA; the paramilitary wing of the National Socialist Party), on whose word the case rested, was an unreliable witness. The consequence was that Metzger's right to act in treason cases was withdrawn; the SA informant's testimony was taken to be true. Events such as this inevitably brought Metzger into conflict with the Nazi authorities, as, for instance, when a stern reprimand was delivered to him indirectly at the beginning of 1942 from the Reichsjustizministerium (Reich Justice Ministry).[21] He was also warned, in the same year, that he was under surveillance by the Gestapo. Understanding that the situation was likely only to deteriorate for Metzger if he remained in Germany, his right-hand man, Ludwig Engel, encouraged him to leave for Luxembourg. In Berlin, Engel had made the acquaintance of Alfred Kulemann, the director of the Deutsche Umsiedlungs-Treuhand-Gesellschaft (DUT; German Resettlement Trust), who, in private conversation at least, did not hide his disdain for Hitler and was seeking lawyers whom he might be able to employ in Luxembourg. After a visit to Kulemann in Berlin, Metzger took over direction of the DUT in Luxembourg. In truth, Metzger was extremely fortunate that his move to Luxembourg left him comparatively politically protected; nevertheless, his general strategy throughout the war years seems to have been to do what was possible 'without placing either himself or his family in danger'.[22] His activity and position as a lawyer had enabled him to do that in Darmstadt until 1942, and this was remembered by many on his return after the end of the war. Though Metzger was later a leading figure in Hessian, national, and European politics – he became education minister for Hesse in 1951, a member of the Bundestag representing the SPD (Sozialdemokratische Partei Deutschlands; German Social Democratic Party) in 1953, and a member of the European Parliament in 1957 (ultimately serving as vice-president between 1966 and 1970) – in the immediate aftermath of the war, his concern was with his home city of Darmstadt.

---

[21] Király, *Ludwig Metzger*, 86–9. [22] Ibid., 113.

Introduction: music after catastrophe

Metzger had passed the last days of the war in Beerfelden in the Odenwald south of Darmstadt and, learning that the city had come under American occupation, made the roughly thirty-five-mile journey home on foot, reaching the city's outskirts on 24 March 1945. On the following day, a Sunday, Metzger attended a communion service held by the protestant clergyman Wilhelm Weinberger in emergency accommodation in the city. Later that same afternoon Weinberger and a Catholic priest, Wilhelm Michel, were asked whom they would recommend to head the civil administration of Darmstadt. Metzger, no doubt in memory in part of his prior activities defending local people against what looked like Nazi persecution, and probably in light of his well-known Christian faith too, was named by both. Metzger was rapidly summoned to the Residenzschloss, where the Americans had established a temporary headquarters, and asked whether he would be prepared to serve as mayor. Although he was certainly aware that he would be called upon to make a large number of unpopular decisions – and would be potentially in thrall to the requirements of American military administration – Metzger agreed.[23]

Metzger was faced with a wide variety of serious day-to-day challenges in terms of bare essentials – food and housing – in Darmstadt, as in Germany more generally, but the rebuilding of cultural life was seen as central. Even if, as Adorno would later opine, 'both cultural enthusiasm and political abstention were the result of collective self-deception', it seemed vital to many to bring about a resurgence in that part of German life which had bound the idea of 'Germany' together, long before the political state existed.[24] As Lepenies observes, '[p]olitics seemed to be discredited forever; a remilitarization of the country was unthinkable, only culture – not least because of the "internal exile" in which so many intellectuals had take refuge – was left with a legitimate past and hopes for the future.'[25] It was in this context, too, that approaches to culture in Darmstadt developed.

In any case, Metzger's approach to culture could hardly be seen as 'neutral', at least not from the perspective of personnel.[26] Metzger relied largely on personal contact and knowledge; the system that developed in Darmstadt, for the initial construction of the city's civil service more broadly, as well as in its culture department, was a function of Metzger's personal network of trusted individuals. The appointment of Wolfgang Steinecke as head of culture for the city was no exception to this.

As Metzger later recalled, the artist Willi Hofferberth, who was himself born in Darmstadt and, with Paul Thesing, founded the Neue Damstädter

---

[23] Király, *Ludwig Metzger*, 155–7. [24] Lepenies, *The Seduction of Culture*, 136. [25] Ibid., 146.
[26] Gerberding, *Darmstädter Kulturpolitik*, 37.

Sezession as early as the autumn of 1945, brought Steinecke to the attention of Metzger through the offices of Metzger's trusted aide Ludwig Engel. As Metzger's own memoir recalls, Hofferberth said to him, 'Ludwig, I've got to know a man, a well-known music critic, who would be prepared to work with us in Darmstadt. His name is Dr Wolfgang Steinecke. I think you might be able to make good use of him.'[27] Metzger's description of the meeting he immediately organised with Steinecke gives a strong impression of the character of Darmstadt's future head of culture:

> I asked the man to come to see me and we talked for a long time. He was full of ideas. We needed people like this. He became the city's head of culture. Steinecke was no fiery go-getter, but rather had a sensitive disposition and would often content himself with a gentle 'Mm' when he agreed, but had an unbelievable tenaciousness when he wanted to achieve something. His effectiveness in bringing well-known figures to Darmstadt, without excessive expense, was astonishing. He was aware that we Germans had been cut off from the world not only spiritually but also musically for many years and had little connection or knowledge even amongst ourselves. He was a master of bringing people together, without making a huge fuss about things.[28]

Steinecke's appointment in some senses, then, was quite this simply achieved; he was appointed initially for a trial period from 1 August 1945 until 31 October 1945.[29] At this point, he retained his position as a music correspondent with the *Mittag* in Düsseldorf.

In another sense, Steinecke's appointment was more complex, and bears closer examination. By 23 June 1945, Steinecke had already applied to the city – rather than directly to Metzger – offering his services for work in cultural fields and suggesting that his previous experience made him suitable for work in music programming for the radio, work in the culture department at either municipal or state level, cultural journalism, or a leading position in the theatre.[30] The beginning of a subsequent letter, dated 5 July 1945, suggests that Steinecke received no response to his earlier letter, again lending credence to the idea that Metzger was more interested in personal recommendation than in direct application:

---

[27] Ludwig Metzger, *Im guten und in schlechten Tagen: Berichte, Gedanken und Erkenntnisse aus der politischen Arbeit eines aktiven Christen und Sozialisten* (Darmstadt: Reba, 1980), 104–5.
[28] Ibid.
[29] Steinecke's *Dienstvertrag* is reprinted in Michael Custodis, *Tradition - Koalitionen - Visionen: Wolfgang Steinecke und die Internationalen Ferienkurse in Darmstadt* (Saarbrücken: Pfau, 2010), 31.
[30] Michael Custodis, '"Unter Auswertung meiner Erfahrungen aktiv mitgestaltend": Zum Wirken von Wolfgang Steinecke bis 1950', in Albrecht Riethmüller (ed.), *Deutsche Leitkultur Musik? Zur Musikgeschichte nach dem Holocaust* (Stuttgart: Franz Steiner, 2006), 153.

> On the request of the local American military government, I made myself available for work in cultural areas. My application and curriculum vitae, etc. were, after being checked for any political dubiousness, forwarded on. Since my attempt to come into personal contact with you this way has failed, I would like to provide you in these few lines a brief portrayal of my background and personal circumstances to date, on the basis of which you might perhaps regard a personal conversation as fruitful.[31]

It is clear already here, as Custodis notes, that Steinecke was keenly aware of the importance that a clean political record would have.

Steinecke never undertook a formal denazification process. Nevertheless, he completed a *Fragebogen* (personal information questionnaire) supplied by the city, and dated 4 August 1945, which stated that he had neither been a member of the National Socialist Party nor of any affiliated or similar organisations. This may well have been true, since Steinecke has no entry in the *Zentralkartei* (the central files) of the NSDAP (the Nationalsozialistische Deutsche Arbeiterpartei; the National Socialist German Workers' Party),[32] but his answer to the fifteenth question on the form was arguably not. In this question he said that he had not written or spoken publicly in a political context during the Nazi era.[33] A letter from the Office of the Military Government, dated 1 December 1945, confirmed that Steinecke's *Fragebogen* had been vetted and found acceptable.[34]

While Steinecke's letter to Ludwig Metzger, dated 5 July 1945, did reveal many of Steinecke's activities, it was silent on others. He certainly worked at the film production company Terra-Filmkunst in Berlin between 1941 and 1943, a fact he did not mention. While there is little to tie Steinecke in to any particular activity at Terra-Filmkunst – he was employed first as an 'associate' and later as a 'consultant' – certainly the company produced a number of racist and propaganda films during the period during which he was involved with them, including *Quax, der Bruchpilot* (1941), *Wir machen Musik* (1942), *Die Feuerzangenbowle* (1944), and *Große Freiheit Nr. 7* (1944).[35] The precise nature of Steinecke's work there, though, remains unclear.

He did, however, list newspapers with whom he had worked, naming in particular *Der Mittag* and the *Deutsche Allgemeine Zeitung*. As noted above, to say that Steinecke had made no political comment in print during the years of NSDAP rule would be a hard position to defend. Yet, in a certain

---

[31] This letter is reprinted in full in Custodis, *Tradition – Koalitionen – Visionen*, 104–6.
[32] Fred K. Prieberg, *Handbuch deutsche Musiker 1933–1945* (Auprès des Zombry: self-published, 2004), 6844.
[33] Custodis, "'Unter Auswertung meiner Erfahrungen aktiv mitgestaltend'", 154.
[34] This letter is reprinted in Custodis, *Tradition – Koalitionen – Visionen*, 34.
[35] Custodis, "'Unter Auswertung meiner Erfahrungen aktiv mitgestaltend'", 150–2.

sense, the vast majority of Steinecke's wartime journalistic writings were remarkably cautiously constructed. To be more precise, Steinecke only very rarely expressed anything that might bring him directly into line with the regime in his own words. Almost without exception, Steinecke quoted or gave reported speech in such cases. Reviewing the première of Fritz von Borries's *Magnus Fahlander* (1937), performed as a part of the Niederrheinische Kulturwoche in Düsseldorf, for example, Steinecke suggested that 'the plot, in which a leader [*Führer*] rises from the people themselves in order to set them free, aims to provide a "copy of the immense conflict of our time"'.[36] His review of the *entartete Musik* exhibition, also in Düsseldorf, works in similar ways: 'The exhibition provides an effectively arranged illustration of the diverse manifestations of post-war musical life. Hindemith, Stravinsky, Kurt Weill, and Arnold Schoenberg are represented by numerous rehearsals of their work, alongside "little cultural Bolsheviks" like Alban Berg, [Ernst] Toch, [Karol] Rathaus, [Josef Matthias] Hauer, Hermann Reutter, and others.' Were it not for the words that Steinecke is careful to quote from elsewhere, indeed, this review would barely be worth mentioning. Later in the review, he is cautious enough to place scare quotes around the ostensible subject of the exhibition itself: 'So far as music, even "degenerate music", allows itself to be understood in the context of an exhibition [. . .] a show is taking place here that fulfils its aims in effective and strongly impressive ways, meaningfully extended through the numerous plaques announcing the basic views of the new German musical politics.'[37] Nevertheless, elsewhere Steinecke was less well able to avoid commitment, not least when reviewing the work of his own doctoral supervisor, Friedrich Blume, who published the notorious essay 'Music and Race' in *Die Musik* in 1938, as well as the later *The Racial Problem in Music*.[38] Blume delivered an earlier version of his *Die Musik* essay during the *entartete Musik* exhibition, and it was this that Steinecke was reviewing:

> German music history portrays a string of invasions of foreign artistic expressive forms, but it [German music] somehow remains at the same time thoroughly German in its manifestation. This is an argument, then, that the foreign can be absorbed, without diluting core racial stock. It would be a poor testament to our race if one were to allege that foreign influences could

---

[36] Prieberg, *Handbuch deutsche Musiker*, 650 (original in *Neue Musikblatt*, vol. 16, no. 31 (November 1937), 5).
[37] Prieberg, *Handbuch deutsche Musiker*, 6844 (original in *Deutsche Allgemeine Zeitung*, 25 May 1938).
[38] Friedrich Blume, 'Musik und Rasse: Grundfragen einer musikalischen Rassenforschung', *Die Musik*, vol. 30, no. 11 (August 1938), 736–48; Friedrich Blume, *Das Rasseproblem in der Musik* (Wolfenbüttel: Kallmeyer, 1944).

Introduction: music after catastrophe

endanger our basic racial stock. It is precisely in the melting and re-melting of foreign forms that the strength of the 'racial soul' is evident.[39]

Steinecke's suggestions that non-German influences ought to be acceptable to the regime – since they would, in any case, 'become' German in the hands of a German composer – are certainly some way distant from the extremes of Nazi ideas of *Blut und Boden*. However, even in the case of a writer who can elsewhere be seen ensuring that it is the words of others that incriminate (and here too, he makes clear that 'racial soul' is Blume's coinage rather than his own), he does nevertheless refer both to 'racial stock', twice, and to 'our race', inevitably placing it into opposition to other 'races'. It is worth noting, too, that in this case the writing is not reported speech either. Though it *is* a report of what Blume had to say, the case in which it is written means that the reader is led to believe that this is Steinecke's opinion too. Something very similar had appeared from Steinecke's pen only the previous year, in an article on 'Smetana and Czech National Music':

> The question of whether there could ever be an 'international music' is today finally decided. Only somebody in a period of uncertainty regarding their national feeling could believe that music might be an Esperanto born of something other than the spirit of the nation, an artificial language, whose development is bound up with no racial conditions and laws. We know more strongly today than ever that a music can first have international (trans-national) validity only when it is honestly and genuinely fed by the strength of one's own folklore, when it is in the first place national.[40]

The distance from an administrator who would be responsible for international new music courses in the post-war era is palpable, not least because multiple serialism was itself, in many respects, an 'artificial' language.

Steinecke was undoubtedly no anti-Semite, much less a supporter of Nazism, but he was no inner emigrant either. The broad spread of his writing suggests that his strategy of quoting and reporting was probably an intentional attempt to avoid writing anything that would compromise him. Nevertheless, pieces like the review of Blume's 'Music and Race' indicate that even an author who had developed strategies like this still existed within a culture, presuming that they did indeed remain within the German-speaking world, in which it was sooner or later a practical impossibility to avoid having one's writing infected by the language of Nazism.

---

[39] Wolfgang Steinecke, 'Musik und Rasse: Vortrag Professor Blumes bei den Reichsmusiktagen', *Deutsche Allgemeine Zeitung*, 28 May 1938, quoted in Custodis, '"Unter Auswertung meiner Erfahrungen aktiv mitgestaltend"', 147.

[40] Wolfgang Steinecke, 'Smetana und die tschechische Nationalmusik', programme booklet of the Duisburger Opera, quoted in Custodis, '"Unter Auswertung meiner Erfahrungen aktiv mitgestaltend"', 146.

The problem was, indeed, hardly an uncommon one. The British Quaker relief worker Grigor McClelland wrote in a letter of 12–13 July 1945: 'I met today one of the men who produce the Oldenburg German-language newspaper – a staff sergeant. The main trouble, he says, is shortage of staff – both on the English side, and in getting non-Nazi German journalists. Even men of good will have a Nazi style of writing – it was so drummed into them in their job – quite unconsciously.'[41] Doubtless Custodis is right that one reason why Steinecke's wartime activities in respect of publications which could be regarded as political were not discussed in relation to the vetting of his *Fragebogen* was that the sheer volume of applications was unmanageable, especially given that a full and comprehensive check would have involved hard-pressed officials examining a wide range of disparate press sources for ideological nuance. These sources, where they could be obtained at all, were naturally available only in German. Monod observes that 'disorder prevailed in the American zone until August 1945' in the case of denazification, and that it was only with the establishment, then, of the ICD that this procedure became either standardised or efficient.[42] The process that developed appears to have been more complex than the one which Steinecke completed: where he submitted a single, 131-point personal information questionnaire, in accordance with the United States Forces European Theater (USFET) directive of 7 July, from this point anyone applying to work within the arts in the American zone had to complete four *Fragebögen*, four further questionnaires concerning their business or career activities to date, three questionnaires for the military government, and four work application forms. With the introduction of a new law on 5 May 1946, however, the system had changed again, as control of denazification was handed back to German hands in local denazification courts (*Spruchkammer*). Certainly, Steinecke may have benefited to some degree from this disorder, but equally the situation in Darmstadt provided a highly specific and contentious backdrop for the submission of *Fragebögen* to the Americans.

As Király reports, in August 1945 the American military government became aware that Ludwig Metzger increasingly regarded it as a 'problem' to balance the city's need to find suitably qualified individuals to take up sometimes specialised positions with the military administration's demands that all employees of the civil service be politically impeccable.[43] The dispute which developed between Darmstadt and the Americans centred on 150 city

---

[41] Grigor McClelland, *Embers of War: Letters from a Quaker Relief Worker in War-Torn Germany* (London: British Academic Press, 1997 [1945]), 31.
[42] Monod, *Settling Scores*, 51.   [43] Király, *Ludwig Metzger*, 173.

employees who had been NSDAP members. The attitude of the Americans was simple: all of them should be dismissed. Indeed the American attitude was that they ought to go further and investigate all of the lower-level civil servants too. Metzger, by contrast, wanted to distinguish between those who had been only 'nominally' party members and those (he estimated the number at between twenty and thirty) who were 'truly' Nazis, all of whom, he later stated, had already been removed from their posts. In short, Metzger's position was 'I know my Darmstädter better than the Americans.' The stand-off between Metzger and the Americans in Wiesbaden lasted until October 1945, at which point American patience was seemingly exhausted, and Metzger was relieved of office. There was some suggestion that Metzger might himself have engaged in activities in Luxembourg on behalf of the NSDAP, which would have disbarred him from office in any case. The sort of loyalty which Metzger seems to have inspired is shown in the fact that Major Wilson W. Williver travelled to Luxembourg not to gather evidence against Metzger but, on the contrary, to clear his name, returning with 'glowing references' for him and food parcels for the Metzger family from various families he had known in Luxembourg. Metzger also received strong and persistent support from all the other leading figures in Darmstadt's local politics and perhaps more pertinently from Ludwig Bergsträsser, who acted as regional president for Hesse. The SPD demanded Metzger's reinstatement, and, by the time the issue reached the office of Lucius Clay, it was clear that the situation was becoming untenable. Metzger was, thus, reinstated by February 1946 and elected officially as mayor on 26 May 1946 in local elections. Nevertheless, in August 1946 he, too, was forced to fill out his 131-question *Fragebogen*, receiving his final clearance from the German-administered *Spruchkammer* in April 1947.[44]

In short, Metzger won his skirmish with the Americans, even if it took a substantial amount of time and the good offices of some extremely influential members of both the SPD and the American administration. Though it would be impossible to provide substantive proof of this, it is surely plausible that, rather than stir up a major diplomatic incident for a second time, Metzger's administration might have been treated with a lighter touch than was the case elsewhere. Certainly this would be one explanation for how it could be that Wolfgang Fortner came to lecture at the Darmstadt New Music Courses at a point when he was officially (and very recently) blacklisted, as I will discuss below. The other, of course, might be that the city of Darmstadt itself took a relatively cavalier approach to denazification

---

[44] See ibid., 173–7, and Metzger, *In guten und in schlechten Tagen*, 107–8.

after Metzger's reinstatement, in line with his general thoughts that he was better placed than an American questionnaire to identify ideological Nazis.[45] In this context, even if there had been some questions regarding Steinecke's suitability, it seems likely that these issues would have been regarded as trifling compared with the major incident surrounding Metzger.

Whatever the reasons, Steinecke's wartime writings slipped through the net and his musical activities as the city's head of culture had already begun by late September 1945. A series of seven concerts began on 29 September 1945 with a performance where the music of J. S. Bach, Buxtehude, Beethoven, and Leonhard Lechner was presented alongside poetry by Hölderlin. A second concert series began on 3 November 1945, with Sunday evening performances of music by Schubert, Brahms, and Dvořák. On 11 November 1945, Hindemith's *Ludus tonalis* (1942) was given its German première as a part of the 'Tag der jungen Kunst', an especially appropriate 'early' musical performance, given Hindemith's membership of the original Darmstädter Sezession.[46] On 12 May 1946, Hermann Heiß's *Symphonisches Konzert* (1944) for piano and orchestra received its (unofficial) première in the Orangerie, south of the city centre. The piece had originally been projected for a première in the city on 16 October 1944, a performance which, in the wake of the bombing, never occurred.[47]

Hermann Heiß and Wolfgang Fortner

For all that Beal observes that 'Ferienkurse participants had to receive a clearance issued by the Music and Theater Branch' of the American military government and that, further, 'early IFNM [Internationale Ferienkurse für Neue Musik] programs were stamped with OMGUS publishing licenses', in the case of Darmstadt, the Americans cannot always have made especially careful checks.[48] Plausibly this was, in part, a result of the experience with Metzger outlined above. Even so, clearances granted for the early courses are surprising. A letter to Steinecke from Gerhard Singer at the Music and Theater Branch in Wiesbaden on 12 August 1946 – under two weeks before the start of the first courses – granted clearance to Hermann Heiß, Karl

---

[45] For a comprehensive overview of denazification, including its ramifications after denazification had officially come to an end, see Perry Biddiscombe, *The Denazification of Germany: A History, 1945–1950* (Stroud: Tempus, 2007).
[46] Elke Gerberding, 'Darmstädter Kulturpolitk der Nachkriegszeit', in Rudolf Stephan, Lothar Knessl, Otto Tomek, Klaus Trapp, and Christopher Fox (eds.), *Von Kranichstein zur Gegenwart* (Stuttgart: DACO, 1996), 31.
[47] Henck, *Hermann Heiß*, 387–8.
[48] Amy C. Beal, *New Music, New Allies: American Experimental Music in West Germany from the Zero Hour to Reunification* (Berkeley, CA: University of California Press, 2006), 38. OMGUS was the Office of Military Government, United States.

Wörner, Heinrich Strobel, and fourteen others to attend the courses. The following year, a letter from Singer, dated 4 June 1947, cleared the attendance of Heiß, Strobel, Wolfgang Fortner, Hermann Scherchen, Hans Heinz Stuckenschmidt, and eleven others.[49] While Hermann Heiß was cleared to deliver lectures at the courses in 1946, Fortner assuredly was not. The differences between their two respective positions may help to clarify the reasons for this, even if, since Fortner did teach at Darmstadt in 1946 anyway, it seems highly likely, as Thacker contends, that 'the Intelligence Branch of the ICD did not know about Darmstadt in any detail in either 1946 or 1947, and that it was not kept informed by either the Education Branch in Hesse, or by Radio Frankfurt, which sponsored the first courses'.[50]

Heiß's *Fragebogen*, dated 24 April 1946, included his statement that he had not belonged to any of the fourteen named Nazi organisations and confirmed that he had been a member of the Reichsmusikkammer (Reich Chamber of Music) between 1936 and 1945, for which he paid less than RM 1 per month, and had paid a total of about RM 9 into the coffers of the Nationalsozialistiche Volkswohlfahrt (National Socialist People's Welfare) in 1943. He gave his occupation as 'freelance composer, pianist, choral director, music teacher' and confirmed his taxable income for many of the previous years (from a low of RM 600 in 1934 to highs of RM 6,000 and 7,000 in 1943 and 1932 respectively). He suggested, too, that he had already been vetted by the Second Military Government Battalion in Dieburg, near to Darmstadt, receiving a 'positive' response on 5 February 1946.[51] In answer to the question 'to what category do you belong under the law?', Heiß answered: 'none'. The law in question was the one of 4 May 1946, from which, for example, Steinecke had been found exempt on grounds of his earlier *Fragebogen*, filled in while denazification had been undertaken by the American military administration. Thus, Heiß declared that he fell into none of the following categories:

1. Hauptschuldige (major offenders)
2. Belastete (incriminated persons)
3. Minderbelastete (less-incriminated persons)
4. Mitläufer (fellow travellers)
5. Entlastete (non-incriminated or exonerated persons)

---

[49] See Amy C. Beal, 'Negotiating Cultural Allies: American Music in Darmstadt, 1946–1956', *Journal of the American Musicological Society*, vol. 53, no. 1 (2000), 113 n. 29.
[50] Toby Thacker, *Music after Hitler, 1945–1955* (Farnham: Ashgate, 2007), 79.
[51] As Henck observes, it is extremely difficult to make any checks against Heiß's claim of this earlier vetting, given that the document, if it survived at all, would be somewhere within OMGUS files in Washington, DC, scattered across twenty-seven folders containing some 5,300 pages, without any index. See Henck, *Hermann Heiß*, 411.

Heiß justified his answer thus:

> 1933 sacked because of my opposition to National Socialism. Very few opportunities in Berlin as a recognised cultural Bolshevist. 1941 position at Heeresmusikschule Frankfurt-am-Main, sacked without notice 1942 because of refusal to join civil air defence, = lawsuit against the Reich lost. My increased earnings in 1943 relate to private commissions from the *Süddeutscher Musikverlag* in Hamburg, which was like me anti-fascist.[52]

Heiß doubtless, and understandably, over-stated his case a little. On the one hand, he had been associated in Berlin with twelve-tone composers, particularly with Josef Matthias Hauer, but also with Schoenberg, and had found himself pilloried in the press following a concert in Berlin's Bechsteinsaal on 17 March 1934, in which he presented his own work and Bartók's alongside the pianist Else C. Kraus, a recognised interpreter of Schoenberg's music. Some of the reviews made the link between Heiß, Schoenberg, and 'Jewishness' absolutely explicit.[53] Heiß himself suggested after the war that the concert was intended as a protest against the state, which had cut his projected piece, *Das Jahresrad* (1931–2), from the Cultural Olympiad of 1936 for which it was planned probably in late 1933 or early 1934.[54] Heiß's suggestion that he was sacked without notice in 1942, too, gives a misleading impression. He was reported as being a staff member in the school in February 1943 in an article in *Die Musik*. Even allowing for the possible delay in publication, which could have meant that he had been dismissed in 1942, the performance of the 'Festliches Konzert' there in May 1943 certainly suggests he was not regarded as persona non grata.[55]

Heiß, however, had admitted that he had written music in support of the German war effort, including 'soldiers' songs', commissions for the Luftwaffe and other military music. Thacker describes an application he made to the state for artists' funding on 22 June 1940 in connection with this, observing that Heiß's economic means were certainly severely limited by this stage.[56] Yet many of the pieces he wrote which either directly or indirectly seemed to support the regime existed long before that. In 1936 and 1937, he wrote lieder on texts by the Nazi poet Josef Weinheber ('Distel', 'Christblume', and 'Herbstzeitlose'; 'Thistle', 'Christmas Rose', and 'Autumn Crocus'), as well as the song cycle *Blumenlieder* (*Flower Songs*), on texts by the same poet.[57] More damningly, he composed numerous songs on his own texts for the Luftwaffe song book, including 'Kein Tor

---

[52] Ibid., 411.
[53] Ibid., 146–65. There were positive reviews of the concert, from Josef Rufer and Fred Hamel (writing under the pseudonym Hans Lyck) not least, but these were in the minority.
[54] Ibid., 146.   [55] Ibid., 328–32.   [56] Thacker, *Music after Hitler*, 78.
[57] Henck, *Hermann Heiß*, 187–90.

Introduction: music after catastrophe   17

der Welt ist uns zu hoch' ('No Gate in the World is Too High for Us'),
which he revisited in *Jagdfliegermarsch* (*Fighter Pilot March*; 1940), and
co-authored a cantata dedicated to the Luftwaffe – *Wir sind des Reiches
leibhaftige Adler: Eine Fliegerkantate* (*We are the Reich's Spirited Eagles: A
Pilots' Cantata*) – with Karl-Heinz Kelting, which was premièred in
Neustadt-Glewe in November 1939.[58] Nevertheless, Heiß's statement
regarding Willy Müller's *Süddeutscher Musikverlag* certainly seems to
have the ring of truth. As Henck puts it,

> [f]rom the aesthetic point of view, after coming into contact with Müller
> in 1942, Heiß again broke with the requirements of National Socialism,
> which is to say how music had to sound under the Third Reich. There was
> no further politically motivated music, like that he had written or
> worked on for the Reichsluftfahrtministerium [Reich Air Ministry] in the
> years between 1938 and 1941. In 1944, and even before his move to
> Jamnitz, Heiß seemed to have rediscovered his relationship with
> twelve-tone music.[59]

One might conclude, then, that Heiß's interests lay principally with twelve-tone music, but that financial necessity caused him to make compromises from which he retreated once it became possible to earn his living by other means. Even if this was the case, Heiß's compositions for the Luftwaffe ensured that he was, for a time, blacklisted.[60]

If the situation of Heiß was a comparatively complex one – with promotion (and indeed composition) of that which was clearly *entartete Musik* on the one hand and pro-regime popular (and populist) military songs on the other – the case of Wolfgang Fortner was more straightforward, from the American perspective at least. As Thacker describes his activities: 'Fortner had earlier written a song called *Tag der Machtübernahme*; he specialised in "festive music" for the HJ [Hitlerjugend], and conducted the HJ orchestra in Heidelberg.'[61] These activities led to his being regarded by the NSDAP as 'a good comrade [...] politically reliable and unobjectionable'.[62] Michael Kater's judgement of Fortner is damning. Fortner was certainly, more than anything else, recognised as a composer of church music, but Dibelius's proposal that Fortner sought 'refuge' from Nazism in the church

---

[58] Ibid., 239–307.
[59] Ibid., 342. Heiß had moved to Jamnitz, Moravia (now Jemnice in the Czech Republic, then a part of the German protectorate of Bohemia and Moravia), in October 1944.
[60] Thacker, *Music after Hitler*, 78.   [61] Ibid.
[62] Matthias Roth, *Ein Rangierbahnhof der Moderne: Der Komponist Wolfgang Fortner und sein Schülerkries 1931–1986. Erinnerungen, Dokumente, Hintergründe, Porträts* (Freiburg im Breisgau: Rombach, 2008), 29.

is, whether or not 'embarrassing', as Kater finds it, certainly erroneous.[63] Alongside his work with the Hitler Youth, Fortner had worked as a guest conductor for the Nationalsozialistische Betriebszellenorganisation (National Socialist Factory Cell Organisation) before that organisation was absorbed by the Deutsche Arbeitsfront (German Labour Front) in 1935. He also staged new work for a Nazi celebratory event at the University of Göttingen in 1937, joined the party in 1941, and described twelve-tone composition as 'evidence of uprootedness'.[64] Matthias Roth takes a more sympathetic line, suggesting that Fortner was coerced into joining the NSDAP and that, moreover, his homosexuality gave him reason to fear prosecution for a 'bio-political crime' against Paragraph 175 of the Reich's criminal code, which carried with it the sentence of imprisonment in a concentration camp.[65] Moreover, like Heiß, in the mid 1930s Fortner was briefly suspected of musical Bolshevism through the ministries of the dramaturge Otto zur Nedden and the Nazi functionary Hans Severus Ziegler. The latter had joined the party early, in 1925, had the ear of both Hitler and Goebbels, and organised the concert of *entartete Musik* in Düsseldorf in 1938, plausibly in the wake of a concert at the 1936 Weimar Musikfest which had featured Fortner's music alongside that of Hermann Reutter, Ernst-Lothar von Knorr, Heinz Tiessen, and Hugo Hermann.[66]

Although Roth claims that Fortner 'came relative quickly and easily through denazification', he was nevertheless blacklisted by the American authorities in June 1946, as a part of the fifty-page 'supplement' to an earlier hundred-page-long document of April 1946, meaning that he was regarded as 'not suitable for employment in any Information Control Media'.[67] That this followed so swiftly after the submission of Fortner's *Fragebogen* on 2 May 1946 suggests that, even if the *Spruchkammer* had felt willing to exonerate him ('letting him off lightly', as Roth has it),[68] the American administration was not. Fortner remained blacklisted as late as March 1947, along with thirty other composers, including Richard Strauss and Carl Orff,

---

[63] Michael Kater, *The Twisted Muse: Musicians and their Music in the Third Reich* (Oxford University Press, 1997), 170. Dibelius's defensiveness becomes more explicable when it is remembered that Fortner was a family friend of Dibelius's as well as a regular musical colleague in Heidelberg. See Roth, *Ein Rangierbahnhof der Moderne*, 32–7.
[64] Roth, *Ein Rangierbahnhof der Moderne*, 30, 85–6, and Kater, *The Twisted Muse*, 170–1.
[65] Kater, *The Twisted Muse*, 170–1. As Richard Evans notes, the same law remained in force after the close of the war; in the twelve years of Nazi rule 50,000 men were arrested under it, while a staggering 100,000 were arrested between 1953 and 1965. See Richard J. Evans, *The Third Reich in Power* (London: Penguin, 2006 [2005]), 529–35.
[66] See Roth, *Ein Rangierbahnhof der Moderne*, 45, and Frederic Spotts, *Hitler and the Power of Aesthetics* (London: Pimlico, 2003 [2002]), 276.
[67] Thacker, *Music after Hitler*, 51–2.   [68] Roth, *Ein Rangierbahnhof der Moderne*, 82.

Introduction: music after catastrophe   19

suggesting that the American occupiers at least regarded him as politically highly suspect.[69]

It was hardly only Heiß and Fortner, though, who were involved with events at Darmstadt in the first two years and were, simultaneously, blacklisted by the Americans. Udo Dammert led the piano class in 1947, despite being a former NSDAP member whom the Americans had caught lying on his *Fragebogen*. In the same year, Bruno Stürmer taught conducting classes in choral music (alongside Scherchen's conducting masterclass and Carl Mathieu Lange's class on opera conducting), despite having been downgraded by the Americans from 'Grey – Unacceptable' to 'Black'. The music of the blacklisted composers Helmut Degen, Hugo Distler, Paul Höffer, and Ernst Pepping was also performed in 1946.[70]

In sum, this adds further credence to the idea that, in the earliest days at least, the Americans simply cannot have truly known about events at Darmstadt in full, even if William Dubensky mentioned the courses in his 'Weekly Activity Report, Film, Theater and Music Branch, ICD' on 25 July 1946: 'A public instructional course on contemporary music is taking place in Darmstadt's Schloss Kranichstein under the sponsorship of the Darmstadt cultural authorities. It is intended to give a concise panorama of the contemporary music scene for those individuals who find it of importance for their profession and will spread this knowledge in their own circles.'[71] That Dubensky observes that the courses were 'under the sponsorship' of the cultural authorities in Darmstadt is particularly notable. In truth, Frances Stonor Saunders's regularly cited claim that the courses were 'a bold initiative of the American military government' is almost certainly without foundation, at least as far as the years before currency reform are concerned.[72] Though Beal cites the case of the delivery of a Steinway, confiscated from the Nazis, to Schloss Kranichstein by American soldiers in 1946,[73] and Gerberding notes that the Americans gave their agreement to the procuring of scores from abroad in the same year,[74] these

---

[69] Thacker, *Music after Hitler*, 54.
[70] Ibid., 79. Thacker suggests that Dammert also led piano classes in 1946, but I can see no evidence to suggest that anyone other than Georg Kuhlmann was responsible in that year. It was Kuhlmann who performed in the vast majority of concerts where piano was involved, so if Dammert was present he, at least, was there only in the most informal of capacities. Dammert was, in any case, already regarded as 'trouble' by the Americans, having been caught performing in Berchtesgaden in December 1946, in spite of having been explicitly barred from so doing. It is worth noting that, for instance, Distler never had an opportunity to clear his name, since he committed suicide at the age of thirty-four in 1942, perhaps to avoid conscription into the Wehrmacht. See Roth, *Ein Rangierbahnhof der Moderne*, 38.
[71] Quoted in Beal, *New Music, New Allies*, 37.
[72] Frances Stonor Saunders, *Who Paid the Piper? The CIA and the Cultural Cold War* (London: Granta, 1999), 23.
[73] Beal, *New Music, New Allies*, 38.   [74] Gerberding, *Darmstädter Kulturpolitik*, 52.

Introduction: music after catastrophe

were probably isolated incidents until roughly 1948, when the programme booklet for the courses received an introductory note from the American military officer Harold P. Radigan:

> The American military government welcomes and supports the development of these courses and their associated *Internationale zeitgenössiche Musiktage* because they represent an event which is suited for supporting the rebuilding of German cultural life in a spirit of freedom, of progress, and of the promotion of mutual understanding between nations. We wish success to the city of Darmstadt and the initiative they have taken.[75]

As Beal observes, '[r]equests by Steinecke and others to the military government for money, performance space, bedding, and food were frequent and frequently granted'.[76] However, the letters that Beal cites in support of this date from between 1948 and 1949, after currency reform. Similarly, as Geberding and Beal both observe, the OMGUS Music Branch in Wiesbaden was the primary sponsor of the *Patenring*, a fund to pay for scholarships for those who would otherwise be unable to attend the courses. A sum of DM 4,000 was obtained, yet this funding began only in 1949.[77] Doubtless a range of factors brought about genuine American interest in the courses, and not only the introduction of the Deutsche Mark.

The presence of Everett Helm, a Harvard music graduate and sometime composer, as music officer at Wiesbaden seems to have led to the idea that the Darmstadt courses were somehow 'cooked up' almost fully formed in a meeting between Metzger, Steinecke, and Helm at OMGUS's Wiesbaden offices.[78] There is no doubt at all that Helm played a significant part in providing monies to Darmstadt, and indeed he seems to have been responsible for the provision of the *Patenring* funds, but the idea that Metzger, Steinecke, and Helm devised the Darmstadt 'project' jointly is spurious. Such stories may stem, at least in part, from Elliott Carter's 1959 report that '[a]s a U.S. Army Theatre and Music Officer in Wiesbaden, [Helm] helped to establish the Darmstadt School after the war and at various times since has saved it from being overwhelmed by numerous situations that have threatened its existence.'[79] However, Helm simply could not have helped to 'establish' the Darmstadt New Music Courses (if it is presumed that that is what Carter means here by the 'Darmstadt School') by virtue of the mere fact that he had not been appointed in 1946. In 1946, William Dubensky was head of music for Hesse, having taken over the post in January of that year.[80]

---

[75] Ibid., 56. [76] Beal, *New Music, New Allies*, 38.
[77] See ibid., 38, and Gerberding, 'Darmstädter Kulturpolitik der Nachkriegszeit', 34.
[78] See, for instance, Christopher Fox, 'Music after Zero Hour', in Paul Attinello, Christopher Fox, and Martin Iddon (eds.), *Other Darmstadts* (Contemporary Music Review, vol. 26, no.1 (2007)), 9.
[79] Elliott Carter, quoted in Beal, *New Music, New Allies*, 39. [80] Monod, *Settling Scores*, 106.

Introduction: music after catastrophe 21

As was clear from his report on the Darmstadt New Music Courses cited above, while Dubensky may have been aware that they were taking place, he had certainly not visited them, and gave no indication that they were of particular interest to the Americans as, presumably, they would have been had an American financial investment been at stake.

Helm acted as music officer in Hesse for OMGUS only between 1948 and late 1950 (by which stage the Music and Theater Branch no longer existed in any case), though he did indeed channel funds to the courses, especially in 1948 and 1949.[81] Between 1949 and 1951 the American High Commission funded roughly 20 per cent of the total costs of the courses, in addition to the *Patenring* funding. It financed, too, the attendance of Edgard Varèse at the courses in 1950.[82] Yet the principal source of funding remained the city of Darmstadt itself. That funding, though, was not unrelated to the support of the Americans. As Monod observes:

> Although the amounts contributed were small, American support was critical to the seminar's survival because it placed pressure on local governments to fund the organization. As a result, Hesse and the city of Darmstadt maintained the Ferienkurse with vital subsidies. Land contributions of DM 4,500 in the late 1940s were raised to DM 10,000 in 1951, but this amount pales before the municipal subsidy of between DM 50,000 and 85,000 per annum. Because the institute earned only DM 10,000 to 15,000 a year, it was clearly an entirely public organization. Government patronage of the Ferienkurse, as an 'international institution … with support in American circles', continued in spite of recognition that its market was 'relatively small and would remain so'.[83]

Even if it was only for a brief few years that American funding was vital, these were arguably the foundational years of the Darmstadt courses 'proper'. The earliest courses – in 1946 and 1947 – had been ramshackle affairs in most respects. Indeed it is probably closest to the truth to regard them as experiments in finding out what the courses could be and how they might function. It is far from unreasonable to claim that the 'real' courses began with the 1948 courses and with the arrival of Helm at Wiesbaden. Though the original idea of the Darmstadt New Music Courses was not the result of conversations between Metzger, Steinecke, and Helm, there may still be reason to think that Carter's assertion of Helm's importance is not that far from the mark.

In this context, a closer examination of Saunders's claim is, too, instructive. The source on which she principally draws, Ralph Burns's 'Review of Activities', written in his position as chief of OMGUS's Cultural Affairs

---

[81] Thacker, *Music after Hitler*, 105.   [82] Ibid., 177–8.   [83] Monod, *Settling Scores*, 198–9.

Branch, dates from July 1949 and refers quite clearly to the courses of that year. The presence of René Leibowitz – who was a faculty member in composition only in 1948 and 1949, and then, much later, in 1955 – is a clear marker, as is the reference to an article written by Holger Hagen for the *Neue Zeitung* in the same month. Saunders quotes at length from Burns's report:

> It was generally conceded that much of this music was worthless and had better been left unplayed. The over-emphasis on twelve-tone music was regretted. One critic described the concerts as 'The Triumph of Dilettantism' … The French students remained aloof from the others and acted in a snobbish way [and] their teacher, Leibowitz, represents and admits as valid only the most radical kind of music and is openly disdainful of any other. His attitude is aped by his students. It was generally felt that next year's [course] must follow a different, more catholic programme.[84]

In this case, Saunders's description of the courses as having fundamentally to do with the Americans becomes more plausible: if the beginnings of Darmstadt (after relatively messy, homespun versions had been attempted in 1946 and 1947) can be instead centred shortly thereafter, then a claim for the impact of the Americans, at least in the person of Everett Helm, on the shape of the courses is more easy to understand.

This also ties in with the end of denazification and the cessation of vetting by the ICD:

> In November 1946, McClure informed all his subordinates that future decisions on the licensing and registration of musicians and artists would not need clearance from the Intelligence Branch, and in January 1947 Music officers were told that 'the authority granted Information Control to apply a higher standard than Spruchkammer, or similar clearances … will not apply to conductors, artists and musicians'. After this, excluded musicians in the American Zone were able, one by one, to resume their former way of life.[85]

By 1948, blacklisting had come to an end, and so even compromised individuals such as Heiß and Fortner were able to lecture at Darmstadt without any threat of sanction (as indeed they did: Heiß taught in 1948, 1953, and 1954;[86] Fortner yet more regularly, in 1948, 1949, 1951, 1953, 1955, and, for the last time, 1959).[87]

---

[84] Saunders, *Who Paid the Piper?*, 23–4.   [85] Thacker, *Music after Hitler*, 53.
[86] See Carla Henius, 'Genie-Blitze in der Waschküche: Erinnerung an Hermann Heiß', in Stephan et al. (eds.), *Von Kranichstein zur Gegenwart*, 44–8.
[87] Fortner was supposed to lead the composition courses in 1957, but was prevented from attendance through illness. Wolfgang Fortner to Wolfgang Steinecke, 6 July 1957, IMD. See also Peter Cahn, 'Wolfgang Fortners Kompositionskursse in Darmstadt (1946–51)', in Stephan et al. (eds.), *Von Kranichstein zur Gegenwart*, 36–43, and Roth, *Ein Rangierbahnhof der Modern*, esp. 189–208.

The early years

While the above gives a sense of who the major figures in Darmstadt's early years were, whose initial idea the Darmstadt New Music Courses were remains unclear. Though Gerberding suggests bluntly that '[t]he programme of the Ferienkurse was conceived by Steinecke', this seems highly unlikely, not least given his own scholarly interests.[88] His musicological work towards the end of the war is typical in this sense: an incomplete habilitation draft, 'Der Geist der Barockmusik', a biography of Buxtehude, and a history of protestant church music in the seventeenth century, as well as sketches for a history of Baroque music in Darmstadt.[89] This is hardly the resumé of a man who might be expected to found an institution dedicated to the performance of new music.[90] Kovács's account, as Thacker pithily observes, 'reports, and dismisses, Wolfgang Fortner's claim in 1981 to have suggested the outline of the summer school to the Darmstadt Kulturreferent, Wolfgang Steinecke'.[91] Yet perhaps the claim is too quickly passed over. Fortner was certainly already known to Steinecke. In April 1946, in collaboration with the Neue Darmstädter Sezession – whose Willi Hofferberth had, as noted above, brought Steinecke to Metzger's attention in the first place – a 'composition evening with Wolfgang Fortner' was arranged which, as Gerberding describes it, sounds not wholly dissimilar in aim from that which dominated the early new music courses. It understood its purpose as, quite simply, the raising of awareness of contemporary music.[92] If Fortner is to be taken at his word, it also suggests an additional reason why Steinecke would have felt his presence necessary, despite the complexities of his position with respect to the Americans.

This might be compared, then, with the rather more developed version of this idea which was published as Steinecke's introduction to the programme booklet for the 1946 courses, which is worth quoting from at some length:

---

[88] Gerberding, *Darmstädter Kulturpolitik*, 52.
[89] Custodis, *Tradition – Koalitionen – Visionen*, 26.
[90] Steinecke's early compositional efforts do not, either, suggest any strong interest in new music, representing a largely effective but already outmoded style. See ibid., 100–3. This said, Herbert Eimert's doctoral dissertation, which focussed on formal structures in seventeenth- and eighteenth-century music, would have given little indication that he, too, would be a leading figure in new music in post-war Germany. His case, however, is certainly a little different from Steinecke's, since he had also published his *Atonale Lehrbuch* in 1924, an event which led to his departure from the Musikhochschule in Cologne, directed as it was against the conservative thinking of one of his teachers there, Franz Bölsche (Christian Blüggel, *E. = Ethik + Ästhetik: Zur Musikkritik Herbert Eimerts* (Saarbrücken: Pfau, 2002), 9–10).
[91] Thacker, *Music after Hitler*, 78. The original reference may be found in Inge Kovács, 'Die Institution – Entstehung und Struktur', in Gianmario Borio and Hermann Danuser (eds.), *Im Zenit der Moderne* (Freiburg im Breisgau: Rombach, 1997), vol. I, 67.
[92] Gerberding, *Darmstädter Kulturpolitik*, 50.

> Behind us lies a time in which almost all the essential powers of new music were disconnected from German musical life. For twelve years, names like Hindemith and Stravinsky, Schoenberg and Krenek, Milhaud and Honegger, Shostakovich and Prokofiev, Bartók, Weill, and many others were proscribed. For twelve years a criminal cultural politics robbed German musical life of its leading figures and its continuity [. . .] Today, the narrow boundaries which enclosed German musical life for a decade have fallen. Possibilities for free development have been returned to us [. . .] Only if our new musical blood comes into contact with the true creative forces of our time can these possibilities fruitfully renew German musical life. It is from the recognition of this need that the Ferienkurse for international new music have been conceived [. . .] The Darmstädter Ferienkurse represent a serious attempt actively to come to terms with the problems of composition and representation which new music presents.[93]

Though Steinecke would keep to this line throughout his tenure as director of the courses – an essay of his published in the *Darmstädter Beiträge zur neuen Musik* shortly after his death suggested that 'the torn threads had to be laboriously re-tied' – it is the sense that this was ongoing labour that is most pertinent to his description.[94] Despite Steinecke's successor, Ernst Thomas, making the claim in 1959 that 'the first years of the Ferienkurse stood entirely under the sign of "making good"',[95] the first years of the new music courses at Darmstadt were reactionary too. Sometimes this was expressed in ways which would seem pertinent only later, but in some cases there were composers featured who flourished in the Nazi era. As mentioned above, Helmut Degen, Hugo Distler, Paul Höffer, and Ernst Pepping were all featured, despite their blacklisted status. Not only that, but Degen gave the first of five 'Composer Self-Portraits' on 26 August 1946, and Hugo Herrmann (who had published an arrangement of the 'Horst-Wessel-Lied' for accordion, led the Swabian Gauchor, district choir, of the German

---

[93] Wolfgang Steinecke, introductory note for the 1946 Darmstadt Ferienkurse programme booklet, reprinted in Borio and Danuser (eds.), *Im Zenit der Moderne*, vol. I, 25. Kovács is quite right, however, to observe that in the early years of the courses especially, the matter of what precisely they were and what they were for was in some flux. At points Darmstadt certainly was a centre for the communication of international new music, just as an examination of the early years would suggest; at others, it was close to a new music festival, with discourse surrounding new music at a low level. Rather later, in the mid 1950s, it developed more of the character of a teaching space, essentially a compositional masterclass. By this point, all three aspects were in play, but in truth their relative importance to one another never wholly settled. Thus, even if Fortner did play a key role in the initial framing of ideas, many (if not most) decisions were taken by Steinecke, often on an impromptu, improvised basis. See Kovács, 'Die Institution – Entstehung und Struktur', 67.

[94] Wolfgang Steinecke, 'Kranichstein – Geschichte, Idee, Ergebnisse', *Darmstädter Beiträge zur neuen Musik*, vol. 4 (1962), 10.

[95] Ernst Thomas, 'Darmstadt: Internationale Ferienkurse für Neue Musik', in German Section of the International Society for New Music (eds.), *Neue Musik in der Bundesrepublik Deutschland: Dokumentation 1958/59* (Mainz: Schott, 1959), 26.

Introduction: music after catastrophe

Sängerbund, and was a party member after 1939) gave the third. Ottmar Gerster, whose position regarding the Nazi regime was, to be sure, ambiguous, but who was nevertheless listed as one of the most important cultural figures of the Third Reich in the so-called *Gottbegnadeten-Liste* ('God-gifted list') of 1944, gave the fourth. For all that, Siegfried Mauser's assessment is essentially correct.[96] First, concert proceedings were dominated by the music of Hindemith, with performances of two piano sonatas, two flute sonatas, a horn sonata, a violin sonata, *Ludus tonalis*, four songs from *Das Marienleben*, and his String Quartet in E flat. Not only this, but the participants of the courses themselves also performed his *Lehrstück* (twice), the *Meditation* for violin and piano, and *Die junge Magd*. Second, there were no lectures which focussed either on questions of aesthetics or on compositional technique. Instead what predominated were, exactly as Steinecke's description of his aims would suggest, presentations on the new music of the Soviet Union (Karl H. Wörner), England (Fred Hamel), France (Heinrich Strobel), and the United States (Holger E. Hagen), and ones which focussed on music characterised by genre or style: Georg Kuhlmann discussed contemporary piano music, Fred Hamel presented orchestral music, and Friedrich Noack gave an introduction to contemporary choral music, while Hermann Heiß presented an introduction to twelve-tone music. There could be little sense, though, from Heiß's lecture that any of the Second Viennese School composers could have any great significance for Darmstadt. Certainly, no music by Schoenberg, Berg, or Webern was played in 1946, and, if Edwin Kuntz's description is any indication, the results of discussions around Heiß's lectures suggested quite the opposite: 'Schoenberg's creations – this is the upshot too of the examinations and discussions carried out in Darmstadt – are seen today as fruitless and wholly transcended'.[97] As far as the other, ostensibly more 'advanced', trends in new music were concerned, these too were marginal: Bartók was represented through a single performance, that of the early *Two Rumanian Dances* (1909–10), while two pieces of Stravinsky were on the programme: the *Duo concertant* (1931–2) and the *Serenade en la* (1925). These first courses were barely recognisable as being of the same nature as those of the 1950s. Indeed, both their length (four weeks in total) and their closing not with music but with Schiller's *Mary Stuart* mark 1946 out as an exceptional year.

The situation was already a little different by 1947. In place of generality, presentations in this year focussed on 'Leading Masters of New Music', with

---

[96] Siegfried Mauser, 'Emigranten bei den Ferienkursen in Darmstadt (1946–1951)', in Horst Weber (ed.), *Musik in der Emigration 1933–1945* (Stuttgart: J. B. Metzler, 1994), 242–3.
[97] Edwin Kuntz, 'Zeitgenössiche Musik', *Rhein-Neckar-Zeitung*, 3 October 1946, quoted in Mauser, 'Emigranten bei den Ferienkursen', 243.

lectures on Berg (Hans Mayer), Schoenberg (Hans Heinz Stuckenschmidt), Bartók, Alfredo Casella, and de Falla (dealt with in a single presentation by Karl Holl), and Stravinsky (Heinrich Strobel). Music by all of these composers was performed but, again, there was certainly no sense of any 'party line'. Alongside them could be heard Milhaud, Debussy, Honegger, and even Ravel. Orff's newly revised *Der Mond* (1937–8) was premièred, and a chamber version of Bach's *Art of Fugue*, prepared by Roger Vuataz, was performed too, by the orchestra of the Landestheater of Darmstadt, under the direction of Hermann Scherchen.[98] Inevitably, Hindemith still stood at the centre of proceedings, even if he was, himself, absent. As Mauser rightly observes, however, by 1947 Hindemith was already seen by some as essentially conservative. In 1948 and 1949, the number of pieces by him at the courses decreased markedly, and his music was heard only sporadically in the early 1950s. The feeling was by that stage mutual. Willy Strecker, the director of Schott, wrote to Hindemith on 14 July 1949, directly after the close of that year's courses: 'Sadly, there was a fair number of young people there who are now totally confused and no longer have any idea what they ought to do, and (amongst other pieces) would now throw your more recent music, like the Cello Sonata and the Piano Concerto, on the scrap heap.'[99] For Hindemith, whatever the young composers at Darmstadt might think was ultimately an irrelevance. He replied to Strecker a few days later: 'Darmstadt Music Days, hahaha. That's exactly what I think. To be on the scrap heap is a badge of honour.'[100]

The change, which is to say the beginnings of the foundations of what Darmstadt would become, occurred in 1948. With currency reform, as noted below in more detail, the courses' finances stood in a desperate situation. However, at the same time, travel between the Western zones of occupation became easier (though this had been less of an issue between the British and American zones since the creation of the jointly administered territory, Bizonia, at the beginning of 1947), and, much more significantly, international travel into and out of what would become West Germany was more straightforward. In this year, the sense that the courses would be an

---

[98] See Helmut Mendius, 'Aus der Sicht der Orchestermusikers', in Stephan et al. (eds.), *Von Kranichstein zur Gegenwart*, 58–9, and Joachim Lucchesi, 'Um in ihnen mehr Klarheit zu schaffen: Hermann Scherchen in Darmstadt', in Stephan et al. (eds.), *Von Kranichstein zur Gegenwart*, 60–4.

[99] Willy Strecker to Paul Hindemith, 14 July 1949, quoted in Gianmario Borio, 'Kontinuität der Moderne?', in Borio and Danuser (eds.), *Im Zenit der Moderne*, vol. I, 165.

[100] Hindemith to Strecker, 19 July 1949, quoted in Borio, 'Kontinuität der Moderne?', 165. In his Norton lectures at Harvard, Hindemith had referred to twelve-tone music as being akin to an 'epidemic of measles', from which affliction it was to be hoped that the composers recovered (Paul Hindemith, *A Composer's World: Horizons and Limitations. The Charles Eliot Norton Lectures 1949–1950* (Cambridge, MA: Harvard University Press, 1952), 122).

Introduction: music after catastrophe

ongoing event was formalised by the city, with the official foundation of the Internationales Musikinsitut Schloss Kranichstein and, perhaps more importantly, the rebranding of the courses themselves from 'Courses for International New Music' to 'International Courses for New Music'. Although it would not be until 1949 that the courses became truly international (rather than merely *presenting* music which was), this was a significant change, and was reflected in the lecturing staff whom Steinecke was able to win with the altered situation regarding visas. Fortner and Heiß continued to lead the composition seminars, but René Leibowitz came from Paris, bringing his interests in twelve-tone music *à la* Schoenberg with him and,[101] of more practical significance, Rolf Liebermann came from Switzerland to lecture on 'applied music', specifically focussing on music for the radio. It was not in his lectures, though, that Liebermann made the greatest impact. Liebermann brokered funding from the Swiss Pro Helvetia Foundation which enabled the purchase of a wide range of scores and parts, which formed the basis of the Musikinstitut's holdings.[102] This, combined with Heiß's approach to Vienna's Universal Edition, meant that the stranglehold that Schott (based in Mainz, relatively close to Darmstadt) had had on the scores available to the courses was broken. Steinecke's excitement about this is evident in a letter to Heiß of 2 December 1947: 'What your triumphal information regarding Universal Edition really means is that you have shown me the way in which I can obtain scores from them. I have in any case tried to get study and performance materials from them in every way available to me; as you know yourself, at present that is near to impossible.'[103] Though there is nothing in the record to suggest that Schott pursued any active determination of the programme of the courses, in the first two years Darmstadt was restricted by what it was possible to acquire in terms of performance materials and, for the most part, this meant Schott.[104] Nor was Schott's Willy Strecker unaware of the fortuitous situation in which he found himself, writing to Hindemith on 16 August 1946:

> From here I can report only good news about the ongoing interest in your works. It's a real stroke of luck that all of your works are available here and that performance materials stand at the ready. The twelve-year hiatus hasn't done any damage, since we were always working underground and, notwithstanding the quality of the works, everyone is grabbing whatever is readily available.

---

[101] See Reinhard Kapp, 'René Leibowitz in Darmstadt', in Stephan et al. (eds.), *Von Kranichstein zur Gegenwart*, 76–85 for a fuller account of Leibowitz's presence.
[102] Kovács, 'Die Institution – Entstehung und Struktur', 92.
[103] Steinecke to Hermann Heiß, 2 December 1947, quoted in Kovács, 'Die Institution – Entstehung und Struktur', 85.
[104] Kovács, 'Die Institution – Entstehung und Struktur', 85.

> Almost all the other publishers can't deliver. Therefore Krenek, Schoenberg, Bartók, Weil [sic], Alban Berg, etc., etc. have fallen right into oblivion, and, of the whole group from that time, only you and Stravinsky have been spared.[105]

That Steinecke would have been relieved to distance himself from Schott may be explained in other respects, too. As Thacker observes, though the French occupying forces in Mainz felt that Ludwig and Willy Strecker 'made a favourable impression, and appeared to be good anti-fascists with an international outlook', it would not have been difficult to come to an opposing view:

> Schotts had been a major publisher of Nazi and militarist music, as must have been evident from even a cursory examination of their catalogues. The Strecker brothers may have spoken excellent French, but they had not made Schotts Germany's largest music publisher before 1945 by resisting the Nazis. Ludwig was apparently a Party member, and Willy had written enthusiastically about the Nazis to Stravinsky in April 1933: 'This movement has so much that is healthy and positive about it ... a welcome cleaning-up has been undertaken ... in an attempt to restore decency and order'.[106]

It was, in some respects, ironic that it was through Heiß's ministries that Steinecke was able to loosen the grip that a seemingly compromised publishing house had on the direction of the courses, since Heiß's own record was, as shown above, far from straightforward. Yet Steinecke's use of Heiß and Fortner, as well as of composers like Degen, Distler, Höffer, and Pepping, and of Schott as a publishing house, gives a strong indication of at least two things. First, in the immediate post-war era, if the courses were to take place at all, Steinecke had to make use of those figures and publishers who were available to him: it is little surprise in this context, then, that Heiß was a Darmstadt composer, Schott was based in nearby Mainz, and Fortner was, at least comparatively, local in Heidelberg. Second, and no less importantly, Steinecke was *willing* to make such decisions, which is to say that, from his perspective, that 'culture' be returned to Darmstadt's day-to-day life was obviously more important than the precise nature *of* that culture. Steinecke's decisions, especially in the early years of the courses, were evidently guided more by contingency than by ideology.

The music presented in 1948 should give some impression of just how slowly trends changed at Darmstadt. Hindemith was, once again, a

---

[105] Strecker to Hindemith, 16 August 1946, quoted in Kim H. Kowalke, 'Music Publishing and the Nazis: Schott, Universal Edition, and their Composers', in Michael H. Kater and Albrecht Riethmüller (eds.), *Music and Nazism: Art under Tyranny, 1933–1945* (Laaber, 2003), 174. I am grateful to Ian Pace for drawing my attention to this source.

[106] Thacker, *Music after Hitler*, 64. See also Kowalke, 'Music Publishing and the Nazis', 170–218.

Introduction: music after catastrophe

strong presence, represented by the Solo Viola Sonata, op. 25, no. 1 (1922), the Cello Concerto (1940), the Sixth String Quartet (1945), the prelude to *When Lilacs Last in the Door-Yard Bloom'd* (1946), and *Das Marienleben* (1922–3, rev. 1936–48), as well as a studio concert of extracts, performed by the participants. Yet alongside this strong showing by Hindemith (as noted above, rapidly becoming of less apparent interest to the participants themselves) were Boris Blacher, Karl Amadeus Hartmann, Stravinsky, Prokofiev, Kodály, Walter Piston, Honegger, Messiaen, Bartók, Britten, and de Falla. There was also the first major set of performances of the music of the Second Viennese School, including the first performance of Webern at the courses. As well as Schoenberg's Second Chamber Symphony, op. 38 (1906–39), Schoenberg's Piano Concerto, op. 42 (1942) and Webern's Variations for piano, op. 27 (1935–6) were given their German premières by Peter Stadlen, who, as a result of the easing of travel restrictions, came to Darmstadt from London in that year. Yet there was no sense in which the Viennese composers dominated.

For a long time, Steinecke operated with almost total autonomy in Darmstadt's cultural office. Although a clerical assistant, Günther Michel, was appointed in December 1945, until the end of 1947, in the culture of austerity that pervaded post-war Germany until currency reform, only Steinecke, Michel, and a secretary were employed by the Kulturverwaltung (culture department). At the beginning of 1948, however, a further administrator was engaged: Georg Pfarrer. Since Steinecke had become used to running the office 'his way', unsurprisingly there were frictions between Pfarrer and Steinecke, principally focussed upon what parts of Steinecke's role now fell to Pfarrer and what Steinecke retained.[107] In any case, the problem did not last long. On 6 April 1948, Steinecke wrote to Metzger that he had received an offer from *Die Welt* to take over as head of its culture department, which would provide him with a substantially greater income than he received from Darmstadt as its culture chief. The subject of Steinecke's salary had been a bone of contention between Steinecke and the city administration ever since he took office, and he took the opportunity to remind Metzger that he regarded his current position as 'on the same level as the cleaners who sweep the town hall'. Moreover, he had stressed on an ongoing basis that the repeated short-term contracts he had for his work made it impossible to plan for the city's cultural life – the new music courses not least – in anything more than piecemeal fashion.[108] If Steinecke had thought that the city would give in to his demand for a higher

---

[107] Gerberding, *Darmstädter Kulturpolitik*, 39.
[108] Steinecke to Ludwig Metzger, 6 April 1948, SAD.

salary and a longer-term contract, he was mistaken. On the contrary, the decision was taken that it would be better to let Steinecke take the job with *Die Welt*, with his contract ending on 31 July 1948. When Steinecke left the culture department, Pfarrer took over as head of culture for the city.[109]

1948 was, in general, a parlous year for the courses. Notwithstanding Steinecke's departure, the currency reform which led to Germany's economic recovery – and, indeed, in time the so-called economic miracle – had left the finances of the courses in ruins. Darmstadt was still dominated by German participants – in 1946 0.8% of participants came from outside Germany; in 1947, the figure stood at 1.4%; by 1948, it was still only 6% – and currency reform meant that it was practically impossible to accept participants from the Russian zone, who had only a currency which was now useless in the Western zones. Though the courses proceeded, with the support of Metzger, he had to face stern criticism from local communist politicians. Nevertheless, Metzger held firm to his conviction that support for new music was precisely what it meant for him to be committed to Darmstadt as a cultural centre. Perhaps his defence, a written response to the communists dated 10 September 1948, would have been less strong had Steinecke truly left the scene.[110] Yet by the close of the 1948 courses, it seems that Steinecke had devised a plan which would ensure their survival, testament not least to his own apparent belief that they were his greatest success as head of culture in Darmstadt. It can hardly have hurt that 1948 was the first year in which the courses had begun to receive serious press attention and, as detailed above, had genuinely come to the attention of the Americans. As early as 3 August 1948, Steinecke sent a proposal to the city that he become director of the Kranichsteiner Musikinstitut, with ultimate responsibility for the Ferienkurse, alongside his work for *Die Welt*. He estimated that he could devote ten days per month to the role, travelling to Darmstadt from Essen four times each month, and could take six weeks' unpaid leave during June and July each year to ensure that final arrangements were in place and to oversee the courses. He proposed that positions be created (or continued) to ensure smooth running: he proposed that Hellmuth Vriesen act as head of the library and as Steinecke's proxy in his absence and that W. W. Göttig be director of the logistical aspects of the organisation. He also argued that continued secretarial support would be vital.[111] The city authorities responded promptly, on 16 August, that they were in agreement with all of Steinecke's suggestions. The only issue that

---

[109] Gerberding, *Darmstädter Kulturpolitik*, 39. [110] Ibid., 56–61.
[111] Steinecke to the office of the Oberbürgermeister of Darmstadt, 3 August 1948, SAD.

Introduction: music after catastrophe 31

remained unclear by this stage was whether Schloss Kranichstein, the venue for the first three courses, would continue to be available.[112]

Schloss Kranichstein, in fact, was not the property of the city. Darmstadt rented it from Prince Ludwig von Hessen-Darmstadt, who decided not to renew the lease, handing it instead to the Central Committee of the Quakers of West Germany.[113] A later director of the Darmstadt courses, Friedrich Hommel, speculated that Ludwig's concern may well have been that the courses were already growing to such a size that the Schloss could become subject to a compulsory purchase order, which he would have had no intention of allowing.[114] Steinecke was personally inconvenienced by this, since he and his wife, Hella, had been living in a flat at the Schloss. A solution at least to the problem of a venue for the new music courses was found through the Seventh-Day Adventists, who had recently taken possession of the Seminar Marienhöhe, a little way south of the city centre of Darmstadt.[115] The Seminar Marienhöhe presented only one major difficulty: its new owners insisted upon a strict ban on alcohol and tobacco, though ultimately Georg Pfarrer negotiated a compromise on these issues.[116] Despite the move to the Marienhöhe, many critics and composers persisted in referring to the courses as the Kranichsteiner, rather than Darmstädter, Ferienkurse for many years afterwards, even though Kranichstein had been the seat of the courses for a mere two years, and a two-year period that most had never experienced.

While Messiaen attended the courses in 1949, he was not, as Hill and Simeone suggest, really there as a member of lecturing staff, and he neither taught students nor lectured, though he performed *Visions de l'amen* (1943) in its German première with Yvonne Loriod on 23 June of that year.[117] Borio's pithy summary of Messiaen's time in Darmstadt in 1949 as a 'brief visit' is about right.[118] Nor is it really possible to suggest that Messiaen's composition there of *Mode de valeurs et d'intensités*, which would of course become of vital importance for the younger generation, was anything other than, ultimately, coincidental. As Hill shows, Messiaen's conceptual path to the *Quatre études de rythme* (1949–50) had begun long before:

> As early as 1945 an entry in Messiaen's diary (22 July) shows him speculating on applying serial organisation to tempo. The first mention of 'rhythmic studies' came in 1947: Messiaen's notes clearly show that he had systematic

---

[112] Feick (city treasurer) to Steinecke, 16 August 1948, SAD.
[113] Gerberding, *Darmstädter Kulturpolitik*, 39. [114] Ibid., 162 n. 206. [115] Ibid., 59.
[116] Ibid., 162 n. 210.
[117] Peter Hill and Nigel Simeone, *Olivier Messiaen: Oiseaux exotiques* (Aldershot: Ashgate, 2007), 11.
[118] Borio, 'Kontinuität der Moderne?', 272.

experiment in mind: '... look for melodic movements, chords, rhythmic figures from beyond my language – make myself a little dictionary.' When work on the *Études* began in Darmstadt in June 1949, the first to be completed – *Mode de valeurs et d'intensités* – put into effect an idea sketched three years earlier; at that time Messiaen was planning a ballet on the subject of Time, in which pitch, duration, dynamics and timbre would all be derived from a single 12-note 'serial theme'.[119]

In Germany as a whole there were few senses of any flickerings of the new either. Hindemith's visit to Germany in 1949, under the auspices of the American military, saw him state publicly that he could find nothing new in the German musical scene either in the West or the East. Hindemith wrote to William Glock that 'the musical life is now quite normal with Furtwängler playing Brahms and Bruckner in the same way as nothing happened in the past. All the hopes that something has changed since 45 are gone.'[120] It was certainly not until 1950 that the first signs that something genuinely 'new' might be about to take place in Darmstadt could be seen, and even then only fleetingly, as I outline in what follows.

By 22 September 1949, Steinecke had returned to acting as a freelance journalist. He was released by *Die Welt*, not least because he had found himself in increasing ill-health. Throughout this whole period he was suffering from recurrent bouts of nephritis, which meant that he found himself regularly hospitalised. On this date, Bürgermeister Schroeder proposed that Steinecke act as director of the Kranichsteiner Musikinstitut on a part-time basis,[121] a proposal that the city, now in rather better financial health, agreed to a little over a week later, though it was stipulated that this contract should not be ongoing, but should run only until 31 March 1950.[122] It would not be until 1953 that Steinecke actually received any sort of long-term contract from the city, occasionally acting in the interim as a freelance administrator, occasionally as an official employee of the city. In any case, he remained in regular dispute regarding the precise terms of his service at least until 1957. By this stage, however, the importance of the Ferienkurse to Darmstadt was self-evident, and Steinecke was clearly no longer, in this context, replaceable.

---

[119] Peter Hill, 'Messiaen Recorded: The *Quatre études de rythme*', in Christopher Dingle and Nigel Simeone (eds.), *Olivier Messiaen: Music, Art and Literature* (Aldershot: Ashgate, 2007), 80.
[120] Thacker, *Music after Hitler*, 119.
[121] Bürgermeister Schroeder to the Darmstadt city magistrate, 22 September 1949, SAD.
[122] Darmstadt Stadtoberinspektor to Bürgermeister Schroeder, 30 September 1949, SAD.

PART I

The accidental serialists

1 Arrivals

Maderna and Nono

The first sounds to be heard from the composers who would become known as the 'Darmstadt School' were, in a sense, barely audible. There was little sign at the earliest stages that the first two of those composers to make their presence known at Darmstadt would become figureheads of the courses. It was, in any case, Maderna who would be the first on the scene.

Though it is often held that it was Hermann Scherchen who was responsible for bringing Maderna (and, for that matter, Nono) to Darmstadt,[1] the correspondence between Steinecke and Maderna suggests that Steinecke made the first move, on the recommendation of Karl Amadeus Hartmann. Steinecke wrote to Maderna to enquire whether he had any music which might be suitable for inclusion in a projected 'Music of the Younger Generation' concert on 9 April 1949, suggesting too that he would be delighted if Maderna wished to attend the courses in person.[2] Maderna responded almost a month later with great enthusiasm, excusing his delay in replying on the grounds of having been away in Sicily for much of the preceeding four weeks, and suggesting four possible pieces for inclusion: the Fantasia and Fugue for two pianos (1948), the Double Piano Concerto (1947–8), the *Tre liriche greche* (1948), and his first *Composizione* for orchestra (1948).[3] Though Steinecke showed enthusiasm for all four pieces, suggesting that in principle he had the resources to have any one of them performed,[4] Maderna rapidly withdrew the *Composizione* and the *Tre liriche greche*, on the grounds that the performance materials were not ready.[5] Steinecke then planned to have the concerto performed; indeed this was the plan as late as 22 June 1949, by which time the Hessischer Rundfunk's New Music Week concerts – held in collaboration with the Darmstadt courses – had already begun.[6] Two days later, Maderna clearly intended to be in attendance, sending Steinecke his passport details in order to deal with his visa requirements.[7] Yet in the event Maderna did not reach Darmstadt in

---

[1] Raymond Fearn, *Bruno Maderna* (Chur: Harwood, 1990), 7.
[2] Steinecke to Bruno Maderna, 9 April 1949, in Rossana Dalmonte (ed.), *Bruno Maderna–Wolfgang Steinecke: Carteggio/Briefwechsel* (Lucca: LIM, 2001), 23–4.
[3] Maderna to Steinecke, 11 May 1949, in ibid., 25–6.
[4] Steinecke to Maderna, 15 May 1949, in ibid., 26–7.
[5] Maderna to Steinecke, 6 June 1949, in ibid., 29.
[6] Steinecke to Maderna, 22 June 1949, in ibid., 33–4.
[7] Maderna to Steinecke, 24 June 1949, in ibid., 35.

1949 and, frustratingly, the telegram which explains the reasons for this has not survived. In any case, Maderna's absence caused Steinecke to take the decision to remove the concerto from the final concert and, instead, programme a performance of the double-piano Fantasia and Fugue, given by Carl Seemann and Peter Stadlen. This may well have been the right decision on several grounds: Hans Heinz Stuckenschmidt had observed that Maderna's piece was 'technically brilliant', but also noted that the quality of performers in general terms was wildly uneven, with Seemann and Stadlen picked out as two of the few high-quality exceptions.[8] Steinecke communicated the success of the première to Maderna in a letter of 19 August 1949, adding that it was his hope that Maderna would attend in person in the following year.[9]

Maderna was already well aware of the music of the Second Viennese School, not least because 'keeping in touch' with the music that was being written abroad was much more straightforward in Mussolini's Italy than it had been in Hitler's Germany. As early as December 1943, Maderna had conducted Webern's Variations for orchestra, op. 30.[10] Yet the Darmstadt audience could have had little indication of a developing relationship to twelve-tone music from the Fantasia and Fugue. Like Webern's String Quartet, op 28, it is based on the B–A–C–H motif, but while Webern built a twelve-tone row from these four notes, Maderna kept to only eight notes and restricted himself in terms of available pitches to only these eight pitch classes for the vast majority of the piece (although the fugue reaches the complete chromatic). In terms of figuration Fearn is right to observe that a Bartókian character is in greater evidence than a Webernian or Schoenbergian one, and the presence of a direct quotation from the chorale *Vor deinem Thron tret'ich hiermit* recalls Berg rather than the more austere brands of twelve-tone music that one might more typically associate with the name Darmstadt.[11]

Even if Scherchen was not the person from whom Steinecke first learned of Maderna, it was almost certainly under his aegis that Maderna's second performance at Darmstadt arose: his *Composizione II* (1950) for chamber orchestra was performed by the orchestra of the Darmstadt Landestheater under Scherchen, who was also the piece's dedicatee, on 26 August 1950.[12] Fearn is keen to distance this, too, from any sense that it might be regarded

---

[8] Hans Heinz Stuckenschmidt, 'Apokalyptische Gespräche und Klänge: Nachwort zum Sommer der Neuen Musik in Darmstadt', *Neue Zeitung*, 7 August 1949.
[9] Steinecke to Maderna, 19 August 1949, in Dalmonte (ed.), *Bruno Maderna–Wolfgang Steinecke*, 36–7.
[10] Fearn, *Bruno Maderna*, 5–6.
[11] Fearn gives a much fuller analysis of the Fantasia and Fugue. See ibid., 8–16.
[12] Steinecke to Maderna, 24 May 1950, in Dalmonte (ed.), *Bruno Maderna–Wolfgang Steinecke*, 36–7.

Arrivals

as a 'Darmstadt work'. In point of fact, Fearn links it more closely to that which at the very beginning of the 1950s *was* predominant at the courses, at least in part. He suggests that

> it might almost be thought rather anachronistic in its mixture of elements: in its 'Neo-classical' or 'Expressionistic' usage of popular dance-forms as a major part of the structure, in the employment of an Ancient Greek melody (the famous *Epitaph of Seikilos*) at the beginning and end of this one-movement piece, in the distinctly Bergian writing in the Waltzes, the Webernesque pointillism of the Rumba, and in its overall quality of lyrical expressivity as the main impetus.

Maderna's 'visiting-card' was not as unusual as Fearn suggests. On the one hand, its expressionism and neo-classicism found analogues in much of the rest of what was presented at Darmstadt in 1950 – Bartók was the most heavily featured composer, alongside Krenek, while Schoenberg, Berg, and Hauer received a single performance each – and, on the other hand, as I hope will become clear below, the idea that a typical Darmstadt work might be held to be identifiable is dubious.[13]

In any case, Maderna's *Composizione II* was overshadowed in 1950 by the première of Luigi Nono's *Variazioni canoniche sulla serie dell'op. 41 di Arnold Schoenberg* (1950) for orchestra, Nono having been recommended to Steinecke by both Maderna and Scherchen.[14] Though Nono's accompanying letter is lost, he sent the score of the *Variazioni canoniche* to Steinecke on 14 May 1950.[15] Steinecke confirmed to Nono that his score had been selected by the Darmstadt jury for performance roughly two months before its scheduled performance on 27 August 1950.[16]

The performance was a disaster, or a major scandal at least. According to Hans Heinz Stuckenschmidt's report, almost the whole audience joined in with whistling and catcalling, though intermingled with applause and shouts of 'bravo', and the second movement, 'with its ejaculatory style, its disruption and ripping to shreds of the melody, its overlong pauses and breaks of timbre was incomprehensible to the unprepared'. For Stuckenschmidt, the piece was comprehensible, just about, as an experiment, but was certainly not yet music. That said, Stuckenschmidt's report seems to have been either completed in haste or rather poorly edited, since it is littered with errors, two of the more obvious ones being the identification of Nono's home city as Rome and that Schoenberg's op. 41, the series of

---

[13] Fearn, *Bruno Maderna*, 55.
[14] This is suggested in a letter from Steinecke to Maderna, 24 May 1950, in Dalmonte (ed.), *Bruno Maderna–Wolfgang Steinecke*, 39–40.
[15] This is confirmed in Steinecke's reply to Nono, 25 May 1950, ALN.
[16] Steinecke to Luigi Nono, 26 June 1950, ALN.

which was at the heart of Nono's piece, was the Piano Concerto (in fact, op. 42 of 1942) rather than the *Ode to Napoleon Buonaparte* (1942).[17]

Stuckenschmidt's verdict was, though, positively effusive in comparison with the judgement of the correspondent of the *Frankfurter Allgemeine Zeitung*: 'The work is, for a public concert, out of the question, and only really suitable for a workshop [...] This indigestion of a musical stammerer, this corpse of a compositional figure ought not to have got through the barricade of a jury.' Nono had 'sinned against all that is human in music'.[18] Wilhelm Hermann proposed that perhaps it would be best 'to find a collective name other than music'.[19] It can hardly have helped, if Nono's recollection of events was accurate, that Scherchen himself insulted the audience, loudly, calling them 'a bunch of pigs'.[20]

Elsewhere, there were pleas for greater indulgence. The *Aachener Nachrichten*'s correspondent argued that the *Variazioni canoniche* were, at the very least, the most original of the pieces played and that, moreover, 'one must get to know the work better; most especially one must hear it in a performance which has greater authority than what Scherchen was able to achieve in only a few rehearsals'.[21] Josef Rufer, too, defended Nono, praising his 'astounding musical and sonic fantasy' and observing that it was regrettable that unfamiliarity had seemed to lead to rejection of Nono's music.[22] Notwithstanding the few voices of support amongst the press, there could have been little expectation that Nono would become one of Darmstadt's leading figures.

It seems difficult in retrospect to imagine that the pluralist style of Maderna's *Composizione II* would lead particularly strongly to associations with twelve-tone music, but both he and Nono seem to have been branded in some quarters 'young Italian dodecaphonists', Walther Harth making the specific association in *Der Kurier*,[23] while Humphrey Searle observed that

---

[17] Hans Heinz Stuckenschmidt, 'Spielerei, Pathos und Verinnerlichung: Abschluß der Darmstädter Konzertreihe', *Neue Zeitung*, 30 August 1950.
[18] 'Protest nach zwei Seiten: "Musik der jungen Generation" in Darmstadt', *Frankfurter Allgemeine Zeitung*, 30 August 1950.
[19] Wilhelm Hermann, 'Die jüngste Komponistengeneration: Internationaler Wettstreit bei den Darmstädter Ferienkursen', *Badisches Tagblatt*, 4 September 1950.
[20] Luigi Nono, 'Un'autobiografia dell'autore raccontata da Enzo Restagno' [1987], in *Scritti e colloqui*, ed. Angela Ida De Benedictis and Veniero Rizzardi (Lucca: Ricordi, 2001), vol. II, 495. This interview is also available in German as 'Ein Autobiographie des Komponisten Enzo Restagno mitgeteilt' [1987], in *Luigi Nono: Dokumente, Materielen*, ed. Andreas Wagner (Saarbrücken: Pfau, 2003), 34–138, or as *Incontri: Luigi Nono im Gespräch mit Enzo Restagno*, ed. Matteo Nanni and Rainer Schmusch (Hofheim: Wolke, 2004). There are no compelling reasons to prefer one version over another.
[21] [K.], 'Musik der jungen Generation: Studienkonzert für Alban Berg und Ernst Krenek – das Ende der Experimente in Kranichstein', *Aachener Nachrichten*, 5 September 1950.
[22] Josef Rufer, 'Darmstädter Thema mit Variationen', *Der Mittag*, 7 September 1950.
[23] Walther Harth, 'Musik-Olympiade der Jüngsten', *Der Kurier*, 8 September 1950.

Maderna's idiom was 'somewhat derived from Webern'.[24] Steinecke's own broadcast for Radio Basel is arguably closer to the mark: 'the tonal material [...] is here placed radically into question, becoming a style which developed in the music of Anton Webern, disrupted and broken apart. Not only Schoenberg's method, but also the spirit and style of his musical language are here the starting point for a fresh confrontation.'[25]

Yet the relationship to Schoenberg is certainly more one of spirit and style than it is of technique. For his own part, Nono was clear: the *Variazioni canoniche* 'deal with some elements which are composed in a canonic way', and those canons were particularly to do with the study of fifteenth-century puzzle canons, which Nono had undertaken together with Maderna.[26] Though the working of the canons through the piece may well be rigorous, they are generated, initially at least, through canonic, rather than serial, permutations of the intervallic content of the Schoenberg series, although as this discussion progresses, it may become clear that the boundary between serial and canonic procedures is probably far from a clear one.[27] Nevertheless, Nono's working on a rhythmic level begins to come very *close* to systematic procedure (though it would be going too far to claim, as Rizzardi does, that Nono's base rhythm operates as a 'true rhythmic series').[28] The base rhythmic series, such as it is, is as shown in Figure 1.1.

As Roderick shows, at the beginning of the fourth movement of the *Variazioni canoniche*, the 'Allegro violento', Nono begins to rotate his rhythmic units, tying them directly to particular dyads, which results in the following sequence between bars 153 and 164:

Pitches	8–9	5–4	12–1	3–2	6–7	11–10
Rhythmic unit	1	2	3	4	5	6
Pitches	11–10	6–7	5–4	8–9	3–2	12–1
Rhythmic unit	6	5	2	1	4	3

---

[24] Humphrey Searle, 'Young Composers at Darmstadt', *Halle: Magazine for the Music Lover* (October 1950), 9.
[25] Wolfgang Steinecke, '2. Vortrage: Darmstadt', broadcast, Radio Basel, date unknown but presumably late 1950, transcript IMD.
[26] Nono, 'Un'autobiografia dell'autore', 489–90.
[27] See Martin Iddon, 'Serial Canon(s): Nono's Variations and Boulez's Structures', in Lisa Colton and Martin Iddon (eds.), *Recycling and Innovation in Contemporary Music* (*Contemporary Music Review*, vol. 29, no. 3 (2010)), 265–75, and Peter Roderick, 'Rebulding a Culture: Studies in Italian Music after Fascism, 1943–1953' (unpublished PhD dissertation, University of York, 2010), 285–306.
[28] Veniero Rizzardi, 'La "nuova scuolo veneziana": 1948–1951', in Gianmario Borio, Giovanni Morelli, and Veniero Rizzardi (eds.), *Le musiche degli anni cinquanta* (Florence: Leo S. Olschki, 2004), 12.

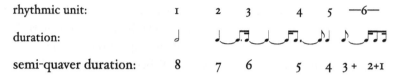

Fig. 1.1 Rhythmic 'series' of Luigi Nono, *Variazioni canoniche*

Yet there is no sense of a slavish adherence to a system. Roderick notes that 'much of the texture is achieved through octave doubling (and even at the fourth), rests are added at will, and note repetition is frequent',[29] though the direct linkages between individual dyads and particular rhythmic cells finds resonance in the sorts of procedures utilised by Karel Goeyvaerts in his Sonata for Two Pianos, to which I return below (see Example 1.1).

In the end, it made little difference whether Nono's procedures in this piece related closely to those of Schoenberg or Webern or anybody else, at least not in terms of the continuing reception of his music at Darmstadt. After the performance, the apparently unique copy of the score for the *Variazioni canoniche* was lost (along with, one presumes, all the orchestral parts). According to a letter from Steinecke to Nono, they were despatched from Darmstadt in the first week of November 1951, but seem never to have reached Venice. Only thirty-five years later did Nono recover the parts and, from them, reconstruct the score, such that the piece received only its second performance on 12 July 1985 in Freiburg im Breisgau, under the direction of Michael Gielen.[30] In the same letter, Steinecke reassured Nono that for his part 'despite all the difficulties' he regarded it of genuine importance that the *Variazioni canoniche* had been presented, adding that he hoped that Nono and Maderna would return to Darmstadt in 1951.[31]

Perhaps more important in the long run than his orchestral première was Nono's encounter with Edgard Varèse at the 1950 courses, which was to prove to be Varèse's sole visit to the courses.[32] Varèse's recollection of his time in Germany, reported in the *New York Times* later that year, is indicative of what a vital position Darmstadt already held as a forum in which ideas could be exchanged, given that there was little opportunity otherwise:

> I told them that since 1945 they could have caught up a little more on modern music. They gave me an answer I couldn't reply to. They said that they wanted to but couldn't find books or scores. This I found to be true. In all Germany, for instance, there is not a Webern score available. Do you realize that? Many

[29] Roderick, 'Rebulding a Culture', 294–5.   [30] Stenzl, *Luigi Nono*, 19.
[31] Steinecke to Nono, 13 November 1950, ALN.   [32] Beal, *New Music, New Allies*, 46–7.

Ex. 1.1 Luigi Nono, *Variazioni canoniche*, bb. 153–64

books are out of print. In all of Germany it is the same. But the young Germans want to learn. It is pernicious propaganda that they don't. But how can they be taught if there is nothing to learn with?[33]

Doubtless, Varèse exaggerated, but the underlying notion that new music was hard to come by is accurate. It is notable, too, that he identified that same cultural hunger of which Adorno had written, with surprise, to Mann. Varèse's mention of the stylistic norms of the music he had encountered in Germany also seems prescient: 'As for the young school of German composers, it is Mr. Varèse's belief that the post-romantic tradition of Mahler, Strauss and Pfitsner [sic] is dead. The new "German school", he thinks, is going off on a tangent – not hypermodern, not exactly neo-classical either,

[33] Harold C. Schonberg, 'U.S. Role Abroad: Varèse Says our Influence must be Cultural Too', *New York Times*, 8 October 1950.

Ex. 1.1 (cont.)

but toward a lean, cryptic style.'[34] Varèse gave only one lecture at Darmstadt in 1950, on the sound-world of electronic music, and received only one performance (of *Ionisation*, sandwiched between Schoenberg's *A Survivor from Warsaw* (1947) and Krenek's Fourth Symphony (1947)). Though Humphrey Searle's review of the courses is effusive, terming *Ionisation* 'an astounding work [...] which exploits every conceivable sonority with the utmost precision and effect', in terms of the German reception, Varèse was largely overshadowed by Schoenberg.[35] Nevertheless, Varèse appears to have been quite active in the field of teaching composition to the young

[34] Ibid. [35] Searle, 'Young Composers at Darmstadt', 9.

participants who had enrolled, even though, as Borio observes, there is little concrete record of the content of those sessions.[36] Alongside Nono, other participants in Varèse's composition course included Heinz-Klaus Metzger, who would become a major critical presence in the Darmstadt of the 1950s, and Dieter Schnebel, an important compositional voice in the Darmstadt of the 1960s and the editor of the first three volumes of Stockhausen's *Texte*.

Nono recalled that before the courses he had had no idea who Varèse was, and had not even ever heard his name.[37] Yet the degree of impact Varèse had was great:

> On the day after the performance I went into his class and he asked me for the score. He analysed it for an hour or more and then, instead of giving me his opinion, confronted me with problems, let me see the problems that this score threw up, and by doing this showed me what I – in many cases without knowing it – had done.[38]

For Nono, Varèse's influence was one which might seem, in retrospect, a fairly conventional reaction to his music, which is to say the 'emancipation' of percussion. Varèse's use of percussion as the central (or only) timbral resource seemed to Nono to be something wholly new on the European stage, even if one might argue that what this showed was the relatively narrow band of music known to Nono at the time.[39] Regardless of the underlying reasons, Varèse seemed to give Nono a sort of permission to think differently about how both timbre and material might be allowed to function in his music. Yet the impact of Varèse was only a part of the story, which is to say that it was important that the meeting of Nono and Varèse, from Nono's perspective, happened when it did. In 1948, during Scherchen's conducting course, Nono had encountered the Brazilian pianist and composer Eunice Katunda (sometimes Catunda), who was visiting Venice as a part of Hans-Joachim Köllreuter's Música Viva ensemble. Katunda was influential politically: she was a communist and, though both Nono and Maderna had already strong leftist inclinations, the example of Katunda was a further spur for them to join to the Partito Comunista Italiano (the Italian Communist Party) in 1952. Musically, however, she was no less significant. She introduced the two Italians to the work of Federico García Lorca and to 'the rhythms of the Mato Grosso [one of Brazil's western states], which anticipated in certain respects what Varèse taught'.[40] It was the combination of the Brazilian rhythms introduced to Nono by Katunda and the timbral 'permissions' of Varèse that led to Nono's second piece for Darmstadt,

---

[36] Borio, 'Kontinuität der Moderne?', 267.   [37] Nono, 'Un'autobiografia dell'autore', 495.
[38] Ibid., 495.   [39] Ibid., 497–8.   [40] Ibid., 501.

Polifonica–Monodia–Ritmica (1951), which, though scored for flute, clarinet, bass clarinet, alto saxophone, horn, piano, and percussion, leaves the winds and brass behind in its final section in exclusive favour of percussion (especially if the piano is considered a percussion instrument). As Nono observed, this piece, like his later first Lorca epitaph, *España en el corazón* (1952), was based not on a row, but on popular musics, in this case a Brazilian song: 'Everybody said that it [*Polifonica–Monodia–Ritmica*] harked back to Webern, while it was actually based on the song 'Jemanja' ['Yemanjá'] [...] I took this material and used it in *Polifonica–Monodia–Ritmica* from both an intervallic and a rhythmic standpoint.'[41] In this sense, though Heile is quite correct in taking Born to task for her claim that 'modernist serialism' made no reference to non-Western musics, the earliest piece that Heile makes reference to in this context is Stockhausen's *Telemusik* (1966).[42] Such a claim can certainly be made in the case of *Polifonica–Monodia–Ritmica* too; even if one might more properly regard it as proto-serial, it is doubtless one of the foundational pieces of the idea of the 'Darmstadt School'.

Nono would write to Scherchen on 2 June 1951 that the first section of the piece, 'Polifonica', was based wholly on permutations of a rhythm he had from Katunda,[43] and, as Nono's sketches for the piece suggest, this is precisely how the rhythmic material is derived in, for instance, the Allegro (from bar 59 onwards). Nono's process for generating fresh rhythms here come from, first, displacing each beat-long section of the basic rhythm by a crotchet and then, second, swapping the first and third crotchet beats of the basic rhythm. Finally, Nono provides retrogrades of both rhythms. As this section of the piece progresses, the rhythms are displaced by smaller values, such that Nono generates, near enough, every possible rhythmic variant available down to displacements by a semiquaver, hardly coincidentally the smallest rhythmic value in the basic rhythm itself (see Figure 1.2 and Example 1.2). However, even if the material is *generated* according to the permutation of a limited range of rhythmic materials, as was the case with *Variazioni canoniche*, there is no sense that the distribution of rhythms as a polyphonic whole is rigidly determined. Indeed, as with the first entry of the clarinet, and the saxophone entry in bar 68, Nono breaks off the complete statement of the basic rhythm. In his recollections of precisely this period, Nono observed: 'The concept of the twelve-tone row actually hasn't got to

---

[41] Ibid.
[42] Björn Heile, 'Darmstadt as Other: British and American Responses to Musical Modernism', *twentieth-century music*, vol. 1, no. 2 (2004), 168. Born's original claim may be found in her *Rationalizing Culture: IRCAM, Boulez, and the Institutionalization of the Musical Avant-Garde* (Berkeley, CA: University of California Press, 1995), 57.
[43] Rizzardi, 'La "nuova scuolo veneziana"', 16.

Arrivals

Fig. 1.2 Rhythmic permutations in Luigi Nono, *Polifonica–Monodia–Ritmica*

do with a mechanical procedure that exhausts the four possible presentations of the row; it is a principle that, in discussion with itself, is constantly shifting, a thought that seeks other possibilities, exactly as happened during the Flemish period.'[44] Even though Nono operated procedurally in terms of both pitch and rhythm by this stage, this was probably influenced more by his study of fifteenth-century polyphony than it was by the music of the Second Viennese School composers directly.

Nevertheless, although rhythms derived from Brazilian popular song are at the heart of *Polifonica–Monodia–Ritmica*, the general effect is for the most part both still and austere. In the light of Adorno's presentation on Webern's music, delivered on 4 July 1951, to which I return below, it was perhaps unsurprising that the critics should have made links, in the first place, to Webern, following its première on 10 July 1951. If the judgements of influence were erroneous, the response was strong. Wolf-Eberhard von Lewinski for one regarded the piece as 'extreme', but was certainly impressed: 'Utmost, but successful, economy and ordering of the material, huge (in the first part, too much) space between pitches and surrealistic atmosphere masterfully turn this study into a work. The rhythmic study – if one can judge just that aspect on its own – aroused an uncanny fascination, as well as huge applause.'[45] It was Antoine Goléa, though, who made the most direct comparison with Webern: 'The strictest twelve-tone composition that there has been since Webern becomes here a vehicle for a widened sensibility of the most extreme refinement.'[46] The correspondent for the *Kölner Stadt-Anzeiger* took pains to draw a contrast between the 'angry whistling' that had met the performance of the *Variazioni canoniche* and the stamping and the calls of 'bravo' that had occurred at the close of

---

[44] Nono, 'Un'autobiografia dell'autore', 497.
[45] Wolf-Eberhard von Lewinski, 'Musik der jungen Generation: Die letzten Kammer- und Orchesterkonzerte', *Darmstädter Tagblatt*, 12 July 1951.
[46] Antoine Goléa, 'Die Musik der jungen Generation: Fünf Studiokonzerte der Darmstädter Ferienkurse', *Der Mittag*, 17 July 1951.

Ex. 1.2 Luigi Nono, *Polifonica–Monodia–Ritmica*, bb. 63–72

Arrivals

Ex. 1.2 (cont.)

Polifonica–Monodia–Ritmica, praise which was wholly justified in the reviewer's mind. Like Goléa's, this report describes the resulting music as 'terse, almost aphoristic, seemingly twelve-tone music'.[47]

Nono was already becoming a stick to beat the less successful with; Albert Rodeman commented that, in comparison with *Polifonica–Monodia–Ritmica*, 'entirely the opposite appears in the *Music for Trumpet, Violin, and Piano* by the Swedish composer Bengt Hambraeus. There is nothing there for future development.'[48] Only Hans Mayer, the East German critic and literary scholar, was unimpressed, though the degree to which he thought the Darmstadt audience had misjudged Nono was striking:

> Then came a 'work' from the twenty-three-year-old Italian Luigi Nono; it had a priceless advantage: the whole thing lasted only six minutes. First movement: some snoring, some yawning. End. The second movement was dominated by a single drum which banged away for some two minutes in rather dull fashion. End. Then came, under the title of polyphony, some entirely unconnected pitches, one after the other, which presented exactly the opposite. After two minutes this 'melody' was at an end. What happened then was shocking. For more than ten minutes the hall was in rapturous uproar (mainly young snobs).

[47] [S.], 'Neue Musik in Kranichstein: Zwölftonkongreß – Woche der jungen Generation', *Kölner Stadt-Anzeiger*, 18 July 1951.
[48] Albert Rodemann, 'Musik der jungen Generation: Musikalische Jugend aus aller Welt in Darmstadt', *Allgemeine Zeitung*, 17 July 1951.

> Again and again Mr Nono appeared on the stage, waving both hands as a sign of thanks like a boxer after delivering a knock-out blow.[49]

Mayer's description of the piece he had heard, though, bears little relationship to either the score or the Darmstadt performance, even if one might suspect that in the process of listening he had managed to confuse the order of the sections enough to have been expecting 'polyphony' when what was on offer was 'monody'.

Varèse's presence influenced Maderna, too, but in rather different ways. While the moves of other composers towards electronic music came from wholly different directions, it was Varèse who was the seminal figure for Maderna. While most composers who turned to electronic music initially, at least, effected an impermeable barrier between those pieces composed for electronic and those for acoustic means, Maderna followed, in the first place, the example of Varèse's *Déserts* (composed in the year in which Varèse and Maderna first met, 1950) in attempting to fuse the 'two dimensions' of live and tape music.[50] Even if it was the exemplar of Varèse's work which made Maderna strike out in the direction of a combination of electronic and acoustic sound, it was with the assistance of Werner Meyer-Eppler, at the University of Bonn's Institute for Communications Research and Information Theory, that Maderna prepared the tape part for the first version of his *Musica su due dimensioni* for flute and tape (1952), which would be premièred at Darmstadt in 1952, as a part of the so-called 'Wunderkonzert'. Maderna met Meyer-Eppler, too, at Darmstadt in 1951 as a part of the workshop focussing on music and technology.[51] I shall return to both this workshop and the 'Wunderkonzert' below.

Schoenberg and Adorno

Steinecke had tried for several years to bring Schoenberg to Darmstadt as a member of the composition faculty. His first invitation dates from a letter of 24 February 1949, in which he informed Schoenberg that he had heard from all sides – in a long list, Steinecke names René Leibowitz, Wolfgang Fortner, Willi Reich, Josef Rufer, Hans Heinz Stuckenschmidt, Peter Stadlen, Tibor Varga, Maurits Frank, Rolf Liebermann, Margot Hinnenberg-Lefèbre, Heinrich Strobel, and Eduard Zuckmayer – that Schoenberg's attendance should be a central aim of the courses. It is clear from the letter, too, that

---

[49] Hans Mayer, 'Beton und Krach: Amerikanismus in einer westdeutschen Stadt', *Freies Volk*, 11 September 1951.
[50] Fearn, *Bruno Maderna*, 70.   [51] Ibid., 78.

Steinecke had already made strides to ensure that it would be easy for Schoenberg to say yes: he advised Schoenberg that John Evarts – who was by this point stationed in Berlin, though he still coordinated the work of music officers like Everett Helm in Hesse – had already agreed he would make all the necessary arrangements from the American perspective and that Ludwig Metzger would be pleased to accommodate not only Schoenberg, but also his family for the duration of the courses.[52]

Schoenberg's reply must certainly have given Steinecke hope that the plan would come to fruition: 'I have already heard from numerous people about your courses, and I find the idea very interesting.' Yet in terms of actual attendance, Schoenberg was definitive that his precarious health meant that he could not be certain of being well enough to travel until close to the date when he would have to do so. It also seems clear from the letter, though, that Schoenberg would find himself more strongly minded to come to the courses if monies were made available to commission a new piece.[53] In any case, Schoenberg did not come. He wrote to Steinecke on 9 May 1949: 'My health simply won't allow it [. . .] It is a matter of great regret to me, since I might have seen all my friends together there [. . .] So I must hope that there will be another, better opportunity in the future. If not, then this comes too late for this life.'[54] One must presume that Steinecke had not yet received this letter when he wrote to Maderna on 15 May 1949 that he still had hopes that Schoenberg would direct one of the composition courses.[55]

Though a small amount of Schoenberg's music had been performed at Darmstadt in 1947 and 1948, in 1949 Schoenberg was very heavily featured. The concerts in 1949 were arranged in conjunction with the Hessischer Rundfunk's 'Woche für Neue Musik' (as the 1948 concerts had been affiliated to the Südwestfunk), which took place in nearby Frankfurt, the course participants travelling between Darmstadt and Frankfurt by bus as and when necessary: Darmstadt effectively piggy-backed onto the Frankfurt celebrations of Schoenberg's seventy-fifth year.

The concert series began on 19 June 1949 with Schoenberg's Variations on a Recitative for organ, op. 40 (1941), performed by Michael Schneider, and featured two performances of the Fourth String Quartet, op. 37 (1936), by the Amsterdam Quartet. The quartet was given its German première on 25 June, directly following Josef Rufer's lecture on Schoenberg's music, and a

---

[52] Steinecke to Arnold Schoenberg, 24 February 1949, in Heinz-Klaus Metzger and Rainer Riehn (eds.), *Darmstadt-Dokumente I* (Munich: text+kritik, 1999), 30.
[53] Schoenberg to Steinecke, 2 March 1949, in Metzger and Riehn (eds.), *Darmstadt-Dokumente I*, 30–1.
[54] Schoenberg to Steinecke, 9 May 1949, in ibid., 32.
[55] Steinecke to Maderna, 15 May 1949, in Dalmonte (ed.), *Bruno Maderna–Wolfgang Steinecke*, 27.

second performance the following morning. The major event, though, came that night – the evening of 26 June – with an all-Schoenberg performance, given by the Radio Frankfurt Symphony Orchestra under the direction of Winfried Zillig, with Tilla Briehm as the soprano soloist and Tibor Varga – also a member of the Darmstadt faculty – the violin soloist, in performances of the Five Orchestral Pieces, op. 16 (1909), the 'Lied der Waldtaube' from the *Gurrelieder* (1900–11), the Violin Concerto, op. 36 (1934–6), and the Variations for orchestra, op. 31 (1926–8). His String Trio, op. 45 (1946), was performed by members of the New York-based Walden String Quartet a week and a half later on 5 July, under the auspices of OMGUS.

Schoenberg still seemed dissatisfied. He wrote to Steinecke on 15 July 1949 that he was concerned that an expected performance of his solo piano music by Else Kraus seemed to have fallen through, adding, 'I know that Aaron Copland and Everett Helm are behind it all.'[56] Steinecke endeavoured to persuade Schoenberg once again to attend the courses and assured him that the absence of the Kraus concert was really related to Schoenberg's own absence and that, moreover, 'no-one has interfered with the planning of things from behind the scenes, least of all Dr Everett B. Helm, about whom I can say nothing beyond that he has genuinely made possible and unstintingly supported the planning of the courses.'[57] Again, Schoenberg's ill-health made travelling impossible for him, but it is notable that Steinecke had already begun to promote Schoenberg's music outside the main run of the courses: the Amsterdam Quartet reprised its performance of the Fourth String Quartet in February 1950 for the Kranichsteiner Musikgesellschaft. This performance received an introduction by one Theodor Wiesengrund Adorno, who presumably impressed Steinecke since, in the first place, Adorno replaced Stuckenschmidt as Darmstadt's faculty member for 'music criticism' in 1950 and, perhaps more strikingly, Steinecke's plans for the 1950 courses appear to have been marked by Adorno's *Philosophie der neuen Musik*: he wrote to Schoenberg that the forthcoming course would 'not as previously lay out the broad spectrum of all sort of new music. Instead all the lectures and courses will focus intensively and exclusively upon your work and the work of Stravinsky.'[58] Nothing of the kind happened; there was none of Stravinsky's music at the 1950 courses at all and only one piece of Schoenberg's, albeit a major one: *A Survivor from Warsaw*, op. 46 (1947), was given its German première on 20 August 1950 at the hands of Hermann Scherchen and the chorus and orchestra of the

---

[56] Schoenberg to Steinecke, 15 July 1949, in Metzger and Riehn (eds.), *Darmstadt-Dokumente I*, 32.
[57] Steinecke to Schoenberg, 13 September 1949, in ibid., 33.
[58] Steinecke to Schoenberg, early February 1950, in ibid., 33.

Darmstadt Landestheater, with Hans Olaf Heidemann acting as the narrator. Yet Steinecke had clearly already recognised that Adorno – or Adorno's thought at least – could be an important adjunct to proceedings at the courses.

Though Schoenberg agreed in principle to come to Darmstadt for the 1951 courses, it always seemed likely that he would ultimately decline to come. In the first case, his health was clearly not improving, and he would die on 13 July 1951, days after the end of the courses. He had also shown little desire to return to a Germany which he felt was hostile to him. He had written to Steinecke on 29 January 1951 that he had 'read in a press clipping that last year, at an event which concerned me, an apparently strong Nazi demonstration against me took place'.[59] Despite Steinecke's assurance that what had happened was nothing of the kind – on the contrary, Steinecke said, the only protest had come from a small number of relatively unimportant people within the city council who had, some time *before* the performance, expressed concerns regarding the content of *A Survivor from Warsaw* – and that the whole event had been exaggerated out of all proportion in the press, this can hardly have made the already ailing Schoenberg think that Germany was, even yet, ready for what he had to say.[60] Thus it happened that Schoenberg found himself replaced as composition lecturer with probably his foremost German exegete, Adorno, a former Alban Berg student. Nor was Schoenberg absent musically speaking: the centrepiece of the 1951 courses was the Second International Congress on Twelve-Tone Music. As well as Josef Rufer's presentation on Schoenberg, 'Der Tanz um das goldene Kalb' ('The Dance around the Golden Calf') from *Moses und Aron* (1930–2) was premièred on the evening of 2 July.

Goeyvaerts and Stockhausen

It was Adorno, then, who, alongside Fortner and Heiß, led composition courses at Darmstadt in 1951. More properly, those two more senior composers led courses; Adorno was engaged to lead a working session for young composers, in which studio performances of new work and work-in-progress would be presented. The studio proved to be decisive not only for two of the young composers who took part – Karel Goeyvaerts and Karlheinz Stockhausen – but also for Adorno himself. The story of Goeyvaerts and Stockhausen's encounter with Adorno at the 1951

---

[59] Schoenberg to Steinecke, 29 January 1951, in ibid., 35.
[60] Steinecke to Schoenberg, early February 1951, in ibid., 35.

Darmstadt courses is well known, yet it is of such paramount importance for the reception of new music in that context that it bears another retelling.

Goeyvaerts's reason for applying to the courses was quite simple. In the spring of 1951, even though he was certainly aware that this was something of a gamble, Steinecke had advertised that Schoenberg would lead composition classes at Darmstadt. Goeyvaerts was, in this sense, 'ahead of the game'. He already knew Webern's music – having made analyses of the Variations, op. 27, and the Symphony, op. 21 (1927–8) – and had, moreover, studied in Paris with Messiaen. At the 1951 courses at Darmstadt, Goeyvaerts was perhaps the only composer to whom the music of John Cage was already known: he had encountered Cage and his music during Cage's long visit to Paris in the spring and summer of 1949, while he was still a Messiaen student. Goeyvaerts's recollection was that Messiaen himself had regarded Cage's *Sonatas and Interludes* as 'his most riveting musical experience since he had first discovered Çarngadeva's *Deçitâla*'.[61] While Goeyvaerts likewise proclaimed himself to have been spellbound, it was certainly the sort of organisation that he had found in the Second Viennese School composers that held his attention more and, hearing that Schoenberg would be in attendance at the 1951 courses, he sent his *Music for Violin, Contralto, and Piano* to the Darmstadt jury; it was accepted and received its première on the evening of 8 July 1951.[62] Yet this piece, though it was a première, dated from 1948, and showed little of the work that Goeyvaerts had done since then and which, in the form of the second movement of his Sonata for Two Pianos (1951), would be the notorious centre of his Darmstadt experience.

Stockhausen had applied initially to Darmstadt to have his Three Lieder for alto and chamber orchestra (1950) performed at the 1951 courses. For him, it was not obviously an interest in encountering Schoenberg that caused him to apply. The second page of the letter contained his professional *curriculum vitae* to date, which closed bluntly with: 'Public performances to date: none.'[63] Shortly thereafter, he received word that the jury had not selected his music. In Cologne, in the following months, Stockhausen came to know Herbert Eimert, who had been a member of that jury. Eimert advised him that 'the texts were felt to be too gruesome

---

[61] Karel Goeyvaerts, 'Paris – Darmstadt 1947–1956: Excerpt from the Autobiographical Portrait', *Revue belge de musicologie*, vol. 48 (1994), 40. Çarngadeva's *Deçitâla*, mentioned by Goeyvaerts here, had played a decisive role in the development of Messiaen's approach to rhythmic organisation.

[62] Ibid., 44.

[63] Karlheinz Stockhausen to the Kranichsteiner Musikinstitut, 11 January 1951, in Imke Misch and Markus Bandur (eds.), *Karlheinz Stockhausen bei den Internationalen Ferienkursen für Neue Musik in Darmstadt 1951–1996: Dokumente und Briefe* (Kürten: Stockhausen, 2001), 6–7.

Arrivals

and the music too old-fashioned'.[64] Nevertheless, Eimert obviously felt that Stockhausen might have something to offer: he had his Sonatine for violin and piano recorded and broadcast on the Westdeutscher Rundfunk on 24 August 1951 and, rather more significantly, advised Stockhausen that he should attend the Darmstadt courses that summer, despite their refusal of his piece.

It cannot have taken long for Goeyvaerts and Stockhausen to encounter one another. While both were attending Adorno's seminars, Stockhausen seems, initially at least, to have been the only person who took Goeyvaerts seriously. Goeyvaerts had brought his Sonata for Two Pianos, which operated according to a principle he termed a 'synthetic number' (explained in fuller detail below). As Goeyvaerts recalled:

> There was only one young man who saw something in it and asked me more about it: Karlheinz Stockhausen. I can well recall how he tried to explain the 'geistliche Gründe' [spiritual basis] of my novel technique to the others over lunch. When I explained all of this to him I had to resort to a mixture of German and English, yet despite my inadequate efforts he understood immediately [. . .] Before even my Sonata for Two Pianos came up for discussion in the class, Stockhausen knew it inside out.[65]

That Stockhausen had understood the piece well in practical terms is evident in the recording of the performance of the second movement, which he and Goeyvaerts performed for Adorno and the other students. It is, to be sure, far from perfectly accurate but, given the degree of complexity involved and the brief period Stockhausen must have had to study his part, the performance is impressive. Before turning to Adorno's examination of it, it is worth outlining the way in which the second movement of the piece functions.[66]

The pitch material of the second movement is generated from two overlapping heptachords. The overlaps, on E♭ and A, appear in each of Goeyvaerts's two sets of material, and act as hinges, appearing twice as often in the movement as any other pitch class (see Example 1.3). These two heptachords are, across the course of the movement, consistently alternated. On each occurrence, each pitch class is displaced upwards by an octave, but across an increasingly narrow total range. The exceptions to this rule are the

---

[64] Michael Kurtz, *Stockhausen: A Biography*, tr. Richard Toop (London: Faber, 1992 [1988]), 31.
[65] Goeyvaerts, 'Paris – Darmstadt', 45.
[66] The analysis here is drawn in large part from Mark Delaere, 'Auf der Such nach serieller Stimmigkeit: Goeyvaerts' Weg zur Komposition Nr. 2 (1951)', in Orm Finnendahl (ed.), *Die Anfänge der seriellen Musik* (Berlin: Wolke, 1999), 15–19. Delaere's essay itself draws on Herman Sabbe's commentary in *Karlheinz Stockhausen: . . . wie die Zeit verging . . .* , ed. Heinz-Klaus Metzger and Rainer Riehn, Musik-Konzepte, vol. XIX (Munich: text+kritik, 1981), 7–11.

Ex. 1.3 Heptachords in Karel Goeyvaerts, Sonata for Two Pianos, second movement

Ex. 1.4 Disposition of heptachords in Karel Goeyvaerts, Sonata for Two Pianos, second movement

two hinge pitches of E♭ and A, which remain absolutely static and, as the available range of the movement decreases, are left as the outer pitches (Example 1.4).

A further degree of stasis is emphasised by the way in which these heptachords are scored for the pianos. On each occasion, Piano 1 performs I then II, while Piano 2 performs II then I, such that the formal structure is simply achieved (see Table 1.1). Goeyvaerts's hinge pitches, however, have a further function, and this is specifically to do with his notion of 'synthetic number'. Each pitch is allocated a numerical value, from 1 to 3, according to its distance from the hinge pitches, which are themselves allocated a value of 0 (see Example 1.5). Each other parameter, too, is allocated a series of values, such that Goeyvaerts is able to construct, in principle at least, a system where each musical point acquires the same value of 7. Goeyvaerts restricted the other parameters far more than he had restricted pitch (see Figure 1.3).

Goeyvarts was not utterly rigid. Occasionally, individual points (and this is, surely, point music *par excellence*) actually add up to numbers other than 7 according to this parametric count (in Example 1.6 see the first note of bar 4 in Piano I). Similarly, duration refers only to the distance until the next sounding pitch, not the actual duration of a pitch, such that rests are largely

Arrivals

Table 1.1 *Sketch formal outline of Karel Goeyvaerts, Sonata for Two Pianos, second movement*

Piano I:	AI	AII	|	BI	BII	|	CI	etc.
Piano II:	AII	AI	|	BII	BI	|	CII	etc.

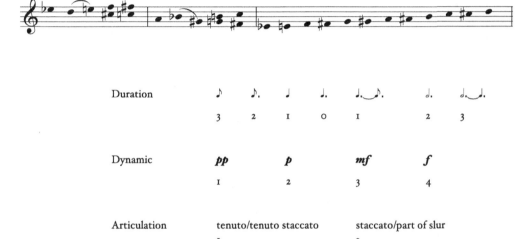

Ex. 1.5 Pitch values in Karel Goeyvaerts, Sonata for Two Pianos, second movement

Fig. 1.3 Synthetic number values in Karel Goeyvaerts, Sonata for Two Pianos, second movement

freely interpolated. Sometimes, too, Goeyvaerts 'cheats', counting the actual duration towards his synthetic number and then adding rests in afterwards (see Example 1.6). Nevertheless, Goeyvaerts's piece was the most rigorously determined piece to have been presented at Darmstadt by that point and would remain one of the most highly deterministic pieces, in terms of pre-compositional decision-making, across the years to come.

Goeyvaerts's sonata raised much discussion, most of it from the corner of Adorno, who was shocked. His initial, obviously perplexed, response was to ask: 'Why did you compose that for *two* pianos?', and he went on to query, with little understanding of the piece's structural procedures it seems, why there was no sense of phrase, which is to say no obvious cadence between antecedent and consequent.[67] Though Stockhausen endeavoured to explain,

[67] Kurtz, *Stockhausen*, 35.

Ex. 1.6 Karel Goeyvaerts, Sonata for Two Pianos, second movement, bb. 1–8

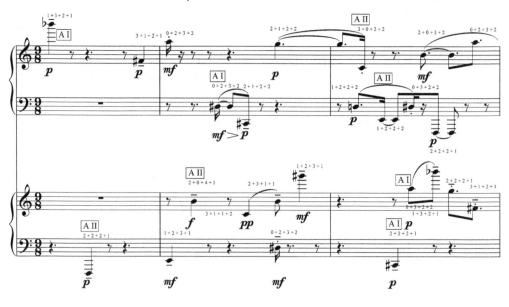

delivering what Goeyvaerts regarded as a 'penetrating analysis' of the movement, Adorno appears to have been left none the wiser about *why* a composer might choose to operate in this way.[68] The session culminated

[68] Goeyvaerts, 'Paris – Darmstadt', 45.

Ex. 1.6 (cont.)

with a by now obviously frustrated Stockhausen retorting to Adorno: 'Professor, you are looking for a chicken in an abstract painting.'[69]

For Adorno, this contretemps with Goeyvaerts and Stockhausen remained at the heart of almost all of his own critical responses to multiple serialism throughout the 1950s. Goeyvaerts recalls that Adorno dubbed the pair of them 'Adrian Leverkühn und sein Famulus', in reference to Thomas Mann's *Doktor Faustus*. Though Stockhausen would soon find his career in the ascendency, there can be little doubt that, at the time, it was Goeyvaerts who represented the Faustus figure, with Stockhausen relegated to the position of his exegete, Serenus Zeitblom. The parallels were reasonably clear. For Goeyvaerts the principle of the 'synthetic number' also had transcendent overtones, just as Leverkühn had drawn relations between mystical numbers and the elements of composition, as first signalled by Mann in the placement of Leverkühn's etching of a magic square above his piano, 'always buried under music, some of which he had written himself'.[70] It would be this magic square that Zeitblom would later identify as that to which the material of a twelve-tone composition could be reduced,[71] leading to Leverkühn's reply: 'Reason and magic [...] surely meet and become one in what is called wisdom, initiation, in a

---

[69] Kurtz, *Stockhausen*, 36.
[70] Thomas Mann, *Doctor Faustus: The Life of the German Composer Adrian Leverkühn as Told by a Friend*, tr. John E. Woods (New York: Vintage, 1999 [1947]), 102.
[71] Ibid., 206.

belief in the stars, in numbers ... '.[72] Such a distinction, expressed in just these literary terms, was exactly what was at stake for Goeyvaerts: 'After we had talked about it for a long time, Karlheinz thought he had discovered a resemblance to Hesse's *Glass Bead Game*. I did not agree at all, since Hesse is dealing with an image of human knowledge and not with something as intangible as the trace of a mode of existence – without time and space.'[73]

Even if Adorno was, somehow, using the figures of Leverkühn and Zeitblom to direct a wagging, admonitory finger towards Goeyvaerts and Stockhausen, the press paid little enough attention to the events of Adorno's working group, though doubtless few had been present in order to make a report possible. A review of the courses by someone who had been a student at them, Ruth Rehmann, certainly did mention Goeyvaerts (and she mentioned no-one else by name who had been a student at those sessions): 'Beyond the others, the Belgian Karel Goeyvaerts weaves his ideas of an equilibrium of pitches, expressed through numbers, which create an impression of a static music and lead, followed through to the logical conclusion, to an annihilation of pitch, to silence.'[74] Antoine Goléa was the only person engaged as a journalist as Darmstadt who felt this was important enough to warrant printed discussion, seeming to rate it as the most significant event to have happened in those sessions with Adorno. Goeyvaerts's recollection of events at the time suggests a different stance from that which Goléa's review shows. Goeyvaerts's suggestion that Goléa had told him that his *Music for Violin, Contralto, and Piano* was 'by far the best and the most progressive he had heard in Darmstadt' is largely borne out by Goléa's review, in which he describes it as 'one of the most enthralling events of this year's courses *in toto*'.[75] Yet the implication of Goeyvaerts's autobiographical account that Goléa was somehow more supportive of this earlier piece than of the Sonata for Two Pianos does not wholly ring true.[76] As near-enough the only contemporary eyewitness account of the event (alongside Rehmann's brief description), Goléa's report is worth quoting in full because of its evident strength of feeling:

> During one of the composition seminars, confidently well run by Theodor W. Adorno, the participants experienced what one might think of as a private première of a composition for two pianos by Goeyvaerts which lies at the most extreme point of what is theoretically and practically conceivable. Alongside his teacher Messiaen and his French colleague Pierre Boulez, Goeyvaerts scales

---

[72] Ibid., 208.   [73] Karel Goeyvaerts, quoted in Kurtz, *Stockhausen*, 35.
[74] Ruth Rehmann, 'Insel der Unseligen: Zu den Darmstädter Musiktagen', *Rheinische Merkur*, 20 July 1951.
[75] Goléa, 'Die Musik der jungen Generation'.   [76] Goeyvaerts, 'Paris – Darmstadt', 46.

the heights of thinking and sensation which can, to be sure, only come through a mastery of metaphysics. Rules applied here with iron rigour and extreme consistency lend the music the status of world affairs, the eternal properties of which bear comparison with the precession of the stars. That Adorno himself shied away, and at the same time admitted that this musical flow became suddenly 'comprehensible', is not least characteristic of the icy-hot, angelic horror of this music.[77]

Goléa's suggestion that Adorno was both repelled and attracted by Goeyvaerts's sonata meshes neatly with the rest of his hot–cold, heavenly–hellish imagery, though there is little in Adorno's later writing – and he returns to this event repeatedly – to suggest that he ever truly 'comprehended' what Goeyvaerts was trying to do. Nonetheless, over a period of ten years, he would seemingly find it difficult to view anything else as paradigmatic of the sorts of constructivist trends he saw in the new music.

Goléa was, no doubt, more closely acquainted with Stockhausen and Goeyvaerts than he had been with any of the other younger participants. Though Goléa reported on the courses as a journalist, he had also been engaged to deliver a lecture on 'The Situation of New Music in France' on 26 June 1951. Alongside recordings of Honegger's Fifth Symphony (1950) and Jolivet's Piano Concerto (1949–50), he had played extracts from the soon-to-be-released Columbia disc of Messiaen's *Quatre études de rythme*, which included *Mode de valeurs et d'intensités*, the earliest of the four, composed, as mentioned above, during Messiaen's own residency at the Darmstadt courses in 1949. The piece clearly struck a chord with Stockhausen and Goeyvaerts, who cornered Goléa after his lecture and demanded that they be able to listen to it again. Though no score was available at the courses, Kurtz recounts that they played the disc three or four times.[78] In Goléa's almost certainly exaggerated recollection only a few years later, Stockhausen played the piece roughly thirty times back to back.[79] Certainly the relationships to Goeyvaerts's sonata were tangible, as they would become, too, in

---

[77] Goléa, 'Die Musik der jungen Generation'. Goléa's allusion here to 'stellar motion' is hardly as contrived as it might at first seem. The reference is doubtless a sly dig at Adorno, obviously related as it is to Severus Zeitblom's first reaction to Adrian Leverkühn's explanation of his version of the twelve-tone system in *Doctor Faustus*: 'One would gain from it an extraordinarily self-contained, unified voice, a conformity to almost astronomical regularities.' Mann, *Doctor Faustus*, 205.

[78] Kurtz, *Stockhausen*, 37.

[79] Antoine Goléa, *Musik unserer Zeit*, tr. Antoine Goléa and Willi Reich (Munich: C. H. Beck, 1955 [1954]), 198. Peter Hill observes that the impression that Stockhausen and Goeyvaerts may have received of the piece from listening to the recording alone probably gave a rather skewed picture of the piece itself, since Messiaen's own recording (of which Goléa must have had an early pressing, the disc not being officially released until October 1951) is 'thickly pedalled' and 'impressionistic', far from the sharp crispness of later recordings (Hill, 'Messiaen Recorded', 85–90).

Stockhausen's *Kreuzspiel* (1951). In Messiaen's *Mode de valeurs et d'intensités*, parameters are 'fixed' to one another, even if mobile in and of themselves, according to three modes, which are themselves fixed to particular staves.

Though not a flexible construct like Goeyvaerts's synthetic number – in that, for Goeyvaerts, each pitch could acquire a range, even if a limited one, of different durations, dynamic values, and modes of attack and still come to the same numerical tally – the way in which points were constructed was evidently close to Goeyvaerts's conception. This too was doubtless 'point music'. Similarly, though Messiaen had much more freedom than Goeyvaerts would have allowed in the dispersal of his fixed materials through the piece, the alignment of modes with individual staves may have suggested to Goeyvaerts that what Adorno had read as compositional conceit might have a stronger claim for validity through Messiaen's example.

Goeyvaerts and Stockhausen also encountered Nono during the 1951 courses and seem to have had friendly relations. In any case, there was little sense of rivalry in that earliest meeting. Goeyvaerts remembered that Doris Andreae, Stockhausen's fiancée, later his first wife, captured their discussion when sprawled on the grass outside the Marienhöhe.[80] He recalled too the content of that discussion:

> While chatting with Luigi Nono we were quick to observe that his lyric temperament was at considerable odds with what I was doing. Luigi did not pursue the experiment with the *Polifonica*. He was too bound up with the power of the text, too involved with its semantic meaning, in short too attached to the extra-musical element a text represented.[81]

Years later, it would again be the question of text that would lead to the first major break between Stockhausen and Nono. In any case, for Stockhausen it was Messiaen who was the major figure of the older generation, and Goeyvaerts who was the leading representative of his peers. Only a few weeks after the end of the courses, Stockhausen would write to Goeyvaerts: 'I now feel closer to Messiaen than ever',[82] having assured Goeyvaerts too that 'whenever asked with whom he had studied, he would mention only my

---

[80] Goeyvaerts almost certainly confuses two memories here, since the photo of Goeyvaerts and Nono in discussion comes, instead, from 1952. The photo, when seen in full, shows, from left to right, Boulez, Stockhausen, Nono, Goeyvaerts, and Maderna. It is, thus, one of the very small number of photographs to show all members of the group which Nono would dub the 'Darmstadt School' in Darmstadt together. It is reproduced in, amongst other places, Borio and Danuser (eds.), *Im Zenit der Moderne*, vol. III, 658.
[81] Goeyvaerts, 'Paris – Darmstadt', 46.
[82] Stockhausen to Karel Goeyvaerts, 30 July 1951, in Misch and Bandur (eds.), *Karlheinz Stockhausen bei den Internationalen Ferienkursen*, 14.

[Goeyvaerts's] name'.[83] Stockhausen would soon follow Goeyvaerts's example in other respects, moving on 8 January to Paris, where he would come, for the first time, into contact with Pierre Boulez.[84] Peyser suggests that, at some unspecified later stage, when Stockhausen was 'trying to undermine Boulez', he had observed that Goeyvaerts's sonata predated the first book of Boulez's *Structures* (1952) by some margin. According to her account, Boulez was dismissive, claiming that the Belgian was 'an invention of Stockhausen's. He was to me what Hauer was to Schoenberg.' Her judgement that 'Boulez's depreciation of Goeyvaerts's talent is echoed by other specialists in the field' may well have truth given the long view, but in 1951, Goeyvaerts seemed to be a composer to watch.[85]

The distinction that Boulez made between Hauer and Schoenberg was evidently a significant one at the time. Hermann Heiß, reporting on the first day of the International Congress on Twelve-Tone Music, which was to have been held in connection with Schoenberg's hoped-for attendance, suggested without ambiguity that Hauer's and Schoenberg's were the two available routes a composer might take towards a twelve-tone technique. Schoenberg's route, Heiß proposed, would lead to 'an absolute isolation of the human', and he suggested that this was Adorno's thinking, too, when he claimed that new music was the 'true message in a bottle'. Yet Heiß is not critical of this; he hardly could be given his own decisive return to twelve-tone writing after the war: his suggestion seemed to be that neither Schoenberg (who for Heiß developed the twelve-tone method in the horizontal, which is to say melodic, direction) or Hauer (who Heiß suggests worked the series into verticalities) were adequate for post-war purpose.

Heiß's argument is one which would become familiar – which was, in some senses, *already* familiar, to Goeyvaerts or Messiaen: that metre and rhythm had found no place in the methods of either Schoenberg or Hauer, and that what ought to be expected was the 'concresence', the growing together, of 'twelve-tone' treatments of pitch and rhythm.[86] Heiß would not take that route himself, but for Goeyvaerts this was already the plan. After their meeting, Stockhausen was intent on following his lead. Nono, too, was working in related directions, though there was no real sense in his music to date that there was any *unity* of systematic procedures, just that pitch and rhythm were both being treated in ways that moved towards systematisation. In this sense, though the International Congress on Twelve-Tone Music may well have been of symbolic importance for Darmstadt itself,

---

[83] Goeyvaerts, 'Paris – Darmstadt', 45.   [84] Kurtz, *Stockhausen*, 45.
[85] Joan Peyser, *Boulez: Composer, Conductor, Enigma* (London: Cassell, 1977 [1976]), 77.
[86] Hermann Heiß, 'Zwei Wege der Zwölftonmusik', *Darmstädter Echo*, 3 July 1951.

for those young composers what was under discussion was not truly relevant to them. It was, seemingly, not only Stockhausen and Goeyvaerts who felt this. Gertrud Runge, writing in the *Welt am Sonntag*, reported that 'a well-known composer of the Schoenberg school formulated the issue well when he said: "Enough with feeling and alcohol! I am an engineer!"'[87] Schoenberg and Hauer, too, were already in the past, although, as I will suggest below, the relationship between Hauer's theorisation of serialism and Eimert's aesthetics was to become a potent one.

Certainly, Adorno's presentation on Webern must have made a greater impression than Heiß's, not least because what Adorno had to say on the subject of Webern is so clearly reflected in what Rehmann and Goléa had said about Goeyvaerts. The *Darmstädter Tagblatt*'s report is indicative of the similarities:

> Anton Webern's music, about which we heard during the meatiest lecture during the past few days of the courses, has at its heart an ideal: to achieve a higher harmony (not in the narrow musical sense) between the interior and the exterior of being. It aims to bring about an indifference between subject and object, the 'balanced equation between the furthest distance and the nearest proximity'. So Webern's music becomes a music of silence [...].[88]

The report suggests that much of what Adorno had to say in 1951 on the subject of Webern remained unchanged in 1959, when his article on the composer was published in *Merkur*, although his move from a symbol of indifference to one of hope is notable:

> Webern's musical minimalism is founded on the expressive requirement that it excludes any independent phenomenon that is not at the same time expressive. This economy comes to influence expression itself – to the point of silence [...] The absolutely transitory, the toneless beating of wings, as it were, becomes in his music the faintest, but most persistent, seal of hope. Disappearance, an ephemerality that fixes on nothing that exists anymore, or even that objectifies itself, becomes the refuge of a defenceless eternity.[89]

By contrast, the press largely felt that Schoenberg probably went quite far enough, even though the performance of his music was widely held to be a triumph. Karl H. Wörner wrote in the *Mannheimer Morgen* that Schoenberg's 'Tanz um das goldene Kalb' represented 'a compelling sonic

---

[87] Gertrud Runge, 'Gefahren der Neuen Musik', *Welt am Sonntag*, 8 July 1951.
[88] [ski], 'Schoenberg, Webern, Berg: Die Vorträge zum Internationalen Zwölftonkongress', *Darmstädter Tagblatt*, 5 July 1951.
[89] Theodor W. Adorno, 'Anton von Webern' [1959], in *Sound Figures*, tr. Rodney Livingstone (Stanford University Press, 1999), 105; originally published in *Merkur*, vol. 13, no. 3 (March 1959).

document, which testifies to the expressive force of this system in the hands of a great composer'.[90] For Humphrey Searle, too, it was 'the outstanding event'.[91] The reviewer for the *Bochumer Anzeiger* was one of relatively few dissenting voices, suggesting that the piece was 'bloodless' and 'bores more than it unsettles',[92] though Walther Wehagen's review for the *Wiesbadener Kurier* raised the fell spectre of Richard Strauss: 'Written fifty years after Richard Strauss's *Salome*, it shows a decline in terms of ideas, as well as in text and music.'[93] For Goeyvaerts, too, it may well have been better that Schoenberg was not there, since he would only have been disappointed, but in quite the reverse manner from those reviewers just mentioned. Though he may well have been exaggerating, there was no doubt a degree of truth in his observation to Yvette Grimaud that, on hearing Schoenberg's 'Tanz um das goldene Kalb', his first reaction was '[c]'est du Verdi serie!' ('it's serial Verdi').[94] One should not, though, take it that Goeyvaerts was wholly the aesthetic firebrand some of this might suggest. In the midst of his reminiscences of times at Darmstadt, he still had time to recall performances in Paris of his 'beloved *Rosenkavalier*'.[95] For Stockhausen, though, there was no turning back.

Elsewhere at the 1951 courses the sometimes brutal response of the Darmstadt audience, for which it became renowned, was in evidence. As Heinz Enke described it in the *Frankfurter Rundschau*, one of the pieces in the first orchestral concert of the 'Musik der jungen Generation' series of concerts, which brought the 1951 courses to a close, dragged on for such a long time that, when an apparent close to the piece came, the audience began such a welter of whistling that Scherchen stormed off, ending the concert there and then.[96] Doubtless Enke exaggerated. A more measured and a detailed account from Willy Werner Göttig insisted that, though Scherchen certainly left the podium in a huff, he did at least wait until the close of the concert, though Göttig's report suggested that the majority of the audience might have wished he had gone sooner. The first piece, Max Baumann's *Concerto grosso* (1950) for string orchestra, showed Baumann to be 'not without talent', but the piece as a whole was unconvincing, the first movement of Gottfried Michael Koenig's *Horae* (1950) was 'thin

---

[90] Karl H. Wörner, 'Jugend diskutiert über sich selbst: Die sechsten Kranichsteiner Internationalen Ferienkurse', *Mannheimer Morgen*, 13 July 1951.
[91] Humphrey Searle, 'Frankfurt ISCM – Darmstadt Summer School', *Monthly Musical Record* (September 1951), 185.
[92] [GE], 'Darmstädter Musikkurse werfen Probleme auf: Bloße Beherrschung des "Materials"'. Zwölftonkongreß: Nichts Neues', *Bochumer Anzeiger*, 18 July 1951.
[93] Walther Wehagen, 'Neue Musik in der Sackgasse', *Wiesbadener Kurier*, 20 July 1951.
[94] Goeyvaerts, 'Paris – Darmstadt', 46.   [95] Ibid., 40.
[96] Heinz Enke, 'Gestörtes Konzert', *Frankfurter Rundschau*, 9 July 1951.

blooded', and the first movement of Gottfried Schnabel's Sinfonie (1950) 'endlessly long'.[97] Only the skills of Peter Stadlen, as soloist in the slow movement of Kurt Schäfer's Divertimento for piano and orchestra (1950), seem to have made the whole event bearable at all. After Walter Faith's Sinfonietta (1950), throughout the performance of which the audience had been visibly (intentionally visibly, if Göttig's report is to be trusted) yawning, Scherchen did not acknowledge the audience's applause. Relations between the conductor and the audience did not improve. After the following piece, Schnabel's Sinfonie, rather than applauding, large parts of the audience whistled instead. Scherchen's somewhat undignified response was to shout at them: 'What sort of slobs are you, to have so little respect for the work the orchestra has done?' Though Göttig felt that Scherchen had gone rather too far, he also observed that 'through the cliquery and claquery of the Ferienkurse participants, applause has been rather sadly discredited at Darmstadt.'[98]

If Scherchen's orchestral concert seemed to belong to the past, the way forward might have seemed to belong to the new possibilities afforded by electronic sound. As early as the first Ferienkurse in 1946, recording technologies had been foregrounded at Darmstadt. Then it was in Hans Joachim von Braunmühl's presentation 'Technology and the Care of Music', though that lecture, in truth, had little to do with the way technology would come to be important for Darmstadt, focussing as it did, first, on electronic instruments which could do the work of acoustic ones and, second, upon the way in which tape could be used as a recording device for the recording of acoustic music. It would not be until 1950 that electronic music, as it later came to be understood, figured at the courses, in the persons of not only Varèse, but also Robert Beyer and Werner Meyer-Eppler.

Varèse's thoughts regarding electronic music had come to Meyer-Eppler's attention with the 1949 publication of his essay 'Musik auf neuen Wegen' in *Stimmen*.[99] Here, Varèse had argued that making distinctions between the scientific and artistic aspects of music was erroneous; since music's position in this respect fluctuated according to history and culture, music was *both* art

---

[97] Only the first movements of Koenig's and Schnabel's pieces and the slow movement of Schäfer's were performed, for reasons which, according to the slip of paper handed to audience members on arrival, had, rather vaguely, to do with 'difficulties regarding performance materials and technical problems'. Many seemed to blame Scherchen, though what precisely he was supposed to have done wrong was hardly less nebulous than the description of the performance problems.

[98] Willy Werner Göttig, 'Hermann Scherchen rügte Pfeifkonzert in Darmstadt', *Abendpost*, 10 July 1951.

[99] This is reprinted in Borio and Danuser (eds.), *Im Zenit der Moderne*, vol. III, 92–7, though it is, curiously, dated there '1950'.

and science. Meyer-Eppler was certainly interested enough to contact Varèse directly, as he had done as early as October 1949.[100]

For his part, Robert Beyer had written to Steinecke on 29 January 1950 to propose three lectures on 'The Sound World of Electronic Music', and received a prompt affirmative response.[101] Beyer delivered one lecture, on 'The Meaning of Electrified Sound-Production for the Music of the (Coming) Future', on 21 August, and one the following day, on 'Space as a Form-Determining Moment in the Photography of Sound: Its Meaning for Electronic Music'. The title of the second lecture should give some indication of what comparatively tentative and early thoughts these were. Meyer-Eppler's lecture on 'The Problem of Timbre in Electronic Music' followed on 23 August. It is a matter of great regret that all that survive of Meyer-Eppler's presentation are the keywords about which he planned to speak and the examples of studio work he brought with him. Nevertheless, along with a detailed report of the event from Antoine Goléa, it is possible to recover some sense of what Meyer-Eppler (and Beyer) delivered.[102]

Beyer's lectures seem to have drawn links with historical forebears, suggesting that the production of sound in the studio and the music of Busoni, Schoenberg, and Messiaen shared a certain sort of 'perspectival hearing'. Nevertheless, his interest was more than anything else in the accurate recorded reproduction of acoustic sounds, phonographic sound being more 'accurate' in this sense than the ears of a live audience. Goléa described it thus: 'The deep embeddedness of sound in a well-made orchestral recording, which makes it possible to hear the complete idea of a composer in, so to speak, a perfect light, is only the first consequence of the electric revolution in the area of music.'[103] Meyer-Eppler's lecture was probably of more interest. In it the expanded resources in terms of timbre which the studio made available were already literally audible. He demonstrated the transformations of sound which were possible through the application of a variety of filters, both ones which limited the total frequency bandwidth of a pre-recorded sound and ones which filtered the sound according to vocal formants. Meyer-Eppler's presentation, then, moved from accurate reproduction to inventive timbral production. Perhaps the most astounding of Meyer-Eppler's materials was the 'score of the future' that he projected onto the wall of the Marienhöhe, which, from Goléa's

---

[100] M. J. Grant, *Serial Music, Serial Aesthetics* (Cambridge University Press, 2001), 53.
[101] Elena Ungeheuer, 'In den Klang und in die Welt – elektronisches Komponieren in Nordrhein-Westfalen', in Heike Stumpf and Matthias Pannes (eds.), *Zeitklänge: Zur Neuen Musik in NRW 1946–1996* (Cologne: Studio, 1996), 47.
[102] Elena Ungeheuer, *Wie die elektronische Musik 'erfunden' wurde ... : Quellenstudie zu Werner Meyer-Epplers Entwurf zwischen 1949 und 1953* (Mainz: Schott, 1992), 104–5.
[103] Antoine Goléa, 'Die Klangwelt der elektronischen Musik', *Der Mittag*, 29 August 1950.

report, appears to have shown a frequency diagram, probably quite similar to the score Stockhausen would later produce for *Studie II* (1954). It drew what Goléa termed an 'unearthly mumur' from the hall.[104]

Beyer and Meyer-Eppler returned to Darmstadt in 1951 as a part of a conference on music and technology, which featured their work (without any performance of actual music) on 9 July and the work of Pierre Schaeffer and Pierre Henry on the following day, including performances of both *Symphonie pour un homme seul* (1949–50) and *Orphée 51* (1951). If Maderna's *Musica su due dimensioni* would represent the first piece to combine tape with an acoustic instrument, it was preceded by *Orphée 51*, which combined voice with tape. The audience was, seemingly, impressed. Goléa reported that rapturous applause followed the performance.[105] As for Meyer-Eppler, his aim was, now, to show the potential autonomy the studio might provide to the composer:

> Is the composer condemned to compose *only with paper and ink*? Can he not, like the painter or sculptor, execute his work in an adequate form himself? It is an old *pipe dream* of the composer that he can *interpret* his music *himself*. To date only a few have managed to meet the technical requirements needed to achieve this. The modern *magnetophone technology* promises to change this.[106]

Nevertheless, it was the way in which it was possible to generate previously unheard timbres that excited the most interest. Though Meyer-Eppler does not appear to have spoken of a division of sound by parameter as such, the idea that timbre might be worked on *independently* of pitch, duration, or dynamic appears already to have been present in embryo.[107]

As Grant observes, though Meyer-Eppler was not the first to develop the idea of parametric thinking, his conception of it was certainly influential, at least in the case of Stockhausen.[108] Parametric thinking already existed in a very limited form in some of the music already presented at Darmstadt; Meyer-Eppler's presentations might be seen as a contemporaneous extension of this. Nono's *Polifonica–Monodia–Ritmica*, for instance, treated pitch and rhythm independently of one another, while Goeyvaerts's Sonata for Two Pianos constructed relationships between parameters divisibly, with the parameters only later recombined into singular points. Yet neither of these truly presented what Meyer-Eppler's theory would come to suggest: that independent parametric strands could therefore be treated systematically.

---

[104] Ibid.
[105] Antonie Goléa, quoted in Ungeheuer, *Wie die elektronische Musik 'erfunden' wurde* ... , 114.
[106] Werner Meyer-Eppler, 'Möglichkeiten der elektronischen Klangerzeugung', in Borio and Danuser (eds.), *Im Zenit der Moderne*, vol. III, 102.
[107] Ungeheuer, *Wie die elektronische Musik 'erfunden' wurde* ... , 112–17.
[108] Grant, *Serial Music, Serial Aesthetics*, 62.

Although Maderna worked with Meyer-Eppler earlier, in the preparatory work for the 1952 première of *Musica su due dimensioni*, of the composers who were to come to prominence at Darmstadt, it was for Stockhausen that Meyer-Eppler would become central.[109] Stockhausen would not study with Meyer-Eppler directly until autumn 1953, with his studies lasting until 1956, but he certainly knew of Meyer-Eppler's work rather earlier, both through attendance at the 1951 Music and Technology conference and also, as time went on, through his writings and through Herbert Eimert at the Westdeutscher Rundfunk. Nevertheless, by the close of the 1951 courses, it was not Stockhausen who was seen as the next composer, after Nono, likely to make a major impact. Rather, it was Karel Goeyvaerts.

This was not how events were to turn out. Steinecke had apparently noted that Goeyvaerts had caused a stir in some quarters. He wrote to Goeyvaerts on 18 January 1952 that he thought it would be important for him to be represented musically at the 1952 courses, and proposed his Second Violin Concerto (1951). Steinecke also advised Goeyvaerts that Messiaen was again invited to the 1952 courses, and hoped that Goeyvaerts would be able to assist with translation.[110] Though Goeyvaerts's immediate response was a positive one with regard to Messiaen, he clearly aimed to have his *Opus 2 for 13 Instruments* (1951) performed instead of the violin concerto, which was older only by a matter of months but by this point, from Goeyvaerts's perspective, hardly representative of his music.[111] Yet by 10 April he was resigned, asking to enrol in the seminars of Messiaen and Yvonne Loriod.[112] Hearing that the expected soloist, André Gertler, might hand the work over to a student of his, Goeyvaerts tried a final time to swap the Second Violin Concerto for *Opus 2*, but to no avail.[113] Steinecke simply assured him that Gertler would definitely undertake the role himself.[114] Goeyvaerts's dissatisfaction is palpable in the part of the biography he sent to Steinecke for the programme booklet which deals with the older piece: 'The Second Violin

---

[109] Meyer-Eppler, for his part, was wholly unconvinced by Maderna's idea of combining acoustic instruments with electronic sound, querying whether such a combination was, in point of fact, 'licit'. He worried, too, that the reception of the piece would almost literally divide the listeners' attention into 'two columns'. Finally, Meyer-Eppler was concerned that the amount of time Maderna had set aside for his work in the studio would be insufficient to produce any beyond the essentially improvised. Werner Meyer-Eppler to Maderna, 14 May 1952, quoted in Roderick, 'Rebulding a Culture', 310.

[110] Steinecke to Goeyvaerts, 18 January 1952, IMD.

[111] Goeyvaerts to Steinecke, 20 January 1952, IMD.

[112] Goeyvaerts to Steinecke, 10 April 1952, IMD.

[113] Goeyvaerts to Steinecke, 2 May 1952, IMD.

[114] Steinecke to Goeyvaerts, 15 May 1952, IMD. Steinecke was clearly not wholly against *Opus 2*, though he seems to have given little consideration to a performance in Darmstadt, since he did try to help Goeyvaerts have the piece performed at the Venice Biennale, as a letter which doubtless crossed with Goeyvaerts's of 2 May shows. Steinecke to Goeyvaerts, 3 May 1952, IMD.

Concerto, which is performed here, belongs to a set of orchestral and chamber compositions the aesthetic of which I have left behind.' The biography went on to discuss the Sonata for Two Pianos (now *Opus 1 for Two Pianos*), *Opus 2*, and *Opus 3 with Bowed and Struck Tones*, all of which, it is clear, Goeyvaerts regarded as of much greater import than the concerto.[115] It is no less clear that, in terms of any sort of ongoing Darmstadt career, Goeyvaerts was right to have the misgivings he did. The Second Violin Concerto barely made any impact. Even Antoine Goléa, Goeyvaerts's staunchest defender in the previous year, could say nothing more positive than that Goeyvaerts was a 'talented young composer', listing him alongside Henze and Hans Ulrich Engelmann in this category.[116] In terms of the press reception of what was important at Darmstadt in 1952, there can be no doubt that two concerts, and four composers, received the lion's share of the attention: Yvonne Loriod's performance of Boulez's Second Piano Sonata on 19 July 1952, and three premières on 21 July – Stockhausen's *Kreuzspiel*, Maderna's *Musica su due dimensioni*, and Nono's *España en el corazón* (1952) – which, together with Camillo Togni's *Omaggio a Bach* (1952) and Jacques Wildberger's Quartet for flute, clarinet, violin, and cello (1952), comprised the so-called 'Wunderkonzert'. This is hardly to say that those reviews were necessarily positive – far from it, as I show below – but more that Goeyvaerts had been absolutely correct that the performance of the Second Violin Concerto represented a backward step which would do his career in Germany no favours.

After this, Goeyvaerts, despite his hugely promising entry onto the Darmstadt stage, was not to return. No Leverkühn, he was not even a Zeitblom, there to report on the success of the composer who took, adapted, and ran with his ideas, becoming ultimately the composer most associated with the name Darmstadt: Karlheinz Stockhausen.

The 'Wunderkonzert', 1952

On the evening of 21 July 1952, a concert occurred at Darmstadt which came to be seen as far more important than its contemporary impact would have suggested: the so-called 'Wunderkonzert'.[117] Though it is tempting to think that this was to have been the first occasion on which the composers who would later be dubbed the 'Darmstadt School' were performed together

---

[115] Goeyvaerts to Steinecke, 21 May 1952, IMD.
[116] Antoine Goléa, 'Ausklang in Kranichstein: Problematik und Meisterstil', *Der Mittag*, 29 July 1952.
[117] See Inge Kovács, 'Neue Musik abseits der Avantgarde? Zwei Fallbeispiele', in Borio and Danuser (eds.), *Im Zenit der Moderne*, vol. II, 55.

on the same programme, it is hard to find much evidence to support this, notwithstanding later descriptions of the concert as having featured Boulez, Maderna, Nono, and Stockhausen. The programme did, however, consist entirely of premières, three of them of significance in this context: Stockhausen's *Kreuzspiel*, Maderna's *Musica su due dimensioni*, and Nono's first Lorca epitaph, *España en el corazón* were joined by the rather less obviously 'progressive' *Omaggio a Bach* by Camillo Togni and Jacques Wildberger's Quartet, scored for flute, clarinet, violin, and cello. Though it is certainly true that Steinecke and Boulez had agreed that the first book of *Structures* would be performed at the 1952 courses,[118] the plan was that this would have been performed by Yvonne Loriod and Boulez himself alongside Boulez's Second Piano Sonata (which Loriod did perform) in the first chamber concert of the 'Musik der jungen Generation' series on 19 July 1952.[119] There was never any intent that it would feature on the 21 July programme. Though *Structure Ia* was completed by April 1951, according to Boulez's dating,[120] and had been premièred by Boulez and Messiaen in Paris as early as 4 May 1952, it would not be until 13 November 1953 that the whole of the first book of *Structures* would be premièred by Yvette Grimaud and Yvonne Loriod in Cologne. Even if *Structures Ib* and *Ic* were ready in principle – Boulez wrote to Cage in mid May 1952 that 'we [Boulez and Messiaen] should play the three that are written in Darmstadt, Germany in July and on Cologne Radio' – in practice they could not be played. Therefore, the Second Piano Sonata was the only representation of Boulez's music at Darmstadt in 1952.[121]

Though it is obvious that Steinecke felt strongly that Boulez would have been a natural addition to the Darmstadt offering, Boulez does not seem to have been at all interested. Two letters from Steinecke to him went unanswered and, though Steinecke arranged for Boulez to have a stipend for the courses, which meant that they would have cost him nothing, he seems to have been present only for a brief few days, simply to hear his own work: as well as Loriod's performance of the Second Piano Sonata, Boulez's *Deux études concrètes* (1952) were given their German première as a part of the concert of electronic music and musique concrète on the afternoon of 21 July. It is possible, but by no means certain, that Boulez stayed into the evening and heard the 'Wunderkonzert'. He certainly stayed little longer. Indeed, it would not be until 1955 that Boulez returned to Darmstadt and

---

[118] Pierre Boulez to Steinecke, undated but probably early–mid June 1952, IMD.
[119] Steinecke to Boulez, 23 April and 29 May 1952, IMD.
[120] Lev Koblyakov, *Pierre Boulez: A World of Harmony* (Chur: Harwood, 1990), 110.
[121] Boulez to John Cage, undated but before 21 May 1952, in Jean-Jacques Nattiez (ed.), *The Boulez-Cage Correspondence*, tr. Robert Samuels (Cambridge University Press, 1994 [1993]), 128.

then only for a few days. 1956 would be the first occasion on which Boulez was to attend the courses for their full duration.[122]

The young composers in the 'Wunderkonzert', the third chamber concert of the 'Musik der jungen Generation' series, were all, from the perspective of the Darmstadt institution itself, still definitely 'participants' (the distinction between participants and faculty members being stark), even if the music of Maderna and Nono (and, to a lesser extent, Stockhausen) had begun to make some impact on the press. Nono, indeed, attended the 1952 courses on a full scholarship.[123] How exactly those particular composers came to be selected for the concert is not clear: even if there was a jury system as had operated in previous years, it can hardly have harmed the chances of either Maderna and Nono that they were both busily engaged in 'propaganda' activities in favour of the courses in Venice, approaching newspapers, conservatoires, and the radio.[124] As early as November 1951, Maderna expected his new piece to be performed, writing to Steinecke that he had already begun work on a new piece for Darmstadt for 1952.[125] Again, since it was through Maderna's auspices that Severino Gazzelloni (who would première Maderna's *Musica su due dimensioni* in the 'Wunderkonzert') was won as Darmstadt's flute lecturer for 1952, the impact of 'making oneself useful' at Darmstadt is clear.

As for Stockhausen, work on the piece that would become *Kreuzspiel*, initially entitled *Mosaike*, had begun in earnest not long after the close of the 1951 courses. The crossing points which would characterise *Kreuzspiel*, formally speaking, were planned in sketch form as early as 10 August 1951,[126] and had been sent (albeit in a handwritten copy) to Darmstadt as a submission for the World New Music Days, which were to take place in Salzburg that year.[127] Stockhausen had actually missed the submission deadline for Salzburg by a couple of days, though *Kreuzspiel* was nevertheless considered for performance there; Kurtz relates that, on having sight of the score, Eimert had warned Stockhausen, 'If you make music like this, you will have to be patient for twenty years until you get a

---

[122] Pascal Decroupet, 'Boulez: Schlüssige Kompositionssysteme. Dem flexiblen Musikdenken Vorrang eingeräumt', in Stephan et al. (eds.), *Von Kranichstein zur Gegenwart*, 226.

[123] This scholarship was in recognition both of the performance of *España en el corazón* and of the fact that Nono had agreed to act as a translator for Severino Gazzelloni's flute class. Though Nono's German was, even in later years, highly idiolectic, it was also probably fluent enough to do this reasonably effectively even in 1952. Steinecke to Nono, 22 April 1952, ALN.

[124] Maderna to Steinecke, 12 April 1952, in Dalmonte (ed.), *Bruno Maderna–Wolfgang Steinecke*, 61; Nono to Steinecke, 15 April 1952, ALN.

[125] Maderna to Steinecke, 18 November 1951, in Dalmonte (ed.), *Bruno Maderna–Wolfgang Steinecke*, 45.

[126] Stockhausen to Goeyvaerts, 10 August 1951, in Misch and Bandur (eds.), *Karlheinz Stockhausen bei den Internationalen Ferienkursen*, 15.

[127] Stockhausen to the Secretariat of the Kranichsteiner Musikinstitut, 26 October 1951, in ibid., 16.

performance.'[128] The judgement of the Salzburg jury was little better, regarding *Kreuzspiel* as 'unperformable'.[129] As matters turned out, Stockhausen did not need to wait anything like twenty years, though it surely helped a great deal that Stockhausen, like Nono and Maderna, was willing to do things to assist with the smooth running of the courses. Based in Paris as he was from the beginning of 1952, he was ideally placed to negotiate with Messiaen regarding his hoped-for engagement for the 1952 courses: as Eimert wrote to Stockhausen on 11 January 1952, '[h]e [Steinecke] wants to attempt to win Messiaen for this year's courses, but has no route to him whatsoever. Could such a connection be established by you via Goeyvaerts?'[130] It took Stockhausen little time to achieve this: he wrote to Steinecke that he had met with Messiaen and had reached an agreement, in principle at least, that he would come to Darmstadt.[131]

By the end of January, Stockhausen had moved from having no options for a performance of *Kreuzspiel* to having two: one in the Frankfurt New Music Weeks and one at Darmstadt, even though Steinecke had not by this stage given a firm commitment.[132] The idea that the Hessischer Rundfunk might snatch the première of *Kreuzspiel* from Darmstadt seems to have spurred Steinecke into giving that firm commitment, although it was also clear that Steinecke regarded paying for the services of nine players and their rehearsal time as an expense he could barely afford.[133] Before the première, Stockhausen must have felt he had made the right decision as, though the Hessischer Rundfunk's Heinz Schröter was obviously disappointed that Stockhausen had decided Darmstadt to be the right venue for *Kreuzspiel*'s first performance, he also wrote to Stockhausen that he hoped it would be possible to record *Kreuzspiel* for broadcast by the Hessischer Rundfunk at a later date.[134] Stockhausen had also renewed his contact with Nono in advance of the 1952 courses, though he wrote that '[y]ou will doubtless have forgotten our brief encounter at Darmstadt.'[135] Nono did remember, replying that 'the two of you [Stockhausen and Goeyvaerts] were really the only ones interested in music; and after Darmstadt I've thought of you both many times, unhappy that we were together too little at the Marienhöhe'.[136] Stockhausen and Nono were, doubtless, looking forward to renewing their

[128] Kurtz, *Stockhausen*, 41–3.
[129] Misch and Bandur (eds.), *Karlheinz Stockhausen bei den Internationalen Ferienkursen*, 30 n. 1.
[130] Herbert Eimert to Stockhausen, 11 January 1952, in ibid., 26.
[131] Stockhausen to Steinecke, 20 January 1952, in ibid., 28.
[132] Eimert to Stockhausen, 26 January 1952, in ibid., 31.
[133] Steinecke to Stockhausen, 14 February 1952, in ibid., 33.
[134] Heinz Schröter to Stockhausen, 28 Febuary 1952, in ibid., 38.
[135] Stockhausen to Nono, 10 March 1952, in ibid., 39.
[136] Nono to Stockhausen, 13 March 1952, in ibid., 40.

musical acquaintance. The Henze who, in 1957, would be upset, if not surprised, that Nono accompanied Boulez and Stockhausen's 'walk out' during the première of his *Nachstücke und Arien* at Donaueschingen would probably have been disappointed to read 'his friend Gigi' writing to Stockhausen in 1952 that he had been 'at the première of Henze's *Boulevard Solitude* in which one finds no music and is also wrongly called an "opera"', comparing this situation unfavourably with his hopes for the relationship he thought might develop amongst the 'real' Darmstadt composers:

> I believe that you and Goeyvaerts are like me and Maderna. When we work and live together, I believe that something genuinely good and beautiful can be achieved musically. At the Marienhöhe we will see together, clearly, how and with whom it can be done. It must be a brotherhood; if something is done against one of us, it will be as if it were done against all of us. But we should talk about this, it's easier.[137]

At this early stage, then, it is already possible to see the sort of impetus that would make Nono seek to find commonalities amongst his peers, while Stockhausen's interests were already turned more inwards, towards his own music. Moreover, implicit in Nono's letter to Stockhausen and its reply are notions that suggest their presumptions regarding their forebears. Nono observed that, in the time he and Maderna had spent working with Eimert in Cologne in the early months of 1952, they had begun afresh with study of twelve-tone technique; one might wonder whether he and Maderna were actually encountering the matter of Eimert's *Lehrbuch der Zwölftontechnik*, which had greater interest in the sort of constructivist model of twelve-tone composition suggested by Hauer than by Schoenberg.[138] In any case, Nono's letter implies a renewed interest in twelve-tone music, which had probably not been of particular pertinence for Nono since the close of the 1940s. Stockhausen's reply suggested that working together at Darmstadt would leave Nono with a thorough command of the Webernian idiom, an idiom which appears to have been largely unknown to Nono at the time, regardless of what the press reception (on which more below) would suggest.[139]

As for Stockhausen's compositional work, as presented at the 1952 Darmstadt courses, *Kreuzspiel* certainly bears the imprint of both Goeyvaerts

---

[137] Hans Werner Henze, *Bohemian Fifths*, tr. Stewart Spencer (London: Faber, 1998 [1996]), 146; Nono to Stockhausen, 13 March 1952, Misch and Bandur (eds.), *Karlheinz Stockhausen bei den Internationalen Ferienkursen*, 41.

[138] Nono to Stockhausen, 13 March 1952, in Misch and Bandur (eds.), *Karlheinz Stockhausen bei den Internationalen Ferienkursen*, 41; Herbert Eimert, *Lehrbuch der Zwölftontechnik* (Wiesbaden: Breitkopf & Härtel, 1950).

[139] Stockhauen to Nono, 20 March 1952, in Misch and Bandur (eds.), *Karlheinz Stockhausen bei den Internationalen Ferienkursen*, 44. The comment is curious in that, as I suggest below, Stockhausen appears to have known little of Webern's music before 1953.

and Messiaen, though it is simultaneously more ambitious and less rigorous in its application of technique than either *Mode de valeurs et d'intensités* or the Sonata for Two Pianos. A brief analysis of its first section, up to bar 91, gives some indication of the ways in which Stockhausen both appropriates and extends the ideas found in those two earlier pieces.[140]

Stockhausen does work from a literal twelve-tone row, as Goeyvaerts did not, but the way in which this row is treated across the piece's first major structural division (from bar 14 to bar 91, following a brief introductory passage) is redolent of Goeyvaerts's procedures. First, the series itself is treated according to a permutational system of shuffling, in which every move of an individual pitch class in one of the series's two hexachords must be mirrored in the other. Thus in Stockhausen's first transformation, the first note of the series is moved six places to the right in the second version of the row. This means necessarily that the twelfth, and last, note of the series must move six places to the left, in only one of many structural crossings within the piece. In this first transformation, then, there is only one mirrored crossing, but over the eleven transformations (thus generating twelve series, before returning to the opening series), Stockhausen utilises a pattern of numbers of 'pitch crossings' which is, too, a mirror: 1–2–2–4–4–6–4–4–2–2–1. As Blumröder's table showing this demonstrates, however, this is not an absolutely fixed process. Though the general shape of the motions is clear, Stockhausen certainly acted upon the crossings to change what the strict results would be (see Figures 1.4 and 1.5).

Rhythmic decisions appear to have begun following Messiaen's example, in that particular durations were to be bound to particular pitch classes. Blumröder's tabulation of the durations allocated to the various pitch classes of the first large structural phase of the piece shows the residue of this mode of working, along with the duration that Stockhausen had sketched for each pitch class. In the end, certain pitch classes were more or less fixed in duration, while others had flexible durations within certain limits, thus ensuring the sorts of control which would enable particular pitches or figures to be highlighted or disguised more flexibly (see Figure 1.6).

Nevertheless, *Kreuzspiel* should still be regarded more as 'point music' than as serial music, not least because this remains a closer analogue to the experience of hearing the music, even though Stockhausen's approach begins to develop a more developed horizontal focus alongside the vertically isolated points.

---

[140] The analysis presented here is largely drawn from Christoph von Blumröder, *Die Grundlegung der Musik Karlheinz Stockhausens* (Stuttgart: Franz Steiner, 1993), 44–69.

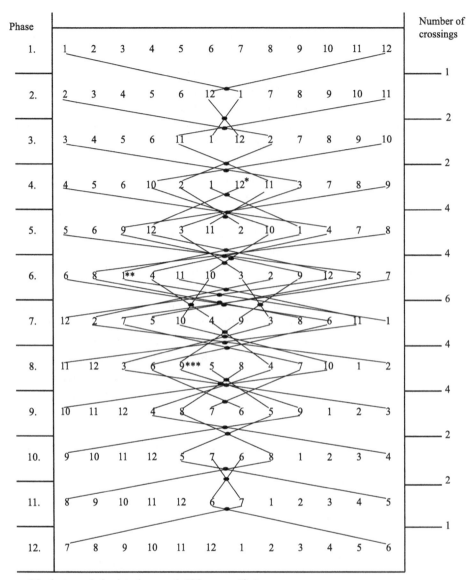

* In the transcription into the score 1–12 becomes 12–1
** 8–1 becomes 1–8
*** 11–12–3–6–9 becomes 12–3–11–9–6

Fig. 1.4 Blumröder's table of pitch 'crossings' in the first part of Karlheinz Stockhausen, *Kreuzspiel*

The technical resources that Nono's *España en el corazón* displays are arguably simpler than Stockhausen's (though the reduced pitch material with which Nono operates is redolent on this background level of what Stockhausen was doing in Klavierstück III, a piece to which I return below).

Arrivals

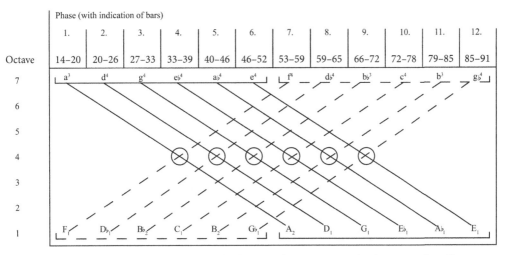

Fig. 1.5 Blumröder's table of octave dispositions in the first part of Karlheinz Stockhausen, *Kreuzspiel*

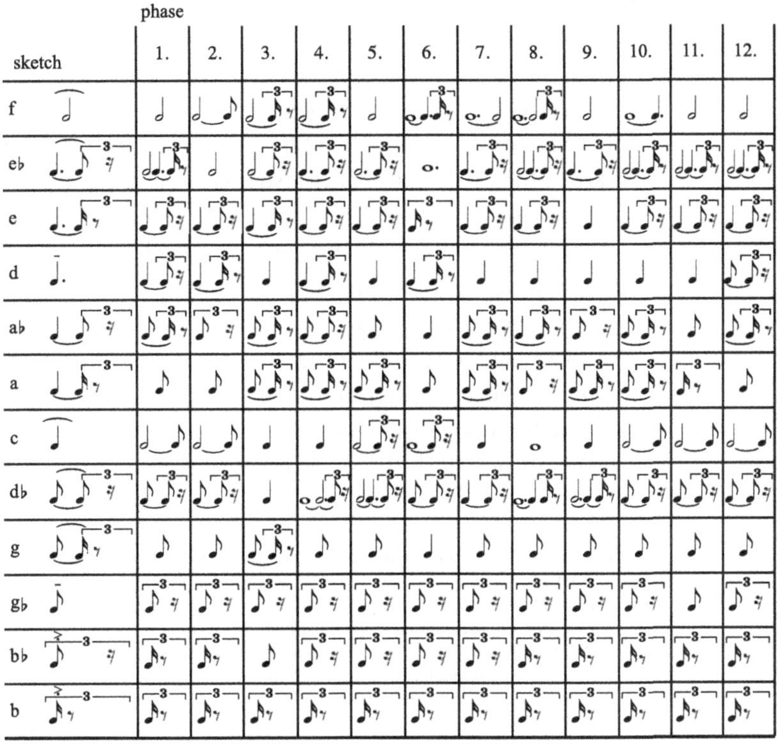

Fig. 1.6 Blumröder's table of rhythm distribution by pitch class in the first part of Karlheinz Stockhausen, *Kreuzspiel*

Table 1.2 *Core permutations in Luigi Nono, 'Tarde'*

1	3	2	4					2	1	4	3				
				<u>4</u>	<u>3</u>	2	<u>1</u>					2	<u>4</u>	<u>1</u>	3
1	3	2		4				2	1	4		<u>3</u>			
			4		3	2	1				<u>2</u>		<u>4</u>	<u>1</u>	3
1	3		2		<u>4</u>			<u>2</u>	1		4		3		
		4		<u>3</u>	<u>2</u>	1		<u>2</u>				<u>4</u>		1	<u>3</u>

If the procedures are simple, the level of compositional choice and decision is far higher.[141] Nevertheless, in one respect at least, the pieces can be seen to have a similarity: Nono also moves a little more in the direction of the horizontal. In truth, this is more of a return in Nono's case, since polyphonic lines were hardly absent from the *Variazioni canoniche*. Really, *España en el corazón* is a fusion of the sense of line exhibited in the *Variazioni canoniche* and the more explicitly procedural approach of *Polifonica-Monodia-Ritmica*.

The beginning of 'Tarde', the first part of *España en el corazón*, is exemplary in this regard. Here, Nono begins with the same sort of shuffling of resources he had undertaken with the Yemanjá rhythm in *Polifonica-Monodia-Ritmica*, though in this case pitches are used. In the first section of 'Tarde', the pitch material is restricted to a single tetrachord: F♯–C♯–E–F (numerically 1, 2, 3, and 4 in Table 1.2).[142]

These permutations do not appear in 'Tarde' in any form that is recognisable, however. They are, truly, pre-compositional, even if not dodecaphonic. Within Table 1.2, certain numbers are marked in bold: it was only these which Nono actually used in the process of generating pitches and durations.

Durational characteristics were linked to the pitches chosen or, more accurately, to intervals, and here Nono introduced a further element of choice. In principle, the notes either side of an interval were to be of the

---

[141] The analysis presented here relies upon those presented in Gianmario Borio, 'Tempo e ritmo nelle composizioni seriali: 1952–1956', in Gianmario Borio, Giovanni Morelli, and Veniero Rizzardi (eds.), *Le musiche degli anni cinquanta* (Florence: Leo S. Olschki, 2004), 70–6, and Juan José Raposo Martín, *Luigi Nono: Epitafios Lorquianos. Estudio musicológico y analítico* (La Palma del Condado: Hergué, 2009), 64–95. For a fuller account, the reader is advised to examine these two analyses, ideally with relation to one another, since Raposo Martín helps to amplify various aspects of Borio's analysis.

[142] Raposo Martín notes that both this and Nono's second pitch grouping (G♯, G♮, D–E, B♭, which is utilised *as* a tetrachord in the piece, even though the third pitch D is consistently elided with an E 'held over' from the first tetrachord) can be seen as having been 'extracted' from archetypically Spanish modes based on C♯ and G respectively. Raposo Martín, *Luigi Nono: Epitafios Lorquianos*, 74.

Arrivals

minor second	=	♩ ♩
major second	=	♪ ♪
minor third	=	♩. ♩.
major third	=	♪. ♪.
perfect fourth	=	♩ ♩

Fig. 1.7 Transformation of interval to duration in Luigi Nono, 'Tarde'

Pitch:	F♯	E	C♯	F	
Interval:		2	3	4	0
Durations:	♪	♪	♪.	♪.	
		♩.	♩.		
Selection:	♪	♩.	♩.	♪.	

Pitch:	F	E	C♯	F♯	C♯
Interval:		1	3	5	5
Durations:	♩	♩	♩	♩	♩
		♩.	♩.		
Selection:	♩	♩	♩.	♩	♩

Fig. 1.8 Derivation of rhythmic line from intervallic content in Luigi Nono, 'Tarde'

same duration, according to the scheme shown in Figure 1.7. Inevitably, however, this led to occasions where more than one option was possible for a duration, as shown in the opening of Nono's calculations (see Figure 1.8). From this, Nono constructed a source melodic line, as shown in Example 1.7. Yet even this did not appear in 'Tarde' in literal form. Having constructed the source melodic line, Nono would cut away further pitches from it, until only the pitches in his original permutational arrays which are shown both in bold and underlined remain in the piece itself (see Example 1.8).

Nono was utilising a complex set of pre-compositional resources, and was by this stage deriving both pitch and rhythm from a common source. Yet he acted so strongly on this material that, on the page itself, there was little to show the degree of work undertaken. If the permutational ideas used in *Polifonica–Monodia–Ritmica* were relatively straightforward, here they

Ex. 1.7 Source melodic line in Lugi Nono, 'Tarde'

Ex. 1.8 Luigi Nono, 'Tarde', bb. 1–5

were pushed much further, though the most potent development was that additional levels of pre-compositional structuration were mirrored with increasing degrees of decision-making regarding which of those aspects to retain and which to do away with. It is notable, too, that Nono's pitch language is far from stereotypically dodecaphonic: while the total chromatic is revealed within 'Tarde', Nono concentrates for the most part on restricted parts of it, such that it is not really meaningful to speak of a 'series' in the case of this part, at least, of *España en el corazón*, even if the materials are treated according to two separate parameters and permuted. It is also worth noting that, just as 'Yemanjá' figured in *Polifonica–Monodia–Ritmica*, so too did the rather more politically charged song of the Italian labour movement, 'Bandiera rossa', feature in *España en el corazón*.[143]

The sorts of permutation that appeared in Nono's *España en el corazón* were also utilised in Maderna's *Musica su due dimensioni*, though in a rather more developed form. The sort of multi-layered shuffling of elements which Nono had begun to formalise, from the *Variazioni canoniche* through to *España en el corazón*, was an idea which he and Maderna shared and termed a

---

[143] Mário Vieira de Carvalho, 'Towards Dialectical Listening: Quotation and *Montage* in the Work of Luigi Nono', in Stephen Davismoon (ed.), *Luigi Nono: Fragments and Silence* (*Contemporary Music Review*, vol. 18, no. 2, 1999), 42.

Arrivals

Table 1.3 *Displacement array in Bruno Maderna,* Musica su due dimensioni

C	B♭	F	A♭	G♭	E♭	C♯	B	A	E	D	G
11	9	11	15	12	9	12	10	11	11	13	10
15	11	9	11	9	12	9	11	10	9	10	13
9	11	15	11	9	12	9	10	14	13	11	9
11	15	11	9	12	9	12	14	10	10	9	11
11	13	10	9	10	14	11	9	12	11	9	11
9	10	13	11	14	10	10	12	9	15	11	9
13	11	9	10	10	11	14	12	9	9	11	15
10	9	11	13	11	10	10	9	12	11	15	11
9	12	9	12	9	11	15	11	9	10	10	14
12	9	12	9	11	9	11	9	11	11	14	10
12	9	12	9	11	15	11	13	10	10	10	11
9	12	9	12	15	11	9	10	13	14	11	10
10	10	11	14	13	10	9	11	15	9	12	9
11	14	10	10	10	13	11	15	11	12	9	12
10	10	14	11	11	9	10	9	11	12	9	12
14	11	10	10	9	11	13	11	9	9	12	9

'tecnica degli spostamenti', a 'technique of displacements'. Here, Maderna's 'b' series (itself permutationally generated from the 'a' series which was used for *Musica su due dimensioni*'s opening electronic part) forms the basis of the central solo flute section.[144] Maderna showed this basic pitch material on a twelve-by-twelve array, but also had a separate 'displacement array', which moved the notes of the series along by a certain number of positions, such that their position in the order would change (and that it was possible to end up with series arrays which contained duplications or no instances of a particular pitch class). The displacement array itself provided sixteen 'displacements' for each pitch class, in columns in which the total number of displacements all added up to 176, ensuring a 'wrap-around' to the original series (see Tables 1.3 and 1.4).[145]

---

[144] Christoph Neidhöfer analyses this opening section in 'Bruno Maderna's Serial Arrays', *Music Theory Online*, vol. 13, no. 1 (March 2007), www.mtosmt.org/issues/mto.07.13.1/mto.07.13.1.neidhofer.html (accessed 25 April 2011). In this first section, it is worth nothing that rhythmic values are not truly serialised. Rather they are bound directly to particular pitch classes (a simpler version, in some senses, of Goeyvaerts's punctual system), in multiples of a crotchet: A was worth a crotchet, D♭ a minim, C, E, F♯, and D a dotted minim, and F and D a semibreve, with the remainder of the pitch classes each lasting five crotchets.

[145] A much fuller description of Maderna's procedures in the second section of *Musica su due dimensioni* may be found in Roderick, 'Rebulding a Culture', 309–23. Roderick's analysis is the source of what is presented here.

The accidental serialists

Table 1.4 *Serial arrays 1–4 in Bruno Maderna,* Musica su due dimensioni

	1	2	3	4	5	6	7	8	9	10	11	12
A									•			
B♭		•										•
B							•					
C	•											
C♯						•						
D											•	
D♯					•							
E										•		
F				•								
F♯					•							
G		(•)										•
G♯				•								

	1	2	3	4	5	6	7	8	9	10	11	12
A									•			
B♭												•
B						•						
C	•											
C♯								•				
D												
D♯					•							
E										•		
F				•								
F♯							•					
G											•	
G♯								•				

	1	2	3	4	5	6	7	8	9	10	11	12
A								•				
B♭												•
B							•					
C					•							
C♯						•						
D	•											•
D♯						•						
E										•		
F	•											
F♯					•							
G												
G♯								•				

	1	2	3	4	5	6	7	8	9	10	11	12
A											•	
B♭												
B					•							
C			•									
C♯				•								
D												•
D♯						•						
E										•		
F				•								
F♯	•											
G	•										•	
G♯							•					

Even though this meant that Maderna had access to core materials (in the form of sixteen arrays) which were themselves no longer obviously 'twelve-tone', while still being generated *from* a twelve-tone row, Maderna was not minded to leave this material as it was. As Roderick shows, he used the material of only the first twelve arrays (using the remaining four in the piece's second electronic section), and modified or adapted the fifth, ninth, tenth, and twelfth presentations. Even if he had used the unaltered arrays, though, the 'tecnica degli spostamenti' would already have meant that *Musica su due dimensioni* 'is unified only at the ontological level (*i.e.* in its origins) not at the phenomenological level (*i.e.* in its sound)'.[146] The piece would not be justified on the grounds of how faithfully it reproduced its generative processes, but on its sounding immanent surface.

It was hardly the treatment of pitch material in *Musica su due dimensioni* that was problematic, but precisely the two dimensions themselves, the acoustic and the electronic. As Meyer-Eppler had feared, the result, in this piece and at this point at least, was not that the musical elements were fused, but merely that they were contrasted, as the critics (to whom I return below) were quick to note. As Roderick states, Maderna's aim 'was not to layer audio effects to compose a stand-alone composition, but to create a seamless whole that integrated an electronic tape and a live flute and piano line'.[147] *Musica su due dimensioni* had three panels: tape, solo flute, and tape, but the projected mixture of the tape and the flute never occurred (the piano having

[146] Ibid., 321.   [147] Ibid., 313.

been relatively quickly dropped, and the cymbal contributing nothing more than a single strike at the very close of the piece). This may not have been wholly Maderna's fault, except that he failed to comprehend quite how serious Meyer-Eppler's warnings of the time Maderna would need in the studio were. While Maderna's later descriptions of electronic music became elegantly imagistic – 'cold hallucination', 'soft, undulating sounds', or 'sheet metal' – here he 'emerged from the Bonn studio with a compromised work'.[148]

Later, Steinecke (albeit in an essay published posthumously) would reinvent the events of the 'Wunderkonzert' in his own description of the history of the Ferienkurse. It can be little more than wishful thinking (and, indeed, a wilful failure to check the details of that year's programme) that Steinecke would claim not only that the pieces by Maderna, Nono, and Stockhausen that *were* performed were a part of the 'Wunderkonzert', but also that he recalled the first book of Boulez's *Structures* being performed within the same concert. This enabled Steinecke quite literally to backdate the idea of the 'Darmstadt School' – a notion which was not conceivable at this point – to these foundational years.[149] Steinecke was also able to make further spurious claims in this retrospective reinvention of the Ferienkurse:

> With the four works that were performed in that Darmstadt concert of 1952, four different ways of looking at the problem were simultaneously posed. Luigi Nono's Lorca epitaph was the first attempt to fuse serial music with a new vocal style, and we know from Nono's later work that, since then, the problem of new music for voice has been central for him. Karlheinz Stockhausen's *Kreuzspiel* presented a model example of the punctual style, that style of a pointillist individuation of the tone, which we recognise today as a passage from Schoenberg's thematic dodecaphonic technique to serial compositional techniques. Pierre Boulez's *Structures* already represent a textbook example of serial compositional techniques, which were presented here according to a strict and almost dogmatic manner. Bruno Maderna's *Musica su due dimensioni* of 1952 is interesting because it makes the first use of the new sonic means of electronic music in this context. With these keywords – punctual and serial music, new vocal music and electronic music – that concert in 1952, with the work of Stockhausen and Boulez, Nono and Maderna, outlined a new thematic, which was of particular significance for the stylistic development within the framework of the generation of the new music.[150]

While it is true that Boulez's *Structures* represent just such an example of multiple serialism, they were, as noted above, not premièred until 13 November the following year in Cologne, and were not heard at

[148] Ibid., 316. [149] Steinecke, 'Kranichstein – Geschichte, Idee, Ergebnisse', 15. [150] Ibid., 15.

Darmstadt until 2 June 1955, when they were performed by Yvonne Loriod and Hans Alexander Kaul. Rather curiously, even at the time, one reporter, the *Rheinische Post*'s Paul Müller, seems to have been rather confused, since he, too, suggested that Boulez's first three *Structures* were performed.[151] Where Müller's confusion originated is unclear, since no other reporter made the error.[152] In any case, as has been often stressed in scholarship on Boulez's serial practice, the first book of *Structures* is aberrant in terms of the ways in which Boulez generally operated,[153] nor does it represent a paradigmatic example of serialism as generally practised at Darmstadt. According to the example of the 'Wunderkonzert' such a paradigm would be hard to imagine: Nono's music utilised some quite strict procedures on the background level, but most of the material thus generated became transformed by compositional decision-making (mainly by eliminating elements thrown up by the process). Nor was Nono's music concerned with a twelve-tone row. What Nono did concerned a certain procedural approach to creating material in both the parameters of pitch and duration, but the material, once generated, could largely be acted upon freely by the composer. Whatever the problems of Maderna's piece, it is notable that he was already keen to put some distance between his music and that of the twelve-tone composers, using procedures to ensure that his material was no longer obviously dominated by a chromatic equality of pitch classes, but also changing the results of processes at will in sections of the piece. Stockhausen was process-driven and was, genuinely, twelve-tone too, but also introduced changes both at the pre-compositional level and once he had begun to work with the material he had generated. In truth, the similarities are so limited as to make it difficult to imagine a model which usefully encompassed these practices. What links the composers is little more than existence of pre-compositional work which includes independent consideration of more than one parameter, typically pitch and rhythm (though more than two are, of course, possible). Gottfried Michael Koenig suggested that '[i]n the beginning, one's attention was focused on pitches,

---

[151] Paul Müller, 'Schmelztiegel der Neuen Musik: Abschluß der Kranichsteiner Tage', *Rheinische Post*, 30 July 1952.

[152] The mistake is perpetuated, though in a less strong form, by Kurtz, who notes that '*Kreuzspiel* had been accepted for the younger generation concerts at the Darmstadt Summer Courses and put on a programme with works by Boulez, Maderna, Nono, Camillo Togni and Bernd Alois Zimmermann' (Kurtz, *Stockhausen*, 52). Lothar Knessl, too, repeats a slightly different version in his claim that Boulez's Second Piano Sonata was on the programme (Lothar Knessl, 'Das Dezennium des großen Aufbruchs: Rückblick-Notizen – ohne (?) Verklärung', in Stephan et al. (eds.), *Von Kranichstein zur Gegenwart*, 141).

[153] See, for example, Thomas Bösche, 'Auf der Suche nach dem Unbekannten oder Zur Deuxième Sonate (1946–1948) von Pierre Boulez und der Frage nach der seriellen Musik', in Orm Finnendahl (ed.), *Die Anfänge der seriellen Musik* (Berlin: Wolke, 1999), 37–96.

durations, intensities, and timbres. Then other qualities or issues became pressing: groups, which consisted of many notes; spatially conceived sound events; new musical instruments or new ways of playing old ones; liberties given to performers; musical action.'[154] Yet even according to such a conservative view, the Italian composers would have been excluded. Maderna's and Nono's trajectory had little to do with such a model, even if it may reasonably well describe what happened in Germany. What the composers themselves had to say hardly exhibited much unanimity either, as I show below in the context of presentations made by them on the occasion of the Webern evening in 1953. Nevertheless, as Boulez would implicitly observe at that event, one important unifying characteristic was that the material which was pre-compositionally generated, regardless of whether or not it was followed in a slavish way in the composition proper, led to the structure and form of the piece, rather than being suspended in an extant formal shape. This was an idea which would, much later, preoccupy Adorno, amongst others.

In such a context, perhaps it is unsurprising that Steinecke's description of the origins of the 'Darmstadt School' made no mention of the fact that, on the one hand, Maderna's *Musica su due dimensioni* would not reappear until 1958,[155] and, on the other, that Stockhausen's *Kreuzspiel* was withdrawn by its composer immediately following the performance (and would not be available for performance again until 1959, when it was performed at the courses on 3 September, with the number of percussionists reduced from four to three). Taruskin observes that '[w]ithin the ascetic world of "total serialism," at any rate, *Kreuzspiel* counts as easy listening. That may be one reason why Stockhausen suppressed constant pulsation in the works that followed and also withheld *Kreuzspiel* from publication for nearly a decade, despite positive audience reactions.'[156] It is difficult to see where Taruskin would have found the idea that *Kreuzspiel* received a positive response from its audience. It did not, and the last thing the Darmstadt audience of 1952 regarded it as was 'easy listening'. Albert Rodemann's review of *Kreuzspiel* was probably about the norm:

> Why Karl Heinz [sic] Stockhausen entitled his music for oboe, bass clarinet, piano, and four percussionists *Kreuzspiel* ['Cross Play'] is incomprehensible.

---

[154] Gottfried Michael Koenig, quoted in Marcus Zagorski, 'Material and History in the Aesthetics of "Serielle Musik"', *Journal of the Royal Musical Association*, vol. 134, no. 2 (November 2009), 273–4.

[155] That version bore only tangential relation to the one premièred in 1952, notwithstanding Maderna's claim in 1959 that 'I felt the necessity for this synthesis for the first time in 1952, and was very happy with it'. Maderna, quoted in Roderick, *Rebulding a Culture*, 309.

[156] Richard Taruskin, *Music in the Late Twentieth Century*, The Oxford History of Western Music, vol. V (Oxford: University Press, 2010 [2005]), 48.

Arrivals

> Following a system of 'static music', the indefensibleness of which Theodor Adorno already demonstrated the previous year to its Flemish inventor [i.e. Goeyvaerts], the sound of the piece goes far beyond that which we have been accustomed to call music. That he finds a few devotees to celebrate his work [. . .] doesn't change things a jot. Every idea finds its prophets. And its sect.[157]

The correspondent of the *Abendpost* seemed to be making some reference to what Rodemann had said, in observations that are striking because of how early a criticism that would become familiar was made, and made explicitly:

> Most of what was on offer in Kranichstein left the listener cold. The twelve-tone row has become a fetish and its propositions have become empty phrases. As justification, the pseudo-geniuses present their scores and point to interesting graphic images of their musical logarithms. With that the music degenerates into only its visual appearance and could, finally, be replaced by a film of the score. That would involve less effort and less noise. Only: it wouldn't be music any more.[158]

In truth, though the criticism is one which already sounds familiar, the only concrete event to which reference can have been being made was the session on electronic music and musique concrète on 21 July, which featured Eimert, Meyer-Eppler, Goléa, and Boulez, especially in the light of the 'score of the future' that Meyer-Eppler had shown in 1950, since otherwise the lecture series was dominated by Strobel's six-part introduction to 'the complete works of Igor Stravinsky'. Even if Stockhausen might later have explained his work in these ways, by 1952 he was not in any position, institutionally speaking, to do so.

Nevertheless, a few commentators exhibited some comprehension of what Stockhausen, at least, was attempting. Gustav Adolf Trumpff explained the principles behind *Kreuzspiel* with reasonable accuracy and suggested that, once those had been understood, one could comprehend the way in which the piece is shaped. Trumpff went further: 'One might doubt that this can really come to a final, musical result, one might style this music an example of mathematical calculation, but one ought to consider the possibility for or the fact of real inspiration which is vital for creative mathematicians too. Understood in this way, Stockhausen's work is notable because of its consequences.'[159] Perhaps the most damning report, however, when viewed with a knowledge of the impact Stockhausen would ultimately have, came in

---

[157] Albert Rodemann, 'Ein Tag des Experimentes: Zwei Veranstaltungen in den Kranichsteiner Ferienkursen', *Darmstädter Tagblatt*, 23 July 1952.
[158] [N.], 'Die Jugend der Neuen Musik in gefährdendem Zwielicht', *Abendpost*, 28 July 1952.
[159] Gustav Adolf Trumpff, 'Es geht um eine neue Musikästhetik: Versuche mit elektronische Musik – Karl Heinz [*sic*] Stockhausen's *Kreuzspiel*', *Darmstädter Echo*, 24 July 1952.

Walther Friedländer's pithy observation that '[p]ieces like Karl Heinz [*sic*] Stockhausen's *Kreuzspiel* for chamber ensemble and Renzo dall'Oglio's *Cinque espressioni* for orchestra, both written in the "punctual" manner, can hardly be distinguished from one another.'[160] By all accounts the close of Stockhausen's piece divided the audience strongly, being 'as heavily applauded as it was whistled', as Heinz Enke had it.[161] In fairness to the critics, the performance at the 'Wunderkonzert' was, especially in the final section, only just recognisable as *Kreuzspiel*. It is clear that Romolo Grano, who performed the oboe part, was extremely nervous throughout, with rather shaky, hesitant entries. It is also plausible that there is some truth in Kurtz's description of Friedrich Wildgans having deliberately sabotaged the piece by playing the bass clarinet part comedically loudly at points.[162] The performance was, moreover, exceptionally slow. Precisely the rhythmic drive which gives *Kreuzspiel* so much of its character simply could not have been perceived by critics at this first performance. For that reason, Maconie's assessment too – that '[l]isteners were offended by the cool, personal self-sufficiency of *Kreuzspiel*, and also by its seeming to defer, by its salon-jazz character, to the vulgar influence of the occupying American culture' – must be rejected.[163]

In truth, though Stockhausen was hardly well received, it was probably Maderna who was hit worst by the press, in no small part because most of the reviews were relatively kind, almost paternalistic, in their explanation of why Maderna's music was simply not good enough. Engler's review was probably the most scathing: 'Maderna presented a "composition" made up of train station noises, plus flute and cymbal. That these things can be used in the fringe areas of *Gebrauchsmusik* isn't a question; to go further would be rather premature.'[164] 'Premature', too, was exactly the word Wilhelm Herrmann used to describe Maderna's attempt to bring acoustic and electronic music

---

[160] Walther Friedländer, 'An den Grenzen der Hörbarkeit: Internationale Ferienkurse für Neue Musik in Darmstadt', *Der Standpunkt*, 8 August 1952.
[161] Heinz Enke, 'Anton von Weberns Geist über Kranichstein: Die junge Generation bei den Internationalen Ferienkursen', *Allgemeine Zeitung*, 26 July 1952.
[162] Kurtz, *Stockhausen*, 52. Certainly, in Reinhard Kapp's interview with Gösta Neuwirth, it seems clear that Wildgans probably had little time for *Kreuzspiel* personally, though the recording suggests that he was one of the more accurate of the players. See Markus Grassl and Reinhard Kapp (eds.), *Darmstadt-Gespräche* (Vienna: Böhlau, 1996), 30.
[163] Robin Maconie, *The Works of Karlheinz Stockhausen* (London: Oxford University Press, 1976), 22. This remark is not retained in Maconie's more recent volume devoted to Stockhausen's music, but some of its sentiment remains, as Maconie makes comparisons with Glenn Miller's 'A String of Pearls' and 'the gently nudging style of Paul Desmond's alto sax in the Dave Brubeck Quartet'. (Robin Maconie, *Other Planets: The Music of Karlheinz Stockhausen* (Lanham, MD: Scarecrow, 2005) 61–3).
[164] Günter Engler, 'Musik der jungen Generation? Experiment und Manier bei den "Ferienkursen"', *Neue Zeitung*, 23 July 1952.

together,[165] while for Rodemann, the problem was that, despite the brilliance of Gazzelloni's performance, the instrumental and the electronic parts simply did not mesh, meaning that the piece failed to achieve its principal goal.[166] For Goléa, the same difficulty was in evidence. *Musica su due dimensioni*, in this version, was 'an experiment in juxtaposition, but hardly ever resulting in a fusion of the "normal" and electronic instruments'.[167]

Only Nono appeared to come out of these events relatively unscathed, *España en el corazón* being, for Engler, impressive in the way it was able to marshal the varied resources of singing and speaking voices and percussion.[168] In comparison with Stockhausen, Nono was, for Rodemann, neither doctrinaire nor sectarian, and could be 'justifiably picked out as the father of the Kranichstein model of the young compositional generation'. The aural experience of Nono's work, in Rodemann's description, already feels very close to that of rather later pieces, like *Il canto sospeso* (1955–6):

> At the heart of the short, three-part composition lie texts of Spanish freedom poets – the murdered Garcia Lorca and Pablo Neruda, who died in exile – which Nono sets neither syllabically nor illustratively. They become for him the basis of a bold and charged abstraction, in which the instruments, speaker, speaking choir, and both singing voices create an atmosphere which, even in the space of autonomous music, points towards the content of the poems.[169]

The reporter of the *Aachener Nachrichten*, too, drew comparisons between Stockhausen and Nono:

> The punctual style, which leads back to Anton Webern, and which the young H. K. [*sic*] Stockhausen still handles clumsily in his *Kreuzspiel* [...] has found its master in Luigi Nono. His *Espana* [...] is a beautiful piece. Tautly constructed, captivating in its dabs of orchestral colour, immediate in effect. The enchanted listeners demanded an encore, which Maderna, conducting, finally allowed. For Luigi Nono, who only two years ago was strongly criticised and lampooned, it was a major evening.[170]

Trumpff, too, reported that the response to *España en el corazón* was so positive that it had to be encored immediately.[171] According to Günter

---

[165] Wilhelm Herrmann, 'Internationale Ferienkurse für Neue Musik: Kritischer Rückblik [*sic*] auf das Darmstädter Treffen', *Rhein-Neckar-Zeitung*, 1 August 1952.
[166] Rodemann, 'Ein Tag des Experimentes'. [167] Goléa, 'Ausklang in Kranichstein'.
[168] Engler, 'Musik der jungen Generation?'
[169] Rodemann, 'Ein Tag des Experimentes'. It is not clear whom Rodemann has mistaken for Neruda here, but he is certainly in error, since Neruda, in the first place, was Chilean, rather than Spanish, and in the second, did not die until 1973. Nevertheless, it is the case that Neruda was exiled from Chile at the time of the première of *España en el corazón*.
[170] [Kemp.], 'Die "Neue Musik" und die Gesellschaft: Für wen denn eigentlich schaffen unsere Jüngsten?', *Aachener Nachrichten*, 25 July 1952.
[171] Trumpff, 'Es geht um eine neue Musikästhetik'.

Engler, though, with the exception of Nono's contribution, the concert as a whole represented 'a skeleton of music, with no flesh on it. (To refer to Webern in this context borders on the libellous.)'[172] Hille Moldenhauer's review was similarly disparaging: '"Punctual Music" is the shibboleth for this skeleton, whose secrets only its composers know. Thankfully it is, as yet, only a part of proceedings, since this system is in decay.' Nevertheless, Moldenhauer was, like everyone else, impressed by Nono's new piece.[173]

What is intriguing in these reports is the way in which Nono's procedures became reconstructed. Although his compositional method was radically different, and concerned at all points with *line*, Nono was recontextualised in many reports as an Italian analogue to the German 'pointillists',[174] although Nono was accorded, consistently, rather more praise. Furthermore, Heinz Enke's report, in the *Allgemeine Zeitung*, also made the link between the aphoristic style that had been noted in Nono's music in the previous year and that of Webern (as had Engler, though only as a ploy to say that the comparison was spurious).[175] Even if Nono's own permutational devices, which he had derived principally from fifteenth-century models rather from Webern, were the basis for the composition of *España en el corazón*, and even if any relationship Stockhausen had to Webern in *Kreuzspiel* was largely mediated by the example of Goeyvaerts, the press was starting to construct a recognisable idea of who the composers at the heart of young Darmstadt were. The truth of the matter, as far as *Kreuzspiel* is concerned, is probably close to Harvey's description:

> The only influences detectable in *Kreuzspiel* [...] are Messiaen, Indian music (suggested by high drum patterning), a pointillistic piece by the fellow Darmstadt student Goeyvaerts – Sonata for 2 Pianos whose middle movements also cross registers, and just a sniff of Webern in the purity and austerity of texture (he [Stockhausen] only knew Webern's Five Movements for String Quartet, op. 5).[176]

---

[172] Engler, 'Musik der jungen Generation?'
[173] Hille Moldenhauer, '"Punktuelle" Musik und Filzpantoffeln: Eindrücke von den Internationalen Ferienkursen für Neue Musik', *Hamburger Echo*, 26 July 1952.
[174] See, especially, Wolf-Eberhard von Lewinski, 'Geräuschrhythmik und Dodekaphonie: Die 7. Internationalen Ferienkurse für Neue Musik in Darmstadt', *Wiesbadener Tagblatt*, 31 July 1952. This said, Lewinski also regarded Henze as a representative of 'statistical' music, suggesting the degree to which such a construction was founded on dubious ground.
[175] Enke, 'Anton von Weberns Geist über Kranichstein'.
[176] Jonathan Harvey, *The Music of Stockhausen: An Introduction* (Berkeley, CA: University of California Press, 1975), 16. Stockhausen's letter to Nono of 20 March 1952, mentioned above, would appear to suggest, however, that Harvey is wrong to say that Stockhausen probably *could not* have shown the influence of Webern, even if he is largely correct in his assertion that it *need not* be held to be a Webernian piece. Nevertheless, though Stockhausen may have known a little more of Webern's music than the Five Movements, op. 5, it would not be until the following year that he would come to know Webern more fully.

Nevertheless, the distance of such reportage from the actuality of what they were doing is, for the most part, an irrelevance, since the young composers did little themselves to redress the impression (even though it was, in fairness, some years before any of the young composers was in a *position* to be able to query the accuracy of the descriptions). In terms of influence, it might be noted that, although Nono had not yet been exposed to Messiaen's mode of working with rhythm directly, in 1952, as noted above, Messiaen was a Darmstadt faculty member (he would repeat the visit the following year, on that occasion with Goléa acting as translator, rather than Goeyvaerts), and Nono was enrolled not only in his composition classes, but also in his special course on rhythm.[177] Even if Messiaen appears not to have made a huge impact upon Nono, he too, like Boulez, Goeyvaerts, and Stockhausen, had experienced his teaching.

Other decisive changes certainly occurred at the 1952 courses. Nono and Maderna moved from being on professional terms with Wolfgang Steinecke to being on personal terms, the three men addressing one another as 'Du' from this point onwards. This relationship was one which Stockhausen would not reach until after the 1959 courses. Though the rather more ebullient Italians, especially the affable Maderna, were more likely to be on 'Du' terms sooner than Stockhausen was, it bespeaks a position of importance and influence on the Darmstadt institution on behalf of Maderna and Nono which neither Stockhausen nor Boulez had, even if Boulez would probably have had little interest in guiding the courses at Darmstadt at this point.

The Webern evening, 1953

Although no new piece by Nono was to be played in 1953, Steinecke nevertheless invited him to play a role at the courses. Eimert and Steinecke had jointly planned two events which concerned the younger generation. First, they had projected a concert to mark the seventieth anniversary of the birth of Webern; second, they proposed a discussion evening on the music of the younger generation, to feature recordings of Boulez's *Polyphonie X* (1951), Stockhausen's *Kontra-Punkte* (1952–3), and Nono's second Lorca epitaph, *Y su sangre ya viene cantando* (1952). That the first of these two events concerned Stockhausen and Nono should appear a little surprising: Stockhausen did not know Webern's music particularly well, and it was only one of a very wide range of influences on Nono and certainly not the

---

[177] Steinecke to Nono, 22 April 1952, ALN. See also Borio, 'Tempo e ritmo nelle composizioni seriali', 64.

most pressing of those, despite claims in the press of Webern's importance for both. In any case, it was Steinecke's and Eimert's plan to have Webern's music discussed by the younger composers: as well as live presentations by Stockhausen and Nono, there were readings of prepared texts by Boulez and Goeyvaerts. This was followed by an all-Webern programme: the Six Bagatelles, op. 9, for string quartet (1911–13); the Three Short Pieces, op. 11, for cello and piano (1914); the Three Lieder, op. 23 (1933–4); the Four Pieces, op. 7, for violin and piano (1910–14); and the Five Movements, op. 5, for string quartet (1909). The whole event was recorded for broadcast on the Nordwestdeutscher Rundfunk, hence Eimert's involvement and interest. Notably, it seems that no-one considered that Maderna might speak about Webern, though he was the only one of the younger composers who received a performance at Darmstadt in 1953, conducting the première of his own *Quattro lettere* (1953) in the final concert on 30 July. He did, however, take part in the discussion of the music of his contemporaries, alongside Messiaen and Heiß, in a roundtable under the title 'Positions and Possibilities in Today's New Music', chaired by Goléa.

Though the models for Nono's music may not have been especially Webernian, that is certainly not to say that he did not know the music.[178] Steinecke wrote to him to ask whether, although it had proved impossible to put any of his music into the course programme, he would still be willing to come to Darmstadt and whether he would speak for no more than ten minutes on the subject of Webern.[179] Nono's answer could hardly have been more effusive, regarding both his strength of feeling regarding Webern and his commitment to Darmstadt:

> I said to you once that if and when you ask something of me for Kranichstein and it's within my power to do it, you don't need an answer from me, because you must know how my heart is bound to Kranichstein. UNDERSTOOD?!?!?!?! Especially in this case: to say something new about Webern, against the mentality that holds Webern up as an almost high-abstract mathematics and against those who would speak of his music with formulae.[180]

Regardless of what the members of the press may have intimated, Nono for one was obviously critical of any attempt to describe Webern with charts and tables.

---

[178] The earliest extant piece of Nono's writing, a brief commentary on Dallapiccola's *Sex carmina Alcaei*, mentions that the fragmentation of phrases and the generally quiet dynamic range of that piece might be considered a part of the way in which it represents a homage to Webern. Luigi Nono, 'Luigi Dallapiccola e i *Sex carmina Alcaei*', in *Scritti e colloqui*, ed. Angela Ida De Benedictis and Veniero Rizzardi (Lucca: Ricordi, 2001 [*ca.* 1948]), vol. I, 4.
[179] Steinecke to Nono, 17 June 1953, ALN.   [180] Nono to Steinecke, 19 June 1953, ALN.

Stockhausen, for his part, was in Darmstadt for only one day in 1953, since Doris Stockhausen was expecting the birth of their first child, Suja, but that one-day visit was made to present his essay on Webern's Concerto for nine instruments, op. 24 (1934), a piece which he had only come to know relatively recently, Universal Edition having provided him with the scores of everything it had in print by Webern in June 1953, in advance of his Darmstadt presentation. Regarding the Webern Concerto, Stockhausen wrote to Goeyvaerts on 20 July 1953: 'I am showing only the first movement, and only what's most essential. What Webern anticipates is immense. I have only just come to realise this, as I have, little by little, come to know the music.'[181] If Stockhausen was excited by what he had found in Webern, he was significantly less enthused by the invitation to take part in the other roundtable.[182] In this respect, Stockhausen observed that it seemed to him

> not to make sense for the composers themselves (least of all me) to be active participants in a discussion regarding 'Positions and Possibilities in Today's New Music'. The 'position' is clear: Webern died in 1945 – it is 1953 today. The 'possibilities' are no less clear: what is possible is what occurs to one – mindful (or reminded) of the historical 'position' (in which respect Webern's music is a benchmark). What occurs to me [. . .] is what seems to me to be possible – and that is different for each and every composer. How can one, then, discuss these 'possibilities'?[183]

Though Stockhausen stated that he thought that it might be fruitful to show the ways in which points of contact between composers in France, Germany, Belgium, Italy, and the United States suggested a new mode of speech that was in certain respects common, his principal stress was on difference. From Stockhausen's perspective, if Webern might be regarded as some sort of role model for young composers, what each of them took from that was rather different and, in any case, the route of a particular composer did not, or should not, represent a 'possible' route for *other* young composers to follow. Even if Webern came to represent a significant model for Stockhausen's approach to serialism, this could hardly have occurred any earlier than 1953, since he did not know Webern's music in any depth before this. Any suggestion that Nono's response to Webern might represent a sort of cold calculatedness is surely belied by his own reaction, mentioned above, which is expanded upon below. Vitally, this was already

---

[181] Stockhausen to Goeyvaerts, 20 July 1953, in Misch and Bandur (eds.), *Stockhausen bei den Internationalen Ferienkursen*, 71.
[182] Steinecke asked him by letter on 9 July 1953 whether he would participate (ibid., 69).
[183] Stockhausen to Steinecke, 14 June 1953, in ibid., 69–70.

some time after the two composers had begun to develop their own techniques, which already implied particular takes on compositional practice.

Eimert at least was well aware that what the Webern evening represented had the potential to make history (or to revise it). He was, as Kovács points out, no 'neutral observer'.[184] His introductory words make this clear:

> We begin to understand that Webern was not just a student of Schoenberg who developed the twelve-tone system until it reached a final abstract zone, behind which there seems to be nothing but silence – we begin to understand too, much more, that this putative end of music is simultaneously a beginning, a beginning for a group of young composers [...] who, through an unshakeable belief and firmness of faith in Webern, may be seen unquestionably as the leading masters of the new music.[185]

These words from Eimert should be recalled through much of what follows, since they mark the press coverage of the Webern evening starkly. There can be little doubt that the faith in Webern outlined here is, almost wholly, of Eimert's own invention, even if it would later seem prescient. Eimert explicitly set his stall out against Adorno, who had opined in *Philosophie der neuen Musik* that

> [t]he self-proclaimed law of the row is truly fetishized in the moment when the composer puts his trust in the supposition that this law has meaning in itself. In Webern's Piano Variations and in his String Quartet the fetishism of the row is blatant. They feature nothing more than monotonously symmetrical presentations of serial marvels [...] In Webern the musical subject, falling silent, abdicates; Webern abandons himself to the material, which assures him indeed of nothing more than the echo of muteness.[186]

Eimert argued that such a criticism was no more or less accurate (especially when extended to the 'newer' music of Boulez, Goeyvaerts, Nono, and Stockhausen) than that which Pfitzner had ranged against a then-'newest' music in the 1930s.[187] In truth, that this would be Eimert's stance could probably have been predicted by any reader of his *Atonale Musiklehre* (1924) or his later *Lehrbuch der Zwölftontechnik* (1950). The first of these drew on Hauer as a model much more than Schoenberg and, in particular,

---

[184] Kovács, 'Webern zwischen gestern und morgen: Die Rezeption seiner Musik bei den Ferienkursen der fünfziger Jahre', in Stephan et al. (eds.), *Von Kranichstein zur Gegenwart*, 183.
[185] Herbert Eimert, 'Junge Komponisten bekennen sich zu Anton Webern' [1953], in Borio and Danuser (eds.), *Im Zenit der Moderne*, vol. III, 58.
[186] Theodor W. Adorno, *Philosophy of New Music*, tr. Robert Hullot-Kentor (Minneapolis, MN: Minnesota University Press, 2006 [1949]), 86–7.
[187] Eimert, 'Junge Komponisten', 59. One might recall in this context that Pfitzner had, for instance, managed to have Schoenberg's *Der glückliche Hand* (1908–13) removed from the programme of the Duisburg Tonkünstlerfest in 1929 (see Michael Kater, *Composers of the Nazi Era: Eight Portraits* (Oxford University Press, 2000), 147).

the 'rather cerebral' aspects of Hauer's technique.[188] Indeed, it was perhaps in comments such as Schoenberg's (that Hauer 'sought his solution in the cosmos. I limited myself to the human brain available to me') that specific relations can be found with the way in which Goeyvaerts conceived of his systematic procedures as concerned with unveiling a particular mode of 'being', and a rather different one from the sort Boulez described in his comments on Webern.[189] Eimert's later volume near enough shared its title with Hauer's own *Lehrbuch der Zwölftontechnik: Vom Wesen des Musikalischen* (1923). This volume suggested that Hauer's intellectual constructivism ought be seen as no less important or valid than the music of the Second Viennese composers, but also that writers (other than Eimert himself) had failed to come to terms with the technical and theoretical aspects of twelve-tone music, focussing for the most part only on the aesthetic. Named specifically in this context is Adorno, with the judgement that 'strange to say, music theoretical knowledge has remained wholly trapped within the primitive beginnings of the compositions of that first "dawn"'.[190] Unsurprisingly, the way in which Eimert constructed both Webern and the young composers too found resonance in Adorno's response a few years later in 'Das Altern der Neuen Musik' ('The Ageing of the New Music'). It would exaggerate only a little to suggest that the composers who spoke at the Webern evening were, unknowingly, deployed by Eimert in this ongoing private dispute with Adorno.

Nevertheless Boulez was little less enthusiastic than Eimert regarding Webern, even if his particular stance was different. Webern was 'the only composer of the last musical epoch to have a consciousness of a new sonic dimension, to have abrogated the distinction between the vertical and horizontal and to have seen in the row nothing other than a means to "structure a sonic space"'.[191] Webern had also broken with Schoenberg and Berg:

> In certain respects, Alban Berg and Schoenberg limit composition with rows to the semantic part of the language; they introduce elements which are combined in a rhetoric which is not of the row. By contrast, in the case of Webern the row technique itelf is extended to become the plan for this rhetoric. Thus the first elements of a musical thought occur [...] which does not lead back to traditional fundamental schemes. Webern's historical importance lies in the fact that he discovered a new sort of musical being.[192]

---

[188] Arnold Whittall, *Serialism* (Cambridge University Press, 2008), 25.
[189] Arnold Schoenberg, 'Hauer's Theories' [1923], in *Style and Idea*, ed. Leonard Stein, tr. Leo Black (London: Faber, 1975), 212.
[190] Eimert, *Lehrbuch der Zwölftontechnik*, 59.
[191] Pierre Boulez, in Eimert, 'Junge Komponisten', 60.   [192] Ibid..

This new start – a rhetoric of the row, rather than one which simply made use of it – was not to be found in Berg or Schoenberg:

> In order to solve the problem of polyphonic composition via the principle of the row, Webern was compelled to delimit structure and invention, which is why his works are relatively short, simple in material, and clear in construction. It is first in his late works that he introduces materials of greater richness and complex rhetoric. In Webern, there is never a disagreement between being and consciousness, between the aesthetic reality and the consciousness of musical problems which must be answered.[193]

It is not too difficult to hear in this assessment the echo of Boulez's earlier judgement in 'Schoenberg is Dead' that '[p]erhaps we might, like this Webern, investigate the musical EVIDENCE arising from the attempt at generating structure from material.'[194] Yet, though it is tempting to stress Boulez's proposal that '[p]erhaps we might generalize the serial principle to the four constituents of sound: pitch, duration, dynamics/attack, and timbre',[195] what seems to underline Boulez's stance is that structure should be a product of material, rather than material being something which is introduced into a pre-determined structure. It is this mode of thought, much more than any strict approach to the generation of material itself, that characterised Boulez's method.

Goeyvaerts's response shared certain ideas with Boulez's. He argued, too, that Webern should not be seen in the same light as either Schoenberg or Berg, stating that Webern's achievement was 'the use of pitch materials as a means for the realisation of the structural network', which implied a desire for total objectivity. This last idea was not one which had appeared in Boulez's commentary. On the contrary, from the same starting point Boulez argued that such a desire would be one which wanted to create a musical ordering which placed itself under continual interrogation. If, for Goeyvaerts, the idea of generating structure from smaller elements led to an objectivisation of the material, for Boulez it led, instead, to a reflexive, questioning practice. This same reflexivity looked to Goeyvaerts like hermeticism: 'Music becomes an image of its own essence; the composer becomes a tone-craftsman. The tone becomes a structural building block and requires only those of its characteristics which are structurally motivated.'[196] Nevertheless, as far as Goeyvaerts was concerned, the division of parameters was already becoming outmoded (and, as he observed, the *color*

---

[193] Ibid., 61.
[194] Pierre Boulez, 'Schoenberg is Dead' [1952], in *Stocktakings from an Apprenticeship*, tr. Stephen Walsh (Oxford University Press, 1991), 214.
[195] Ibid.   [196] Karel Goeyvaerts, in Eimert, 'Junge Komponisten', 61 n. 1.

and *talea* of the isorhythmic motet already pre-empted such thought in most fundamental respects), not least because electronic means had shown that divisions between parameters did not necessarily hold in practice. What was important was the way in which musical structures might be viewed as projections in space and in time. It is notable that these two ideas would form the central trajectories of Stockhausen's subsequent thinking in '… wie die Zeit vergeht …' and 'Musik im Raum'.

By the time the introduction to the pieces on the Webern evening had reached Eimert's radio broadcast, Goeyvaerts's text had been replaced with a wholly new one which in some respects clarified, in others confused, his earlier statements. Here he described just the sort of purity for which many would criticise the Darmstadt composers:

> [O]ne finds in Webern and in the composers who have developed his ideas regarding the objectivisation of structure a gradual purification of sound complexes: first through the development of closed particles, which are juxtaposed; next the whole musical work is imagined in all aspects of its sounds as the passage of time; later the substance of the sounds is structurally determined in its entirety by the smallest element (the pure sine tone) upwards.[197]

If anything what Goeyvaerts 'clarified' was Boulez. Where Boulez had suggested nothing more than that the series might be used to generate structure (i.e. working bottom-up rather than top-down) and, indeed, that Webern's work was really just a simple experiment (until the latest pieces) in this respect, in Goeyvaerts's hands this became a musical programme.

Nono was probably a little taken aback by Goeyvaerts's version of Webern. Goeyvaerts was likely to have represented exactly the sort of 'charts and tables' approach to Webern that Nono had feared. Yet his own presentation was perhaps too vague, too romantic in its relationship to Webern, to stem the flow. Where Boulez had stated that 'In Webern, there is never a disagreement between being and consciousness, between the aesthetic reality and the consciousness of musical problems which must be answered' and Goeyvaerts had argued that 'a musical work today is no longer a complex of pitches constructed through tensions [*Spannungen*]', Nono would counter that 'In Webern I see a new human who has that serenity and sureness, two qualities which allowed him to animate contemporary life through interior tension [*Spannung*]. The tension in Webern's music is the same tension as that which rules the dialectic between nature and life.'[198] Thus, even if it was a different dialetic from the one that Goeyvaerts had suggested characterised

---

[197] Ibid., 62.   [198] Luigi Nono, in ibid., 63.

common-practice music, it was nevertheless a question of dialectical tension between aesthetics and reality from Nono's perspective. Yet it was not here that Nono saw the greatest difficulty: 'It would be a gross error and serious danger if one were only to understand Webern's creative force through technical schemata and if one were to aim to understand his technique only through a "ready reckoner"'.[199] For Nono, what mattered about Webern was precisely his clarity, which offered a direct explanation of the essence of music. In essence, Nono and Goeyvaerts actually agreed that Webern's music was a paradigmatic example of the 'being' of music, even if they disagreed on what it might signify. Only a few years later, Nono too would be guilty of speaking about serial practice in terms of just these charts and tables, even if he would apologise on that occasion for having failed to go beyond the technical toward the aesthetic.[200] Yet it is hard to imagine how Nono could have been regarded as interested in 'pure' structures, working as he did with all manner of 'external' materials: as well as 'Yemanjá' and the 'Bandiera Rossa', Nono had made use of the 'Internationale' in his second Lorca epitaph.

At the 1953 Webern evening, however, it would be Stockhausen who would demonstrate what he thought he had found in Webern in more recognisably analytical form. That this was a relatively recent set of discoveries did not lead Stockhausen to any caution with his words: 'I honour Anton Webern as the most forceful, clear, and acute composer of the tradition', he began.[201] It would only be after working with Meyer-Eppler a little later that Stockhausen would add timbre to his list of parameters; in the music of Webern, he found just three: duration, pitch, and dynamic (and these three, and only these, he regarded as the dimensions of the acoustic world at this point). Following his analysis of Webern's Concerto, op 24, which was excised from the version broadcast on the radio, Stockhausen believed he had discovered in Webern 'a polyphony of polyphonic principles', which was to say the extension of ordering principles (and, vitally, not the 'row' as such) to all parameters, as he perceived them at the time: ordered groups of pitches, ordered groups of durations, and ordered groups of volumes.[202] For Stockhausen, as he himself said, the consequences were clear:

---

[199] Ibid., 63–4.
[200] Luigi Nono, 'Die Entwicklung der Reihentechnik' [1957], tr. Willi Reich, *Darmstädter Beiträge zur neuen Musik*, vol. 1 (1958), 37.
[201] Karlheinz Stockhausen, in Eimert, 'Junge Komponisten', 64.
[202] Karlheinz Stockhausen, 'Weberns Konzert für 9 Instrumente op. 24: Analyse des ersten Satzes' [1953], in *Texte*, ed. Dieter Schnebel, vol. I (Cologne: DuMont, 1963), 30; originally published in *Melos*, vol. 20, no. 12 (December 1953), 343–8.

> Previous instrumental music will be replaced by the electronic production and reproduction of music. The old twelve-division chromatic pitch system will be expanded to the whole range of frequencies; the smallest entity with which one can compose is pure, which is to say a sine tone with no overtones. The interrelationships between pitch, duration, and volume are exposed. The structure of a work is to be educed from a unifying principle. This principle marks out the proportional fields of the three named dimensions; composition becomes statistical, which is to say each value employed in a structure is relative.[203]

This must have sounded like something of a bold proposition (even if, on closer examination, one might wonder, as Goeyvaerts surely did, whether Stockhausen was inadvertently reinventing a fourteenth-century isorhythmic wheel). Whatever the case, the Webern evening certainly stirred things up. Stockhausen wrote to Goeyvaerts on 23 August:

> I was in Darmstadt for one evening. So I can only tell you what I heard later: the summary of your words, of the Boulez article and my analysis stirred up a hornets' nest! During the night, Herr Schibler wrote an extremely foolish polemic against us and distributed it to everybody. It even reached the minister. We were a group who wanted to liquidate humanity and so on. And finally it was claimed that we were communists and how could one give us publicity like this ...[204]

Schibler appears to have been furious with what had happened, suggesting that Boulez, Goeyvaerts, and Stockhausen (he did not name Nono as a part of his polemic) had fundamentally misunderstood Webern, particularly because of a focus on late Webern in which, according to Schibler's reading, 'the work with rows threatens to becomes an abstract process which suppresses every declaration of humanity'. Stockhausen's report of the pamphlet was quite accurate: Schibler concluded that, by taking this part of Webern's oeuvre as a touchstone, the young composers he mentioned sought the 'elimination of the human element from art'.[205] Schibler's judgement of the results of what he saw as the adoption of this aspect of Webernian thinking in the music of Boulez, Goeyvaerts, and Stockhausen was no more positive. Though he agreed that their output to date might be regarded as having some sort of historical value, in that they stared the collapse of European civilisation in the face, he felt that to hold this moment up as some sort of epiphany was simultaneously to sanctify it, supporting a

---

[203] Karlheinz Stockhausen, in Eimert, 'Junge Komponisten', 64–5.
[204] Stockhausen to Steinecke, 23 August 1953, in Misch and Bandur (eds.), *Stockhausen bei den Internationalen Ferienkursen*, 72. By 'the minister', Stockhausen almost certainly meant Ludwig Metzger, by this time culture minister for Hesse.
[205] Armin Schibler, 'Rundschreiben', in Borio and Danuser (eds.), *Im Zenit der Moderne*, vol. III, 66.

conscious regression into anonymous collectivity and control mechanisms.[206] Stockhausen was the central object of Schibler's dissatisfactions, although it was clear too that, as far as Schibler was concerned, Eimert was also to blame for allowing such abhorrent ideas to take a central place at the courses (and later, for that matter, on the radio). It is even plausible that Stockhausen may have represented a proxy for Eimert in Schibler's attack. For his part, Stockhausen must have been disappointed that it was Schibler's Second String Quartet, op. 30 (1951), which, along with Peter Racine Fricker's Four Impromptus for piano, op. 17 (1950–2), gained the most positive reviews of all the music performed at the 1953 courses.

Yet what was ultimately most significant about the reception of the Webern evening was hardly Schibler's outrage, but a form of construction that was made by the press, which endeavoured to 'make sense' of these confusing young composers. Most immediately notable was the headline of Rodemann's response: 'An unknown gives rise to a school'.[207] Here was the first sense, in the press, that Webern's example might represent the guiding principle of a young 'school' of composers gathered at Darmstadt, whose representatives, as Rodemann had it, were Nono, Boulez, Goeyvaerts, and Stockhausen. Rodemann was distinctly unimpressed with Stockhausen's presentation, suggesting that it was delivered 'in the distinterested tone of a castellan surveying a castle'. While noting parallels between Webern's music, the isorhythmic motet, and the canonic art of the fifteenth century, to which attention had been drawn by Eimert, Rodemann argued that it was vital that Webern's work be 'protected from false prophets and saved from music-theoreticians', just the same concerns that Nono had expressed in advance to Steinecke.

While it would be a fair judgement, in part, to suggest that Boulez and Goeyvaerts were influenced by Webern in the way in which Rodemann described it, Nono's response was a quite different one, and Stockhausen had only very recently come to know the music of Webern in any significant way. Nevertheless, the relationship was drawn across the reportage, with Ernst Thomas suggesting that the conclusions Stockhausen had drawn from Webern in the composition of *Kontra-Punkte* were the most dangerous of all: 'a total objectivity and complete elimination of the subjective expressive will. His *Kontrapunkte I* [sic] follows an ordering principle, which is imprisoned by its material: he himself does not compose, rather he obeys the intellectually independent material.'[208] Turning to the younger

---

[206] Ibid., 67.
[207] Albert Rodemann, 'Ein Unbekannter bildet Schule: Anton-Webern-Gedächtnis-Konzert im Seminar Marienhöhe', *Darmstädter Tagblatt*, 25–26 July 1953.
[208] Ernst Thomas, 'Die Situation des "kaputt"', *Darmstädter Echo*, 27 July 1953.

generation's own music, Rodemann's judgement was similar, regarding *Kontra-Punkte* as wholly a product of chance, 'an abstract, dehumanised art'. Nevertheless, Rodemann regarded what Nono was doing as something quite different. Though he persisted with the notion that Webern was Nono's model, he identified in the recording of the second Lorca epitaph, *Y su sangre ya viene cantando*, that the rhythms of different Spanish dances were employed at some level in the construction of the score. Even if Rodemann agreed that, in total distinction to Stockhausen, Nono was concerned principally with a 'human element', this piece fell short of the impact of *España en el corazón*.[209] Those distinctions, though, were unusual. For most in the press, Boulez, Stockhausen, and Nono (and, mentioned by some, Goeyvaerts) were tarred with the same brush: under the sign of Webern they aimed at 'total objectivisation; the composer is only a tool for the materials, complete in and of themselves'.[210] Gertrud Runge made no more distinction between the young composers, observing that

> [t]here is a group of young composers who want to see in this music [Webern's] neither an isolated case nor an end stage, but rather a new point of departure. They step further along the path toward the abolition of the senses, atomisation, and mathematicisation of music [. . .] Pitches are, for them, 'material', out of which something can be constructed.

Runge argued that it could hardly be any surprise that such attitudes found an analogue in the composition of 'electronic music'.[211] This was the other link that was made: Lewinski, though he suggested that Webern and Schoenberg had a role to play, stressed that it was electronic music that had led to the 'static' music of the young guns. He observed that, following the impact of the division of sound into parameters in the studio, 'some young composers make use of these material consequences, which can be worked with without concession in the studio, even for music with conventional instruments'. Lewinski cited Boulez's *Polyphonie X* and Stockhausen's *Kontra-Punkte* as examples.[212] Yet only Stockhausen's presentation allowed for the making of such a link, which, as Kurtz suggests, portrayed 'the structural proportions [of Webern's Concerto, op. 24] as

---

[209] Albert Rodemann, 'Musik der jungen Generation III: Bandaufnahmen und Diskussions-Quartett im Radio Frankfurt', *Darmstädter Tagblatt*, 27 July 1953.
[210] G. N. Herchenröder, 'Darmstädter Ferienkurse: Musik-Klänge der Maschinen-Zeit', *Abendpost*, 1 August 1953. See, too, Fritz Bielwiese, 'Im Grenzgebiet der musikalischen Wirkungen', *Kölner Stadt-Anzeiger*, 4 August 1953, and Heinz Enke, 'Im Zeichen Schönbergs und Weberns: Die Internationalen Ferienkurse in Darmstadt', *Allgemeine Zeitung*, 5 August 1953.
[211] Gertrud Runge, 'Ergebnis der Darmstädter Ferienkurse: Anschluß an die Weltmusik endlich wiedergewonnen', *Welt am Sonntag*, 2 August 1953.
[212] Wolf-Eberhard von Lewinski, 'Die neue Musik am Scheidwege: Aufschlußreiche Ergebnisse der Kranichsteiner Ferienkurse 1953', *Düsseldorfer Nachrichten*, 3 August 1953.

antecedents of timbre composition, that is, of electronic music'.[213] Much later, Stockhausen recalled the event:

> When people have something specific in mind, something they want to put into practice, they look for justifications. And that is why my analysis of the Webern Concerto was so savagely attacked at the time. They said that was not what Webern meant, he was up to something quite different, he was thinking in terms of motives [...] They did not understand that of course it was a one-sided interpretation, because I too had something specific in mind, and said that that was already implicit in some works bequeathed by tradition. Perhaps we see in these works only the things that we find personally important, and that is why we can constantly reinterpret traditional music: we always have new ideas of how to do things, and so we find ourselves modernizing a composition that is not widely regarded as important, or a composer, or the whole style of an epoch.[214]

It was hardly the first time Stockhausen would be taken to task for interpreting the work of another composer while really speaking about himself. Here, already in 1953, the distance between what Stockhausen and Nono thought was important about Webern was really quite great.

That the three composers, Boulez, Nono, and Stockhausen, should be regarded together – though not yet quite as a 'school' – was hinted at by Trumpff as well, though his response was rather more subtle than either Rodemann's or Thomas's: 'The bravery of the experiments, even when some remote paths are being trodden, and the exchange of personal experience are the secret strengths of these youngsters'.[215] In short, whatever the reality of the situation compositionally speaking, after the Webern evening, for the most part the press had unified Boulez, Nono, and Stockhausen into some sort of composite entity, working forward from the exemplars of Webern, on the one hand, and electronic music on the other. It is a recognisable picture, but it is also one which is belied by the composers' own individual positions, which were clearly divergent, sometimes strongly so, on many issues. If the foundations of the idea of the 'Darmstadt School' can be found here, those foundations are based on a construction of the press and of Herbert Eimert's invention, which does not necessarily map neatly onto compositional practice. Even Steinecke made little attempt to suggest that anything else was the case in terms of what the young composers represented. Though he made a stark distinction between the 'total organisation' of Boulez and Stockhausen and the 'humanistic' content of Nono's work,

---

[213] Kurtz, *Stockhausen*, 61. [214] Karlheinz Stockhausen, quoted in ibid., 61–2.
[215] Gustav Adolf Trumpff, 'Musik der jungen Generation: Eindrücke von den Darmstädter Ferienkursen', *Göttinger Presse*, 30 July 1953.

he proposed that both sides of this particular coin were derived from Webern.[216]

In the light of all of the above, the report of the *Sozialistische Volkszeitung*, headed 'Nothing to Do with Music', takes on an almost comic quality since, for the reviewer, it was neither Webern nor the young composers who had caused offence – in fact, Maderna's *Quattro lettere* is reported as representing a good idea, poorly executed – but instead it was Bartók's Divertimento (1939) and Milhaud's *La Mort d'un tyran* (1932) that represented the major offences against the 'musical'.[217] The review was of only the final concert, which had also included Fortner's *Mitte des Lebens* (1951). One shudders to think what the correspondent would have made of the Webern evening.

Very shortly after the close of the courses, Nono wrote to Steinecke about how pleased he was with how they had gone for him personally (as well as his despondency regarding Cologne, where he was living at the time):

> I want to thank you again for this year, in particular for the ever stronger and better friendship we share. Now I am truly, after Kranichsteinecke [*sic*], quiet and more sure with wholly new ideas and plans for work: I believe a new period begins for me now; in every sense. The Webern evening with the violent discussion, in the night with Stockhausen, was very important for me, and I believe that just as Stockhausen gave me something, so did I to him, just as it should be between two friends. I am certain that Stockhausen will become an increasingly important and vital musician. Here all is DEATH and SHIT; the people believe that Bruno and I come from Mars, but I am more than ever a pure Italian and of this earth.[218]

Even though Stockhausen's approach had represented just that which Nono had, in advance, railed against, it was this that Nono returned to as the moment in which he had had to pause for thought. Nono doubtless had time for further discussion with Stockhausen during his stay in Cologne in 1953. Despite his immediate rejection of the Cologne scene, Nono seemed briefly to have found some enchantment with the city, writing to Steinecke: 'Here things are so lovely, and so simple. And so humane that I find it hard to believe. One can really live here.'[219] Yet only a few weeks later, another letter reached Steinecke: 'Already back in Venice. Because I must work right away and stay in Cologne no longer. In Cologne everything seen and

---

[216] Wolfgang Steinecke, 'Positionen der neuen Musik heute', broadcast, Hessischer Rundfunk, 18 September 1953, transcript IMD.
[217] [Gallus.], 'Mit Musik nichts zu tun: Schlußkonzert der Internationalen Ferienkurse für Neue Musik in Darmstadt', *Sozialistische Volkszeitung*, 3 August 1953.
[218] Nono to Steinecke, 8 August 1953, ALN. [219] Nono to Steinecke, 25 October 1953, ALN.

understood: there is much, much nonsense [...] I will stay a long time in Cologne next year serenely: but it is not easy.'[220]

A question of priorities?

Boulez would later claim to Célestin Deliège that Darmstadt was characterised by number fetishism of exactly the sort that Nono had warned about. They must both have had this idea from somewhere, but it is certainly not borne out in what was performed there in the period around 1953 and 1954. Boulez stated that '[s]ome of the concerts at Darmstadt in 1953/54 were of quite lunatic sterility and academicism, and above all became totally uninteresting. One could sense the disparity between what was written and what was heard: there was no sonic imagination, but quite simply an accumulation of numerical transcriptions quite devoid of any aesthetic character.'[221] Notwithstanding the fact that Boulez was hardly in any position to make this judgement – he was present in neither year, having been in Darmstadt for only a couple of days in 1952, and did not attend the courses for their entire duration until 1956 – an examination of the music that actually *was* presented, taking 1954 as an example, suggests that Boulez exaggerated not only the dominance of serial thought but also his rejection of it.[222] There were pieces performed that might, just about, fit Boulez's characterisation, and one of the lecture series that year, René Leibowitz's, focussed on Webern's late music, but Darmstadt was hardly a bastion of the most extreme of serialists.

Despite a deliciously partisan appraisal of the Piano Sonata of his fellow Briton Alexander Goehr, David Drew's review of the 1954 courses for *The Score* is both accurate and lucid. Vital is his observation that the new music heard in the 'Musik der jungen Generation' concerts 'constitute[d] about one-third of the music heard at Darmstadt. The other two-thirds consist[ed] of music by twentieth century masters, and by established composers of our

---

[220] Nono to Steinecke, 11 November 1953, ALN.
[221] Pierre Boulez, *Conversations with Célestin Deliège* (London: Eulenburg, 1976), 64.
[222] This sort of misremembering permeates composerly accounts of Darmstadt. Berio's recollection of his first year of attendance at the courses, 1953 according to his own account, is no less erroneous. Berio claimed that '[i]n 1953 Stockhausen was the theoretical pivot of the Ferienkurse, Pousseur provided the speculative machinery, Boulez the analytical spirit and Maderna was a benign father-figure' (quoted in Whittall, *Serialism*, 194). As already noted, Boulez was not present at Darmstadt in this year and Pousseur did not arrive at Darmstadt until 1954. Of those mentioned, only Maderna would have had anything like sufficient institutional authority to occupy a position of centrality. Stockhausen, it should be remembered, spoke in an official context at Darmstadt in 1953 for the first time; this hardly suggests that one could reasonably speak of him as the 'theoretical pivot'. His description suggests rather more that Berio is thinking of the relationships he developed on a personal level with Stockhausen, Pousseur, Boulez, and Maderna in the years following meetings at Darmstadt in 1953.

own day.' The list of those by the 'established composers' shows how inaccurate perceptions were that everything that Darmstadt touched turned to numbers. Furthermore, some of Drew's parenthetical comments are notable: Gunther Schuller's *Dramatic Overture* of 1951 ('neo-Straussian') and Giselher Klebe's Rhapsody of 1953 were performed in 'a concert that might have been entitled "aspects of contemporary romanticism"'; elsewhere there were performances of Henze's *Ode an den Westwind* of 1953 (Henze had 'become an unabashed Romantic') and Krenek's *Medea* of 1951–2 ('another curious and unexpected lapse into the nineteenth century'). Drew suggested that Nono's new *La Victoire de Guernica* (1954) showed 'a crippling deadweight of both academic and *avant-garde* cliché [. . .] and the few moments of lyrical charm (always Nono's strong point) do not redeem the overall banality of invention'. Of the 'masters', it would be hard to identify a tendency to promote one trend over another. Though Webern's orchestral Variations, op. 30, were performed, as was Schoenberg's Piano Concerto (1942), so were Stravinsky's *Capriccio* (1928–9), Messiaen's *Quatuor pour la fin du temps* of 1940–1 ('abominably played, with the exception of Mlle. Loriod at the piano') and *Cantéyodjayâ* (1949), Britten's *Lachrymae*, op. 48 (1950), Dallapiccola's *Quaderno musicale di Annalibera* (1952), and even Ravel's *Frontispiece* (1918) and Debussy's *Lindraja* (1901). This is hardly the programme line-up of a hotbed of fervent serialist revolutionaries.

Looking to the young composers, it is still hard to see whence Boulez's criticism could have arisen. Two pieces were essentially tonal: Hans Eklund's *Kleine Serenade* (1954) ('harmlessly juvenile') and Juriaan Andriessen's *Hommage à Milhaud* (1948) ('fulfilled the sinister expectations aroused by its title'). Two pieces were products of an extended tonality: a Piano Trio (1953) by Heimo Erbse and Karel Husa's Second String Quartet (1953) ('almost slavishly faithful to the structural procedures of Bartók [. . .] the tonal scheme is somewhat primitive, but the argument is exceedingly well-knit'). There were also free atonal and twelve-tone pieces, including, alongside Goehr's Piano Sonata (1951–2), Don Banks's Violin Sonata (1953), Camillo Togni's Flute Sonata (1953) ('beautifully written, classically moulded'), and Jacques Wildberger's Trio for oboe, clarinet, and bassoon (1952). These pieces seem to have been the ones for which Drew had the greatest affection.

This would leave, then, a total of four pieces that might be held to represent the more overtly serial end of the spectrum. Even of these, Drew argues that two, Pousseur's *Trois chants sacrés* (1951) and Bengt Hambraeus's *Gacelas y casidas de Federico García Lorca* (1953), 'stand somewhere between these works [those of Togni and Wildberger] and the extreme *avant-garde*'.[223] This was not to say, though, that Drew had much affection for Hambraeus's piece:

> Hambraeus's position is rather a strange one, for whilst he borrows from the *avant-garde* the principle of continual series-permutation, and, like other composers of this persuasion, applies it to questions of rhythm, tone-colour, etc., he permits certain liberties in the interests of expression. In other words some elements in his compositions are entirely controlled by a series, while others are partly or wholly free. Morphologically, this is nonsense, for the methods he uses *intermittently* were evolved by Boulez, Stockhausen and others expressly as a means of investigating *pure* form. These methods are no more concerned with emotional values than is the work-plan of a scientist, and an attempt to soften their severity by loosening the internal relationships is about as logical as it would be if a physicist substituted one chemical for another during the course of an experiment, simply because he preferred the smell.[224]

In short, in 1954 only Michel Fano's Sonata for Two Pianos (1952) and Stockhausen's first five Klavierstücke (I–IV, 1952–3; V, 1954) really fitted the bill if one were determined to look for pieces which, as Drew described it, 'carry the principles of serialisation as far as they will go – which is some distance beyond the boundaries of music as we know it'.[225]

While Drew may have had a point in stating that Stockhausen was some way beyond the bounds of the 'known' at this stage, a brief examination of Klavierstück III may be instructive to show that, though there is serialisation, there is only a limited degree of pre-ordering (or, at any rate, that very great liberties are taken with the pre-ordered gamut of material). The influence of Goeyvaerts is still visible, though now in much modified form. Rather than Goeyvaerts's heptachords, Stockhausen operated in Klavierstück III with six sets of tetrachords and two sets of trichords. The six tetrachords are partitioned into two groups, thus of twelve pitch classes each, but in the first group the tetrachords are overlaid, avoiding the total chromatic, and developing pitch repetition. This pitch repetition is exaggerated by the fact that, in this first group of pitches, the first tetrachord actually appears twice, the third tetrachord three times, and the central tetrachord only once. Though the tetrachords now do not overlap and thus present the total chromatic, the second group is arranged with similar repetitions, thus preserving the repetition of pitches (see Figure 1.9).

---

[223] David Drew, 'The Darmstadt Summer School of New Music, 1954', *The Score and IMA Magazine*, no. 10 (December 1954), 77–81.
[224] Ibid.
[225] Ibid. It is worth adding that the music of Fano, Stockhausen, and Hambraeus also appeared in the same concert.

Arrivals

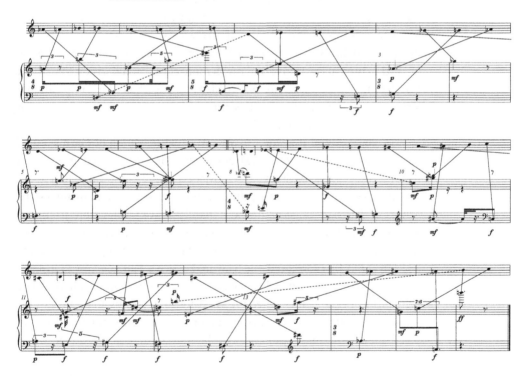

Fig. 1.9 Blumröder's table of pitch distribution and proportions in Karlheinz Stockhausen, Klavierstück III

Ex. 1.9 Dispersal of pitches from underlying skeleton in Karlheinz Stockhausen, Klavierstück III

In the dispersal of the material through the piece, however, there is great flexibility, with Stockhausen seemingly selecting relatively freely from this pre-determined field, as Blumröder shows (see Example 1.9).

It is, perhaps, plausible that there is some systematic procedure to determine the order of selection, but it hardly matters, since the effect is that of free choice in any case. In short, though the pitch material of Klavierstück III *is* dispersed in the way it is, it *could* have been distributed in any number of other ways, without fundamentally altering the pitch spine of the piece.[226] It comes as little surprise that Stockhausen would typically characterise his work with statistical possibilities as aleatoric, in the sense he had learned from Meyer-Eppler.[227] To be sure, one could not possibly hear this sort of organisation, especially not given the shuffling of the pitch resources that go to make up the pre-compositional planning. Indeed, the shuffling is such that it is hardly plausible that one was really *supposed* to hear any such thing in any case, even if Stockhausen may have hoped that the devices used would lend a certain degree of consistency to the piece.

None of this is to say that some of the concerts were not deathly – they must have been – but it is to assert strongly that they were not dominated by serial number crunching, and certainly not by the transcription of numerical elements into sounding form. There was, after all, not much serialism on offer, and, in any case, that which was present (according to the example of Stockhausen at least) involved much more choice and decision than it did pre-determination, which is not to deny that certain pre-compositional structures *were* constructed. It is not the case either that 1954 was an exceptional year in this regard.

It is vital to recall that the progress from participation at Darmstadt to taking a leading role was an extremely slow one. Darmstadt provided a forum for the music of Stockhausen, Maderna, and Nono (and, to a lesser extent, Goeyvaerts and Boulez, though Boulez was relatively firmly established in Parisian musical life and hardly craved validation from the Kranichsteiner). It had also, if only on one occasion, provided an outlet for them to express their views. Yet none of the young composers was quite a fixture. Only by 1956 could one truly make such a claim and, by that stage, the young composers had been faced with a withering assault on their activities from the pen of Theodor W. Adorno. Not only that, but even if ideas of thoroughgoing pre-determination were often emphasised in the press they were only sporadically played out in compositional work,

---

[226] For a much fuller consideration of Klavierstück III, from which the above comments are drawn, see Blumröder, *Der Grundlegung der Musik Karlheinz Stockhausens*, 109–37.
[227] See Werner Meyer-Eppler, 'Statistische und psychologische Klangprobleme', *Die Reihe*, vol. 1 (1955), 22–8.

Arrivals

rigorously worked examples like *Structure Ia* or Goeyvaerts's Sonata for Two Pianos being much more the exception than the norm.

In 1954, too, Henri Pousseur, the last of the 'early' Darmstadt composers, 'arrived on the scene'. In a sense, Pousseur's whole Darmstadt career is probably marked by his having arrived 'too late' to be a part of the early vanguard, associated with the period leading up to the Webern evening, but 'too early' to capitalise upon the position that those composers had established by the end of the 1950s, as, for instance, Kagel, Ligeti, Schnebel (or, to a lesser extent, Bussotti) could do. Pousseur had been recommended to Steinecke by Nono in late 1953, along with Michel Fano, whose music was also played for the first time in Darmstadt in 1954:

> Michel Fano (24 years old) very good: one just needs to make a choice of which one of his pieces for Kranichstein;;;;;;;;;;;;;;;; [sic] Baraque [sic] is almost nothing. In Belgium there's a young man :Poissier (something like that) ask Boulez or Fano directly for more. Stockhausen doesn't want to write music with instruments: only with sine tones. So no première for Kranichstein, except with sine tones. I am, personally, not of Stockhausen's opinion.[228]

It was a little while later that Steinecke wrote to Pousseur, inviting him to submit a score for the 'young generation' concerts.[229] Pousseur delivered to Steinecke the scores of the *Trois chants sacrés* and a more recent score for three pianos tuned in sixth-tones, *Prospection* (1953), on 25 February.[230] *Prospection* was essentially serial in the sense in which *Structure Ia* was, and in many respects is akin to a micro-tonal version of that earlier piece (though, like Boulez, Pousseur made only this single foray into such extremes of control). It was evidently this piece which Pousseur ideally wanted to have played, attempting to persuade Steinecke of its value in a later letter,[231] which followed Steinecke's to him expressing serious concerns regarding the technical viability of the piece, given its requirements in terms of tuning.[232] Ultimately, the earlier *Trois chants sacrés* were the pieces taken into the concert series.[233] In his letter of thanks, Pousseur suggested that he would like, during his time in Darmstadt, to participate in the 'working group' to be run by Boulez as well as in the performance of his *Le visage nuptial* (1946). Neither of these would take place and, indeed, the only one of the events that Pousseur expressed a desire to attend and that actually took place was the performance of Stockhausen's first five Klavierstücke.

---

[228] Nono to Steinecke, 11 November 1953, ALN.
[229] Steinecke to Henri Pousseur, 15 February 1954, IMD.
[230] Pousseur to Steinecke, 25 February 1954, IMD.
[231] Pousseur to Steinecke, 22 March 1954, IMD.
[232] Steinecke to Pousseur, 1 March 1954, IMD.   [233] Steinecke to Pousseur, 12 May 1954, IMD.

1954 was only one of a number of years in which Boulez's disinterest, sometimes bordering on disdain, for Darmstadt was in evidence. The working group of which Pousseur spoke represented an attempt on Steinecke's behalf, first, to bring actual compositional practice into play at Darmstadt – to give the composers something to *do*, practically speaking – and, second, to provide a proper forum for the younger composers. He wrote to Boulez that he envisaged a forum for analysis, discussion, and judgement of the possibilities and difficulties that the new music represented. He had already planned to invite Maderna and Henze, and thought that Boulez might also be interested. Steinecke also advised Boulez that Scherchen planned to perform *Le Visage nuptial*, which he may have hoped would act as an additional enticement.[234] Having heard nothing from Boulez inside a month, Steinecke wrote again, offering a further sop, though this time not for Darmstadt. Steinecke had taken responsibility for a concert as a part of the Nordwestdeutscher Rundfunk's 'Musik der Zeit' series, and he proposed that *Le Soleil des eaux* (1948) might form a part of that concert.[235] Boulez replied with the most cursory of telegrams: 'Return from America 17 August. Visage Nuptial agreed. Seminar impossible.'[236] An undated letter which must, nevertheless, have been written shortly afterwards explained further that Boulez was leaving for the United States on tour with Barrault on 23 April and would not return until 17 August, thus making it impossible to reach Germany until 20 August, the courses in that year running from 12 to 27 August.[237] It is obvious from Steinecke's reply that Boulez's participation in Darmstadt was important to him, since he proposed that Boulez do just what he said was possible: come to Darmstadt for 20 August and lead a part of the working group in the second week of the courses. Steinecke also asked Boulez whether it would be possible for him to provide some recorded examples of Cage's music, so that they could be played during the courses. Boulez agreed to the seminar, and also sent recordings of 'A Book of Music for Two Pianos' and 'Construction of Metal', which suggests that what was played during Wolfgang Rebner's lecture on American experimental music at the 1954 courses may have included one (or both) of these two pieces: *A Book of Music* (1944) for two prepared pianos and *First Construction (in Metal)* (1939).[238]

Though Boulez agreed to attend, it is clear from his correspondence with Stockhausen that he was not especially happy about it and that the real reason

---

[234] Steinecke to Boulez, 26 February 1954, IMD.
[235] Steinecke to Boulez, 27 March 1954, IMD. [236] Boulez to Steinecke, 12 April 1954, IMD.
[237] Boulez to Steinecke, undated but *ca*. 12 April 1954, IMD.
[238] Boulez to Steinecke, undated but marked 9 August 1954 in Steinecke's handwriting on the copy held at the IMD.

Arrivals

why he was willing to come lay in *Le Visage nuptial*.[239] He wrote to Stockhausen: 'Steinecke has asked me to take part in a composition seminar with Maderna and Henze (!!). I gave as an excuse that my arrival would be delayed: 20 or 21 August. But my answer didn't change anything. Also, because he will play *Le Visage nuptial* it's difficult to refuse. I will try to be as discreet as possible. Because as you know I have a horror of all that sort of thing.'[240] By June, however, it was clear that the projected performance would not take place, quite simply, by Boulez's account, because Heugel had failed to provide the performance materials in good enough time.[241] An undated note from Boulez to Steinecke, written on the notepaper of the Societé Génerale de Transports Maritimes of Marseilles (but sent from Dakar on the return journey from the tour according to a letter to Stockhausen),[242] said that he would not be coming to Darmstadt after all, excusing himself on grounds of tiredness after the tour.[243] Nevertheless, it seems that Boulez had taken the decision much earlier, writing to Stockhausen while still on tour that he would not come to Darmstadt since, with no performance of his music to draw him there, he would have to be part of an 'idiotic trinity' with Henze and Maderna,[244] and would also have to put up with Leibowitz's lectures on late Webern, a prospect he regarded as 'supremely stupid'. Finally, the combination of completing work on the first part of *Le Marteau sans maître* (1952–5) and beginning work on electronic music at the Cologne studios in September indicated to Boulez that a week in Darmstadt would be a week that he could better spend devoted to his own work.[245] As he would confess to Stockhausen, his excuse to Steinecke of tiredness was, at least, 'partly true'.[246] Though Boulez would come to Darmstadt in 1955, it should be clear that his attendance in that year would not be a prospect for him to savour.

---

[239] This is certainly understandable, given the performance history of the revised version of that score: it did not receive its première until 4 December 1957, at the Westdeutscher Rundfunk in Cologne, with Boulez himself conducting. Pierre Boulez, 'Erinnerung', in Frank Hilberg and Harry Vogt (eds.), *Musik der Zeit 1951–2001* (Hofheim: Wolke, 2002), 52.

[240] Boulez to Stockhausen, undated but probably *ca.* mid April 1954, in Misch and Bandur (eds.), *Stockhausen bei den Internationalen Ferienkursen*, 81.

[241] Boulez to Stockhausen, undated but probably June 1954 (written from Buenos Aires), in ibid., 81.

[242] Boulez to Stockhausen, undated but probably late July 1954 (written from Buenos Aires), in ibid., 88.

[243] Boulez to Steinecke, undated but *ca.* 17 August 1954, IMD.

[244] In the end, Henze would not lead the working group either; Maderna and Giselher Klebe were left in charge of them.

[245] Boulez to Stockhausen, undated but probably late July 1954 (written from Buenos Aires), in Misch and Bandur (eds.), *Stockhausen bei den Internationalen Ferienkursen*, 86.

[246] Boulez to Stockhausen, undated but probably late July 1954 (written from Buenos Aires), in ibid., 88.

2 Schools

Adorno, 'Das Altern der Neuen Musik'

Though it was of major significance for the aesthetic stance exemplified at Darmstadt, as well as for perceptions of it in its reception, Adorno's critique of the direction that 'new music' was taking was not delivered at Darmstadt but, rather, at the Stuttgart New Music Weeks in 1954. It was broadcast on the Süddeutscher Rundfunk in April 1954, published initially in *Der Monat* in May 1955, and then expanded for publication in *Dissonanzen* in 1956. Its circulation was wide; even if the version which appeared in English in *The Score* in 1956 was, as Hullot-Kentor and Will note, 'a peculiar, abbreviated and completely confabulated paraphrase of Adorno's essay, translated from the French', it is notable that it received comparatively rapid translation into French and English at all.[1] Although Heinz-Klaus Metzger's retort to Adorno's essay, to which I shall return in more detail below, asserted that it was precisely the encounter with Goeyvaerts and Stockhausen at Darmstadt in 1951 that prompted Adorno's critique, Zagorski is doubtless right to suggest that there is rather more at stake. Zagorski suggests that Boulez probably played a part – a view bolstered by Campbell – and there is much material in 'Das Altern der Neuen Musik' to support such a view.[2] However, 'Das Altern der Neuen Musik' also surely responded to Eimert's broadcast of the Webern evening on the Nordwestdeutscher Rundfunk on 12 November 1953, especially given the way in which the reception of that event had seemingly marginalised certain ways of discussing Webern in favour of others and the fact that Eimert had snidely polemicised against Adorno's own assessment of Webern. The link is inadvertently made by Alastair Williams's observation that what Adorno carried out in 'Das Altern der Neuen Musik' was 'in many ways an expansion of Adorno's critique in *Philosophy of New Music* of Webern's "fetishism of the row", which informs

---

[1] Robert Hullot-Kentor and Frederic Will's notes appear at the close of Theodor W. Adorno, 'The Aging of the New Music' [1954, rev. 1955], tr. Robert Hullot-Kentor and Frederic Will, in Adorno, *Essays on Music*, ed. Richard Leppert (Berkeley, CA: University of California Press, 2002), 200. Adorno's original text may be found as 'Das Altern der Neuen Musik' [1956], in *Gesammelte Schriften*, ed. Rolf Tiedemann, vol. XIV: *Dissonanzen: Einleitung in die Musiksoziologie* (Frankfurt am Main: Suhrkamp, 1973), 143–67.

[2] Marcus Zagorski, '"Nach dem Weltuntergang": Adorno's Engagement with Postwar Music', *Journal of Musicology*, vol. 22, no. 4 (Fall 2005), 695; Edward Campbell, *Boulez, Music and Philosophy* (Cambridge University Press, 2010), 74.

the article's central claim that it is delusional to imagine that a focus of technique transcends subjectivity, because the apparent objectivity of an overriding devotion to technique is nothing but an atrophied and impaired form of subjectivity'.[3] This was precisely the view which, Eimert had claimed, turned Adorno into a Pfitzner for the post-war generation.

Adorno began his critique from a particular position, one which informed *Philosophie der neuen Musik* too, which was that new music had 'its essence in the refusal to go along with things as they are',[4] a set of aspects which Zagorski neatly summarises as 'a critical resistance to the existing order; the preservation of subjective freedom; the expression of the individual before the abyss of the administered world'.[5] New music which did not fulfil these criteria was not worthy of the name, and Adorno saw a critical danger in the music that was being composed *as* new music: it was tending towards formalisation with the reification of the 'solution' which serial technique offered. This, so Adorno felt, would represent a 'stabilization of music' in contradiction to the reflexive, questioning nature which made new music what it was: 'it is the result of something actually distressing and confused. Whoever denies this and claims that the new art is as beautiful as the traditional one does it a real disservice; he praises in it what this music rejects so long as it unflinchingly follows its own impulse.' In short, the new music under discussion had lost its 'critical impulse'.[6] For Adorno, too, the idea that paths away from Webern might have purified the raw materials of composition from the 'vestiges of the past' was an irrelevance if this led to a technocratic hegemony of system, especially that of a formalised version of the twelve-tone technique.[7] Vitally, to Adorno's mind, the 'great' achievements of new music – which is to say those of Schoenberg – were 'composed prior to the invention of this technique or independently of it'.[8] In truth, with the development of the twelve-tone technique *qua* technique, Adorno implied that Schoenberg himself had probably effected a retrogressive manoeuvre. Even in the case of Webern, it was the early pieces that Adorno felt should enjoin the greatest interest and the greatest shock:

> One may think, for instance, of Anton von Webern's Five Movements for String Quartet, op. 5, which today sounds as contemporary as on its first day, and technically has not been surpassed. These movements, whose composition now lies forty-five years in the past, had already broken with tonality; they know, as one says, only dissonances; they are not dodecaphonic. A shudder surrounds each of these dissonances. They are felt as something uncanny, and

---

[3] Alastair Williams, 'New Music, Late Style: Adorno's "Form in the New Music"', *Music Analysis*, vol. 27, nos. 2–3 (2008), 194.
[4] Adorno, 'The Aging of the New Music', 181.   [5] Zagorski, '"Nach dem Weltuntergang"', 691.
[6] Adorno, 'The Aging of the New Music', 181.   [7] Ibid., 182.   [8] Ibid., 185.

are introduced by their author with fear and trembling. Right into the treatment of sounds it is possible to follow how carefully Webern took hold of them. Only with hesitancy does he separate himself from each and every sound; each one he holds fast until its expressive values are exhausted. He shrinks away from ruling sovereignly over them while at the same time he respects his own discoveries. This is not the least source of the undiminished power of Webern's tenderness.[9]

It is notable, of course, that just these five pieces closed Eimert's broadcast of the Webern evening. Precisely in these, Adorno countered, one could not find what Eimert had put there. Certainly, there was no cause to look for absolutist controlling structures and systems in Webern at his compositional zenith. Even such a system as might exist 'cannot be conceived without its antithesis, the explosive power of the musically individual, which even today still lives in Webern's early works'.[10] This was, in broad terms, the sum of what Nono had had to say on the subject of Webern; exactly this idea of reflexivity had characterised Boulez's contribution.

The antinomy was between the subjective needs of the individual composer and the organisation of material. Vitally, those materials were themselves historically encoded. Adorno's difficulty with the younger composers was precisely that, unlike Schoenberg in his view, as Zagorski describes it, 'they simply accepted their systems and did not direct their own subjective needs against the compositional tradition that history had bequeathed to them'.[11] Process in Adorno's terms could never represent 'material' in this sense, only its ordering, to be undertaken as a negotiation between the process itself and the composer's needs:

> The same could be demonstrated with the greatest detail in Schoenberg's compositional techniques: thematic construction, exposition, transitions, continuation, fields of tension and release, etc., are all scarcely distinguishable from traditional, especially Brahmsian, techniques, even in his most daring works. It is hardly possible to conceive of composition of a high order other than as the most detailed meaningful articulation of the appropriate musical material. But the available materials, right up to the present, have all grown out of the soil of tonality. When they are transferred to non-tonal musical material, certain inconsistencies result, a kind of break between musical subject-matter and the forming of the music. Schoenberg's musical sovereignty enabled him to master this break.[12]

With late Webern the balance had already shifted away from a dialectic between material and the compositional will, where, in trying to fuse fugue

---

[9] Ibid. Translation very marginally modified. [10] Ibid..
[11] Zagorski, "'Nach dem Weltuntergang'", 689. [12] Adorno, 'The Aging of the New Music', 186.

and sonata form, Webern had come 'very close to renouncing the musical material altogether and reducing music to naked processes in the material, to the fate of the rows as such, though admittedly without ever completely sacrificing musical material entirely'.[13] Even if a process existed, for Adorno it was vital that the composer was willing to act upon what the process suggested and to modify it according to need and will. Moreover, in order to form a critical counterpart to received norms, it was important, too, that musical material with a relationship to tradition be retained. The meaningfulness of the new music was, then, expressive only because of the negative relationship that music had to 'traditional' categories.[14]

The young composers – Adorno named only Boulez, at their head – represented a tendency in opposition to this:

> He [Boulez] and his disciples aspire to dispose of every 'compositional freedom' as pure caprice, along with every vestige of traditional musical idiom: in fact, every subjective impulse is in music at the same time an impulse of musical language. These composers have above all attempted to bring rhythm under the strict domination of twelve-tone procedure, and ultimately to replace composition altogether with an objective-calculatory ordering of intervals, pitches, long and short durations, degrees of loudness; an integral rationalization such has never before been envisaged in music.[15]

For Adorno, such a static conception of music was naïve insofar as it had little relationship with the way in which music was grasped within time. Such a compositional practice would hold that an identical repetition was just that, identical. By contrast, in Beethoven's music, Adorno suggested, '[o]ften the meaning of the preceding passage is only fully established by [a] later recurrence'.[16] Serial procedures aiming at 'secure balance' would be ineluctably undermined by the 'authentic' balances anticipated by musical listening. The material could not speak for itself – could not articulate its own pure forms – and to think that it could do so was to regard it with a blindness for the pitches out of which it had been made. Such modes of thought could be nothing more than fetishism. Pure, mathematical formulae that a composer might follow ('however cosmically they gesture') were always already the product of human intervention: there was certainly nothing 'natural' in them.[17] Rather than making compositional decisions, the composer would be reduced to checking the results of the system, ensuring that no foreign elements entered into its products.[18] In such a situation, not only was the composer no longer a composer: the composer was no longer an individual either.[19] Adorno proposed, in an idea which he

[13] Ibid., 187. [14] Ibid., 189. [15] Ibid., 187. [16] Ibid., 188. [17] Ibid., 194. [18] Ibid., 196.
[19] Ibid., 198.

would endeavour to refine across the next five years or so, that it was 'time for a concentration of compositional energy in another direction; not toward the mere organization of material, but toward the composition of truly coherent music out of a material however shorn of every quality'.[20]

The description of these processes seems to refer to Goeyvaerts's Sonata for Two Pianos, as well as the sorts of 'cosmic gesture' that Goeyvaerts made in his suggestions of the metaphysical possibilities of compositional systematisation. It was he who had consistently argued that what was unveiled in the sort of processual musics he undertook was 'being', a 'mode of existence' as Goeyvaerts himself had put it in 1951. Given Goeyvaerts's position as revealed in his correspondence with Stockhausen around 1951–2, what is described here almost certainly refers quite literally to the defence of Goeyvaerts made by Stockhausen during Adorno's 1951 seminar. It is, moreover, in this passage that Adorno's criticism probably reaches its zenith:

> Even meaninglessness can become meaningful, as a contrast to and a negation of meaning, just as in music the expressionless is a form of expression. But the newest musical efforts have nothing to do with this. In them meaninglessness becomes the program, though sometimes dressed up with Existentialism: in place of subjective intention, Being itself is supposed to be heard. But as a result of the abstract compositional procedures in which it originates, this music is anything but that of primal sources; it is subjectively and historically mediated to the extreme. But if this music is not the pure voice of Being, what then is the *raison d'être* of this purified music? Its schematic organization takes the place of the *raison d'être*, and the organization of material becomes a substitute for the renounced goal. As a result of the atomistic disposition of musical elements, the concept of musical coherence [*Zusammenhang*] is liquidated, a concept without which nothing like music really exists.[21]

Adorno's critique of serial music is largely familiar. Its underlying description of serialism is a pervasive (and now, quite literally, textbook) one; Paul Griffiths's description of *Structures* relies upon a similar basis: 'he [Boulez] began with twelve-piece scales of durations, dynamics and attacks as well as pitches: each aspect is strictly controlled according to serial principles, and the result is perpetual change at every level'.[22] Similarly, Griffiths continues, 'the composers of total serialism saw themselves as concerned primarily with structure and organisation, as architects or engineers in sound. They pursued their ideas with quasi-scientific rigour; there was much talk of "research", and much mathematics in their technical writings.'[23] For all

---

[20] Ibid., 191. [21] Ibid., 191–2.
[22] Paul Griffiths, *Modern Music: A Concise History* (London: Thames & Hudson, 1994), 133.
[23] Ibid., 136.

the persistence of this essentially Adornian view, such a version of serialism could hardly be attributed to either Nono or Maderna in the music thus far mentioned; it was precisely the 'human element' that Nono had sought to highlight directly *against* process-driven composition. Even the more obviously systematic Stockhausen freely intervened in the results of his systems, as in the composition of Klavierstück III.

Boulez was assuredly culpable, in Adorno's terms, of dissolving the dialectic between compositional will and material in the way in which he had discussed Webern: though Adorno and Boulez would have agreed that the unity between the form and content of the row characterised later Webern, only for Boulez was this a positive dimension. If that had been where Boulez had stopped, he would have been guilty as charged, according to the rubric of 'Das Altern der Neuen Musik'. No less would Goeyvaerts have been implicated, with the idea that music would self-reflexively express itself, being generated from the single pitch. Stockhausen, too, had expressed an almost identical desire. Even so, compositional practice itself was already on the move. The Boulez who described Webern thus had already moved on from such a position in terms of the music he himself was writing, as I outline below. For Adorno too, even if Boulez had been a part of the circle of composers whom he had thought to critique in 'Das Altern der Neuen Musik', by the autumn of 1955 he had changed his mind. He wrote to Eduard Steuermann on 14 April 1954 – in advance of Steuermann's attendance at that year's courses – that many of the composers there would be under Boulez's 'questionable influence'.[24] By the end of 1955, Adorno had actually met Boulez, probably, according to Boulez's own recollection, when sitting in a café after a concert at the 1955 Darmstadt courses.[25] Boulez was, it transpired, someone with whom one could have a conversation about music, 'a highly gifted person and a real musician', as a later letter to Steuermann proposes. By contrast, Stockhausen and the music critic Heinz-Klaus Metzger were characterised as 'unfortunate' and 'little', respectively.[26] Though Nono and Maderna were unmentioned in the essay, they had been construed as being part of a broader scene earlier in 1955, in Adorno's 'New Music Today', which condenses Adorno's thinking on the Darmstadt composers admirably, as well as showing the distance of his thought from the actuality of compositional work, which was already – as Adorno would later have it sternly pointed out to him – some distance from Webern:

---

[24] Theodor W. Adorno to Eduard Steuermann, 14 April 1954, quoted in Campbell, *Boulez, Music and Philosophy*, 69.
[25] Campbell, *Boulez, Music and Philosophy*, 68.
[26] Adorno to Steuermann, 14 October 1955, quoted in ibid., 69.

Late Webern combines an undreamed-of density of twelve-note relationships with stark compositional simplicity, in a fashion comparable to the paintings of Mondrian. This reduction has often made his music 'pointillist' [*punktuell*]; but even the barest of those contructs contain barely a note that does not have some highly precise and convincing meaning, however skeletal. It is against such musical sense that the rebellion of this group of young composers – highly diverse within itself – is directed; it includes Boulez in France, Stockhausen in Germany and Maderna and Nono in Italy. Objective construction is now supposed to encapsulate all elements mathematically, in particular rhythmic ones; the aim, to put it drastically, is the liquidation of composition in each composition [. . .] Some have compared their aims to the cybernetic efforts of science and industrial automation; they are so automatic in their realization that, as E. I. Kahn put it, a form of 'robot music' is beginning to emerge.[27]

If meeting Boulez had caused Adorno to modify his position, it was only by a little. He stated at the close of 'New Music Today' that 'Stockhausen has admitted a threshold of "indeterminacy", and an eminently talented composer such as Boulez seems capable of casting off his self-imposed shackles and, drawing on all the experiences gained through ascetic discipline, writing convincing music'.[28] It is significant, too, that regardless of claims for Adorno's influence on the direction of compositional practice, the composers were already well ahead of him.[29]

Getting institutionalised: an atelier for autonomous music?

At Darmstadt in 1955 Steinecke tested a new forum. Though he had often placed value on music criticism as a part of the Ferienkurse – from 1946 to 1950, there was always at least one music critic on the faculty: Fred Hamel, Heinrich Strobel, Hans Heinz Stuckenschmidt, and Adorno himself had all acted for Darmstadt in this respect – the practice had, to some extent, fallen away as composers, especially young ones, came into the limelight. In 1955, Steinecke put music criticism back at the centre of the agenda, inviting Claude Rostand, Luigi Rognoni, and Stuckenschmidt to offer three roundtable discussions on 'Music since 1945', 'The New Works of Young Composers', and 'New Aspects and Tendencies'. That Steinecke's selected critics came from France, Italy, and Germany, respectively, mirroring Boulez, Nono, and Stockhausen, hardly seems likely to have been a coincidence. Yet precisely this sort of roundtable discussion was not one to which

---

[27] Theodor W. Adorno, 'New Music Today' [1955], in *Night Music: Essays on Music 1928–1962*, ed. Rolf Tiedemann, tr. Wieland Hoban (Calcutta: Seagull, 2009), 398–9.
[28] Ibid., 400.
[29] See, for example, Max Paddison, *Adorno's Aesthetics of Music* (Cambridge University Press, 1997 [1993]), 265.

Steinecke returned, though it was obviously, given his commitment to compositional working groups run by several of the young composers in common, the *sort* of idea that appealed to him. Part of the reason why the idea was dropped may have been that it led to little debate or interest. The *Darmstädter Tagblatt*'s correspondent noted that, first, the three critics impressed by not backing their own 'national horses' and that they were in agreement to a remarkable degree, but that, second, the best debates were heard by only a handful of listeners.[30] Like it or not, it seemed that the participants came to Darmstadt to listen to composers, not to critics. One of the few points of disagreement, however, was notable, since it concerned Stockhausen: while one of the critics (and the report gives no indication as to who said what in this respect) defended Stockhausen, another painted him as an 'uncalled-for martyr, who has no desire to be understood, even though the public this year has shown itself willing to engage with the most extreme matters'.[31] Other correspondents gave little indication that there had been any debate on the matter, however; Herchenröder gave the impression that the judgement of all three critics on the young composers (he suggests that it was the names of Boulez and Stockhausen that came repeatedly into the debate) was that '[t]hey themselves have no desire to compose, but are, rather, obedient to the material which is already complete in and of itself. The music they create is not an art which the listener who has no experience of theory and psychoacoustics can understand. It is open only a few.' This, then, was 'music on the borders of silence'.[32] It is hardly difficult to hear the voice of Adorno ventriloquised through this critique, especially since the proximity of music to silence is such a distinctive mark of his own understanding of Webern.

There were more influences discerned than Webern, however. While for Werner Oehlmann, Webern was the 'central figure in the music of our epoch' so far as the young composers were concerned,[33] Claude Rostand had said in the discussion sessions with Rognoni and Stuckenschmidt that the new post-war music should be traced back to the curious students whom Messiaen had taught and that, thus, the 'new style' had already existed, from a French perspective at least, since 1944 or 1945.[34] When Ernst Thomas came to review the courses, it was Schoenberg whom he placed at the beginning, literally and figuratively: 'The decisive symptom: serial

---

[30] [ski], 'Die Diskussion der Kritiker: Stuckenschmidt, Rostand und Rognoni zur neuen Musik', *Darmstädter Tagblatt*, 8 June 1955.
[31] Ibid.
[32] G. N. Herchenröder, 'Musik an der Grenze des Schweigens', *Abendpost*, 8 June 1955.
[33] Werner Oehlmann, 'Die junge Generation in Darmstadt: Instrumentale und elektronische Musik', *Der Tagesspiegel*, 10 June 1955.
[34] Ibid.

composition, a massive evolution of Schoenbergian principles, has taken hold. Schoenberg's name stands symbolically at the beginning of the representative concert series.'[35] This was not a proxy way of a correspondent making a tacit claim for the composer whom he was, personally, 'backing' (Messiaen standing for Boulez, Schoenberg for Nono, and Webern for Stockhausen), though there may well have been a hint of that too, but rather a signal that, even if later it would become 'obvious' that it had been Webern all along who had been the exemplary figure, in 1955 it was still not clear how the mythology would be constructed. It should go without saying that the state of affairs in 1955 feels rather closer to the truth of the matter – a flood of influences, and not only Messiaen, Schoenberg, and Webern, of differing weights of significance for the different composers – even if the press had already started to tilt at a more unified narrative.

That the story of new music at Darmstadt was already far from unified ought really to have been symbolised in Boulez's lecture that year, which explicitly aligned his own output with not only Webern, but also Debussy. The point, as Boulez saw it, was that what he found in Debussy had little to do with calculation – the serial transformations of the series – as one might find in Webern, but much to do with morphology and with form, as well as with orchestration.[36] Where Webern's formal principles, however 'advanced' the materials inserted into them, harked back to classical models – and here Boulez distanced himself from Eimert's position that Adorno had erroneously found the fusion of fugue and the sonata principle in Webern – in Debussy one found fluid formal principles which were developed from the chromatic material in play, even in pieces which appeared, at first blush, to be composed according to a simplistic ABA schema. The Second Viennese School, Boulez opined, had not written for orchestra, but had, on the contrary, done little more in their orchestral scores than orchestrated what was truly chamber music.[37] It was obvious in Boulez's presentation that he was describing a manoeuvre which he felt a composer ought to effect: it was Boulez who needed to fuse the Debussian with the Webernian, rather than that the two composers could be heard already in relationship to one another. That that relationship could, literally, be heard in Boulez's contemporaneous music is signalled by Arnold Whittall's observation that, at the beginning of the third movement of *Le Marteau sans maître*, there is already 'a sense of the not-so-distant presence of one of Boulez's most admired precursors, Debussy'.[38]

---

[35] Ernst Thomas, 'Werkstatt für Neue Musik: Die Darmstädter Ferienkurse im Jubiläumsjahr', *Düsseldorfer Nachrichten*, 9 June 1955.
[36] Pierre Boulez, 'Claude Debussy et Anton Webern' [1955], tr. Heinz-Klaus Metzger, in Metzger and Riehn (eds.), *Darmstadt-Dokumente I*, 75.
[37] Ibid., 77–9. [38] Whittall, *Serialism*, 178.

A year later, Boulez would go rather further – admittedly in a publication in France rather than Germany on this occasion – suggesting that one might consider setting up 'a Debussy–Cézanne–Mallarmé axis as the root of all modernism'.[39] While Boulez was probably not wholly serious, it was becoming clear in both Germany and France that he was outlining a gradual distancing from Webern. Boulez's lecture was given an impromptu translation into German by Heinz-Klaus Metzger, whose translations in more formal ways – not least of Boulez's later lecture, 'Alea', and of Cage's third Darmstadt lecture, 'Communication' – would have an impact on the development of the aesthetic debate at Darmstadt.

The link, too, was emphasised in performance. Directly following Boulez's lecture, Yvonne Loriod performed the third, tenth, eleventh, and twelfth of Debussy's *Douze études* (1915) juxtaposed with a performance, the German première, of the first book of *Structures* by Loriod and Hans Alexander Kaul. Neither the performance nor the lecture elicited much response at the time, with *Structures* representing, for Lewinski at least, nothing very important in terms of its own musical substance and forming instead a vital point of departure.[40] Yet, even for Boulez, *Structures* was no real point of departure, but more – much like Messiaen's *Mode de valeurs et d'intensités*, whose pitch material Boulez adapted into the series for *Structure Ia* – an experiment at the limits of a particular mode of serial organisation, and it is hardly typical for Boulez's working in more general terms.[41] Nevertheless, Stuckenschmidt took the first book of *Structures* to be 'symptomatic' of the problems of the new serial music. He raised one of the regular concerns regarding pre-determination of serial material: 'when *fortissimo* and *pianissimo* have equal rights, the stronger always wins.' Whether Stuckenschmidt intentionally meant to make the political comparison explicit or not, his use of the word *Stimmrecht*, more literally 'suffrage' or 'franchise', to mean equal rights, was certainly suggestive of the Adornian notion that a fully pre-determined serial system was redolent of totalitarian political ones. In any case, he argued that one of the other difficulties was the degree to which the ear tired of such textures, and suggested that Boulez had overstepped the maximum duration for which such music could be tolerated.[42]

As far as the reception of Stockhausen's music at the 1955 Darmstadt New Music Courses was concerned, it was, as Ernst Rittel said, amongst

---

[39] Pierre Boulez, 'Corruption in the Censers' [1956], in *Stocktakings from an Apprenticeship*, tr. Stephen Walsh (Oxford University Press, 1991), 20.
[40] Wolf-Eberhard von Lewinski, 'Debussy – Webern – Boulez: Yvonne Loriod und H. A. Kaul spielten auf der Marienhöhe', *Darmstädter Tagblatt*, 4 June 1955.
[41] See Bösche, 'Auf der Suche nach dem Unbekannten', 46–50.
[42] Hans Heinz Stuckenschmidt, 'Leidenschaftlich suchen Komponisten nach neuen Ordnungen und Formen der Musik', *Die Welt*, 8 June 1955.

the most controversial subjects of discussion.[43] In particular, it was Marcelle Mercenier's performance of his second cycle of Klavierstücke, numbers V–VIII (1954–5), which attracted the greatest attention, though only indirectly because of the music. Stockhausen was acting as Mercenier's page-turner, but was, at some point in the performance, angered by the laughter and 'ironic applause' of some listeners. He stormed off the stage, and had to be coaxed back by Mercenier to continue his role until the end of the performance.[44] Other commentators were less lurid in their descriptions. Stuckenschmidt's report said only that during the concert was there 'protest' against Stockhausen's music, even if he did seem to suggest that the protesters may have had a point: 'It is music without any immediately perceivable structure, dull, but suddenly illuminated by a flashlight. The phenomenally controlled sound of the piano is absolutely fully utilised. Single pitches dash forward, tiny *appoggiature*, arpeggios, fleeting figures. The richness of tension grew at first, then broke off suddenly and flowed into monotony. Stentorian music on the edge, developed with fanatical seriousness.' As in the case of Boulez, Stockhausen's music might be adequate, if it were only shorter.[45] In point of fact, Stockhausen may have been upset by more than the audience response. He wrote to Steinecke after the Hessischer Rundfunk had broadcast Mercenier's performance on 27 July 1955, in a programme moderated by Steinecke himself, that 'for reasons incomprehensible to me, the dreadful Darmstadt recording was played in your Frankfurt broadcast. That does much more damage to our collective work than it does good. I heard the broadcast and was hugely annoyed that you allowed this to happen. Please do not use the recording of the piano pieces again for such purposes.'[46] Stockhausen had already written to Goeyvaerts that, as far as he could tell, Mercenier had not really rehearsed, but that, worse, the audience did not seem to have noticed that and blamed him, the composer, for the problems with the pieces. At some point, in amongst the laughter, whistling, and heckling, it appears that Boulez had shouted out loud: 'Silence, s'il vous plaît!'[47]

---

[43] Ernst Rittel, 'Nachtstudio', broadcast, Südwestfunk, 30 August 1955, transcript IMD.
[44] [hkr.], 'Nur noch routinierte Zwölftonerei: Die Darmstädter Ferienkurse für Neue Musik bald Sektiererei', *Pfälzische Volkszeitung*, 8 June 1955.
[45] Stuckenschmidt, 'Leidenschaftlich suchen Komponisten'.
[46] Stockhausen to Steinecke, undated but after 27 July 1955, in Misch and Bandur (eds.), *Karlheinz Stockhausen bei den Internationalen Ferienkursen*, 111.
[47] Stockhausen to Goeyvaerts, 15 June 1955, in ibid, 112. This event is strongly reminiscent of Cage and Tudor's performance of *12'55.6078"* at Donaueschingen in 1954, detailed below. Audible on the recording of that event, there was a different cry of 'Silence!' during their performance in the forlorn hope of quieting the dissenters. Then, the call came back from the hall, 'Pourquoi?'

Ex. 2.1 Bruno Maderna, *Quartetto per archi in due tempi*, bb. 1–10

Performed by the Drolc-Quartett on 1 June, in the same concert as Mercenier's performance of the Stockhausen Klavierstücke, Maderna's *Quartetto per archi in due tempi* (1955) (in two *stages*, rather than, as might be thought, in two tempi), clearly of Webernian hue, was well regarded by most. Stuckenschmidt said the two movements were 'coherent, melodic music with genuine closes and dramatic climaxes'. Even though this would be Maderna's only excursion into a more fully fledged serial world, it was clear that, from Stuckenschmidt's perspective at least, the model was not absolutely incapable of creating music *qua* music (see Example 2.1).[48] Nevertheless, it is worth noting that Maderna stuck to only two parameters, those of pitch and rhythm. The treatment of those followed a rigorous procedure, determined by a magic

[48] Hans Heinz Stuckenschmidt, 'Drei Generation Neuer Musik in Darmstadt', *Berichte und Information*, 17 June 1955.

122   The accidental serialists

Table 2.1 *Magic square for Bruno Maderna*, Quartetto per archi in due tempi

B	3	10	5	6	9	12	1	4	7	8	11	12	A
F♯	10	5	12	4	7	2	11	8	1	9	6	3	N
C♯	6	9	1	8	11	2	7	4	12	5	10	3	B
D	5	12	4	7	2	11	8	1	9	6	3	10	M
F	9	1	8	11	2	7	4	12	5	10	3	6	C
A♭	12	4	7	2	11	8	1	9	6	3	10	5	L
A	1	8	11	2	7	4	12	5	10	3	6	9	D
C	4	7	2	11	8	1	9	6	3	10	5	12	I
E♭	8	11	2	7	4	12	5	10	3	6	9	1	E
E	7	2	11	8	1	9	6	3	10	5	12	4	H
G	11	2	7	4	12	5	10	3	6	9	1	8	F
B♭	2	7	4	12	5	10	3	6	9	1	8	11	G

square, with the multiplication of basic durations according to a different factor for each horizontal line of the square, labelled A–N in Table 2.1.[49]

Even here, at his most deterministic, Maderna actually used his structural system to introduce ambiguity: the entries of pitch material in the first movement, for instance, 'wrap around' into the retrograde at a seemingly arbitrary moment, allowing Maderna significant fluidity in his contrapuntal serial voice-leading. As Borio schematises the movement as a whole, while the forty 'prime' sets are, to a certain degree, fixed, the twenty retrogrades, even though fixed in the order of their appearance, are free as to the moment of their use (see Table 2.2).

Thus, even in the first stage of the piece, dubbed by Berio 'a rather rigid, sparkling and largely immobile object', there is a relatively rigorously determined layer (the upper one in Table 2.2) and one which is rather more freely distributed (the lower one in Table 2.2). As Berio claimed, in the second stage

> this same object is transformed and re-invented. Bruno here opens up spaces, changes intensities, enlarges the proportions and reveals the melodic characters. This means that he alters things in such a way that the rigid body heard in the first part becomes something different, like a face which is immobile and stiff in one expression, finally beginning to articulate and to express different emotions.[50]

---

[49] A much fuller analysis, from which the matter here is derived, may be found in Borio, 'Tempo e ritmo nelle composizioni seriali', 107–11. A slightly different though complementary analysis is shown in Fearn, *Bruno Maderna*, 95–105.
[50] Luciano Berio, quoted in Fearn, *Bruno Maderna*, 95.

Table 2.2 Row dispersal in Bruno Maderna, Quartetto per archi in due tempi, *first movement*

I	→	II	→	III	→	IV	→
A B C D E F G H I L M N		A B C D E F G H I L M N		A B C D E F G H I L M N		A B C D	
N M L I H G F E D C B A						N M L I H G F E	
			↓				↓
			V				(IV)

Nevertheless, though the quartet may well be 'the work of Maderna's from that period which has received the most critical attention', at the time it was Nono who was, again, the compositional star of the show. As Lewinski reported it,

> Luigi Nono's new, six-and-a-half-minute piece *Incontri* was so praised that Rosbaud repeated it. The thirty-one-year-old Venetian is often named as a promising talent. His newest piece brings the structural methods misused by some young composers to a highly intense and taut conclusion [...] which is, to be sure, exceptionally tightly wrought and demands concentrated listening. Nono's mathematics sound, and turn the calculations of a fugal composition into a communicable, absolute music.

By contrast, Henze's *Quattro poemi* (1955), though 'audibly well worked, disappointed in their substance'.[51] Lewinski was certainly accurate in terms of the audience's reception of Nono's music. Others were hardly so effusive, though. Heinz Pringsheim, in a broadcast on the Bayerischer Rundfunk only days after the concert, observed that, while *Incontri* (1955) was the sensation of the evening, this 'sensation' was positive for some, negative for others. His own view was clear: Nono had 'latterly strayed increasingly decisively down a dead-end street'. That dead end was precisely the one in which composers pre-determined parameters according to 'minutely determined schemes'. This was not music, so Pringsheim suggested, but, in a clearly conscious echo of the title of Boulez's essay in the style, only structures.[52] Everett Helm argued that Nono's 'preoccupation with the "machinery" of composition appears still to hamper and inhibit his freedom of expression',[53] asserting that the break with the past exhibited by pieces written under the sign of Webern (and, for him, it was obvious that it was only Webern that was at stake) was so total that it was 'scarcely possible to judge or discuss the most "advanced" music in conventional music terms; indeed it is hardly possible to judge it at all'.[54] One might wonder whether the problem, at least in part, was that, on the level of pitch, Nono employed a single series, static and unchanging, throughout the course of the piece. The structural 'encounters' of the title took place only in relation to other parameters, thus plausibly meaning that a listener would be unable easily to hear the 'two entities that encounter each other and contend with one

---

[51] Wolf-Eberhard von Lewinski, 'Prominenz der jungen Komponisten: Uraufführungen bei den Kranichsteiner Ferienkursen', *Bremer Nachrichten*, 3 June 1955.
[52] Heinz Pringsheim, 'Kranichsteiner Ferienkurse', broadcast, Bayerischer Rundfunk, 3 June 1955, transcript IMD.
[53] Everett Helm, 'Darmstadt, Baden-Baden, and Twelve-Tone Music', *Saturday Review* (30 July 1955), 46.
[54] Ibid., 35. See also Jeannie Ma. Guerrero, 'The Presence of Hindemith in Nono's Sketches: A New Context for Nono's Music', *Journal of Musicology*, vol. 26, no. 4 (Fall 2009), 481–511.

another but are never subsumed into a greater unity'. Or perhaps it was that the 'social parable' of *Incontri*, as Durazzi describes it, was for just these reasons unclear, leading to the accusations that greater 'freedom of expression' was needed. The figurative level of this aspect of *Incontri* would, perhaps, become clear only when it reappeared in *Intolleranza*:

> This is the scene in which the *Emigrante* first meets his idealized *Compagna*, and it is at this moment that he rediscovers his hope for the future. Now accompanying the dramatic action of the opera, the two complementary and mutually independent entities of *Incontri* take on the characteristics of man and woman as they join forces to face a cruel and unjust world.[55]

In the mid 1950s, however, as far as the influence of Webern was concerned, Helm quoted an unnamed 'apostle' of new music (though Rudolf Kolisch was, fairly clearly, meant) as having suggested that 'Kranichstein should be for all time abandoned, asserting that the influence of this "cult" on young composers leads them down the primrose path to complete sterility and that the localized glorification of this essentially esoteric kind of music gives them an entirely false perspective.'[56] One cannot but wonder whether the response which Nono's work received played a part in the idea of a 'cult', since the critics were faced with music which they, evidently, neither cared for nor understood, but which was nevertheless meeting with a rapturous reception from other younger composers, which suggested either that the older generation was missing something or that the youngsters were in thrall. It was, as far as the critics could tell, only in Darmstadt that quite this level of excitement about the new music could be observed.

Rittel made clear that this 'cult' could be given a name: 'This new work from Nono is a typical example of the so-called Darmstadt style.'[57] Claus-Henning Bachmann, too, made the link between the 'serial' and what he called the 'Darmstadt circle'.[58] Across the coverage of the 1955 courses, certain young composers (Boulez, Maderna, Nono, and Stockhausen are the most commonly named) found themselves described as a group which was both serial and specifically of Darmstadt, even if the name had not yet stuck. Lewinski, too, noted that some sort of consolidation might be seen, in his passing observation that 1955 was the first time he had come to Darmstadt and failed to encounter a 'new name'.[59] This was precisely the sum of Walther Friedländer's review,

---

[55] Bruce Durazzi, 'Luigi Nono's *Canti di vita e d'amore*: Musical Dialectics and the Opposition of Present and Future', *Journal of Musicology*, vol. 26, no. 4 (Fall 2009), 453–4.

[56] Helm, 'Darmstadt, Baden-Baden, and Twelve-Tone Music', 35.   [57] Rittel, 'Nachtstudio'.

[58] Claus-Henning Bachmann, 'Zwischen Kult und Elektronenröhre: Darmstadts Rechenschaftsbericht über die neuen Musik', *Schwäbische Landeszeitung*, 22 June 1955.

[59] Wolf-Eberhard von Lewinski, speaking as a part of the 'Musikalisches Nachtprogramm', broadcast on the Nordwestdeutscher Rundfunk, 23 June 1955, transcript IMD.

126   The accidental serialists

which observed that Kranichstein had not only become stabilised; it had become an institution and, moreover, an institution in which one could begin to sense something of a party line. Even though Friedländer did not deny that there was much more than 'punctual' serialism on show (Milhaud, Bartók, Stravinsky, Hindemith, Berg, Hartmann, Schoenberg, Debussy, and Messiaen made up the bulk of the concert programme in 1955), it was clear that he, too, felt that that was beginning to predominate amongst the pieces by the younger generation which were performed, and that such a centrality for one form of new music – turning serialism into *the* new music – could not in the end be healthy for the institution.[60]

Notably, though Nono received relatively strong praise in the press, Boulez, Maderna, and Stockhausen remained unfavourably treated. In truth, Henze fared no better. The press regurgitated a broadly Adornian line in respect of the young serialists, simultaneously suggesting that Henze had capitulated to the Romantics. Even though the press broadly seemed to feel that Peter Racine Fricker's Three Movements for Viola Solo (1955) represented a moderate way between two extremes, which it was to be hoped composers would follow, the column inches went to those composers more likely to attract controversy. If anything, by the mid 1950s, Stockhausen and Boulez received the majority of the coverage not because their stance had been accepted, but precisely because it had not. For all that, the response to Webern was certainly changing. His Symphony, op. 21, was compared favourably to the music of the young composers by Rodemann, who suggested that 'this piece – written by a master of the art and realised in a masterful performance – is able to have public success despite its esotericism'.[61] The young Darmstädter were not, then, masters yet.

Responding, if indirectly and unknowingly, to Rodemann, Nono wrote to Steinecke:

> Why don't you let the youngsters give lectures during the Ferienkurse??? Like Boulez is supposed to??? I think this would be very good: in the afternoon, young x gives a lecture about.........., afterwards i.e. parallel with the working group (Bruno Boulez Tudor), proper lectures (like Boulez is supposed to on B Debussy – W Wzebern [sic]). But who and about what?[62]

Nono proposed that Boulez might speak about the relationship between text and music (a topic which would become more important for Nono a few

---

[60] Walther Friedländer, '"Kranichstein" muß sich entscheiden: Zu den zehnten "Internationalen Ferienkursen für Neue Musik"', *Frankfurter Allgemeine Zeitung*, 14 June 1955.
[61] Albert Rodemann, 'Konkrete Ziel und abstraktes Ideal: Das Kammerorchester der Nordwestdeutschen Musik-Akademie Detmold', *Darmstädter Tagblatt*, 4 June 1955.
[62] Nono to Steinecke, 25 February 1956, ALN.

years later), that Maderna could discuss the relationship between music, the conductor, and the orchestra, and that Stockhausen might speak about 'his new electronic piece with voice'. Nono was also clear that the 'old guard' ought not to be forgotten: he recommended the retention of Scherchen, Strobel, and Stuckenschmidt. The one person Nono seemed to think had little to offer was Adorno: 'So not only (or not at all any more!!!) doctrinaire academic lectures from Adorno and the like, but really TODAY from people of TODAY for everybody TODAY!!!!!!!!!!'[63] Nono felt that Boulez's lecture on Webern and Debussy suggested a seniority which neither Stockhausen, Maderna, nor he himself had yet been accorded, on an institutional level at least. Nono's position was that all four should, in the Darmstadt context, be seen as equally senior. It would be 1957 before Nono and Stockhausen would find themselves 'elevated' in this fashion. Before that happened, the press would already have identified the grouping that would become known as the 'Darmstadt School'.

Steinecke had evidently felt the sting of the criticisms, raised the previous year, that the Ferienkurse had begun to present a limited fare of new music and had, worse, put forward no new names. In 1956, things were rather different. Claus-Henning Bachmann's note gives the sense of the change: 'it began with Ravel and ended with Hindemith. But in between – oy vey – the reviewer's head buzzes'.[64] In the two weeks of the courses, there were seventeen world premières and a further eight German premières. Yet the hiatus in the introduction of new voices seemed to have solidified the positions of Boulez, Maderna, Nono, and Stockhausen as established Darmstadt 'players', with another generation of young composers following them, even though none of the four held real faculty positions, notwithstanding Boulez and Maderna's working groups. The impression was doubtless heightened by repeat performances of Stockhausen's Klavierstücke V–VIII (though this time in the hands of David Tudor) and Maderna's *Quartetto per archi in due tempi*. Perhaps it was no surprise, then, that Adorno, ostensibly lecturing on the subject of Schoenberg's counterpoint, characterised the Darmstadt courses as an 'Atelier for Autonomous Music', in which young composers would hear their music performed for the first time, become more culturally prominent, and attract greater interest.[65] Adorno was perhaps echoing Ernst Thomas, who had dubbed the Darmstadt courses a 'Workshop for New Music', in an otherwise almost wholly unexceptional essay in the *Düsseldorfer Nachrichten* the previous

---

[63] Ibid.
[64] Claus-Henning Bachmann, 'Sie suchen Rückhalt bei Mozart: Neue Musik in Darmstadt. Handwerk mit Phantasie', *Westdeutsche Allgemeine*, 3 August 1956.
[65] Gustav Adolf Trumpff, 'Atelier für autonome Musik: Zwei Studioveranstaltungen auf der Marienhöhe', *Darmstädter Echo*, 20 July 1956.

year.[66] Now the idea was picked up by others, Stuckenschmidt proclaiming Darmstadt a 'laboratory for the writers of new music'. Stuckenschmidt went further, making perhaps the first direct comparison between Darmstadt and the Bauhaus, though hardly in a wholly complimentary guise. He stated outright, once again, that the Darmstadt style was unambiguously oriented towards Webern's late work, but that the problem with the aesthetic remained that it had separated itself from the traditional forms within which Webern had worked. This, he said, was 'the same narrowing as at the Weimar Bauhaus in 1923, where a red square and a blue circle (or *vice versa*) were more important than the expression of personality'. Even so, Stuckenschmidt felt that personal styles could be felt in, for instance, the jazz-inflected episodes of Bo Nilsson's *Frekvenser* (1955–6) or the melodic syntax of Jacques Calonne's *Trois bagatelles* (1956). He even had praise for Boulez's 'feverish' Sonatine for flute and piano (1946) (if not for his 'atomising' analysis of Webern).[67] In a sense, the press had, through this remark of Adorno's, found a way to understand what Darmstadt represented which was different from the judgements they had previously made. Rather than judging what was presented there as if it were a fully formed, finished product, it was possible instead to regard Darmstadt in general terms as precisely this atelier, or laboratory, in which experiments could be made, following which the composer might amend his or her piece according to the results of a first hearing.[68] It went without saying that such a change would not apply to Boulez, Maderna, Nono, or Stockhausen, who had already 'served their time' in this respect, although it made it possible to re-evaluate the successes and failures of previous years. Lewinski specifically stated, in the context of Tudor's performance of Stockhausen's second cycle of Klavierstücke, that, in this case, one ought not to think of these as 'studio work, which might be decisive for later pieces': this was the finished article.[69] The music of the 'old hands' might be compared to the work of younger student composers: Lewinski's examples were Calonne's *Trois bagatelles*, Luc Ferrari's sonatina *ELYB* (1954), Friedrich Voss's Wind Trio (1956), and Reinhold Finkbeiner's Second String Quartet (1955), all of which received their premières at the 1956 courses.

No matter that some of the now-senior composers had expressly distanced themselves from a post-Webernian mould: the seeds that had been

---

[66] Thomas, 'Werkstatt für Neue Musik'.
[67] Hans Heinz Stuckenschmidt, 'Das Laboratorium der Neutöner: Zehn Jahre Darmstädter Ferienkurse', *Deutsche Zeitung*, 25 July 1956.
[68] Though Darmstadt was to a very great extent dominated by male composers, Gladys Nordenstrom's *Rondo* (1948) was given a rather late première by Gazzeloni and Tudor on 20 July 1956.
[69] Wolf-Eberhard von Lewinski, 'Blick in Kranichsteins Komponisten-Atelier', broadcast, Radio Bremen, August 1956 (exact date unknown), transcript IMD.

planted by Eimert's gathering of composers under that banner in 1953 had come to fruition, in a sense, even if his grouping had included Goeyvaerts, rather than Maderna. It was in just this conjunction that Wehagen, in the first usage to my knowledge of the expression expressed literally, observed:

> If this year roughly 300 participants from twenty-six countries, European and overseas, came to Darmstadt, if many of the composers of yesterday themselves are already active as faculty members – and that is to be sure already to speak of a 'Kranichstein School' – when it is obvious that there is already gathered here a new generation, keen to learn, that speaks for the rightness and viability of an idea which has truly acquired international validity.

As far as Wehagen was concerned, Darmstadt meant more now than mere 'courses'. Steinecke had built a school.[70]

Metzger contra Adorno

In the garbled French and English translations of 'Das Altern der Neuen Musik' which appeared in 1956, a note had been added that 'Boulez intends to free his ultra-constructivist aesthetic from the deadly rigidity which threatens it, without however making any concession as regards the necessity of maintaining a strict discipline.'[71] If Boulez was, as it were, 'off the hook', the same was probably not true for any other composer who might be following (or be perceived to be following) similar automatic, serial paths. It was probably the unnamed – Eimert, Goeyvaerts, and Stockhausen – who were uppermost in Adorno's mind at the time of writing, in any case. It was none of these, though, who would make a direct riposte to Adorno, but rather the 'little' Heinz-Klaus Metzger, sometime student of Max Deutsch and, at the Akademie für Tonkunst in Darmstadt itself, of Rudolf Kolisch, who had been a member of Varèse's composition class with Nono during the 1950 courses. Metzger's influence 'behind the scenes' would come to be belied by his relatively diminutive physical stature.

Metzger's response to Adorno was broadcast on the Westdeutscher Rundfunk on 23 October 1957, under the polemical title 'The Aging of the Philosophy of New Music', and published the following year in *Die Reihe*, with the playful prefix 'Intermezzo I', recalling Adorno's own 'Atonal Intermezzo', originally published in 1929.[72] When it was reprinted in the

---

[70] Walther Wehagen, 'Vor-Ort neuer Musik: Darmstadt hat Schule gemacht', *Das blaue Blatt*, 1 September 1956.
[71] Campbell, *Boulez, Music and Philosophy*, 75.
[72] Heinz-Klaus Metzger, 'Intermezzo I: Das Altern der Philosophie der Neuen Musik', *Die Reihe*, vol. 4 (1958), 64–80; Theodor W. Adorno, 'Atonal Intermezzo' [1929], in *Night Music: Essays on Music 1928–1962*, ed. Rolf Tiedemann, tr. Wieland Hoban (Calcutta: Seagull, 2009).

English-language version of *Die Reihe* two years later, the title was yet more pointed: 'Just Who is Growing Old?'[73]

Metzger's reproaches to Adorno are scathing, not in terms of his methodology but in the evidence he relies upon. Metzger contrasted Adorno's observation in 'Das Altern der Neuen Musik' that there was no reason to worry that his critique was 'a throwback to Schoenberg, and is unable to get beyond him, Berg, and Webern, and that it will ultimately serve reactionary forces' with his earlier self-assigned criterion that '[n]o critique of progress is legitimate save one that names the reactionary element in the ruling unfreedom and thus unapologetically precludes its misuse in the service of the status quo.'[74] Adorno had presumably felt in 1954 that his essay operated in just these ways: he *was* naming the reactionary forces that inhered in post-war serial music – which was to say the excision of a critical relationship with tradition – and his proposal of 'the composition of truly coherent music out of a material however shorn of every quality' could hardly be misunderstood.[75] Yet Metzger observed that it not only could be but *had* been misunderstood: 'On almost the same day as Adorno's lecture, a distinguished Stuttgart music critic took just that intransigent advocate of progress as his unhoped-for authority in order to posit Egk's *Zaubergeige* as precisely that which one henceforth requires.'[76] Even if such a view would have supported precisely the reactionary tendencies that Adorno had, in his earlier writings, been at pains to oppose, it ought, so Metzger suggested, 'to have taken him aback'.[77]

The underlying problems, though, were hardly the idea that progressive musical materials had to be self-critical, but, first, that Adorno had not followed through on one of his own core criteria for valid critique from *Philosophie der neuen Musik*, that '[t]echnical analysis is at every point presupposed and often presented, but it requires in addition the interpretation of the most minute detail if it is to go beyond the characteristic cultural inventorying of the humanities and express the relation of the object to truth.'[78] Metzger would observe that technical analysis was missing at every point from 'Das Altern der Neuen Musik', and that this could only mean that Adorno had 'failed to consult primary sources of any kind, nor had he consulted secondary sources either'.[79]

---

[73] Heinz-Klaus Metzger, 'Just Who is Growing Old?', tr. Leo Black, *Die Reihe*, vol. 4 (1960), 63–80.
[74] Adorno, 'The Aging of the New Music', 195; Adorno, *Philosophy of New Music*, 4.
[75] Adorno, 'The Aging of the New Music', 191.
[76] Heinz-Klaus Metzger, 'Das Altern der Philosophie der Neuen Musik' [1957], in *Musik wozu: Literatur zu Noten*, ed. Rainer Riehn (Frankfurt am Main: Suhrkamp, 1980), 65. See also Kater, *Composers of the Nazi Era*, 22, for an indication of the negative post-war views of Egk.
[77] Metzger, 'Das Altern der Philosophie der Neuen Musik', 65.
[78] Adorno, *Philosophy of New Music*, 24.
[79] Metzger, 'Das Altern der Philosophie der Neuen Musik', 67.

Second, Metzger opined that Adorno's notion of musical material was faulty, in that he had suggested that the material – the tone row itself – of Schoenberg's later music did not bear the mark of the 'historical process' in the way in which free atonal pieces, such as *Erwartung*, had.[80] On the contrary, Metzger suggested that '"[m]aterial" did not adjourn to a place to which Schoenberg, the composer, could not in the end follow, but rather a historic motion of materials is played out in the course of his composing'.[81] Dodecaphony, in its procedural form, was no less a 'token of the historical process' than free atonality had been. Following Webern, Metzger concluded, it was precisely Boulez, Stockhausen, and Pousseur (again, Nono and Maderna are notably absent) who had taken up the challenge to deal with the dialectic between these processes and compositional will. This was exactly what Adorno had suggested would be at the heart of a progressive compositional attitude to material. As Adorno had, in 1951, sought to discover where, in Goeyvaerts's piece, the antecedent or the consequent could be found, so Metzger now observed that '[t]here is musical sense beyond antecedent and consequent phrases, and there is compelling musical coherence beyond any thematic-motivic relationship [...] Does he not know about Stockhausen's group concept?'[82] Thus Metzger tied together his two principal bones of contention: Adorno simply had insufficient knowledge of the music of the young serial composers to offer an informed critique and, had he had that level of information, he would have been forced to concede that their activities already did precisely what he had demanded of them.

Adorno's critique of Boulez (or, perhaps better, *through* Boulez) was taken apart. Where Adorno had held that in Boulez's music (and that of his 'disciples') composition had been replaced by 'an objective-calculatory ordering of intervals, pitches, long and short durations, degrees of loudness', Metzger countered that it was ever thus: 'As a matter of fact even, the scores that have been passed down generally show arrangements of intervals, pitches, long and short durations, and degree of loudness, not as a substitute for composition, but rather as that which is composed. One cannot do without calculation.' Metzger went rather further, suggesting that it was really only with 'objective-calculatory ordering' that it became possible to deviate from traditional numerical strategies, as implied by Adorno's antecedent and consequent phrases, 'where freedom is introduced into regions which were not long ago paralysed by numbers'.[83] In order to say this, Adorno must have been unaware of the activities of Boulez, Stockhausen, and, not least, Cage, who had aimed at 'the most wide-ranging

[80] Ibid., 71.   [81] Ibid.   [82] Ibid., 72.   [83] Ibid., 72–3.

unpredictability of the total form while, as a matter of fact, retaining its unity'.[84] In short, while it might have been possible to make the claim that Adorno did in the case of *Mode de valeurs et d'intensités*, which exhibited a 'decreed system', this would already collapse in an examination of *Structure Ia*, and would become wholly untenable in the light of Stockhausen's Klavierstücke. Adorno's arsenal was, from Metzger's perspective, one which had remained stationary for fifty years.[85] Metzger was, to be sure, hardly mistaken in terms of the examples upon which Adorno had relied, *Erwartung* and Webern's Five Movements, op. 5, both dating from 1909.

Similarly, Adorno's suggestion that the serial composers misunderstood the musical passing of time was regarded with near contempt by Metzger. Adorno's distinction, in Bergsonian vein, between time as measured (*temps espace*) and time as experienced (*temps durée*) showed, for Metzger, little more than that he had either not read or not understood Stockhausen's '... wie die Zeit vergeht ...' ('... how time passes ...').[86] Even in the case of Earle Brown's *Four Systems* (1954) or 'December 1952', Metzger suggested that the performer would deviate from the mere spatial proportions – themselves broadly symmetrical – in order to account for experiential time. The strict proportions indicated by the graphic notation were irrelevant.[87] Going further, Metzger pointed out that flexibility in terms of temporal conceptions was some way beyond that which Adorno seemed to think was possible. Cage, Brown, Feldman, Pousseur, and especially Stockhausen, in *Zeitmasse* (1955–6), had introduced the sort of fluid approach to time that had previously been possible only in solo music. This, rather than pitch material, would represent a new, previously unheard sound-world.[88] In terms of that 'mere' sonic surface, Metzger nevertheless felt that Adorno must have been listening to wholly different musics from him. He admitted that Stockhausen had developed little that was really new in terms of piano timbres, adding a few nuances to pedalling, modes of attack, and the production of harmonics, while even Cage's prepared piano did not extend the available realm of sound further than that which could be produced by an orchestra. Yet as far as electronic music was concerned, Adorno's judgement that it sounded 'as though Webern were being played

---

[84] Ibid., 73.   [85] Ibid., 74.
[86] Ibid., 75. In truth, this is something of an unfair criticism. Since '... wie die Zeit vergeht ...' was not published until 1957 (nor written, by Stockhausen's account, until October 1956), Adorno certainly could not have made use of Stockhausen's thought either in his original lecture of 1954 or in the 1956 printing in *Dissonanzen*. Indeed, Adorno could have heard only one of the pieces with which '... wie die Zeit vergeht ...' deals, Klavierstück V, which had received its première at the 1954 Darmstadt courses, at which Adorno had lectured, with Kolisch and Steuermann, on the subject of the interpretation of new music (Karlheinz Stockhausen, '... wie die Zeit vergeht ...' [1957], in *Texte*, vol. I, 99–139).
[87] Metzger, 'Das Altern der Philosophie der Neuen Musik', 77–8.   [88] Ibid., 84.

on a Wurlitzer organ' suggested that either he had not heard Stockhausen's *Gesang der Jünglinge* (1955–6), Koenig's *Klang figuren II* (1955–6), or Brown's Octet (1952–3), or that his ears functioned in quite different ways from Metzger's own.[89]

Metzger closed by bringing the discussion back to that example which he knew that Adorno *could* rely upon, not least because he had been present during the Adorno seminar in which the confrontation with Goeyvaerts had occurred. Drawing on the quotations from 'Das Altern der Neuen Musik' already mentioned above in connection with Goeyvaerts, Metzger charged that Adorno's article in sum had 'merely substituted the name Boulez for that of Goeyvaerts'. No surprise, then, that Adorno was confused. Had it ever occurred to him to put to Boulez or Stockhausen the same questions that he had addressed to Goeyvaerts regarding the meaningfulness of some element or other within the total context of the piece, the reply would have been quite different, so Metzger proposed, and would have taken Adorno aback. To take Goeyvaerts as a central exemplar and to tar the other young Europeans with the same brush was naïve in the extreme since, although he was 'an artist of integrity in terms of his moral outlook and subjective disposition', he had gone off on the wrong track entirely, as Hauer had earlier.[90] Metzger is close to suggesting that to draw on Goeyvaerts in 'Das Altern der Neuen Musik' made as much sense as substituting Hauer for Schoenberg in *Philosophie der neuen Musik* would have done. In short, Metzger's retort to Adorno said, 'make the totalitarian argument against serial music if you will, but found it upon actual, current evidence'.

For all the polemical tone of Metzger's response, Adorno was certainly not against the idea of entering into direct dialogue, and Metzger and Adorno appeared jointly in a Westdeutscher Rundfunk radio broadcast on 19 February 1958, focussing on the issues Metzger had raised, under the title 'The Most Recent Music: Progress or Regression'. Despite the broadcast date, the discussion had already been recorded in 1957, and it seems likely from its content that it actually took place some time *before* Adorno delivered a further essay on the same theme, 'Criteria of the New Music', at the 1957 Ferienkurse (split across four sessions on 19 and 20 July and then, a week later, on 26 and 27 July). Though the notion of 'criteria' had begun to enter Adorno's thinking – he suggested in passing during the

---

[89] Adorno, 'The Aging of the New Music', 195; Metzger, 'Das Altern der Philosophie der Neuen Musik', 81. Again, this is something of a spurious critique. Adorno may have heard Brown's Octet at Donaueschingen (though it is far from sure that he was present at that performance) but he certainly could not have heard either *Gesang der Jünglinge* or *Klang figuren II* in advance of the publication of *Dissonanzen* since neither was premièred until 30 May 1956 in Cologne.

[90] Metzger, 'Das Altern der Philosophie der Neuen Musik', 87.

broadcast that it would be more useful to think within a framework of 'criteria' than to consider the new music in terms of 'quality' – no reference is made to his Darmstadt presentation of 1957; the discussion is restricted to his *Philosophie der neuen Musik*, 'Das Altern der Neuen Musik', and Metzger's 'Das Altern der Philosophie der Neuen Musik'.[91]

For the most part, this dialogue was, so far as can be ascertained from the transcript, both good-natured and good-humoured, though Metzger may have felt occasionally a little patronised. Yet Adorno gave more ground than Metzger, even if a large part of the broadcast was devoted to clarifying misunderstandings which seemed to have appeared between Adorno's text and Metzger's reading of it. Adorno stressed that he was just as much opposed to judgements of 'worth' as he was to 'worthlessness', and that, as he had stressed elsewhere, his interest was in a 'höhere Kritik', characterised by Zagorski as a '"higher criticism," which attempts to apprehend the work of art as an expression of its historical moment'.[92] If 'value' as such were not the point, the 'instrumentalisation of music in pursuit of the question of truth', as Schubert has it, might well have been.[93] In any case, that the debate might turn on 'truth' and not 'worth' was an issue on which Adorno and Metzger could agree.[94]

In terms of the evidential foundations of Adorno's critique, however, Metzger and Adorno found no real resolution; their discussion dissolved for the most part into a tit-for-tat exchange, with Metzger naming pieces he felt Adorno ought to have listened to and Adorno explaining why he could not have done. Nevertheless, Adorno did not deny that Goeyvaerts – whose Sonata for Two Pianos Adorno decried as 'pure gibberish' – acted as a sort of proxy for those who would propose that composition was now numerically orderable (and Adorno was sure to stress that those he was thinking of were 'very central figures'), noting that Hermann Scherchen had suggested that music had, today, 'entered in a scientific stage, that it had, itself, become a science'.[95] There was little hope of agreement, but neither came well out of their dispute: Adorno was exposed as knowing less about the music than

---

[91] Theodor W. Adorno and Heinz-Klaus Metzger, 'Disput zwischen Theodor W. Adorno und Heinz-Klaus Metzger' [1957], in Metzger, *Musik wozu*, 91.
[92] Zagorski, '"Nach dem Weltuntergang"', 686.
[93] Giselher Schubert, 'Musik gleich Wahrheit? Theodor W. Adornos Einfluß auf die Musikentwicklung in unserem Jahrhundert', in Hanspeter Krellmann (ed.), *Oper aktuell: Die Bayerische Staatsoper 1999/2000* (Munich: Bruckmann, 1999), 109.
[94] Adorno and Metzger, 'Disput', 92.
[95] Ibid., 96. Metzger may have been right in his thinking that, in 'Das Altern der Neuen Musik', the name Boulez stood for someone else. Where he was probably wrong was in thinking that it was Goeyvaerts. If anyone, when Adorno said 'central figures' and named Scherchen, he was probably indicating a figure of the older generation who was nevertheless a composer with institutional 'clout'. It is far from implausible to think that Adorno really *meant* to carry on his dispute with Eimert, without realising that this might actually draw him into an entirely different argument.

Metzger (indeed, simply knowing less post-war music), but Metzger's response, that this or that piece was unrepresentative of his general argument, did not convince. Nevertheless, Adorno conceded that, in the case of the most recent music of Stockhausen and Boulez, Webern was really no longer a factor, even if he remained far from convinced that other unnamed (apart from Berio) young composers had managed to move much beyond Goeyvaerts.[96] In truth, even by the close of the discussion, it was to Goeyvaerts that Adorno again returned, though he did come closer to describing the problem he had had in 1951. The question he wanted answered by the young composers – or, more precisely, the question he wanted young composers to be capable of providing an answer to – was absolutely not 'how is this made?'[97] What Adorno wanted to hear was an explanation from a young composer of the ways in which constellations of meaningfulness accreted to the music they had written, what was meaningful within the context of an (organic) whole, on the basis of the final, written product. How the composer had reached that product was, from Adorno's perspective, fundamentally an irrelevance, and if that was all a composer could say about his or her music, then it probably was the product of mechanistic, crudely objectivist thinking. Metzger could do little more than assure Adorno that neither Boulez nor Stockhausen could be held to be subject to his critique, and, indeed, by the second printing of *Dissonanzen* in 1958, Adorno had added a new foreword which explicitly excepted *Le Marteau sans maître* and *Zeitmasse* from attack, though, as I outline in further detail below, hardly to Metzger's satisfaction.

If Metzger had expected that his conversation with Adorno might have shifted the older thinker's position markedly, he must have been disappointed to hear the 'Criteria of the New Music' that Adorno outlined at Darmstadt in 1957. For all that 'criteria' would not have gone far enough for either Metzger or for the young Darmstadt generation, there was at least a humour that had not been present in 'Das Altern der Neuen Musik':

> Reflection has even become an integral feature of the practice of the composer. Whatever is right for the physicist, who reflects on energy, matter, and causality, must be perfectly proper for the musician too. To complain about this and to bewail the loss of the old naïveté will not do [...] Anyone who has not yet lost his musical virginity cannot be wished anything better than that he should lose it as quickly as possible.[98]

---

[96] Ibid., 101. [97] Ibid., 103.
[98] Theodor W. Adorno, 'Criteria of New Music' [1957], in *Sound Figures*, tr. Rodney Livingstone (Stanford University Press, 1999), 145–6. Adorno's original text may be found as 'Kriterien der neuen Musik' [1957], in 'Klangfiguren', *Gesammelte Schriften*, ed. Rolf Tiedemann, vol. XVI: *Musikalische Schriften I–III* (Frankfurt am Main: Suhrkamp, 1978), 170–228.

Moreover, Adorno would confess that his earlier reliance on the 'given language of music' (by which he meant, not least, the categories of antecedent and consequent, just as much as he meant tonic and dominant) 'stands in need of reappraisal [...] It is not simply that traditional tonality has gone out of fashion and that anyone who considers himself up to date would be embarrassed to compose using such methods. The fact is, these methods have become objectively false.'[99] Adorno would go further and even, to a limited extent, correct his question to Goeyvaerts:

> If, when confronted by a self-evidently senseless constructivist composition, one asks the composer to explain where the antecedent and where the consequent are in a particular phrase, or what the logical function of each note is, he will answer with talk about some parallel or other between pitch levels, volumes, lengths, timbres, and the like, all of which remain external to the flow of the music and are unable to create meaning as long as they fail to articulate the musical phenomenon itself. But to call composers to account in this way is unfair because musical meaning today can probably no longer be readily captured in concepts such as antecedent and consequent that arise indirectly from particular kinds of musical material.[100]

Adorno, it seemed, was prepared to confess that he had experienced a certain loss of innocence, and was aware that there was a 'cultural lag' between the production of music and its reception (by Adorno himself not least) which had an impact on the critic's ability to make judgements upon that music,[101] such that it would be mere 'poetic wish-fulfillment' to think that one could make an assessment of contemporary music in the same way as one might judge Wagner.[102] Adorno stressed that singular, totalising judgements of the state of affairs were probably naïve, since

> [t]he present variety, however, is not one of comparable but diverse products on a single plane, but one of disparate objects. It owes its existence to inconsistency. Some composers simply press on from all sides with the innovations implicit in the state of the musical material, without leaving any preexisting 'parameters' in place, while others merely tackle one particular sector, leaving the others untouched, as if nothing else had changed.[103]

For all this much more finely nuanced, rather self-deprecating commentary, however, Adorno rapidly came to the point, and it was a familiar one. Though it had been erroneous to look for traditional categories in the new 'new music', it was vital that the moves away from such categories went beyond a technocratic obsession with constructivist, scientistic models,

---

[99] Adorno, 'Criteria', 147. [100] Ibid., 159–60. [101] Ibid., 149. [102] Ibid., 163.
[103] Ibid., 151.

which were essentially blind to musical meaningfulness.[104] Though this was not so far away from Adorno's earlier criticism that, without traditional categories, meaning would not occur, the difference here was that he had accepted that meaning *might* occur, while the composers who had created that meaning had yet come to terms with what sorts of meanings those might be. This was the contradiction that Adorno had found in the new music of post-war serialism – the point at which the aesthetic and the technical collided – and it was in this, construed as a dialectical opposition, that a fruitful path forward might be found.[105] However, it was to Metzger that Adorno turned. Metzger had, so he seemed to think, found a way of articulating the precise way in which an autonomous art would hold up the mirror to society, to the culture industry, that Adorno had demanded:

> The fact that works of art once had a purpose, social or liturgical, is something that today, when listening with a musician's ear, we must force ourselves to call laboriously to mind, a memory that is historical only in a dubious sense. Ever since art broke free from the service of rulers, legitimate works have ceased to pursue any very obvious goal external to themselves, and this necessarily has repercussions in their internal technical composition: there is no longer any distinction between articulation and what is articulated, between representation and what is represented. It may well be that art no longer has a purpose, and even that its meaning is its purpose. In fact, no one can say any longer with any assurance what art really is about. All the more anachronistic is the question of the relation between ends and means in its inner technical makeup. But does not its freedom – *l'art pour l'art* – point to its determinate antithesis to society?[106]

For Adorno, such a suggestion – relying as he saw it on a one-to-one correspondence between artistic ends and means – was a massive oversimplification.[107] Nevertheless, the idea continued to preoccupy Adorno, even if he would never accept it, writing in *Aesthetic Theory* that '[t]he claim that there is no difference between articulation and the articulated, between immanent form and content, is seductive as an apology for modern art, but it is scarcely tenable.' His judgement here remained the same as it had been since 1951: 'technological analysis does not grasp the spirit of a work even when this analysis is more than a crude reduction to elements and also emphasizes the artwork's content and its coherence as well as its real or putative initial constituents'.[108] To pursue this argument through to its logical conclusion, Adorno opined that 'Metzger would have to subscribe to a full-blooded relativism of the kind that he and the Darmstadt school

---

[104] Ibid., 155. [105] Ibid., 157. [106] Ibid., 165–6. [107] Ibid., 166.
[108] Theodor W. Adorno, *Aesthetic Theory*, tr. Robert Hullot-Kentor (London: Athlone, 1999 [1970]), 89.

have every reason to reject', making a concrete use of the term 'Darmstadt School' a few days *before* Nono's use of the expression, which was often regarded as foundational.[109] For Adorno, theory (and compositional theory too) had to move beyond technical description of the distribution of row forms in order to be more than a more-or-less accurate description 'of what happens in the conscious and subconscious mind of the artist'.[110]

By the publication of Metzger's 'Das Altern der Philosophie der Neuen Musik' – in German in 1958 and in English in 1960 – the debate had moved on some way. In limited fashion, Adorno had given ground to Metzger's view, now exempting certain pieces by Boulez and Stockhausen from his own critique. Nevertheless, Adorno still felt that something was wrong with the way in which this music was being received, even if he could not pin such problems down to any obvious factor in the immanent musical surface. But Adorno's rethink had not gone far enough for the editors of *Die Reihe*. Having styled Metzger's essay 'Intermezzo I', they followed it with 'Intermezzo II', a title almost certainly from the hand of Eimert himself, although he did not sign it.[111] This is no measured, carefully articulated response. In it quotations from Adorno's 'Das Altern der Neuen Musik' are directly juxtaposed with remarks by Hellmut Kotschenreuther, which disparaged Schoenberg's work. If Kotschenreuther's attitude was one which might be considered a *Blut und Boden* mentality, and Eimert suggested that it certainly could be, then the way in which Adorno's remarks on the new music were framed suggested to Eimert that his critique was little different. As Eimert understood it, Adorno's defence of himself was truly unjustifiable – 'anyone who contradicts him is employing the "thought-control practised in totalitarian societies"' – but the degree to which Adorno's own writing here is re-contextualised as being, broadly, fascistic (hence Eimert's reference to *Blut und Boden*) is surely vicious, not least in Eimert's suggestion that '[o]ne can also read differently – and this is often still more informative – not juxtaposing but regarding the quotations from Kotschenreuther as continuations of the ones from Adorno, as if they came from the pen of the same author.'[112] Adorno's remarks are, in case there were any ambiguity, those shown in the left-hand column below. A few brief examples will probably suffice to give the flavour of what Eimert made Adorno seem to have said:

---

[109] Adorno, 'Criteria', 166. It is possible that Adorno placed the reference to the Darmstadt School into the essay when revising it for publication, although he was not, in broad terms, given to lengthy reworkings of extant texts (and the dedication to Steuermann, July 1957, is suggestive, if gently so, that the text is probably very close to what Adorno actually said at Darmstadt).
[110] Ibid., 167.
[111] This, at least, was Metzger's claim (Heinz-Klaus Metzger, 'Zur Verdeutlichung einer Polemik und ihres Gegestandes' [*ca.* 1958], in *Musik wozu*, 107).
[112] Herbert Eimert, 'Intermezzo II' [1958], *Die Reihe*, vol. 4 (1960), 81.

The confections of serial engineers	Technological processes are made into ideological idols.
The cult of consistency ends in the worshipping of idols.	Procrustes, the ancestor of all ideologists and violators, has become the model for the angry young man.
In the very first bar the listener realises that he must resign himself to being handed over to an infernal machine, which mercilessly runs its course.	... the twelve-tone order thus instituted is fundamentally foreign to material and music, in fact in many ways it is inimical to music.
They have worked out a sure balance on paper; and it does not work out. They need security so badly that they in fact destroy it.	Their need for security is just like that of the overfed bourgeois, and keeps them on the look-out for techniques of composition that will shelter them.[113]

Although Metzger's 'Clarification of a Polemic and its Subject' was not published at the time he wrote it, in or around 1958, it seems, by Metzger's own account, to have formed the basis of many discussions at Darmstadt specifically, and speaks to a strong dissatisfaction with Adorno and what Metzger saw as Adorno's fundamental failure to have learned from his mistakes and to have got to know some new 'new music'.[114] Metzger returned to Adorno's claim – now seen by Metzger as a rather cheap 'get-out' – that he could not have known significant pieces by Boulez or Stockhausen (or, for that matter, Koenig, Brown, Pousseur, or Feldman) at the point of writing 'Das Altern der Neuen Musik'. Metzger insisted that, by the time of the second printing of *Dissonanzen* in 1958, the situation was quite different, both because the availability of materials had altered radically and because Adorno had been alerted by, not least, Metzger to the fact that there were certainly other musics that he really ought to consider before repeating his erroneous judgement of the serialists. Metzger was evidently infuriated by Adorno's new foreword for *Dissonanzen*'s second printing, mentioned above, which was, presumably, intended to offer an apology of sorts. If it was an apology, however, it was a fairly mean-spirited one:

> In the meantime [which is to say between the broadcast and second printing of *Dissonanzen*] the serial school has created works such as *Le Marteau sans maître* by Boulez and *Zeitmasse* by Stockhausen, which no longer have anything in common with bricolage, which is at the heart of 'aging', and which is foreign to composition. Whether the author's critique has played a part in this most recent tendency is not for him to judge.[115]

[113] Ibid., 82–3. [114] Metzger, 'Zur Verdeutlichung einer Polemik', 105. [115] Ibid., 108.

Metzger was clearly outraged, not least by Adorno's implicit arrogance. In the first place, he noted, the first parts of *Le Marteau sans maître* antedated Adorno's criticism. He may well have felt that Adorno had merely inserted as a passing note just that information which Metzger had communicated to him, while making no attempt to come to terms with (or, indeed, even to experience) the products of 'the most recent tendency'. As Metzger would point out, the idea that, in 1958, either *Le Marteau sans maître* or *Zeitmasse* represented that which was 'most recent' was wholly spurious. From Metzger's perspective – and he was probably not far from the mark here – compositional practice was moving at quite some speed, and Adorno was either unwilling or unable to keep pace with it.

Of those composers who had entered into the debate, Metzger gave a long list of performances that Adorno could have heard both before writing 'Das Altern der Neuen Musik' and before the publication of the second printing of *Dissonanzen*: before the broadcast version of 'Das Altern der Neuen Musik', Metzger noted that Boulez's Second Piano Sonata and the Sonatine for flute and piano had been published, and that Adorno could have heard Boulez's *Polyphonie X* at Donaueschingen in 1951 and Stockhausen's *Kontra-Punkte*, the latter in an unfinished version in Cologne in 1953 and in its final version in Paris in January 1954. He pointed out, too, that the first five Klavierstücke had been performed in Darmstadt in the summer of 1954, and that *Studie I* (1953) had received a performance in Cologne in October of that year. Between the broadcast and the *Dissonanzen* publication, it would have been possible to encounter Stockhausen's *Studie II*, Klavierstücke VI–VIII, and *Gesang der Jünglinge*, and the first book of Boulez's *Structures*, as well as his *Livre pour quatuor* (1948–9), and also Koenig's *Klangfiguren II* and Pousseur's *Quintette à la mémoire de Webern* (1955). Finally, Metzger suggested, David Tudor had been performing representative extracts from the piano music of Cage, Brown, Feldman, and Wolff in his 1956 Darmstadt seminar – an event to which I return in fuller detail below – while Adorno 'was reading the proofs of *Dissonanzen*'.[116] By failing to take advantage of any of these opportunities to come to a closer knowledge of the music, Adorno had shown his lack of desire to give an accurate report of it. Nor was it only the composers that Metzger and Adorno had jointly discussed who seemed significant. Metzger was taken aback that Adorno had not seen fit to mention Herman Van San, Bo Nilsson, or Luigi Nono. The last omission might have seemed the most curious since, especially in Nono's music between 1950 and 1954 – which is to say between the *Variazioni canoniche* and *Liebeslied* – Adorno might

---

[116] Ibid., 109.

have found the closest approximation available to his ideal compositional state, even if, by the time of 'Das Altern der Neuen Musik', Nono had turned to serialism in a fuller form. Metzger would hear nothing from Adorno that might approach a revision of his views until 1961, when Adorno presented 'Vers une musique informelle' at the Ferienkurse. From Metzger's perspective at least, after Cage's arrival at Darmstadt, Adorno was, as another product of the 'cultural lag', several years too late.

Nono and Stockhausen: music, language, and serial technique

The plans for Nono's 1957 presentation, 'Die Entwicklung der Reihentechnik' ('The Development of the Row Technique'), were somewhat haphazard. The topic of Nono's presentation was fixed by 12 February.[117] Earlier than that date, however, Nono had already been approached by Steinecke regarding his developing plans to reproduce presentations from the 1957 courses in book form, the project which would become the *Darmstädter Beiträge zur neuen Musik*. Nono was clearly nervous about providing a contribution, writing to Steinecke: 'For the book: that is difffffffffficult!!! You know I have never written anything! But one has to start some time. Of course, I'll do it for you.'[118] Nono delivered his text to Steinecke on 30 April, in a translation from the Italian by Willi Reich.[119]

If Metzger had taken great pains to argue that Webern now had little to do with any serial procedure worth the name and that strict processual devices were long consigned to past history, he must have been rather dispirited by what Nono had to say. Nono's position constituted precisely the sort of ammunition that Metzger felt Adorno could least be trusted with. Nono had taken a distinct route towards his own version of multiple serialism, from a broadly free use of constructivist elements, in a form redolent not least of the fifteenth-century canons he and Maderna had studied together, towards increased systematisation. His own procedures were distinct from those of Stockhausen and Boulez, neither of whom made use of anything which strongly resembled the 'tecnica degli spostamenti'. Nevertheless, 'Die Entwicklung der Reihentechnik' seems to overflow with the enthusiasm of the late convert (though one might equally well claim that the tone had something to do with Nono's relative inexperience in the construction of written texts).

Broadly, Nono's presentation was a reflection on music presented at Darmstadt. Almost all of the examples he draws on had been performed in 1955: Schoenberg's Variations, op. 31, Boulez's first book of *Structures*,

---

[117] Steinecke to Nono, 12 Febuary 1957, ALN.   [118] Nono to Steinecke, 21 January 1957, ALN.
[119] Nono to Steinecke, 30 April 1957, ALN.

Ex. 2.2 Pitch and rhythm series of Anton Webern, Variations, op. 30

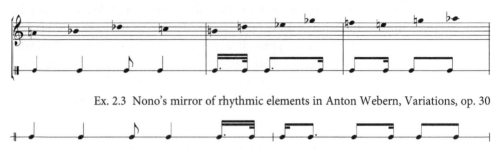

Ex. 2.3 Nono's mirror of rhythmic elements in Anton Webern, Variations, op. 30

his own *Incontri*, and Maderna's *Quartetto per archi in due tempi*. Stockhausen's *Studie I*, which he also mentioned, had not been performed in that year – or at Darmstadt at all – but *Studie II* had. One of his other two examples, Stockhausen's *Zeitmasse*, was integral to the 1957 courses, and his last, Webern's Variations for orchestra, op. 30, had been performed at the 1954 courses. He observed at the close that

> we have consciously restricted ourselves to matters of compositional technique and left the aesthetic out of consideration. This restriction was obvious, to be sure, but here also necessary in order to allow the serial method to emerge sharply in some of its currently developing main features. But it is just as clear that the musical and human results which come from that technical method must be brought into the discussion.[120]

Arguably, this was ultimately a rather weak excuse from the composer who had, only a few years earlier, demanded that discussion of Webern avoid an approach dominated by analytical graphs, since that was precisely the approach that Nono took to both Schoenberg and Webern, and in considerable detail. What was most notable about Nono's description, though, was that it mirrored Stockhausen's in one very precise way: Nono found in both Schoenberg and Webern the image, albeit in a slightly less developed form, of his own rhythmic technique as he had utilised it in the music of the early 1950s. In the case of the Webern op. 30 Variations, Nono proposed that, just as the row itself could be partitioned into three tetrachords made up of minor seconds and thirds, so there were three underlying rhythmic motives (see Example 2.2).

These, when partitioned differently, as a mirror (just as the second hexachord of the row is the retrograde inversion of the first), exhibited similar properties, though the smallest values were doubled, and the largest halved (see Example 2.3).

---

[120] Nono, 'Die Entwicklung der Reihentechnik', 37.

As Nono observed, 'the three rhythmic motives form the rhythmic material for the whole composition. They remain clearly distinguishable even in their variations (through augmentation, diminution, the introduction of fermate), analogous to the three melodic motives into which the row is divided.'[121] The accuracy, or otherwise, of Nono's description of Webern is hardly relevant here; what is significant is the degree to which the procedural (though not strict) treatment of melodic and rhythmic elements is analogous to Nono's own procedures in, for instance, the *Variazioni canoniche*, *Polifonica–Monodia–Ritmica*, or the first Lorca epitaph, despite the fact that Webern had not, at the time, been the model for those pieces.[122] Even though the early press suggestion that Webern was Nono's *Leitfigur* was wrong, Nono himself retrospectively accorded Webern that position.

This starting point was enough to suggest that the work of Schoenberg and Webern had been continued as 'a consequence of the historical development of music' in the music of younger composers. These composers, Nono stated outright, could be termed a 'school of Darmstadt' and could be compared to the Bauhaus of Weimar or of Dessau. In this new music the function of the twelve-tone row had been developed from a thematic element to one determined by the nature of the row itself. The use of the four basic forms (original, inversion, retrograde, and retrograde inversion) was no longer essential in the new music; two rows would suffice (Nono was clearly making reference to his own *Incontri*, where the 'encounter' was precisely that between two parametric structures, though not on the level of pitch), or even just one series (as in *Il canto sospeso*). It was permutation, or transformation, of the row, rather than its literal presentation that was significant now. The results of permutation gave the composer *material*, appropriate for each parameter, out of which the composer 'created' his or her music.[123] It is notable that Nono regarded all of his extant music, including the 'pre-serial' music before *Canti per 13* (1955), as already being a part of the trajectory. Though in retrospect it may be possible to make a division with the composition of *Canti per 13*, it seems likely that Nono saw nothing other than continuity.[124] In this sense, he was insistent that just this part of serial operation – successive serial permutation of the basic series – had been a core part of Bruno Maderna's practice since at least

---

[121] Ibid., 34.
[122] See also Kathryn Bailey, *The Twelve-Note Music of Anton Webern: Old Forms in a New Language* (Cambridge University Press, 1991), 224–7.
[123] Nono, 'Die Entwicklung der Reihentechnik', 34.
[124] It is for this reason that Erika Schaller, for instance, argues that *Canti per 13*, *Incontri*, *Il canto sospeso*, and *Varianti* represent the 'second phase' of Nono's serial compositional work (Erika Schaller, *Klang und Zahl: Luigi Nono, serielles Komponieren zwischen 1955 und 1959* (Saarbrücken: Pfau, 1997), 34–129).

the *Due studi per il 'Prozess' di Kafka* (1950). Whether Nono intended to suggest that this gave a sort of seniority to his and Maderna's procedures or to bring them 'into line' with Boulez and Stockhausen's music of the early 1950s is hardly clear from this throwaway comment. Nevertheless, it was important to Nono to stress that Maderna had been operating in ways like those of Boulez and Stockhausen at least at early as they had.

From Boulez, Nono perhaps unsurprisingly took *Structures* as his model, it seeming no less of a textbook example to him than it would to Ligeti a year later. Nono's conception of what Boulez had done in *Structure Ia*, in any case, seems much less fully developed than what Ligeti would later propose. While Nono correctly deduced the relationship between the transpositions of the tone rows – which is to say that the original row determined the first pitch of each successive entry of the inversion, and vice versa – he did not, it seems, reach the magic square construction that Ligeti would later produce and was, thus, much more vague on how durational values were determined, even if he was aware of the rhythmic series. Nor did he say anything on the subject of the control of dynamics or of mode of attack in *Structure Ia*.[125] In essence, Nono showed here quite clearly that the young composers associated with Darmstadt were not really aware in any detailed way of the work of one another, a criticism he would later level at Stockhausen's claims of certain levels of serial control in *Il canto sospeso*, as I mention below. Any proposal of unity of purpose amongst them, even from the composerly camp, was founded more in assertion than it was in understanding.

Turning to Maderna, Nono was scarcely more detailed. His description of Maderna's *Quartetto per archi in due tempi* is broadly accurate – 'the material is determined by the successive permutation of the basic row with register and duration determined afterwards', and the second movement is essentially a retrograde, in structural terms, of the first – but provides little information regarding *how* Maderna's rhythmic processes functioned, determined as they were, almost uniquely in Maderna's output, by a durational series. Nono's claim that Maderna's generation of durations via the insertion of pauses and the variation of longer durations might represent a 'new compositional element' seems rather undermined by his own outlining of Webern's procedures only a little earlier in his presentation, and his use of the *Quartetto per archi in due tempi* as a paradigmatic example of Maderna's compositional practice is disingenuous, since nowhere else was he quite so pre-determined in his working. One might well feel that Nono was doing his best to bring Maderna into a serial fold where he had no place. This same approach to permutation as a generational device characterised his

---

[125] Nono, 'Die Entwicklung der Reihentechnik', 35.

description of Stockhausen's *Studie I*, which attempted to show how, in the electronic domain, permutational characteristics might be applied to precise overtone frequencies. His description was, principally, literal (though unreferenced) quotation from Stockhausen's own description of *Studie I*, which must, therefore, have been known to him.[126] His description of *Zeitmasse* also took the form of an extended quotation, though this time an acknowledged one, from Stockhausen's own description of the way in which twelve gradations of tempo might operate, similarly, as an additional parameter.

In terms of his own *Incontri*, Nono was yet more vague, though his claims are essentially accurate. Here, he said, the basic row remained unchanged throughout in terms of pitch, while the rows for duration and dynamics underwent successive permutation. While this may be fundamentally true, Nono said nothing of the two structures which guided the disposition of these materials and represented the 'encounters' of the title.[127] Nevertheless, across the course of the presentation, Nono had argued at least four things: first, each of the composers he mentioned thought in terms of parameters, and those parameters were capable of being treated independently of one another at some points; second, those parameters included, but were not restricted to, pitch, duration, dynamic, attack, and tempo; third, not every piece would necessarily dictate *all* parameters; fourth, it was not relevant whether the parameters had anything very much to do with the number twelve: they were determined on their own terms, in reference to the particular parameter under discussion.

The point was probably not to provide analytical detail in any case, even if, in the examples he drew from Schoenberg and Webern, Nono's presentation was heavily weighted in that direction. More importantly, Nono stated outright that there were commonalities of approach between his own work and that of Boulez, Maderna, and Stockhausen, implying that the impression that the press had been developing was fundamentally an accurate one. It is important to note, too, that Nono looked only to these four composers – Boulez, Maderna, Stockhausen, and himself – in his own conception of the 'Darmstadt School'. Goeyvaerts was long forgotten, if Nono had ever given him much thought. Nor was Pousseur mentioned in this context, the insistence upon 1950 as Maderna's 'start date' again suggesting that it was vital for a composer to have 'been there at the beginning', as it were, in order to qualify. Nevertheless, it would not be true to say that Nono really established the idea of the 'Darmstadt School'

---

[126] Karlheinz Stockhausen, 'Komposition 1953 Nr. 2: Studie I, Analyse', in *Texte*, ed. Dieter Schnebel, vol. II (Cologne: DuMont, 1964), 23–36; originally published in *Technische Hausmitteilungen des nordwestdeutschen Rundfunks*, vol. 6 (1954).

[127] Nono, 'Die Entwicklung der Reihentechnik', 36.

here. He did little more than to agree with the prevailing belief that the composers might be thought of as some sort of group, which had been growing in prominence since 1953 and had reached a sort of consensus by 1955, even if Nono must have been aware that linking Boulez with Darmstadt was something of a spurious notion.

However, only a few days after Nono had come out in favour of the idea of the so-called 'Darmstadt School', Stockhausen had already given a presentation which suggested starkly that there might not have been so much unity as Nono seemingly hoped for. Stockhausen delivered his lecture, 'Musik und Sprache' ('Music and Language'), on the evening of 25 July 1957, when it was sandwiched in the lecture programme between Boulez's 'Alea' (on which more follows below in Part II) and the third of Adorno's 'Criteria' lectures.

Late in the previous year, Stockhausen had, in fact, thought to speak on a quite different subject. He wrote to Steinecke on 20 December 1956 that he had had his greatest success to date with performances of *Zeitmasse* and *Gesang der Jünglinge*. Alongside the demand that *Zeitmasse* 'must be played in Darmstadt' (and a hope that David Tudor would perform Klavierstück XI (1956)), Stockhausen proposed that an extension of the essay he had recently completed for *Die Reihe*, '... wie die Zeit vergeht ...',[128] might form the focus of seminars on 'Time-Composition'. He also proposed that an evening concert might be devoted to two performances of *Gesang der Jünglinge*.[129]

With all of this Steinecke was broadly in agreement. There were, though, several notable points in his reply to Stockhausen. First, Steinecke observed to Stockhausen, 'as you know, I want to develop that which we previously called a "working group" for young composers into a forum in which each of you (Nono, Boulez, and you) hold your own, individual seminars'.[130] This was not necessarily so radical a change as all that – in 1956, Boulez, Maderna, and Tudor had all run independent sessions for the 'working group' rather than operating in common as Boulez, Henze, and Maderna had in 1955, and as Maderna and Giselher Klebe had in 1954 – but what it did suggest was that in Steinecke's mind, there were reasons to separate Boulez, Nono, and Stockhausen. The potential reasons for this are legion and need not indicate any suggestion that Steinecke suspected any parting of the aesthetic ways. Steinecke may have wanted simply to get more 'bang for his buck', and having individual sessions from each of the young

---

[128] Karlheinz Stockhausen, '... wie die Zeit vergeht ...', *Die Reihe*, vol. 3 (1957), 13–42.
[129] Stockhausen to Hella and Wolfgang Steinecke, 20 December 1956, in Misch and Bandur (eds.), *Karlheinz Stockhausen bei den Internationalen Ferienkursen*, 136.
[130] Steinecke to Stockhausen, 19 February 1957, in ibid., 158.

composers would have achieved that; equally, he may have felt that this move was one which was only appropriate, in line with moving the younger composers into more 'senior' spots where they would be ready to take over from the likes of Fortner, Heiß, Krenek, and Leibowitz. It is worth remembering in this respect that Fortner, who was scheduled to lead the composition courses in 1957, was ultimately prevented by illness from attending.[131]

In this sense, 1957 became something of a test case to see whether the young firebrands could hold their own. Nevertheless, it is the case that, as Nono was seeking commonality, Steinecke was, like Stockhausen, looking to differentiate. It is notable, too, that one of the results that Steinecke seems to have expected from the separation was that the younger composers would examine music by 'elder statesmen' in their specialist areas, in order to show problems with which they were themselves concerned: Nono might consider Schoenberg, while Boulez might look to Webern. The distinctions between these starting points were clear even at the time, to Steinecke at least. In the end, Boulez did not attend the courses, for reasons which are detailed in Part II below. Nono, though, did offer seminars on Schoenberg, while Scherchen and Pousseur divided the sessions on Webern between them. In case there were any thought that the talk was *exclusively* of the Second Viennese School, it should be added that the Hungarian composer Sándor Jemnitz, himself a former Schoenberg student, offered sessions on the construction of melody in Bartók.

The second notable issue which arose in Steinecke's reply was a request that Stockhausen might provide analyses of more recent music than was to be considered by Nono or Boulez (Stockhausen replied on 20 Februrary that he would look at Boulez's *Structures* and *Le Marteau sans maître* and Nono's *Il canto sospeso*, as well as his own *Gesang der Jünglinge*, *Zeitmasse*, and Klavierstück XI), and might (separately) offer a presentation on 'Musik und Sprache'. Though Stockhausen agreed quickly with the proposed topic, the idea certainly seems to have come from Steinecke.[132]

Third, one of the reasons for Steinecke seeking from Stockhausen a relatively condensed single lecture on a single topic like 'Musik und Sprache' lay in the plans for publication of certain essays from the courses in what would become the *Darmstädter Beiträge*. For the first edition, Steinecke sought up to ten pages, and wanted them by the end of March 1957, which is to say some four months *before* the courses in which they

---

[131] Fortner to Steinecke, 6 July 1957, IMD.
[132] Stockhausen to Steinecke, 20 February 1957, in Misch and Bandur (eds.), *Karlheinz Stockhausen bei den Internationalen Ferienkursen*, 159.

would be presented. Stockhausen, for his part, was a little confused by this, seeking clarification from Steinecke as to whether what was wanted was an essay on the subject of 'Musik und Sprache', or something which dealt with the themes which his seminar at Darmstadt would cover, or both.[133] Steinecke's response was a little clearer, suggesting that what was desired was an *extract* from what Stockhausen would later say in the summer.[134] Stockhausen delivered this promptly, or only a very little late, on 14 April 1957, apologising for having overshot (quite substantially) the ten-page limit.[135] In the end, Stockhausen's promptness was an irrelevance, since anticipated essays from Boulez and Maderna had still not arrived by the end of May 1957, and the projected first volume of the *Darmstädter Beiträge* was ultimately not published until the following year (still without any contribution from Maderna).[136] Regardless of the long wrangling over the publication, the upshot was that Stockhausen's thinking on *Le Marteau sans maître*, *Il canto sospeso*, and *Gesang der Jünglinge* had necessarily crystallised earlier in the year than might have been the case under other circumstances. Stockhausen suggested to Steinecke that, given that he would use only roughly twelve-minute extracts from *Le Marteau sans maître* and *Il canto sospeso*, and since *Gesang der Jünglinge* lasted only a little over thirteen minutes itself, he would need no more than about an hour for the presentation.[137] In the end, it ran to rather closer to two-and-a-half hours.

Part of the reason for this may be found in Stockhausen's delivery of the lecture, which is, in light of a reading of the written text, remarkably impressive. It is clear that Stockhausen was reading from the text that was later published in the *Darmstädter Beiträge*, but at any point in which the written text might be complex to comprehend at a single hearing, Stockhausen not only slowed, but also provided two or three different 'live' paraphrases of what he had said. The content, then, of the live presentation does not differ from the printed version, even though it is significantly longer; the glossed extensions were ways of ensuring comprehension of what Stockhausen had to say. I turn to brief analytical commentary on the three pieces Stockhausen discussed below, but first concentrate

---

[133] Stockhausen to Steinecke, 11 March 1957, in ibid., 160.
[134] Steinecke to Stockhausen, 14 March 1957, in ibid., 163.
[135] Stockhausen to Steinecke, 14 April 1957, in ibid., 165. The published version of 'Musik und Sprache' runs to twenty-five pages in the first volume of the *Darmstädter Beiträge*. Karlheinz Stockhausen, 'Sprache und Musik' [1957], *Darmstädter Beiträge zur neuen Musik*, vol. 1 (1958), 57–81.
[136] Steinecke to Stockhausen, 26 May 1957, in Misch and Bandur (eds.), *Karlheinz Stockhausen bei den Internationalen Ferienkursen*, 167.
[137] Stockhausen to Steinecke, 14 April 1957, in ibid., 166

on the mode of presentation and what Stockhausen implicitly said about the 'state of play' between himself, Boulez, and Nono.

In *Le Marteau sans maître*, as Stockhausen construed the situation, Boulez had come to terms with the problems of setting an extant text to serial music by, in essence, allowing the syntactical sense of the text to dictate the shape of the musical line. Though on the one hand, Stockhausen would state that the verbal and musical articulation were in 'complete agreement', he would, on the other, observe that the example he drew from 'L'Artisant furieux' was typical of the 'support of the formal structure of the text through music'.[138]

Stockhausen claimed that 'the composition of the vocal line thus consistently clarifies the phonological structure of the French text in syllable, word, sentence, and to a large extent also the semantic domain of the words; finally it adheres precisely to the form of the poem'.[139] This was not necessarily to say that Stockhausen was unimpressed by *Le Marteau sans maître*. However, it was clear that, from his perspective, music was subservient here to language, even to the nonsensical (though logically constructed) texts of René Char. The backhandedness of the compliment is clear in his final judgement:

> Since the music of *Le Marteau* is so strongly committed to the text of the poem, bestowing upon it the most elevated form of delivery, it alludes to it particularly strongly: to its form as a poem, to the thoughts which it communicates, to its imagery. To be sure, these poems have no singular meaning in the sense in which spoken information regarding factual data has; precisely here is where their poetic meaning lies: they 'mean' themselves as poems, as forms of high artifice. And Boulez's music clarifies just this meaning outrageously well.[140]

Stockhausen's diagrammatic relationship of the motion between clear semantic meaning and 'musical' meaning in the form of the final movement of *Le Marteau sans maître*, 'Bel edifice et les pressentiments – double', is indeed, as Grant observes, 'almost directly comparable to the levels of semantic clarity he had sketched for his own *Gesange der Jünglinge*'.[141] The similarity is not likely to be coincidental.

Turning to Nono's *Il canto sospeso*, Stockhausen felt he had found a different problem. The texts of *Il canto sospeso*, as is well known, were drawn from letters written by European resistance fighters who had been sentenced to be executed. The text used for the fifth movement is representative: 'If the sky were paper, and all the seas of the world were ink, I could not describe my suffering and all that I see around me. I say goodbye to all of you and

---

[138] Stockhausen, 'Sprache und Musik', 60.   [139] Ibid., 61.   [140] Ibid., 64–5.
[141] Grant, *Serial Music, Serial Aesthetics*, 201.

weep.' Where in *Le Marteau sans maître* the text had dominated musical construction, and problematically so, from Stockhausen's perspective, here the difficulty was that the texts were fragmented, dispersed across various choral voices. Echoing, though disagreeing with, Eimert's review of the première – that 'Nono does not interpret the words, nor does he cover them up' – Stockhausen opined that:

> In certain movements of the *Canto*, Nono composes the text as if he wanted to withdraw its meaning from a public view, in which it does not belong. The texts have moved the composer deeply; it is not only on musical grounds that he wishes to set them. In parts II, VI, and IX, and in some sections of part III too, he makes sounds, or noises, from language. He does not allow the texts to be declaimed, but rather places them in such an indiscriminately strict and dense musical form that one can no longer understand anything of them when listening. Why, then, texts at all, and why these in particular?[142]

As Stockhausen put it, though one encountered a similar problem in the music of Machaut or Gesualdo, the distinction was that, in those cases, the text was one which had a recognisable, already known liturgical function and meaning.[143] Here, that was not an option, especially not since there was, as well as the serial ordering of pitch, rhythm, and dynamics, a process governing the dispersal of vowels, extracted from the source texts.[144] As Stockhausen queried, '[m]ight he not have been better to have chosen sounds in the first place and not texts laden with meaning of this sort?'[145] For all that Stockhausen's analytical approaches may often have been more detailed and more methodical than Nono's, here he was certainly in error. He may even have been aware of this, since the only one of the three composers who had made endeavours serially to order vowels and consonants was Stockhausen himself, and in that case with a liturgical text. Nono would not respond directly until 1960, in a presentation to which I return in Part II.

As Nielinger notes, it was in precisely this area that Stockhausen had earlier criticised Nono, before Nono had written his first strictly serial piece, *Canti per 13*. A letter from Stockhausen to Nono, dated 9 May 1953, argued that Nono failed to pay sufficient attention to the serial organisation of dynamics and duration.[146] Nevertheless, around Christmas 1956, Nono and Stockhausen were on good, friendly terms. A letter from Nono to Stockhausen about this time signalled not only his respect for

---

[142] Herbert Eimert, 'Uraufführung von Nonos *Canto sospeso* in Köln', *Melos*, vol. 23 (1956), 354; Stockhausen, 'Sprache und Musik', 66–7.
[143] Stockhausen, 'Sprache und Musik', 71. [144] Ibid., 72. [145] Ibid., 67.
[146] Carola Nielinger, '"The Song Unsung": Luigi Nono's *Il canto sospeso*', *Journal of the Royal Musical Association*, vol. 131, no. 1 (2006), 97 n. 65.

Stockhausen's work, but also the degree to which he felt it was important for others to encounter it, asking Stockhausen to come to Venice to present on his work (of particular interest to Nono were *Zeitmasse* and the Klavierstücke).[147] Though Nono may have noted the slight, there was nothing to suggest that anyone else had done so.

When Stockhausen turned to his own *Gesang der Jünglinge*, however, and described the way in which it utilised a recognisable liturgical text, fragmented into vowels and consonants which were serially arranged, across seven divisions as he would later clarify,[148] his meaning should have been clear. At this distance, it is almost impossible to read Stockhausen's presentation as anything other than a direct and literal explanation of why, in technical terms, he was 'ahead' in the development of serial technique, with precise demonstrations of the reasons why his contemporaries had failed to come to terms with the new material as effectively as he had. Nevertheless, at the time, it was Stockhausen's briefer presentation, on 'The New Instrumental Style', delivered between two performances of *Zeitmasse*, that seemed to arouse more interest than anything, in Germany at least.[149] Inge Schlösser's report in the *Darmstädter Echo* speaks to her own seemingly keen interest in Stockhausen himself and in what he had undertaken in regard of *Zeitmasse*:

> There can be no doubt that, this time, Stockhausen was a centre and an originator of discussion. His activities, always energised by new impulses, are themselves able to excite even the listeners who accept his proposals only with reservations [...] In the score [of *Zeitmasse*], which has been conceived with utmost clarity, an individual tempo is given for each instrument [...] The score is not divided up with bar lines. Each player reacts to another, the conductor coordinates the various structural networks at particular points of rest. The effect of the work was fascinating: though in this new instrumental style, in which the performers are engaged in the act of production, it seems likely that every performance can be distinguished from every other.[150]

In light of what follows, Schlösser's note regarding the mutability of possibilities in *Zeitmasse* should be kept in mind.

What was, in any case, absolutely clear from the press response around Darmstadt 1957 was that three names ought to be taken as the

---

[147] Nono to Stockhausen, undated but *ca.* Christmas 1956, in Misch and Bandur (eds.), *Karlheinz Stockhausen bei den Internationalen Ferienkursen*, 137.

[148] Karlheinz Stockhausen, 'Musik und Sprache III' [1957], in *Texte*, vol. II, 61–2.

[149] André Boucourechliev mentioned Stockhausen's 'Musik und Sprache' in his review of the courses for the *Nouvelle revue française* (André Boucourechliev, 'Darmstadt 1957', *Nouvelle revue française*, vol. 5, no. 59 (1957), 972).

[150] Inge Schlösser, 'Der neue Instrumentalstil: Darmstädter Aufführung der "Zeit-Maße" von Karlheinz Stockhausen', *Darmstädter Echo*, 25 July 1957.

representatives of the new compositional generation – Boulez, Nono, and Stockhausen – and that those three were, moreover, 'developing from Webern towards the total organisation of musical materials'.[151] In truth, 1957 is the point at which it becomes possible, for the first time, to see at Darmstadt a discourse which is recognisably, wholly 'Darmstadtian'. Steinecke's report for the Hessischer Rundfunk is characteristic in this respect:

> The second phase of this development [of serial technique] appears in the work of Anton Webern, who no longer uses the twelve-tone row thematically, but rather as a building element, as material. It is in this structural principle that the strongest points of connection lie for the young generation of composers who – according to Nono's model – have introduced a third phase in the development of serial technique, a phase which may be recognised through the way in which the dodecaphonic is expanded into a serial ordering principle that includes not only melody and harmony, but also the other musical categories. The ghost of total organisation and of mechanisation, which lurks in this development, has been painted often enough in black colours in recent years by critics of this newest development. Some have spoken of a dead end, without thinking that development at its most extreme points never goes forward with a broad front, but rather a new, legitimate relationship between fixity and freedom must be won on a narrow route.[152]

What is vital to take from this is an understanding that, if one can speak of a recognisable 'Darmstadt School' on the discursive level in 1957, one cannot do the same on a technical level. As Steinecke rightly observed (though perhaps he did not mean anything quite so specific), the development was not a broad one: Boulez's total serial 'moment' occurred with *Structure Ia* in 1952, and with Nono it took until *Canti per 13* in 1955 for him to construct a piece which could genuinely be considered serial in a procedural way. At any particular point in the 1950s, the leading composers of the 'Darmstadt generation' operated on the technical level in ways often wholly distinct from one another, and fully pre-determined pieces of textbook multiple serialism are rare indeed.

It was probably not procedure which seemed most pertinent to Stockhausen as defining what it would mean to be serial, even if that which unified the serial procedures of the Darmstadt composers was relatively limited. In each of the three pieces Stockhausen discussed, there was a

---

[151] Wolf-Eberhard von Lewinski, 'Die neueste Musik von Kranichstein: Bericht von den Internationalen Kranichsteiner Ferienkursen für Neue Musik Darmstadt, Juli 1957', broadcast, Radio Audizioni Italiane, date unknown, transcript IMD.
[152] Wolfgang Steinecke, 'Webern und die junge Generation', broadcast, Hessischer Rundfunk, 24 October 1957, transcript IMD.

common thread, but it was to do with a certain conception of material, and not with process. The only linking characteristic between the three pieces was that the material for the different parameters could be created independently of one another; 'serialism' in this sense was closer to having a definition than it might have been at the start of the 1950s when, if the composers under discussion here had to be unified under some sort of technical rubric, it could be no more specific than that they all treated precompositional material in more or less deterministic fashion. Even so, this meant nothing more than that there was a potential decoupling of the treatment of parameters (representing a reversal, of sorts, of the unities of parameters by which, for instance, Goeyvaerts created his 'synthetic number').

The differences between the composers remained greater than the similarities, continuing the impression that, whatever the press might think, a generalised serial aesthetic, if it existed, could not be grounded in technical procedure. Stockhausen's treatment of individual parameters was, according to the account of Decroupet and Ungeheuer, rigorous, but divided his parameters into seven elements each.[153] Nono and Boulez began from twelve-tone series in *Il canto sospeso* and *Le Marteau sans maître* respectively. However, Boulez created five different chordal 'spellings' of the series, through the rotation of the proportional number series 2-4-2-1-3 (a manoeuvre reminiscent of Nono's permutations of rhythm in *Polifonica–Monodia–Ritmica*). Each of these derivations, then, contains five different groups (such that there is a five-by-five grid of pitch materials). Yet Boulez went further, 'multiplying' each element of the grid by every other element. A simple example of this might be that when the dyad F–E♭ (0–10) is multiplied by itself, this means the creation of another dyad, based on E♭, which has the same interval characteristic as the original: a minor seventh from E♭ thus generates D♭. The multiplication of this dyad with itself, then, generates the trichord F–E♭–D♭. In doing this Boulez generated core material, which he termed domains, in which he could move freely. As the example shown here demonstrates, there was no reason to expect that any domain would contain all twelve pitch classes (and few did), nor was there any reason to place the pitches of a domain in a particular order.[154] In simple terms, it was just this re-found flexibility that enabled Boulez to follow the shape of the poetic line so accurately, and thus the loosening of stricture in precisely this way was what enabled Stockhausen to make his critique.

---

[153] See Pascal Decroupet and Elena Ungeheuer, 'Through the Sensory Looking Glass: The Aesthetic and Serial Foundations of *Gesang der Jünglinge*', tr. Jerome Kohl, *Perspectives of New Music*, vol. 36, no. 1 (Winter 1998), 97–142.

[154] See Koblyakov, *Pierre Boulez*.

Even with an understanding of the underlying devices which help to structure *Le Marteau sans maître*, surely Whittall's observation that '[t]he question inevitably arises: is this music serial at all?' takes on an additional significance.[155] There are serial processes at work here, but they operate in the background, and Boulez acts on them to such a degree, transforming them out of all recognition, that arguably it is not of great significance that the pre-compositional work was serial. The compositional work 'proper' is not serial, and it is here, not in the preparatory work, that *Le Marteau sans maître* takes on its own particular character. Doubtless *Le Marteau sans maître* is potentially *implied* by Boulez's material-generation procedures, but it is only one of a truly vast multiplicity of pieces that Boulez might have chosen following those procedures. There is no sense at all in which the pre-compositional work pre-determines the shape of *Le Marteau sans maître*, except in the most banal of ways.

In *Il canto sospeso*, Nono had developed the 'technica degli spostamenti' a little further than could be found in Maderna's *Musica su due dimensioni*. Here, Nono had constructed magic squares (themselves twelve-by-twelve grids, and therefore effectively 'twelve-tone' from a parametric point of view) to control the entries of series. To oversimplify a little, Nono had created a background series to control the entries of foreground series. The point of this, though, was probably not the control mechanism itself, but a way of mediating between 'strict' stasis and simultaneous flexibility on the surface. Indeed, this background series ensures that the order in which pitches appear in *Il canto sospeso* do not necessarily suggest a twelve-tone row at all. This is to say that, in many movements of *Il canto sospeso*, Nono, like Boulez, uses a particular sort of systematisation to generate a freedom from twelve-tone ordering.[156] Nono's own style of multiple serialism was such that it might be argued that his interest was truly in subverting multiple serialism, turning it against itself to create something seemingly irrational, through rational means. Nono's own statement – that 'it was a real pleasure for me to try to distort systems and systematic elements entirely' – is certainly suggestive of this.[157]

Maderna was now, for the most part, forgotten as a composer, even if Nono attempted to include him; on the other hand, even in his absence (and even if he himself were not all that much concerned with Darmstadt), there was no forgetting that Boulez was a major figure.[158] For all that, Lewinski at least was

---

[155] Whittall, *Serialism*, 178.   [156] See Nielinger, '"The Song Unsung"'.
[157] Nono, 'Un'autobiografia dell'autore', 510.
[158] Even in an expanded view of who might be one of the 'Darmstädter', Maderna remained forgotten: Franz Willnauer suggested that Stockhausen, Boulez, Nono, Pousseur, and Luciano Berio might represent the important names from his perspective. Franz Willnauer, 'Heute: Die "Darmstädter Schule"', *Die Furche*, 7 September 1957.

well aware that any progress towards total organisation (notably not yet achieved in his view) was tempered by the burgeoning interest in chance operations. Elsewhere, Lewinski would observe (or at least his sub-editor would) that 'with the 1957 Kranichsteiner Ferienkurse, a new phase began'.[159]

With the very year in which the 'Darmstadt School' could be spoken of as a 'real' entity, there were already signs perceivable that some members of the new music community gathered there were abandoning serial control, such as it was, in favour of chance operations, although arguably Stockhausen had long viewed statistical procedures as being aleatoric ones, too. Whether the 'Darmstadt School' had any real existence or was largely a fiction of the press, no sooner had it been formalised than it was already in the process of dispersal. Even if the 'Darmstadt School' had meant anything very much as a concept, its life was an exceptionally brief one, at most from 1955 to 1957, and realistically rather shorter than that. If the motion towards chance was one of the reasons for the collapse of the idea, however, its origins were already entering the European discourse earlier, with the arrival of John Cage and David Tudor on the European stage in 1954. In 1958, Cage would arrive at Darmstadt in person. Following this event, any sense of unity amongst the leading participants would be destroyed, as Cage became a figurehead (or, perhaps better, a totem) for precisely the issues which had lain dormant over the past years at Darmstadt but were already beginning to become evident in, not least, Stockhausen's backhanded analyses of serial procedures in *Le Marteau sans maître* and *Il canto sospeso* in comparison with his own work. It took several years for the 'Darmstadt School' to become a recognisable entity, even if it was largely an invention of Eimert and the press. Its fall would be much more rapid. Only two years after it was named, it was clear to everyone involved that it no longer existed if, indeed, it ever had.

---

[159] Wolf-Eberhard von Lewinski, 'Absage an das Idol des Musik-Ingenieurs: Mit den Kranichsteiner Ferienkursen 1957 begann eine neue Phase', *Darmstädter Tagblatt*, 3 August 1957.

Excursus

October 1954, Donaueschingen and Cologne

1954 could have been the year in which Cage came to Darmstadt, having aimed at securing an invitation to the courses in that year, to add to engagements at the Nordwestdeutscher Rundfunk and at Heinrich Strobel's Donaueschinger Musiktage. Yet it was, in part at least, because of such prior agreements that Cage was unable to visit Darmstadt in 1954.

Cage had already excited some interest in Germany, specifically in the minds of Eimert and Stockhausen, through the auspices of Boulez. Boulez wrote to Cage on 1 October 1952:

> Cologne Radio must have written to you (NWDR-Köln); for I spoke to them about you and passed on your records, which they copied. They want to put on a two-hour broadcast about your music and would like some recent recordings and some explanatory notes or things you have written [. . .] If you could send them a recording of your *Music of Changes*, they would be overjoyed. I think it was Stockhausen who wrote to you. He is a young German composer, most remarkable.[1]

Cage may have been able to provide little more to Stockhausen and Eimert than Boulez already had done, since it seems that Eimert's broadcast – the first in Germany of Cage's music – probably included music for prepared piano and the first two *Constructions* (1939, 1940). If the prepared piano was represented by *A Book of Music* (1944), then what Boulez delivered in 1952 was essentially the same music that he would later give to Rebner for his 1954 lecture at Darmstadt, on which more follows below. It was not long after Boulez's letter to Cage informing him of the prospect, on 27 November 1952, that Eimert's broadcast went out as part of the 'Nachtprogramm'. As was the norm with the 'Nachtprogramm', there was an educational element (of sorts), which ran alongside the aim to expose listeners to the sounds of the new music.[2] It was there that the impression that Darmstadt-style serialism was a consequence of devotion to Webern had been most strongly emphasised; Beal is no less right that 'Eimert's portrait of Cage established a view of American music that would come to dominate Germany's reception

---

[1] Boulez to Cage, 1 October 1952, in Nattiez (ed.), *The Boulez–Cage Correspondence*, 134.
[2] For further information see Amy C. Beal, 'The Army, the Airwaves, and the Avant-Garde: American Classical Music in Postwar West Germany', *American Music*, vol. 21, no. 4 (Winter 2003), 483–7.

Excursus: October 1954, Donaueschingen and Cologne 157

of it: he highlighted its rash departure from European tradition and assumed it could sprout only from a place unburdened by – to use Eimert's provocative phrase – "holy eternal criteria of value".[3] While it would overstate the truth of the situation to claim that Eimert intentionally set up a particular image of Cage and a particular conception of a post-Webern 'school' of composers with any expectation that those versions would persist influentially, it is notable that key formative descriptions of compositional activity both at Darmstadt and at New York, which were subsequently rehearsed in the reception more generally of each, came from Eimert's pen.

The interest was, in any case, mutual, even if, in Cage's dire financial situation at the beginning of the 1950s, his own reasons for looking to Europe surely lay substantially in his expectation of it as an almost literal lifeline. Nevertheless, it seems that it was the Europeans who reached out first. Heinrich Strobel wrote to Wladimir Vogel on 12 November 1953: 'Our mutual friend [Rolf] Liebermann tells me that you might have John Cage's address. I'd be grateful if you could let me have it in the next few days.'[4] Twelve days later, Strobel had his reply: 'I'd guess that John Cage is staying with Merce Cunningham at 12 East 17th Str – Cunningham is an extremely highly gifted modern dancer and works with Boulez, Feldman and Cage. He dances to electronic music with his group and is probably at work with Cage right now.'[5]

Shortly afterwards, Strobel wrote to Cage directly to advise him that he had 'long held the desire to present your experiments at this [Donaueschingen], the most advanced music festival in Europe'.[6] Strobel proposed to Cage a single concert, to last three-quarters of an hour, adding that the resources of the Donaueschingen festival were such that it would be important that Cage be in Europe in any case since the payment of travel expenses from North America was probably out of the question, though he noted that a reasonable honorarium, by European standards at least, could probably be achieved. Strobel closed by suggesting to Cage that, if the idea of a Donaueschingen performance interested him in principle, he would welcome any concrete suggestion that Cage cared to make.[7] Cage's suggestions were extravagant (and declined by Strobel, who suggested that Cage may have misunderstood Donaueschingen in terms of both resources and

---

[3] Beal, *New Music, New Allies*, 57.
[4] Heinrich Strobel to Wladimir Vogel, 12 November 1953, in Gisela Nauck, *Risiko des kühnen Experiments: Der Rundfunk als Impulsgeber und Mäzen* (Saarbrücken: Pfau, 2004), 187.
[5] Vogel to Strobel, 24 November 1953, in ibid., 187.
[6] See ibid., 189, and Beal, 'The Army, the Airwaves, and the Avant-Garde', 491.
[7] Strobel to Cage, undated but probably early January 1954, in Nauck, *Risiko des kühnen Experiments*, 189.

scale): three concerts, one of piano music, one of tape music, and one of orchestral music, which would have showcased the music not only of Cage, but also of Brown, Feldman, and Wolff. In the end, the compromises were almost entirely on Cage's side: the resulting programme was a two-piano concert lasting an hour, Strobel demanding of Cage: 'Please, take absolutely into account the length of 60 minutes for your composition. Last year, we had a real scandal at Donaueschingen with a "Musique-concrète"-ballet, just by not respecting the duration of an hour prescribed by us.'[8] Ultimately, Cage and Tudor's anticipated honorarium went to pay their travel expenses. There was also a final condition. Having heard that Cage was investigating the possibilities of concerts with European radio stations, Strobel wrote, 'your contribution to Donaueschingen is possible only if you have neither played on a German radio station nor anywhere else in Germany beforehand. May I ask you to give me your assurance on this?'[9]

Certainly Cage was willing to agree to this stricture. His letter a few days later to Wolfgang Steinecke, hoping for an engagement at Darmstadt, stressed that, now that the date of 17 October was fixed for Cage and Tudor's première European performance, '[o]ne consideration is essential, due to Dr. Strobel's wishes; that is, that no engagement take place before the one at Donaueschingen.'[10] Following that proviso, though, Cage proposed music for piano, or two pianos, from himself, Boulez, Brown, Feldman, and Wolff, or, if desired, music for magnetic tape or even larger forces in a concert to take place at Darmstadt.

Steinecke appears either to have overlooked Cage's letter or to have had little interest in the proposals, since Cage sent a subsequent letter to Steinecke on 8 August 1954 reiterating similar information.[11] Steinecke's reply (promptly written the next day) does not wholly convince in its sincerity:

> Please be so good as to excuse the fact that I have not until now answered your kind letter. Had I had the opportunity to invite you to this year's International Ferienkurse für Neue Musik, I would assuredly have written before. But you mentioned in your letter that you and Mr Tudor will arrive in Germany only in October. Kranichstein is a summer school; in the winter it is merely a music library, although we organise monthly chamber concerts under the auspices of the International Society for Contemporary Music. These though are concerts for which we have hardly any financial support to speak of to pay for an honorarium, such that I cannot venture to invite you here.[12]

---

[8] Strobel to Cage, 21 January 1954, JCC.
[9] Strobel to Cage, 24 March 1954, in Nauck, *Risiko des kühnen Experiments*, 188.
[10] Cage to Steinecke, 30 March 1954, IMD.   [11] Cage to Steinecke, 8 August 1954, IMD.
[12] Steinecke to Cage, 9 August 1954, IMD.

Nevertheless, Steinecke did suggest that, if Cage and Tudor were to stay in Europe beyond their final engagement – which seemed likely at the time, the London concert taking place on 29 October, and the return boat to New York leaving Le Havre on 10 November – Steinecke would try to arrange a recording at the Hessischer Rundfunk in Frankfurt, followed by a performance that evening in Darmstadt for the International Society for Contemporary Music. Steinecke also enclosed a copy of the programme for the Darmstadt courses, noting that, in connection with Wolfgang Rebner's lecture, 'you are represented in the programme, if, sadly, only through recordings'. Cage responded enthusiastically to the possibility of the Hessischer Rundfunk engagement, on 16 August 1954 and again on 24 September 1954, shortly before leaving for Europe from New York. No response was, seemingly, forthcoming. The next correspondence to pass between Cage and Steinecke came from the Darmstadt side, almost four years later, on 8 August 1958. Others showed more interest in Cage and Tudor's tour. In Cage's second letter to Steinecke, he communicated that they had performances arranged in Zürich, Paris, Brussels, Hilversum, London, and, not least, Cologne.

Cage had written to Herbert Eimert, of whom he would have known from the earlier broadcast of his music in 1952, on 13 February 1954, shortly after arrangements for Donaueschingen appeared to have been set in stone, with hopes that something might be arranged in Cologne, in connection with the Studio für Elektronische Musik:

> As you may know all my present work is music for magnetic tape. I shall certainly bring along examples of our work and I hope that my visit will be mutually interesting. I am also writing to ask whether a radio engagement in Köln could be arranged for either Mr Tudor or myself while we are there. Mr Tudor is an extraordinary pianist and plays Boulez's Second Sonata (also the First one), my *Music of Changes* (which you may have seen since I sent a copy to Stockhausen), and many other works by advanced contemporary American composers including Morton Feldman, Christian Wolff, and Earle Brown.[13]

A reply a few weeks later from Eigel Kruttge, then the head of new music for the Nordwestdeutscher Rundfunk, invited Cage to give a performance at the opening of the 1954–5 season of chamber concerts on 8 October. The plan, at that stage, was to present one or two of Cage's pieces for tape alongside the work of Stockhausen, Eimert, and Heiß.[14] The final arrangements were

---

[13] Cage to Eimert, 13 Feburary 1954, in Michael Custodis, *Die soziale Isolation der neuen Musik: Zum Kölner Musikleben nach 1945* (Stuttgart: Franz Steiner, 2004), 106.
[14] Eigel Kruttge to Cage, 9 March 1954, in ibid.

rather different, presumably not least because of Strobel's insistence upon Cage's first performance being at Donaueschingen. Though the programme was divided up, as Kruttge had foreseen, into a first half made up of acoustic chamber music and a second half made up of electronic music ('the first concert performance of purely electronic music'), none of Cage's tape music was performed (nor, for that matter, was any of Heiß's).[15] The first half comprised a duo concert by Cage and Tudor; the second was wholly dominated by the products of the Cologne studio.

Cage and Tudor departed the United States on 2 October 1954, travelling on a Dutch liner, the *Maasdam*, to Le Havre via Cobh and Southampton, and were waved off by Merce Cunningham, M. C. Richards, and Earle and Carolyn Brown. Yet the following day, the *Maasdam* collided with another ship, the *Tofevo*, in thick fog just off the coast of Rhode Island. As Tudor reported the event to Peyser, Cage went 'into a tizzy, screaming "Save the scores!"', since they had with them all the scores by their American colleagues from which they would be performing (and perhaps some European ones too, though surely not any by Stockhausen, as Peyser suggests).[16] Both boats limped back to New York and, after a sit-down protest made by a number of the seafarers who could not afford, in terms of either time or money, to wait for another ship, a KLM plane was chartered to deliver sixty passengers, including Cage and Tudor, to Amsterdam. Cage and Tudor thus arrived in Europe rather earlier than planned and headed to Donaueschingen.[17]

They may, in part, have regretted arriving in Donaueschingen early, and not only because of what had surely been a traumatic experience on the boat (not least one sailing from New York to Cobh and Southampton, the very route, in reverse, of the RMS *Titanic*). Their early arrival gave time for detailed rehearsal of their programme and discussion of its contents with Strobel. In a later interview with Guy Freedman, Cage related his own recollections of these preparations:

> [T]he man in charge of the festival (Heinrich Strobel) was frightened about this music even though he had commissioned it, and he demanded that we give a rehearsal for him and a few others before the public performance. After we played for him, there was a deathly silence, and then he came towards us and said that this music was impossible and could not be presented to the public. The piano piece was 34 minutes long. He said it would have to be shortened, that it simply couldn't be listened to at the original length. We had also brought with us the music of Morton Feldman, Christian Wolff, Earl [*sic*] Brown and my own for magnetic tape, and he found *that* intolerable as well. His reaction

---

[15] Kruttge to Cage, 9 March 1954, in ibid. [16] Peyser, *Boulez*, 106.
[17] David Revill, *The Roaring Silence: John Cage, A Life* (New York: Arcade, 1992), 183.

Excursus: October 1954, Donaueschingen and Cologne

troubled me and I began to feel emotional in the situation. Knowing from experience that I wouldn't work well that way, I said, 'Why don't we simply be silent or separate for thirty minutes or so and then come back together and see if we have a solution for this problem.' What I proposed, and what he accepted, was that we do the first concert as he wished to have it – with all the pieces shortened – and then we would announce to the public that afterwards we would play them as they were intended, at their proper lengths. This satisfied everybody. About one-third of the audience remained for the second full performance.[18]

Strobel was still anxious about what people would make of Cage and Tudor, even after the changes had been made. In his speech, introducing the performance, he described what people were about to hear as a 'demonstration of what is possible and hardly as artistic performances in the true sense of the word'.[19] The piece in particular which horrified Strobel was Cage's *34'46.776"* (1954) (played by Tudor, simultaneously with Cage's own performance of his *31'57.9864"* of 1954). For the concert version, this was indeed shortened to a piece then entitled *12'55.6078"*. The rest of the programme included Christian Wolff's *For Piano II* (1953) and Earle Brown's *Four Systems*, both of which Tudor played on his own, and Morton Feldman's *Intersection 3* (1953), Earle Brown's Octet, and Cage's own *Williams Mix* (1952), all of which were tape pieces. Beal's report of the performance seems to be close to the mark: 'the audience responded with a mixture of shouting, laughter, and general confusion'.[20] This would be much the same reaction which Cage's Darmstadt performances four years later occasioned, though his lectures would certainly modify that response markedly. Beal's commentary notes that several reviews 'compared the performance to a scene from Charlie Chaplin's 1952 film *Limelight*', which 'featured a comic musical performance at a piano by Chaplin and Buster Keaton in tuxedos'.[21] Such a portrayal, too, would continue to dog Cage in the reception of his music and presentations at Darmstadt in 1958. Wolfgang Steinecke's review of the Donaueschingen event regarded the whole thing as 'childish sensationalism'.[22] If Steinecke had had any intention of working on the Hessischer Rundfunk performance, presumably that was now forgotten. It was not only the press that was sceptical. Friedrich Bischoff, the artistic director of the Südwestfunk, wrote to Strobel on 4 November 1954: 'In all seriousness, the question remains [...] could

---

[18] Guy Freedman, 'An Interview with John Cage', December 1976, publication details unknown, JCC.
[19] Nauck, *Risiko des kühnen Experiments*, 188.   [20] Beal, *New Music, New Allies*, 69.
[21] Ibid., 70.
[22] Christopher Shultis, 'Cage and Europe', in David Nicholls (ed.), *The Cambridge Companion to John Cage* (Cambridge University Press, 2002), 31.

experiments like that not have been undertaken with other, less primitive means than those two very likeable people tried out?'[23]

Nevertheless, others were less negative. Hans Curjel's review, published in *Melos*, admitted that Cage had 'not fared well' at Donaueschingen, observing that

> the larger part of the audience reacted negatively, found themselves moved by nothing, and finally allowed the seemingly tedious production to wash over them, more or less bored. The few who were amused by these auguries were stirred by the primitivism with which Cage and Tudor mauled the instruments with sticks and hammers and blew children's whistles here and there.[24]

Curjel insisted, though, that Cage's aim was not to make a scandal or a sensation, drawing attention to his studies with Cowell and Schoenberg to demonstrate his seriousness of purpose. Perhaps most notable in Curjel's review were the links he made with the Europeans. He suggested that the purpose of preparing the piano was, in part at least, to ensure a new start, away from the 'routine' sounds of the piano in its unprepared incarnation. The result was a punctual pitch structure, which was redolent of the sonic structures of Webern. No surprise, then, that Curjel concluded that Cage could be aligned with Boulez, Nono, and Stockhausen as a composer working in the post-Webernian field, even if it would have been impossible to create such a grouping before the Webern evening had concretised Boulez, Nono, and Stockhausen into a single, Webern-influenced entity. In Curjel's terms, even if he could never have thought of the idea of the 'Darmstadt School', Cage would probably have had a reasonable claim to be a member of it in 1954.[25]

In Cologne on 19 October 1954, Cage and Tudor gave a rather different performance. As noted above, the first half included music for piano and prepared piano – Feldman's *Intersection 3* (1953), Wolff's *For Prepared Piano* (1951), Brown's *Perspectives* (1952), and Cage's *23'56.176"* (a further iteration of the shortened versions of *34'46.776"* and *31'57.9864"*) – while the second half comprised electronic music: Stockhausen's *Studie I* and *Studie II*, Eimert's *Glockenspiel* (1953) and *Étude über Tongemische* (1953–4), Goeyvaerts's *Komposition Nr. 5* (1953), Pousseur's *Seismogramme* (1955), and Paul Gredinger's *Formanten I* and *Formanten II* (1954). Cage and Tudor met each of these composers during that part of their tour, later spending two days with Gredinger in Zürich.[26] They probably met Wolfgang Steinecke too, after their 'Musik der Zeit' performance, though there is little reason to suspect that

---

[23] Friedrich Bischoff to Strobel, 4 November 1954, in Nauck, *Risiko des kühnen Experiments*, 188.
[24] Hans Curjel, 'Cage oder das wohlpräparierte Klavier', *Melos*, vol. 22, no. 4 (April 1955), 97–100.
[25] Ibid.   [26] David Tudor to Stockhausen, 8 November 1954, GRI.

his attendance at it altered his initial instincts with regard to what Cage's music represented. Even if the press was broadly unimpressed, Cage and Tudor had begun to develop a strong network of European contacts, and Eimert's broadcast of their Cologne performance on 25 November 1954 gave them a broader exposure.

Cage and Tudor seem to have met with little better response during the rest of their tour, if a letter from Tudor to Stockhausen is any indication. Regarding the Paris performance, Tudor noted: 'We played 17 minutes of the piece for 2 pianos, accompanied by much applause and much booing. Best of all was that before our piece the hall was only 3/4 full, and then was packed to the doors while we played, and again 3/4 full afterward.' Nevertheless, he seemed to feel that they had done some beneficial work, especially with regard to what Pierre Schaeffer had to offer: 'Even the critics remarked that there is a vast gap between our work and Schaeffer. It is obvious that Schaeffer is digging his own grave in Paris – and I hope you will complete the arrangements for his burial in Cologne.'[27] In any case, the meeting with Stockhausen in Cologne appears to have been the most significant of the trip, Tudor claiming that 'it was a great joy to meet and be with you [...] I like your music "the best", and [...] I will devote myself to it and play it wherever possible.'[28]

Regardless of the difficulties, Cage seemed to feel that the tour had been positive as well. He wrote to Kruttge on 3 December that he was particularly pleased to have met Eimert, Stockhausen, Pousseur, Goeyvaerts, and Gredinger, and advised Strobel by a separate letter on the same day that Tudor would shortly give the first performances of Stockhausen's work in America.[29] This performance would take place on 15 December 1954, with the publicity material advertising that Tudor would perform Klavierstücke I–VIII and that, moreover, this would thus represent the world première of Klavierstücke VI–VIII. As well as the Klavierstücke, Cage and Tudor were to play the American première of *34'46.776"* (presumably incorporating *31'57.9864"*). However, what was advertised was certainly not what transpired. A letter from Tudor to Stockhausen suggests that Tudor performed the first five pieces and the eighth and that, though he had hoped to perform the sixth piece, it arrived only the day before the concert, leaving insufficient time for its rehearsal.[30] The reviews of the concert bear striking

---

[27] A similar indifference to Schaeffer may be heard in Cage's letter to Kruttge of 3 December 1954: 'I attempted to let my actual separation from Schaeffer be evident through giving him no information with which to introduce my work.' Quoted in Custodis, *Die soziale Isolation der neuen Musik*, 107.

[28] Tudor to Stockhausen, 8 November 1954, GRI.   [29] Beal, *New Music, New Allies*, 73.

[30] Though the work-list provided by Kurtz gives no première date for Klavierstück VIII, it may be presumed that it was premièred by Tudor at Carl Fischer Hall in New York on 15 December 1954. See Kurtz, *Stockhausen*, 251.

relationships to the responses which the work of Cage had received in Europe, as well as to the European reception of Stockhausen's own work. Tudor quoted from a review by Peggy Glanville-Hicks:

> Where Cage pre-destroys music's material before composing with the rubble, Stockhausen's composition is itself the battle ground for the destruction; a pulverization of the pitch territory is fought like a war on three fronts until not a tone is left standing that bears any logical of expressive relation to any other tone. The gutted ruin presumably is offered as a work of art.[31]

Tudor sent back to Stockhausen the version of the sixth Klavierstück which he had on 3 February 1955, receiving a reply from Stockhausen on 13 March that 'the 6. piece is finished now. It has been changed in many aspects you will see.' Stockhausen also advised Tudor that 'it will be impossible that you play it in April, because I gave the 1st performance to Darmstadt. [Marcelle] Mercenier will play it there in May.'[32] It would not be until 22 April 1957 that Tudor would give another première of Stockhausen's Klavierstücke, this time Klavierstück XI in New York, a performance which was not without ramifications for Darmstadt and the move towards mobile form underway there.

---

[31] Peggy Glanville-Hicks, quoted in Tudor to Stockhausen, 3 Feburary 1954, GRI.
[32] Stockhausen to Tudor, 13 March 1955, in Misch and Bandur (eds.), *Karlheinz Stockhausen bei den Internationalen Ferienkursen*, 101.

PART II

Chance encounters

3 Precursors

Wolfgang Rebner and American experimental music

Even before Donaueschingen, Cage had already come to Darmstadt, in the form of Wolfgang Rebner's 1954 lecture, 'American Experimental Music (with Musical Examples from Charles Ives, Edgard Varèse, Henry Cowell, John Cage, and Others)'. Delivered on the first full day, 13 August, of the 1954 courses, following an all-Krenek concert the night before, it had been immediately preceded by an Adorno lecture – in collaboration with Rudolf Kolisch and Eduard Steuermann – on new music and its interpretation in performance.

Rebner was one of a swathe of German émigrés to the United States – he lived in both New York and Los Angeles – returning to Europe with news of musical life there, precisely in the spirit of musical and cultural exchange which Darmstadt was intended to foster.[1] Though American music had already featured at Darmstadt, both in concert and as a subject of lectures, the music of the American experimentalists, regarded *as* experimental – unless Varèse be considered under that heading – had not. Certainly this appears to have been the first occasion on which Cage formed a subject of debate at Darmstadt.

For the most part Rebner's lecture seems uncontroversial, if stereotypical in its construction of music, whether experimental or not, in the United States.[2] As Beal observes, Rebner characterises Ives, for instance, as a 'rugged individual', exhibiting that 'rebellious American spirit'.[3] The other composers featured – Cowell, Antheil, Peggy Glanville-Hicks, Varèse, and Cage – certainly might be regarded as representing an – albeit unconventional – pantheon of American experimental composers. It is in this context that Rebner's presentation of Cage is most noteworthy. Rebner explicitly links Cowell's expansion of the sonic resources of the piano to Cage's prepared piano and implicitly links Cage with Varèse in his suggestions

---

[1] Rebner returned to Germany permanently in 1955, teaching at the Richard Strauss Conservatory in Munich. See Beal, *New Music, New Allies*, 63.

[2] See Beal, 'Negotiating Cultural Allies', 128–35. Borio and Danuser also reprint Rebner's lecture, but without the handwritten amendments and crossings-out which Beal retains. See Wolfgang Rebner, 'Amerikanische Experimentalmusik' [1954], in Borio and Danuser (eds.), *Im Zenit der Moderne*, vol. III, 178–89.

[3] Beal, 'Negotiating Cultural Allies', 122, 130.

that, in the examples he gave of Cage's music, 'one may recognize principles of accumulative repetition, of density, and of contrast. At times, density seems to replace polyphony.' Following on the heels of his description of Varèse's *Density 21.5* (1936), the comparisons the listener must have been expected to make are clear. It is, though, far from clear precisely what examples of Cage's music Rebner may have played, notwithstanding Boulez's delivery of *A Book of Music* and *First Construction (in Metal)*. As well as his promise to discuss the prepared piano, which was probably represented by *A Book of Music*, the words 'piano concerto' are handwritten into Rebner's text after his description of *Imaginary Landscape No. 4* (1951), regarding which I say more below. This may have indicated Cage's *Concert for Prepared Piano and Orchestra* (1951) but it is impossible to be sure. Though the lecture notes give no indication of it, Beal mentions that Steinecke's resumé of all the music presented at Darmstadt between 1946 and 1958, in the second volume of the *Darmstädter Beiträge*, suggests that Christian Wolff's *For Prepared Piano* was also presented as a part of Rebner's lecture.[4] This idea is strengthened by the mention of Wolff (rendered as 'Christian Wolfe') in Wolf-Eberhard von Lewinski's review of Rebner's lecture, to which I will return presently.

Rebner does not directly suggest that that American experimental music might be considered a 'tradition'. Indeed he is clear that Ives is '[u]ninhibited by prejudices of tradition',[5] but Beal suggests, hardly unreasonably, that the lineage constructed from Ives through Cowell to Cage might be read in just these terms. In such a context the opening of his lecture takes on an added importance. It was here that Rebner explicitly linked experimentalism to Schoenberg's observation that the twelve-tone method would operate as a 'liberator from the shackles of tonality', concluding that 'every individual attempt becomes a solution and every solution becomes an experiment'.[6] In later years, of course, the idea that Cage was an heir of Schoenberg would become a commonplace, yet here it is almost explicit: if the Europeans might consider themselves (even if only some specifically did) successors to Webern, this particular aspect of American music came straight from, as Cage put it, 'the president of the company'.[7]

---

[4] Wolfgang Steinecke, 'Neue Musik in Darmstadt 1946–1958', *Darmstädter Beiträge zur neuen Musik*, vol. 2 (1959), 94. See also Beal, 'Negotiating Cultural Allies', 123 n. 75.
[5] Wolfgang Rebner, 'American Experimental Music', in Amy C. Beal, 'Negotiating Cultural Allies: American Music in Darmstadt, 1946–1956', *Journal of the American Musicological Society*, vol. 53, no. 1 (Spring 2000), 129.
[6] Ibid., 128.
[7] Quoted in David W. Patterson, 'Cage and Asia: History and Sources', in David Nicholls (ed.), *The Cambridge Companion to John Cage* (Cambridge University Press, 2002), 54.

Beal's charge that Rebner may have 'pointed out – perhaps for the first time in Germany – experimental composers' emphasis on the nature of *sound* rather than *system*, thus offering an experiential cousin to the formulaic aspect of total serialism', seems to rely on precisely that, literally totalising, version of serialism which was belied by the activities of the central Darmstadt composers, the Europeans. This is not necessarily to say that the claim is without validity – doubtless the mode of presentation chosen by those composers tended towards descriptions which foregrounded process – but, given that a large proportion of what Stockhausen, for one, was interested in (and spoke *about*) was concerned with what he, following Meyer-Eppler, perceived to be the physical reality and experience of sound, it seems to me that it suggests a confrontation of ideas where there was not *necessarily* one. There are, though, in Rebner's description of Cage the first intimations of a debate – or, more accurately, a misunderstanding – that would lie at the heart of the reception of Cage at Darmstadt. In being the first to speak of Cage at Darmstadt, Rebner was also the first to introduce the idea of indeterminacy:

> Mozart invented a playful musical dice game, in which one could haphazardly piece together, measure for measure, a waltz [*sic*] melody [...] Since then, the factor of unpredictability has no longer been a chosen artistic ally. Is a work like *Imaginary Landscape* for twelve radios perhaps an attempt to bring the forgotten gift of improvisation back to the public? Of course, here, no two versions could ever be identical; every performance in itself becomes a surprise.[8]

It is here that the dread word 'improvisation' was applied to Cage's music. No doubt, Rebner was well aware that *Imaginary Landscape No. 4* contains no elements of performance improvisation *or* indeterminacy; the score, as Nicholls states unambiguously, 'specifies precisely both volume and frequency (that is, the frequencies to which each radio should be tuned)'.[9] Even though Cage would state later that same year that '[w]hen I wrote the *Imaginary Landscape* for twelve radios, it was not for the purpose of shock or as a joke but rather to increase the unpredictability already inherent in the situation through the tossing of coins', what is at stake here is certainly not 'improvisation'.[10] The indeterminate elements of the piece come from whatever happens to be being broadcast at the time of performance, and not from the actions of the performer. Even though Rebner seems to have suggested only that there might be some comparison

---

[8] Rebner, 'American Experimental Music', 134.
[9] David Nicholls, *John Cage* (Chicago, IL: University of Illinois Press, 2007), 55.
[10] John Cage, '45′ for a Speaker' [1954], in *Silence* (London: Marion Boyars, 1968), 162.

to be made between what happens in *Imaginary Landscape No. 4* and the sonic impressions of an improvised performance, that what Cage was asking for was explicitly *not* improvisation was far from clear to many members of the European new music community. Precisely this point tended to characterise many of the criticisms levelled against him and his influence. In any case, Rebner's analogy is, comparatively speaking, subtle (at least in the context of a spoken lecture). It seems likely that listeners who were not extremely attentive might simply take away the association of the name of John Cage and the word 'improvisation'.

Certainly there was some degree of press attention to Rebner's presentation. An earlier article by Rebner on Henry Cowell, written for *Time* magazine, was reprinted in the *Darmstädter Echo* on 14 August 1954, as Beal suggests, at the behest of Steinecke.[11] Rather more coverage was given in a piece for the *Darmstädter Tagblatt* by Wolf-Eberhard von Lewinski, 'American Musicians and the Experiment'.[12]

Lewinski was struck by the lecture, and prepared to defend what Rebner had presented: 'It is vital in the presentation of such work that one judges to what extent they are serious ventures into virgin territory and to what extent more or less spirited gimmickry. If one sometimes has the latter impression, a careful consideration of the situation of music in our century should make one's thinking change quickly.'[13] Describing the experiments of Cage and Wolff with the prepared piano, Lewinski was no less impressed. Cage, he said, would already be known to his readers as an *enfant terrible*, even before the Donaueschingen performances, perhaps from the Westdeutscher Rundfunk's broadcast of the first two of Cage's *Constructions* on 22 November 1952. Even in asserting that the means of sound-production were primitive (certainly thinking of the prepared piano music, but perhaps of those earlier broadcasts too) Lewinski nevertheless observed that this was music which ought – which demanded – to be taken seriously. He concluded not only that Rebner's lecture was both shrewd and well informed but also, and more pertinently, that the pieces he had heard by Cage and Wolff were 'unsettling, but exciting too'.[14] He did sound a word of caution, though, in suggesting that what the music of the American experimentalists represented might turn out to be an artistic programme, but one with no music, only the expansion of sonic resources.

---

[11] Beal, 'Negotiating Cultural Allies', 123. The translation of Rebner's 'Pioneer at 56' was printed in the *Darmstädter Echo* on 14 August 1954 as 'Veteran im Vorfeld der Neuen Musik' ('A Veteran at the Forefront of New Music').

[12] Wolf-Eberhard von Lewinski, 'Amerikanische Musiker und das Experiment: Ein Vortragsabend mit Klangbeispielen bei den Ferienkurse', *Darmstädter Tagblatt*, 16 August 1954.

[13] Ibid.   [14] Ibid.

Yet after that initial flurry of interest, Rebner's lecture faded in its impact, receiving only a passing mention in Albert Rodemann's review of the courses for the *Allgemeine Zeitung* on 31 August 1954, and precious little coverage after the event elsewhere.[15] Even Lewinski had decided that what Rebner had to present was secondary in comparison to the 'Young Composers in Kranichstein' he discussed in his round-up of the courses for the Bayerischer Rundfunk, focussing instead on Stockhausen's first five Klavierstücke, Bengt Hambraeus's *Gacelas y casidas de Federico García Lorca*, op. 37, for voice and ensemble, Henri Pousseur's *Trois chants sacrés* for soprano and string trio, Reinhold Finkbeiner's *Ciacona* for piano (1954), and Camillo Togni's Flute Sonata (premièred by Gazzelloni with Togni himself accompanying).[16] This was the general flavour of the broad press coverage, especially those essays endeavouring to summarise the courses. Indeed, journalists in the main seem to have been split between regarding precisely these pieces – Stockhausen, Hambraeus, and Pousseur attracted the most attention – and the première of Krenek's chamber opera *Dark Waters* (1950–1) in the final concert, on 27 August 1954, as the major 'event' of the year. In short, the press was split between looking forward to the younger European generation and looking backward to the generation of European composers before them, even when those composers were now émigrés residing in the United States. There seemed to be little sense that they ought to be looking towards the *current* generation of American composers.

Stefan Wolpe and David Tudor, 1956

Cage's music (and any official discussion of it) was wholly absent from the 1955 courses; the only American music featured was Everett Helm's *Eight Minutes for Two Pianos* (1943).[17] There was no sense that Rebner's lecture – or Cage and Tudor's performance at Donaueschingen – had awakened a burning desire amongst the young composers at Darmstadt to 'discover' Cage. Tudor had already been recognised as a formidable interpreter of new music, though, even by those who had cared little for his choice of repertoire.

---

[15] Albert Rodemann, 'Neue Musik in Darmstadt: Resumee der Internationalen Ferienkurse', *Allgemeine Zeitung*, 31 August 1954.
[16] Wolf-Eberhard von Lewinski, 'Junge Komponisten in Kranichstein: Bericht über die Kranichsteiner Ferienkurse 1954', broadcast, Bayerischer Rundfunk, Munich, date unknown, transcript IMD.
[17] Even though Krenek, whose *Capriccio* for violoncello and chamber orchestra (1955) was premièred at the 1955 courses on 31 May, had taken American citizenship in 1945, he was still regarded at Darmstadt as a European composer.

Tudor had known the German-born American composer Stefan Wolpe for many years. He had studied the piano with Wolpe's then-wife, Irma, from the mid 1940s, and doubtless met Wolpe himself for the first time in the same period. It had been Irma Wolpe's performance of her husband's Toccata that had first spurred Tudor to seek lessons with her. Before long, Tudor had begun studying composition and analysis with Wolpe, though the sorts of organic unities which Wolpe felt were significant for a composer were already, according to Tudor's recollection, ones he found uninspiring. By 1947, the Wolpes had helped Tudor to move to New York, where he began his performance career in earnest. Tudor returned the favour by acting as the in-house pianist for weekly composition classes at the Wolpes' flat. This was where Tudor first encountered Morton Feldman, whose composition studies with Stefan had been underway for about the same length of time as Tudor's piano studies with Irma. Vitally, too, during this period, Tudor became *the* pianist for Wolpe's music. Wolpe's *Battle Piece* (1943–7) would almost certainly not have been finished without the impetus of Tudor as a pianist, and is dedicated to Tudor, who gave its première on 11 March 1950 in New York.[18] Tudor retained contact with Wolpe throughout the early 1950s, not least through their common commitments to events at Black Mountain College, and, as Beal notes, it was in no small part the financial collapse of Black Mountain College, leading to its closure in 1957, that made Europe – in the form of a Fulbright Fellowship in Berlin and his invitation to Darmstadt – a lifeline for Wolpe.[19]

It is difficult to establish with security whether it was Steinecke or Wolpe who first thought that it would be a boon for Tudor to accompany Wolpe to Europe and to act as the pianist for his music as well as a member of the Darmstadt faculty, responsible for piano teaching alongside Helmut Roloff. It seems unlikely, though, that Steinecke – not least after the debacle, as he had seen it, of Cage and Tudor's Donaueschingen performance – would have been happy to put so much responsibility into Tudor's hands without assurances from someone that that would be a sensible plan. In any case, the surviving correspondence seems to suggest that it was Wolpe who made the offer to Tudor, with Tudor sending a telegram accepting the idea, in principle at least, to Steinecke. Steinecke responded on the same day, with details both of finance and of what would be expected of Tudor.[20] I shall return to the details of Tudor's other activities presently, but the central matter (or, at least, that which had meant he was ideally suited from Wolpe's

---

[18] For fuller details of Tudor's acquaintance with the Wolpes and its relation to his development as a pianist, see John Holzaepfel, 'David Tudor and the Performance of American Experimental Music, 1950–1959' (unpublished PhD dissertation, City University of New York, 1994), 5–11.
[19] Beal, *New Music, New Allies*, 78.   [20] Steinecke to Tudor, 14 February 1956, IMD.

perspective) was that Tudor was to provide live musical examples for Wolpe's lecture, 'On New (and Not-So-New) Music in America', which Wolpe delivered on 19 July 1956, towards the end of that year's courses.

For his part, Tudor was far from enthused regarding the prospect of working with Wolpe. Although Tudor doubtless felt a strong loyalty to Wolpe personally, since it had been he who had, in many respects, made it possible for Tudor to begin his New York performing career, he also felt that Wolpe neither truly knew nor sympathised with the music of the American composers whom Tudor wanted to promote: principally those who would become known as the New York School, which is to say Cage, Christian Wolff, Morton Feldman, and Earle Brown. Judith Malina, the co-founder and co-director of the Living Theatre, recalled in her diary a concert that Cage and Tudor gave on 10 February 1952:

> In the throng I find Stefan Wolpe searching for a seat and I offer him mine because I feel like a hostess. He suggests that I give him the seat of 'whoever is sitting with you'. I agree, if only because he is a composer whose work is being played. So I sit beside Wolpe who, with his contingent, including a sullen, hostile Dylan Thomas, constitutes 'the opposition'.
>
> Cage and Tudor like the opposition to be assertive; it marks the work as being controversial. But it is another matter to sit beside them when listening to music.
>
> Tudor plays the Webern '*Variationen*'. John turns pages.
>
> Henry Cowell's 'Banshee' is a bit of play with the piano strings.
>
> Cage's two 'pastorales'. Sound as we are not used to it, nailing us back to hearing as if we'd forgotten what sound is.
>
> Wolpe and Dylan and their cohorts carry on. Wolpe making throaty sounds, passing notes, and entertaining his friends as loudly as possible.
>
> How could I enjoy Wolpe's piece now?
>
> Serafina [Hovhaness] threatens to boo it and asks to change seats with me so that she may kick Wolpe in the shins. Alan [Hovhaness] restrains her.[21]

Little surprise, then, that Tudor wrote to Stockhausen on 14 May 1956 that his

> last letter came truly like an 'angelic missive'! It arrived in the midst of a great depression over my coming European venture – you will not understand this, it was because I will come to Germany partly in connection with the composer Stefan Wolpe, and I will have to collaborate with him to some extent. He will talk about American music (including Cage etc.), and I frankly do not know whether I will be able to correct all the misinformation he will undoubtedly spread.[22]

---

[21] Judith Malina, *The Diaries of Judith Malina 1947–1957* (New York: Grove, 1984), 210.
[22] Tudor to Stockhausen, 14 May 1956, in Misch and Bandur (eds.), *Karlheinz Stockhausen bei den Internationalen Ferienkursen*, 131.

Stockhausen's reply was supportive: 'Your collaboration with M. Wolpe is a bit stupid; the differences are more and more erased. If he says something which is too blind, you beat very hard on the piano [...] and sweep him away with an old glissando – (presentation finished!).'[23] According to Beal's account, Tudor's later reflections mirrored very closely Stockhausen's observation that the whole affair sounded 'a bit stupid': 'in a way it was a kind of silly lecture, because it was like one-liners about everybody'.[24] It is also notable that, just as Hans Curjel had felt in 1954 that Cage might be regarded as aesthetically close to Boulez, Nono, and Stockhausen, in 1956 Stockhausen agreed that distinctions between the Europeans and the Americans were, at the very least, less pertinent than they had once been.

Tudor's own judgement is understandable on an examination of Wolpe's text. A presentation that contained no fewer than eighteen examples of the music of American composers in a duration which can certainly have been no greater than two hours never stood much hope of being able to do more than scratch the surface of the music under discussion. Of these eighteen examples, half were performed live by Tudor, including examples from Babbitt's Second String Quartet (1954), of which Wolpe had been unable to procure a recording. One might have expected that, if Darmstadt truly had been, in all respects, the serial stronghold it was often considered to be (or, more accurately, in the precise way in which that has been construed), it would have been the discovery of an American composer, Babbitt, who was also operating in the field of multiple serialism, that would have excited. This certainly appears to have been Wolpe's own presumption; about a quarter of the total presentation was devoted to him (thus making the sense that the rest constituted a set of punch lines yet stronger). Yet Babbitt was ignored in Lewinski's report, which mentioned (itself condensing the pithiness even further) only Gunther Schuller, Roger Sessions, Varèse, Feldman, Brown, Cage, and Wolpe himself.[25] Multiple serialism of the sort practised by Babbitt was, it would seem, already 'old news' at Darmstadt.

While noting, perhaps in deference to anticipations of his audience's taste, that they 'must recognize that the prevailing style over in America is become radicalized only very, very slowly', Wolpe stressed too that he felt that serial (or twelve-tone) solutions – which is to say *strictly* serial (or twelve-tone) solutions – were already on the wane, whether in Europe or America. His concern, in this sense, was with those who might refuse to look

---

[23] Stockhausen to Tudor, 20 May 1956, in ibid., 133.
[24] David Tudor in interview with Christian Wolff and Jack Vees, 11 October 1995, quoted in Beal, *New Music, New Allies*, 81.
[25] Wolf-Eberhard von Lewinski, 'Neue und nicht mehr neue Musik aus Amerika: Ein Vortrag von Stefan Wolpe auf der Marienhöhe', *Darmstädter Tagblatt*, 21 July 1956.

back as well as forward since, as he proposed, 'he who limits himself does not progress', noting too that

> those who work with tone rows [...] are becoming impatient with the limitations of such restrictions and are discovering innumerable procedures for delaying and altering the tempo of circulation, for extending concepts of fixed material to each grouping of tones or other auditory sensations, and for navigating in a consciously proportioned musical space in which all elements are structurally predetermined.[26]

Before turning to America, then, Wolpe made clear that he was aware that in Europe, but not only in Europe, any sort of strict serial procedure had long since reached an impasse and was being broken down. In this context, Wolpe proposed, '[e]verything is possible. Everything lies open. That is the historical situation.'[27] Though Clarkson is doubtless right that the 'not-so-new' music of Wolpe's title refers to the more conservative music he played – Schuller, Copland, Keith Robinson, Netty Brown – it is significant in this context that there is little sense that Wolpe is suggesting that the 'progressive' music – Brown, Cage, Feldman, and Wolff at least – is in truth necessarily all that much more progressive. The sum of Wolpe's argument – if an underlying argument can be sensed in what is in many respects an extremely diffuse text – is that 'progress' can be found in many different compositional trajectories, the old at least as much as the ostensibly new. Here, though, it is Wolpe's descriptions of the music of Brown, Wolff, Feldman, and Cage that is of greatest interest; he devoted attention to each of them in turn.

Wolpe's stress in the case of Brown's music was on what he perceived as its 'openness'. His approach to Brown seems, in fact, relatively disparaging. Though initially Wolpe appeared to praise Brown for the creation of 'a mobile, untrammelled space, music entirely without a floor and without a centre of gravity', it becomes clear that he regarded this maximal openness as leading to a result little different from the closed 'tightly clamped' space he had previously identified in Keith Robinson's Twelve Pieces for Piano (1951), one of which Tudor had performed. Following Tudor's performance of (probably) Brown's *Perspectives*, Wolpe concluded that '[b]ecause everything is different, everything is finally interchangeable, and what is interchanged becomes the same because at the same time it is the other.'[28] Brown's music, from Wolpe's perspective, exhibited the same sort of qualities of stasis that Adorno had been horrified by in Goeyvaerts's Sonata for

---

[26] Stefan Wolpe, 'On New (and Not-So-New) Music in America', tr. Austin Clarkson, *Journal of Music Theory*, vol. 28, no. 1 (Spring 1984), 7.
[27] Ibid., 8.   [28] Ibid., 13.

Two Pianos. In Wolff's music, Wolpe again found stasis, but of a rather different kind. His concentration here was on the way in which individual musical events are presented individually, 'suspended in space'. Here, for Wolpe, motion had come to a standstill: 'only as much motion is introduced as is needed to carry the immediately preceding phase of motion forward to a standstill in order to make the act of standing still even more obvious'.[29] Tudor performed an excerpt from either Wolff's *For Piano I* (1952) or, more likely, from *For Piano II*, which he had performed at Donaueschingen.

A similar sort of sparseness was what Wolpe found in Feldman's music, and he suggested that Feldman was 'interested in the remnants of shapes that can barely be heard from a distance'. Any sort of criticism, such as might be educed from the examination of Brown or, to a lesser extent, Wolff, is absent here, in the consideration of Wolpe's own former pupil. In simple terms, it seems as if Wolpe had no idea of how Feldman 'did it', beyond the idea that 'the material is formed in the flow of its spontaneous generation' and that Feldman did not prescribe – which is to say in this sense pre-*order* – any of the pitch sets or harmonic situations of which he made use. Yet, though the sense of critique was removed, a balance much like that which Wolpe identified in Brown's music remained: 'The disjoint elimination of such material is of the same significance as its continued use.' On the level of signification, this too is a case of stasis, since it makes no real difference whether the material changes or stays the same. Given Wolpe's comment that '[b]rought to the brink of dissolution this music is a diabolic test of beauty', one might suspect that the real difference between Brown and Feldman, in such terms, is that Wolpe simply found himself more engaged by the notes Feldman chose to use.[30]

As for Cage, it was again interchangeability that was at stake. Although material might be pre-determined, as Wolpe observed, '[f]or all such elements as tempi, duration, pauses, intensity, sonority, pitch sequences and more developed constellations there are maps with a specific number of prescribed situations whose selection is determined by chance operations – the structuring and ordering of the way in which that material is dispersed through a piece becomes of disinterest.'[31] Where Rebner only implicitly hinted at a 'tradition' of American experimental composers, in Wolpe's hands it is clear – or would have been clear to an attentive listener – that strong links can be drawn, from his perspective, between the four experimental composers he devoted time to, even though that link is little more

---

[29] Ibid., 25.
[30] Ibid., 25–6. It is not certain which piece by Feldman Tudor performed. Since Wolpe refers to it only as 'Piano Piece', it may have been *Piano Piece 1952*, *Piano Piece 1955*, or *Piano Piece 1956 A*.
[31] Ibid., 27. Tudor played the first part of *Music of Changes* as an exemplar.

than the fact that, structurally speaking, their music could play out in any number of ways, each of which would be just as valid as any other. He summarises this briefly: 'The free interchangeability of situations deprives structure of its meaning in favour of "undifferentiated diversity" (that is also the goal), in favour of a panorama of phenomena that criss-cross and follow each other, as in the sounds of traffic, and so on (that might also be a good beginning).'[32] At the same time as many Europeans were trying to find a way to generate plausible larger-scale structures from low-level serial material, Wolpe might have been suggesting that the Americans, or a few of them at least, were implicitly saying that the larger-scale structure was, truly, an irrelevance: what mattered was *what* was being distributed across musical time, not necessarily the order in which it appeared.

There was a second underlying thread to Wolpe's discussion. Even though he did not relate it directly to any of the composers of the so-called New York School directly, Wolpe returned on a number of occasions to jazz and to improvisation. His first reference is perhaps the strongest, since it proposes explicitly that improvisation might be integrated into composition as a means of liberation: 'We have banned improvisation from our scores, from our way of thinking, from our creative assumptions. A few of us wish to liberate our scores again so that improvisation will return as a free, open place in a piece of music, where overall control is suspended for a moment, where something special may happen.'[33] Yet again, though no link is explicitly made, Cageian indeterminacy is juxtaposed with improvisation; moreover, Wolpe's description of Cage's music is concerned with the way in which Cage seeks 'to liberate [himself] from all personal interference in the disposition of the material'.[34] To be sure, what Wolpe meant by improvisation in a compositional sense was already reasonably clear from his earliest remarks: he meant little more than that composers ought not to be restricted by system and that, even in a piece which is largely systematically controlled, space ought to remain for 'improvisation on the page'. Yet it is worth stressing once more that, in the context of a lecture where only fragmentary memories of the specific content are likely to remain after the fact, it is hardly implausible that listeners might have drawn parallels between 'openness' and improvisation. As I have already suggested, and will explain more fully later, this idea is one which recurs repeatedly in the discourse around Cage, and I do not think it is coincidental that the two ideas stand side by side in Wolpe's presentation.

In advance of Wolpe's lecture, Tudor had already given the German première of Wolpe's Passacaglia for piano (1936) in the official opening

[32] Ibid.. [33] Ibid., 8. [34] Ibid., 27.

concert of the 1956 courses on 12 July and that of Stockhausen's Klavierstücke V–VIII on 18 July, and, alongside Severino Gazzelloni, had performed Messiaen's *Le Merle noir* (1951) and the remarkably late world première of Boulez's Flute Sonatine in two separate concerts on 15 July. According to Peyser, Tudor recalled that the performance of the Boulez Sonatine was so successful that they were obliged to repeat it.[35] He would also première Gladys Nordenstrom's Rondo for flute and piano (1948) with Gazzelloni on the afternoon of 20 July. Reviewers again focussed on the impressiveness of Tudor as a performer, with Lewinski describing his performance of Stockhausen's Klavierstücke V–VIII on 18 July as 'admirably intense'.[36] Gustav Adolf Trumpff was more impressed by Tudor than he was by Stockhausen's music itself, suggesting that there were still questions of content and substance to be answered, even when performances were delivered by 'experts' of Tudor's abilities.[37]

Alongside his concert performances and the performance of extracts within Wolpe's lecture, Tudor was engaged to teach piano to the participants, principally, it is clear from the content of Steinecke's letters, in the context of the pieces that attending pianists might perform as a part of the Kranichsteiner Musikpreis competition; in this year, Berg's Piano Sonata, op. 1 (1907–8, rev. 1920) was the obligatory piece. As his free pieces Rolf Kuhnert performed Bartók's Suite for Piano, op. 14 (1916), and Messiaen's *Île de feu II* (1950); Karl Otto Plum and Jorge Zulueta both opted for Schoenberg's *Drei Klavierstücke*, op. 11 (1909). Regardless of what he was *supposed* to be teaching, Tudor's piano seminar also focussed on the performance of Boulez's and Webern's piano music.[38]

Though Peyser quotes Tudor as having said that '[a]ll the invitations I received from Steinecke, beginning in 1956, were arranged through Stockhausen',[39] there seems to be little evidence that this was the case, not only because, as outlined above, it was in connection with Wolpe's attendance that Tudor was first considered, but also because it would overstate the influence that Stockhausen had over Steinecke's decisions of who to bring in to join the Darmstadt faculty. Stockhausen himself moved from participant to faculty member at Darmstadt only a year later, in 1957, and was not entrusted with a composition course until 1959. Indeed, an undated letter (probably from roughly the middle of February 1956) suggests that it was

---

[35] Peyser, *Boulez*, 123.
[36] Wolf-Eberhard von Lewinski, 'Stockhausen – Maderna – Boulez: Zum dritten Studio Konzert der Kranichsteiner Ferienkurse', *Darmstädter Tagblatt*, 20 July 1956.
[37] Trumpff, 'Atelier für autonome Musik'.
[38] Inge Schlösser, 'Zu neuen Interpretationsweisen: Einblick in ein Seminar. Der Klavierkurs David Tudors', *Darmstädter Echo*, 19 July 1956.
[39] Peyser, *Boulez*, 123.

certainly Steinecke who was informing Stockhausen of the plans for Tudor. Stockhausen wrote that Steinecke's 'idea to let Tudor speak in a matinee about piano interpretation in the context of the pieces [Stockhausen's Klavierstücke] is really very, very good. He is the only one who plays them well and with love.'[40] Steinecke developed this idea further into a suggestion to Tudor that he give three two-hour seminars as a part of a working group looking at, principally, new American music. Tudor had endeavoured to persuade Steinecke that music from his repertoire would form a strong evening concert programme. He suggested Cage's *Music of Changes* (1951), Christian Wolff's Suite (1954), Stefan Wolpe's *Battle Piece*, and Morton Feldman's Three Pieces for piano (1954) and *Intersection 3* (1953), as well as, possibly, Earle Brown's *Perspectives*, Wolpe's Two Studies (extracts from several of which had appeared, as noted above, in Wolpe's lecture), and, if a programme that was not all-American was desired, Stockhausen's Klavierstücke V–VIII. As noted above, of the music suggested, only the Stockhausen pieces were performed in concert, and the tone of Tudor's letter suggests that these were the pieces that Tudor thought it *least* important to include.[41]

Steinecke's reply was clear that he regarded the music on which Tudor wished to concentrate as being most appropriate for the working group; he observed that between thirty and forty participants had already registered for it, so there would certainly be no shortage of audience to whom to communicate the ideas that Tudor felt were vital.[42] Tudor's work may well have been more fruitful in this context than in a concert situation in any case, since it would explain what, from Tudor's perspective at least, was so compelling and important about the pieces he presented. The list of participants certainly suggests a healthy interest. Thirty-four registered, including Richard Rodney Bennett, Niccolò Castiglioni, Cornelius Cardew, Friedrich Cerha, Gottfried Michael Koenig, Otto Tomek, Giacomo Manzoni, Richard Maxfield, Toshiro Mayzumi, Wolfgang Widmaier, and Bernd Alois Zimmermann.[43]

Inge Schlösser's piece 'On New Modes of Interpretation: A Look at David Tudor's Piano Seminar', printed in the *Darmstädter Echo* on 19 July 1956,

---

[40] Stockhausen to Steinecke, undated but probably mid February 1956, in Misch and Bandur (eds.), *Karlheinz Stockhausen bei den Internationalen Ferienkursen*, 127.
[41] Tudor to Steinecke, 14 May 1956, IMD.   [42] Steinecke to Tudor, 13 June 1956, IMD.
[43] 'Arbeitsgemeinschaft', undated, unsigned document, GRI. Beal suggests that only two students and six auditors attended Tudor's courses, but this is, it seems, the case only for his *piano* seminars, which is to say his courses for those who had registered for Darmstadt as piano performers. The list of thirty-four participants in the David Tudor Papers at GRI seems highly likely to refer to precisely this working group, tallying neatly as it does not only in title but also in number with Steinecke's description of it. See Beal, *New Music, New Allies*, 82.

focussed specifically on Tudor's work in this respect; she was the only journalist to take this level of interest.[44] Her description of Tudor's work in this respect is worth quoting from at length, since it seems to give a strong flavour of the sessions:

> Alongside his piano course, the thirty-year-old David Tudor is directing a working group, in which he plays music by John Cage. It is here that the fiercest discussions develop. Cage is an American experimenter, who writes works for the 'prepared piano', which incorporate some extra-musical elements. The strings of the piano have, in the design of this music, clothes pegs, wood chips, screws, erasers, and various other objects inserted between them. The player works not only with the keys, but also the pedals, sounding board, piano legs and, in some circumstances, whistles through the spout of a kettle. The action of performance is in this case naturally intensified to the extent that a listener's shock can initially turn to laughter. In any case the experiment gives pause for thought to those who take it seriously. In fact, a little more activity and naturalism wouldn't hurt our performers. Above all, David Tudor takes great pains to bring his students to the point where they do not shy away from experimentation, but look to master even complex problems in the simplest and most natural way.[45]

In these sessions, Tudor expanded discussion of Cage's *Music of Changes*, from which he had performed a few extracts during Wolpe's lecture, to discussion of the first and fourth parts. While Beal's report is sober – 'His public analysis of Cage's chance methods would stimulate both Stockhausen and Boulez, who were exploring open form and semi-indeterminate composition at the time' – Peyser's is lurid (and certainly erroneous in her dating):

> In May 1956, David Tudor played parts I and IV of the *Music of Changes*, the very work that had precipitated Boulez's break from Cage, in a seminar at Darmstadt attended by such formidable figures as Bruno Maderna, Luigi Nono, Stockhausen, and Boulez. After the performance, Stockhausen and Boulez engaged in a fight that, by all counts, lasted at least one hour. Stockhausen fought passionately for the ideas of the work; Boulez fought against them passionately. Tudor says, 'Boulez cared enough about Stockhausen to do everything he could to get Stockhausen to change his mind.' But his efforts were unsuccessful. Stockhausen gave Boulez a kick in the shins.

---

[44] In fairness, she would have been one of only a small number of journalists perhaps easily *able* to have taken this level of interest, as a local reporter, especially since the *Darmstädter Echo* had both her and Gustav Adolf Trumpff at their disposal as reporters, while the *Darmstädter Tagblatt* had only Lewinski.

[45] Schlösser, 'Zu neuen Interpretationsweisen'.

Still, the kick did not produce blood, and the composers persisted in their professional relationship.[46]

Doubtless, the truth lies somewhere in between. Perhaps Stockhausen's own recollection of the events is closest:

> I explained about Klavierstück XI, which I had written shortly before, to Boulez. At first he was taken aback, but then became angry and ranted that he could not understand such nonsense, that I was afraid to set everything down accurately in notation and was trying to cast off responsibility. The whole time, Tudor was laughing whimsically. More than a year went by then, before Boulez sent me the first sketches of the five formants of his Third Sonata.[47]

Not for the last time, it was on the subject of Cage that the Darmstadt composers disagreed, even if, in Stockhausen's description, it is already clear that the debate was really about Stockhausen and Boulez, with Cage acting only as a object of exchange through which the battle could be fought.

As had been the case with Rebner's lecture in 1954, by the time the press came to compile their summaries of the events of 1956 which seemed to them most significant, Wolpe's discussions were largely forgotten, as was Tudor's working group seminar. Of those summative reviews, it was only Steinecke's own, his third report on that year's proceedings for the Hessischer Rundfunk, broadcast on 20 September 1956, which mentioned Wolpe, and that only in passing.[48] Tudor's brilliance as a pianist was a continued focus, although Lewinski's review for Radio Bremen suggested that he at least had no knowledge of Tudor's performance at Donaueschingen, describing him as 'young, phenomenally gifted and as yet unknown in this country'.[49]

Steinecke seems to have been thoroughly convinced of Tudor's gifts, inviting him to give a recital in November 1956 as a part of the series of concerts which the administration of the Darmstadt courses held all year round, outside the main run of the courses.[50] Even if Tudor had been able to return to Darmstadt for the date suggested – 26 or 27 November – the repertoire Steinecke had proposed, including Debussy, Messiaen, Schoenberg, and Bartók, was hardly likely to appeal. Tudor declined,[51] and he and Steinecke had no further communication until February 1957,

---

[46] Peyser, *Boulez*, 121.
[47] Karlheinz Stockhausen and Heinz-Klaus Metzger, 'Vieldeutige Form', in Metzger and Riehn (eds.), *Darmstadt-Dokument I*, 190. I will return in more detail to this essay of Stockhausen's, given as a presentation at the 1960 courses, below.
[48] Wolfgang Steinecke, 'Internationale Ferienkurse für Neue Musik, Darmstadt 1956, III', broadcast, Hessischer Rundfunk, 20 September 1956, transcript IMD.
[49] Lewinski, 'Blick in Kranichsteins Komponisten-Atelier'.
[50] Steinecke to Tudor, 30 October 1956, IMD.   [51] Tudor to Steinecke, 19 November 1956, IMD.

when Steinecke invited Tudor to return as a member of the faculty for the 1957 courses.[52] Tudor sent a brief telegram to accept and, in a fuller letter a few days later, proposed performances of music by Bo Nilsson, Henri Pousseur, Cage, and Wolff, confirming that he would be willing to give two performances of Stockhausen's Klavierstück XI.[53] Tudor also agreed to perform Earle Brown's *Music for Cello and Piano* (1955).[54] Tudor appears not to have noted that Steinecke had requested that he perform Klavierstück XI as a world première at Darmstadt, however, and he gave the world première in New York on 22 April 1957.

Steinecke was, hardly surprisingly, furious with both Stockhausen and Tudor, or at any rate this was Stockhausen's interpretation. Stockhausen wrote to Tudor:

> Steinecke is a tombeau since 8 weeks; in this last time I heard why he does not answer to my letters, to the musicians of the quintet etc.: He became terribly angry when he heard by Nono that you already performed my XI. piano piece [...] in New York and he – Steinecke – had announced it as a 'first performance'. If it is not too much derangement for you: please write him, that I did not know it before your concert (I already said it to him, but he did not believe: I saw him quite short after a concert in the radio) and that you did not know that it would be disagreeable for him if you had played it before Darmstadt; I remember, that I intended to write to you or that I even write to you, that you should play Nr. 7 as a first performance in Darmstadt.[55]

This was precisely what Tudor did only a few days later, writing to Steinecke:

> I am afraid that I owe you an apology about the first performance of the Klavierstück XI of Stockhausen, I had not quite realized that you expected a world première. I assumed that you meant a first European performance, and I am now very much embarassed [sic] by my mistake! The concert in which I performed it was organized so quickly (the whole thing was conceived and executed in 2½ weeks), that there was not time for an exchange of letters between Stockhausen and myself, otherwise the mistake could have been prevented. The fault is entirely mine, and I assure you that in the future I will be more careful about the matter of 'first performances'.[56]

---

[52] Steinecke to Tudor, 12 February 1957, IMD.
[53] Tudor to Steinecke, 7 March and 12 March 1957, IMD.
[54] See Steinecke to Tudor, 13 March 1957; Steinecke to Tudor, 26 March 1957; Steinecke to Tudor, 21 May 1957; Tudor to Steinecke, 31 May 1957; Tudor to Steinecke, 24 June 1957; Steinecke to Tudor, 25 June 1957; and Steinecke to Tudor, 29 June 1957, IMD.
[55] Stockhausen to Tudor, 26 May 1957 (in English), in Misch and Bandur (eds.), *Karlheinz Stockhausen bei den Internationalen Ferienkursen*, 166.
[56] Tudor to Steinecke, 31 May 1957, IMD.

Though presumably it was only small comfort to Steinecke, Tudor offered the world première of Christian Wolff's *For Piano with Preparations* (1955) by way of recompense.[57] The tone of Steinecke's letters to Stockhausen (written on the same day as Stockhausen wrote to Tudor of Steinecke's anger) and to Tudor suggests that worry and anxiousness regarding Tudor's reliability were what had occupied him. As a result of a complex set of forwarding arrangements set up for mail by Tudor, many of Steinecke's letters sent in early 1957 simply did not reach him until much later in the year. Steinecke wrote, then, to Stockhausen: 'Have you heard anything from Tudor? I'm a little worried because, since March, he hasn't answered a single one of my letters.'[58] More pointedly, Steinecke's reply to Tudor began: 'Many thanks for your letter, for which I have long waited and which I was extremely pleased to receive, since it has given me the surety that my proposals for Darmstadt are agreed.'[59] Those proposals would, finally, have included two performances of Klavierstück XI, Brown's *Music for Cello and Piano*, Boulez's Sonatine, Pousseur's *Variations I* (1956), Bo Nilsson's *VIII. Schlagfiguren* (1956), and Wolff's *For Piano with Preparations*.

Ultimately, these arrangements proved an irrelevance: Tudor developed a kidney infection which forced him to cancel his travel plans, sending a telegram to Steinecke to inform him of this on 7 July.[60] Plausibly, this may have been fortunate for Tudor's situation in Darmstadt at least. Had he travelled – presumably that same day, or the one after it – he would have fulfilled an agreement to give a performance of Klavierstück XI at the Festival de l'Art d'Avant-Garde in Nantes-Rezé on 9 July. Steinecke would have been left with a performance that was then only a German, and not even a European, première. In a letter to Stockhausen, Tudor seemed resigned and appeared to have had to agree to the Stockhausen performance in France as amelioration for a different 'offence': 'they are very angry because I have refused to play the Barraqué Sonate. This may make Steinecke furious again, but I am willing to take all the responsibility.'[61] For Darmstadt, Paul Jacobs was engaged at short notice to give the European première of Klavierstück XI, but it was not to a particularly enthusiastic reception. Stockhausen wrote to Tudor that on '[t]he last day in Darmstadt Paul Jacobs played the Klavierstück XI; it was not very interesting for the listeners.'[62] Significantly, though, the word

[57] Ibid.
[58] Steinecke to Stockhausen, 26 May 1957, in Misch and Bandur (eds.), *Karlheinz Stockhausen bei den Internationalen Ferienkursen*, 167.
[59] Steinecke to Tudor, 25 June 1957, IMD.   [60] Tudor to Steinecke, 7 July 1957, IMD.
[61] Tudor to Stockhausen, 25 June 1957, in Misch and Bandur (eds.), *Karlheinz Stockhausen bei den Internationalen Ferienkursen*, 170.
[62] Stockhausen to Tudor, 1 August 1957, in ibid., 176.

'improvisation' was, again, not far from the lips of commentators, Claus-Henning Bachmann, for one, observing that: 'Stockhausen is to a large extent embracing the possibilities of improvisation in his compositions',[63] while Lewinski commented that in Klavierstück XI an 'improvisatory moment returns the human-subjective factor to modern music',[64] and the subheading in a different piece focussing on another of Lewinski's reports from the 1957 courses simply reads: 'Improvisation'.[65] In any case, the possibilities of 'chance' had become central to Darmstadt in 1957, as Pierre Boulez demonstrated.

'Alea', 1957

In his introduction to *The Boulez–Cage Correspondence*, Jean-Jacques Nattiez notes that '[a]s is often Boulez's way, "Alea" does not mention anyone by name; Cage was not however deceived.'[66] Similarly, Amy Beal observes that Boulez's 'Alea' represents a 'thinly veiled critique of Cage's compositional and aesthetic aims as they had been presented in Tudor's 1956 seminars'.[67] Kurtz also identifies the anti-Cageian polemic, suggesting moreover that 'Stockhausen could tell that his words were also intended as a covert side-swipe at Klavierstück XI.'[68] In fact, though doubtless Cage does figure anonymously in Boulez's 1957 presentation, to suggest bluntly that 'Alea' is *about* Cage disguises the degree to which it is about a great deal more, not least the discussion which Adorno and Metzger, most prominently, had already engaged in. Arguably, this view would situate 'Alea' as a rather more important presentation – at least in the context of the Darmstadt avant-garde – than it would be were it *only* a hawkish riposte to Cage, since it brought debates about 'chance' together with debates about serial procedure, and was the first major presentation at Darmstadt to effect such a manoeuvre.

The year 1957 was only the first of several in which Boulez initially agreed to attend the Darmstadt courses and then cancelled late. Steinecke's frustration is clear in a letter to Nono, dated 7 June 1957:

---

[63] Claus-Henning Bachmann, 'Ende der Mechanisierung: Eindrücke von den Tagen Neuer Musik in Darmstadt', *Stuttgarter Zeitung*, 1 August 1957.
[64] Wolf-Eberhard von Lewinski, 'Der musikalische Roboter tritt an: Die modernste Musik zwischen Mensch und Maschine', *Christ und Welt*, 15 August 1957.
[65] Lewinski, 'Absage an das Idol des Musik-Ingenieurs'.
[66] Jean-Jacques Nattiez, 'Cage and Boulez: A Chapter of Music History' [1990], in Jean-Jacques Nattiez (ed.), *The Boulez–Cage Correspondence*, tr. Robert Samuels (Cambridge University Press, 1993), 19.
[67] Beal, *New Music, New Allies*, 91.   [68] Kurtz, *Stockhausen*, 88.

Kranichstein takes more effort than I'd thought (for one thing because of the many, many applications: every day 30–40 letters; then there are always new difficulties, big and small – a large one for the moment must stay between just the two of us: two days ago Boulez cancelled ('je suis fatigué' he wrote!), yesterday I wrote a long letter about the significance of Kranichstein 57 and hope that he will, in the end, come for 1 week – please – no-one knows about this yet, but if Boulez sticks to his cancellations I will have to write to 50 people that he isn't coming – you see: worries and work ...)[69]

Nono was wholly unimpressed with Steinecke's willingness to 'chase after' Boulez, suggesting that this was precisely the sort of thing that would 'lead to his becoming even more of a "prima donna"'. He had, to be sure, sympathy for Boulez's need for time to compose, but not for such a late communication: 'one understands that he has too little time and needs to finish his music, but he could and should have known that in plenty of time, rather than promise and assure you that he could come to Darmstadt for the courses.'[70] Steinecke attempted to persuade Boulez to attend for a briefer period than the whole span of the courses, but to no avail.[71] The absence of Boulez in person was noted with disappointment in the press: 'Boulez, despite being advertised and against all expectations, sadly did not appear.'[72] Lewinski's note in this regard is slightly curious: 'Pierre Boulez, always one of the most prominent young guests at the Marienhöhe, could not come this year.' It is curious simply because of the use of the word 'always' since, as noted previously, Boulez was for the most part notable by his absence from Darmstadt in the 1950s, being present for only a few days in 1952 before coming, still relatively briefly, as a faculty member in 1955.[73]

The upshot was that Boulez's presentation, 'Alea', was delivered for him by its translator into German, Heinz-Klaus Metzger. Metzger had been engaged as early as March to provide a translation of Boulez's 1957 contribution to the courses for publication in the first volume of the

---

[69] Steinecke to Nono, 7 June 1957, ALN. [70] Nono to Steinecke, late June 1957, ALN.
[71] Steinecke to Boulez, 26 June 1957, IMD. Boulez did, however, agree to come to Darmstadt for a performance of the Third Piano Sonata as a part of the run of concerts organised by the Internationales Musikinstitut in late September 1957, outside the main activities of the courses.
[72] Schlösser, 'Der neue Instrumentalstil'.
[73] One might suspect, and with some reason, that the reason why it was possible for Lewinski to make such an otherwise elementary error was the degree to which Darmstadt was increasingly seen as being and, vitally, *having been*, central. In 1958, it fell to Goléa to correct the same misapprehension. Karl Wörner's lecture 'Neue Musik 1948–1958' contained the suggestion that in that ten-year period, all new musical paths had led into and out of Darmstadt. Goléa rejoined that 'Boulez had certainly not been waiting for Kranichstein, and for Messiaen that is definitely not the case.' Antoine Goléa, 'Die neue Musik braucht Kranichstein ... aber es müßte gründlicher geprobt werden – trotzdem gab es herrliche Aufführungen von Nono und Boulez', *Der Mittag*, 17 September 1958.

Darmstädter Beiträge; the essay was sent to Metzger by 31 May.[74] Given the significance of translation for numerous presentations at Darmstadt between 1957 and 1960, it is regrettable that nothing survives in the case of 'Alea' to attest to the ways in which the translation acted upon Boulez's French text. There is no transcript of the version which Metzger delivered in German, nor a recording of the lecture. It is, in this case, possible only to work within the frame of the text published later in the *Darmstädter Beiträge*: although this is *a* translation by Metzger, it is difficult to state confidently that it represents *the* translation, at least not the one which Metzger presented on Boulez's behalf. In any case, Metzger delivered 'Alea' on the evening of 24 July 1957.

That 'Alea' is, in part, a more-or-less bitchy strike against Stockhausen, Cage, or anyone else should not disguise the fact that the opening of the presentation also took apart much of what Boulez regarded as dangerous trends in the European avant-garde as well as recollecting what he had learned of Cage's procedures during the time when they were in regular correspondence. There is no mistaking the first of the 'several composers' of Boulez's generation who exhibited a 'preoccupation, not to say obsession, with chance'. The initial target is, unmistakably, Cage:

> The most basic embodiment of chance is to be found in the adoption of a quasi-oriental philosophy in order to conceal a fundamental weakness in compositional technique: a cure for creative suffocation with a more subtle disease, which destroys the smallest embryo of craftsmanship. I like to call this an experiment in accidental chance – if experiment is the right word where an individual, who feels no responsibility for his work, but out of unconfessed weakness and confusion and the desire for temporary relief, simply throws himself into a puerile mumbo-jumbo.[75]

Boulez's view of this aspect of Cage's procedures did not seem to have moved very far from his perspective in December 1951, when he wrote to Cage that

> [t]he only thing, forgive me, which I am not happy with, is absolute chance (*by tossing the coins*). On the contrary, I believe that chance must be extremely controlled: by using tables in general, or series of tables, I believe it would be possible to direct the phenomenon of the automatism of chance, whether written down or not, which I mistrust as a facility that is not absolutely necessary.[76]

---

[74] Steinecke to Heinz-Klaus Metzger, 11 March and 31 May 1957, IMD.
[75] Pierre Boulez, 'Alea' [1957], in *Stocktakings from an Apprenticeship*, tr. Stephen Walsh (Oxford University Press, 1991), 26.
[76] Boulez to Cage, December 1951, in Nattiez (ed.), *The Boulez–Cage Correspondence*, 112.

If Boulez's perception of Cage's chance procedures had hardly shifted in the five-and-a-half years between these words written to Cage and 'Alea' – and one might well feel that it was this Cage, the Cage whom Boulez knew personally, who was discussed here, rather than the one presented in Tudor's 1956 seminars – his view of his own systematic procedures certainly had. Whatever disdain Boulez may have expressed for 'tossing the coins', it was as nothing compared with that 'more poisonous and insidious form of this intoxication', which is to say 'schematization', the drawing-up of pre-compositional tables: 'number fetishism, leading to straight bankruptcy. We plunge into a statistical stream which has no more (and no less) value than any other. In its All-Objectivity, the work represents a fragment of chance which – I come back to the point – is as justifiable (or unjustifiable) as any other fragment.' Again, it was the absence of imaginative power that Boulez seemed to suggest was most abhorrent, leading to the conclusion that 'these slices of chance are not fit for human consumption, since from the start one wonders why one should consume them!'[77] Although one might imagine this criticism applying reasonably well to a number of serially derived pieces, the piece that must have been utmost in Boulez's mind can hardly have been anything other than *Structure Ia*. While Boulez reserved his most severe criticism for his own music, he also insisted that he had moved on. By contrast, one would think that Cage's music was still dominated by the techniques which had generated the *Music of Changes*.

Alongside Cage and Boulez himself, clearly Stockhausen completed the trinity of malefactors in terms of chance, and it is, no less clearly, *Zeitmasse* that is the particular bone of contention here (which is one sure reason why one cannot find Tudor criticised beneath the surface of what Boulez had to say): 'The notation becomes – subtly – imprecise enough to allow the performer's instantaneous, shifting, iridescent choice to slip through the hypothetical grid. One *could* prolong that rest, one *could* hold that note, one *could* speed up, one *could* ... at every moment ... in short one has chosen henceforth to be meticulously imprecise.'[78] This, though, is roughly where examinations of 'Alea' that would construe it as an attack on this or that aesthetic position tend to leave off, which is to say the point at which Boulez had outlined the problem (that it comes back to '[a]lways a refusal to choose'), but before he had proposed the directions his own thought was taking in terms of developing solutions.

For Boulez this was the nub of the question. Composition had been, classically speaking, 'the result of constant choice', such that from a framework of possibilities, all of which were viable at a certain point in the

---

[77] Boulez, 'Alea', 27.   [78] Ibid., 28.

elaboration of the piece, the composer came to *choose* one. Boulez hardly suggested that this was an objective decision-making process; on the contrary, 'this elaboration once again inevitably involves chance. Is this possibility more "viable" than that? Only because you found it so at that point in your development.'[79] The *point* of composition, and here Boulez and Cage would surely have agreed, remained surprise. Yet it seemed in this case that Boulez was seeking his own personal surprise in the process of composition only. In the writing of the score, as he suggests, despite the composer's vigilance, 'chance survives, sneaking in through a thousand unfillable cracks'.[80] This was the sort of chance which interested Boulez, that which persists *in spite of* any systematic procedure. That he looked here to indeterminacy inhering within the compositional process itself, rather than something which happened in the moment of performance, is clarified by his suggestion that 'musical development could admit "accidents" at various compositional stages or levels'.[81]

As well as describing forms of compositional indeterminacy, Boulez also proposed ways in which performance indeterminacy might take place. The first level he mentioned was, as he himself admitted, elementary: 'If, for example, in a given sequence of sounds I interpolate a variable number of small notes, it is obvious that the tempo of these sounds will be constantly disturbed by the intrusion of the small notes, which each time provoke an interruption, or more exactly a break in the degree of tension.'[82] In such a situation, Boulez suggested, a space would open up between the more-or-less strictly determined (the fixed, written temporal pace of the score) and the more-or-less fluid (the interpolation of the *acciaccature*). It was, most likely, the example of Stockhausen's Klavierstück VI, which is prefaced by a note reading 'small notes are to be played "as quickly as possible", independently of the written tempo indications', which was uppermost in Boulez's mind here. It would only be in a case such as this, where the number of *acciaccature* is so high and their performance is temporally independent, that these notes would be significantly different from *acciaccature* as traditionally conceived.[83]

Throughout 'Alea', Boulez flitted between what might be thought of as performance indeterminacy (where certain decisions are left open to the performer) and the chance vagaries of composition (improvisation, as it were, on the page with given materials), and it is important to distinguish between the two. The latter was a process with which Boulez was wholly in sympathy. His principal mode of operation as a composer at the time seemed to be dominated by it. He might well have been describing either

[79] Ibid., 29.   [80] Ibid., 30.   [81] Ibid.   [82] Ibid., 31.   [83] Ibid., 32.

his own *Structure Ia* or Messiaen's *Mode de valeurs et d'intensités* in making the following (rather lengthy) observation:

> Suppose that I choose series of durations and dynamic intensities and that, assuming a fixed result from the meeting of these two series, I want to attach this result to a pitch series. If I assign fixed registers to the pitch series, it is clear that there will be only one solution for any given note; that is, the note will be ineluctably fixed in register (absolute frequency), dynamic, and duration: a single possibility of encounter for these three systems on this particular sound 'point'.[84]

Thus, Boulez distinguished between fixed relationships between particular parameters – as in the case of the Messiaen study where, for example, the B♮ in the middle of the treble stave would always last for a dotted crotchet with a dynamic of *piano* – and ignoring one parameter at the pre-compositional stage and 'improvising' this parameter's characteristics during what he called the 'writing-up stage':

> [S]uppose we keep the same pitch series without imposing register, and leave the register to be improvised at the writing-up stage, we shall immediately have a 'straight line' of registers, a geometric position for all the 'points' which answer to the three other characteristics: relative pitch-class, dynamics, and duration. By gradually transferring the relativity of registration to the durations, and then to the dynamics, I shall have achieved first a 'plane', then a fixed 'volume', within which to locate my sound 'point'.[85]

This is what Boulez seems to have meant by 'chance' in the context of composition, which is to say from the perspective of the fixed musical score. In any case, however, it is some measure distant from any interpretation of multiple serialism that would have the results more or less fixed at the outset through the various preparational charts and tables. Boulez was clear: such elements were, and ought only to be, merely pre-compositional materials, and the process of composition itself was one by which to *choose* a route through the massively variable labyrinth suggested by these charts of possibilities. In some senses, this is already *musique informelle*, four years before Adorno attempted to theorise it as such. This was also, in Boulez's terms, elementary, if not trivial.

Though it was probably unclear to listeners at the time, what Boulez was tacitly moving into the frame of discussion was his own Third Piano Sonata (1955–7), which had – in provisional form at least – 'solved' some of these problems. Some of the elements that Boulez had already discussed found form in that piece. Koblyakov suggests that Boulez's technique of 'frequency

[84] Ibid., 32.   [85] Ibid.

multiplication' – through which harmonic fields and domains are derived from a core set of pitches – is still in use in the Third Sonata. Moreover, as Koblyakov argues, it is the multiplication itself which, in part, suggests multiple routes through the core material from the outset.[86] That said, even if analytically serial derivations can be found, Alastair Williams is surely right to observe that, in the parts of the second formant, 'Trope', '[i]n Texte and Parenthèse the serial procedure and their derivations, though disguised, are possible to follow. The material of Commentaire and especially Glose is, however, so remote from its origin that it is questionable whether the music is serial at all.'[87] That it is serial is probably not ultimately in doubt; the point made by Williams's observation is that serial derivation of materials can result in musics in which no trace of the process remains, such that any sort of reconstruction of process would be impossible without access to the sketches. In that case, the question of whether the piece is serially derived becomes, surely, much less pressing than the question of what the music actually does in its immanent sounding image.

Those *acciaccature* which may be found in Stockhausen's Klavierstück VI find an analogue in the Parenthèse movement of 'Trope'. Here, rather than small note heads, one finds square note heads which, according to the score's legend, 'have no pre-determined value. They can be completely free, they may also have to be kept within a precise duration indicated between the staves by a horizontal line with an arrow at the beginning and a vertical stroke at the end.' Similarly, different gradations and locations of caesurae interrupt the strict temporal flow. However, it was in terms of structural indeterminacy that Boulez's 'Alea' most clearly recognised the Third Piano Sonata as representing a 'solution' to the two forms of unacceptable chance Boulez had outlined. As Boulez observed:

> In a directed whole, these various structures must be strictly controlled by a general kind of 'phrasing', must contain beginning and end markers, and must make use of different kinds of 'turntable' for purposes of intersection; all this to escape from the complete loss of any global sense of form as well as to avoid falling into a kind of improvisation with no other imperative than free will.[88]

It is clear, again, that the contrast is made between structured, carefully controlled chance and improvisation. In the terms Boulez outlined, if the global sense of form were lost, what remained, even if not improvisation *qua* improvisation, might just as well be the surrendering of compositional will to the performer.

[86] See Koblyakov, *Pierre Boulez*, esp. 3–33.
[87] Alastair Williams, *New Music and the Claims of Modernity* (Aldershot: Ashgate, 1997), 55.
[88] Boulez, 'Alea', 33.

These beginning and end markers are shown in two ways in the extant formants of the Third Piano Sonata. In 'Trope', one route is doubled: a first possible set of routes is given through the piece, such that each individual part can begin, followed by the others in a limited number of possible successions:

Commentaire-Glose-Texte-Parenthèse
Glose-Commentaire-Texte-Parenthèse
Glose-Texte-Parenthèse-Commentaire
Commentaire-Glose-Texte-Parenthèse
Texte-Parenthèse-Commentaire-Glose
Texte-Parenthèse-Glose-Commentaire
Parenthèse-Commentaire-Glose-Texte
Parenthèse-Glose-Commentaire-Texte

Thus, the order is cyclical: Parenthèse-Commentaire-Glose-Commentaire-Texte, except for the fact that Commentaire must be heard only once in a single performance. Second, in both Parenthèse and Commentaire, there are 'free' sections, literally in parentheses, which the performer may choose to play or to omit *ad libitum*.

The centre of the Third Piano Sonata, 'Constellation-Miroir', moves yet closer to what Boulez thought would be the most effective way to introduce chance into composition and yet to master it. His description in 'Alea' of an ideal solution is an almost exact mirror of his practice in this sense:

> Starting with an initial, 'begin' sign, and ending with a concluding, 'finish' sign, the work will put into compositional practice what we were studying theoretically at the outset: a problematical 'course' subject to time – a certain number of aleatoric events within a mobile duration – with, however, a logic of development and a global sense of purpose, allowing for the interpolation of caesuras, whether in the form of silence or sound-plateaux: a course with a beginning and an end. By this means the 'finite' quality of western art, with its closed circle, is respected, while introducing the element of 'chance' from the open circle of oriental art.[89]

That closed circle, to be sure, is the one which 'Trope' foregrounds. The other aspects signalled, however, are those of 'Constellation-Miroir'. Here, across nine large sheets of manuscript, are scattered the various groupings of 'blocks', 'points', and 'mixtures of points and blocks'. Though the instructions are clear that the groupings themselves should be performed in a particular order – Mixture-Points 3-Blocks II-Points 2-Blocks I-Points 1 – in order to fulfil the piece's criterion of alternating points and blocks, after beginning with the mixture, within each grouping there is a

[89] Ibid., 35.

variety of possible routes. Each mixture itself contains a selection of smaller sections, each closing with an arrow, or a number of arrows, to denote the next possible section that can be performed within that grouping. Since Boulez's instructions note that each of these sections must be performed – and, moreover, 'without omission or repetition' – the number of potential routes through the piece is rather smaller than a first look at the score might suggest, but it does afford a limited amount of variety on the structural level. The piece is also, in this sense, radically different from Stockhausen's Klavierstück XI, to which it is in other respects relatively similar, since repetition of structural elements is, in that case, vital not only to shaping the piece but also to knowing where to end, which is to say on the third repetition of an individual group. In Boulez's Third Piano Sonata, the piece does have a defined beginning and end point, even if elements within that span are, within carefully prescribed limits, mobile.

That a relationship might be drawn between Adorno's presentation 'Criteria of the New Music', discussed above, and Boulez's 'Alea' was noted by Andreas Razumovsky, who suggested that their respective polemics against 'material fetishism' and the threats to the criteria of diffentiation, character, and the communicability of both shape and character inherent within serial techniques could be considered analogous.[90] In any case, though, the reaction from the press was less strong than might be expected from the latter reception of 'Alea'. Lewinski regarded Boulez's attempt as being subsidiary to what Stockhausen had presented musically in Klavierstück XI. Indeed, Lewinski suggested that Boulez's thoughts were simply part of a wider trajectory: 'One could, alongside Stockhausen, name Boulez, Nono, and Berio, who are each, in their own way, concerned to defend the freedom of the human against the demands of the machine or the mechanistic in music.'[91] In his annual broadcast for the Westdeutscher Rundfunk, Lewinski returned to Boulez:

> Anyone who has followed the development of new music must say that its force has become worn out. One has waited for this moment, which has now arrived, and for that reason we single it out: the moment of the return of the aleatoric, as Boulez puts it, of the free creative impulse. Put tritely: the rejection of the idol of the music-engineers. Or: the moment of the return of the human into music [...] The artwork should once more be a living organism.[92]

---

[90] Andreas Razumovsky, 'Webern und die junge Generation: Die Darmstädter Ferienkurse 1957', *Frankfurter Allgemeine Zeitung*, 5 August 1957.
[91] Lewinski, 'Der musikalische Roboter tritt an'.
[92] Wolf-Eberhard von Lewinski, 'Kranichstein 1957: Grundsätzliche Gedanken zu den 12. Internationalen Ferienkursen für Neue Musik in Darmstadt', broadcast, Westdeutscher Rundfunk, 25 September 1957, transcript IMD.

In part, one might see here a recognition that composers were, in general terms, no longer adhering to any sort of strict serialism, as noted in the discussion of the dispute between Adorno and Metzger above, and that this was clear even to a regional reporter, albeit a well-informed one (even if Lewinski seems not to have recognised that the apparently strictly serial was only very rarely either strict or serial). What Lewinski was championing was precisely the sort of freedom which Boulez himself outlined: the freedom to work with productive mechanisms as a form of material generation, but to improvise with them on the page. Manfred Gräter's review of the 1957 courses – written for *Melos*, but unpublished by it – struck at precisely this: 'it cannot be denied that this development of the aleatoric in composition can lead to an unquestionably greater degree of differentiation within serial music than has previously been the case'.[93] This sort of improvisation was of the sort that might have been designated in fully notated, fixed pieces through the *title* 'improvisation'. What was meant by the 'free creative impulse' was the freedom to be a 'composer' in the sense in which composers had been before the war. It was, thus, vital that this was a 'return', and not a new development. In short, if there is an underlying critique of pre-existing serial music to be found in Lewinski's commentary, it is very close to Adorno's (or, indeed, Boulez's own), and was already outmoded by the time Adorno (or Lewinski) made it.

Despite the impact which, given a little time to digest, Boulez's presentation appears to have had on Lewinski, 'Alea' was unmentioned in any of Steinecke's broadcasts on the 1957 courses – three for the Heissischer Rundfunk and two for the Bayerischer Rundfunk – though he may, perhaps, still have been smarting from Boulez's absence from the courses themselves. Boulez was represented musically in 1957 only by the Sonatine, which had already been premièred at the previous year's courses, rather than the hoped-for Third Sonata. Similarly, in 1958 Boulez was represented by a revision of an older piece, *Le Soleil des eaux* (1948, rev. 1958). It would be 1959 before Boulez's own musical approach to the aleatory would appear at Darmstadt, and that would happen, vitally, after the arrival 'proper', in person, of John Cage on the Darmstadt stage.

Earle Brown, *Music for Cello and Piano*

Though Tudor did not ultimately attend the 1957 courses, the projected performance of Earle Brown's *Music for Cello and Piano* did take place, on

---

[93] Manfred Gräter, 'Darmstädter Ferienkurse 1957' (unpublished report), IMD.

27 July, performed by the pianist Alfons Kontarsky and the cellist Werner Taube, who had won the Kranichsteiner Musikpreis at the 1956 courses. The suggestion of Brown's music to Steinecke had originally come from Maderna; Steinecke proposed to Brown that a performance of *Indices* (1954, rev. 1957) might be appropriate.[94] In later life, Brown may have had cause to regret declining such a performance (on the grounds that Hans Rosbaud and Strobel had the piece under consideration for performance at Donaueschingen),[95] since it would not be until 16 April 2010, nearly eight years after Brown's own death, that *Indices* would finally be premièred by Ensemble work in progress.

As was often Steinecke's way, his contact with Brown was part of a double game. Doubtless he was wholly sincere in his suggestion that he wanted to bring Brown's music to an official concert at Darmstadt, following the unofficial performance of *Perspectives* during Wolpe's lecture, but he also knew that Brown was in contact with Varèse, whom he wanted to draw into the 'Darmstadt fold' through a Varèse-focussed volume of the *Darmstädter Beiträge*. Steinecke asked Brown whether he could procure detailed biographical information from Varèse as well as precise data on performances – especially premières – of his work.[96] Broadly, Steinecke's attempts to work with Brown in 1957 were an almost complete failure: despite promises from Varèse to Brown, it seems that the materials on his life and works never arrived (indeed, Brown related to Steinecke that, as far as Varèse was concerned, such interests might be regarded as 'necrophilia');[97] Brown himself was unable to attend the 1957 courses, since this would have been possible only through the acquisition of a Guggenheim grant, and Brown's application was unsuccessful; finally, the absence of Tudor meant that Alfons Kontarsky felt he had too little time to put together a strong performance of *Music for Cello and Piano*.[98] Nevertheless, Werner Taube had written to Brown to say that he was pleased with how things had turned

---

[94] Steinecke to Earle Brown, 14 February 1957, IMD.
[95] Brown to Steinecke, 26 Feburary 1957, IMD.
[96] Steinecke to Brown, 24 March 1957, IMD. Steinecke's attempts to entice Varèse to Darmstadt via Brown persisted, with no greater success, into 1961. Though Varèse always made polite noises when he did finally return Steinecke's requests, Darmstadt was clearly of little interest or significance for him.
[97] Brown to Steinecke, 31 March 1957, IMD.
[98] There was no small degree of irony in the fact that it was the piano part that proved the difficulty, as Brown himself noted in a letter to Steinecke, dated 29 January 1958: the problem of finding a cellist who was able to participate had been long been the central difficulty. Initially, Artur Tröster was expected to take this role, though it had taken Steinecke a month to find a cellist willing to take the piece on. Next, Christine Schotte had briefly agreed to perform Brown's music, before Taube was finally agreed upon. Brown to Steinecke, 29 January 1958, IMD.

Precursors

out,[99] and Steinecke assured Brown that the performance had left a strong impression.[100]

Steinecke's assertion of the piece's impact was something of an exaggeration. Largely it appears to have passed the press by. Nevertheless, Steinecke evidently thought enough of Brown's music to feature it on his broadcasts for the Bayerischer and Hessischer Rundfunk, reviewing the 1957 courses. Brown would doubtless have been unimpressed to discover that, in the former case, he was described as a 'Cage student'. Steinecke also put Brown's *Music for Cello and Piano* into the context of Stockhausen's Klavierstück XI, suggesting that both had an interest in the space between serial order and the degree of freedom given to the performer, which lent both pieces a 'certain breadth of variation', and that, moreover, the 'irrational element, which is always meaningful for a piece which is so precisely fixed, is here consciously introduced into the compositional calculations'.[101]

Steinecke was keen that Brown's music appear on the programme for 1958.[102] In the first place this was to have been the delayed performance of *Indices*, under Boulez's direction. Yet Boulez postponed the projected performance by the Domaine Musical of the piece in Paris in March 1958, with the consequence that a Darmstadt performance of *Indices* would also be delayed.[103] Steinecke proposed that he might instead commission a new piece, still for the forces of the Domaine Musical, under Boulez's direction.[104] Brown confirmed the title, *Pentathis*, on 15 April 1958, closing his letter with an observation on the 1958 courses:

> I look forward very much to being in Darmstadt in September. It seems that there will be a great caravan of avant-garde Americans coming to Europe in September......myself, John Cage, David Tudor and now I believe that Merce Cunningham (choreographer and dancer for whom INDICES was written) and my wife (Cunningham's leading dancer) will also come......it is not certain that the dancers will come but they will if they can arrange a tour......I can only speak for PENTATHIS and myself...we will be there.[105]

Brown, perhaps surprisingly, was enrolled at Darmstadt as a student, in the classes of Boulez, Krenek, and Kolisch, though as things turned out, he was unable to take the Boulez seminar. In 1958, however, Cage would come to Darmstadt as a faculty member – of a sort, at least.

---

[99] Brown to Steinecke, 29 January 1958, IMD.
[100] Steinecke to Brown, 19 December 1957, IMD.
[101] Wolfgang Steinecke, '1. Bericht über die XII. Internationalen Ferienkurse für Neue Musik in Darmstadt 1957', broadcast, Bayerischer Rundfunk, 5 November 1957, transcript IMD.
[102] Steinecke to Brown, 19 December 1957, IMD.
[103] Brown to Steinecke, 29 January 1958, IMD.
[104] Steinecke to Brown, 12 February 1958, IMD.   [105] Brown to Steinecke, 15 April 1958, IMD.

4   The Cage shock

Arrangements

The question of how Cage came to be invited to Darmstadt has been a perplexing one. Given that Steinecke had not reacted positively to Cage and Tudor's European concert debut at Donaueschingen, one might find it relatively surprising that he should have been willing to bring Cage to Darmstadt at all. Yet it was not because of Steinecke, originally at least, that Cage was to be in Darmstadt. Despite the issues regarding Tudor's première of Klavierstück XI, Steinecke had written to him in late 1957 to ask whether he would come once again. Steinecke suggested that, alongside classes, he would like to have performances of Boulez's Third Piano Sonata, Cage's *Music of Changes*, and, perhaps to show that the past was forgiven, even if not forgotten, Klavierstück XI.[1] It took a further prompt to elicit a reply from Tudor,[2] but when it came, it was wholly positive, though Tudor advised that he had not as yet seen the score of the Third Piano Sonata and could not commit himself to playing it until he had done so. In respect of Cage, however, Tudor's reply is notable. He stated, quite directly, that '[o]n this visit to Europe John Cage is going to come with me, for concerts and performances of his new work for piano and orchestra. You might like to use this opportunity to have his services at the Ferienkurse also. He is a very able lecturer and teacher, as well as composer!' Tudor proposed that he and Cage might give a piano duo concert, which he expected at that point to feature Brown, Cage, Feldman, Wolff, and William Wilder.[3] Steinecke replied quickly that it would be impossible to give Cage an 'official' position as a faculty member since those positions were already filled: Boulez and Krenek were expected to be the principal composition lecturers, with Boris Blacher speaking about music for stage, radio, and film. Nono and Maderna were jointly entrusted with running the composition studios for discussion and performances of the work of young composers. Nevertheless, what Steinecke proposed was that, as a part of the continuation of Tudor's working group on new performance techniques and the realisation of scores, Cage might speak about his work within that frame.[4] Tudor and Cage discussed this and seemingly agreed quickly, with Tudor proposing the curious title 'Compositorical

---

[1] Steinecke to Tudor, 19 December 1957, IMD.   [2] Steinecke to Tudor, 30 January 1958, IMD.
[3] Tudor to Steinecke, 6 February 1958, IMD.   [4] Steinecke to Tudor, 12 Febuary 1958, IMD.

Questions – Europe–America'.[5] Thus it was that Cage was taken onto the Darmstadt programme and was advertised in the promotional material as giving a lecture, jointly with Tudor, entitled 'New Piano Music in the USA and Europe', which was to focus on precisely the three pieces Steinecke had proposed.[6] The first that Stockhausen knew about this, it seems, was in a letter in which Tudor suggested that he had perhaps already heard from Otto Tomek at the Westdeutscher Rundfunk that Cage was coming with Tudor to Europe between August and October. The letter largely concerns the details of the piece Cage was at that point writing for performance in Cologne (though first in New York): his *Concert for Piano and Orchestra* (1957–8). Darmstadt was mentioned in passing only. Nevertheless, Stockhausen did write to Steinecke on 1 March 1958 and proposed to him that Cage should have a complete composition course, stating that he was 'worth 10 Kreneks'.[7] By the time this idea came under any serious discussion, however, Stockhausen's advice was apparently not decisive; indeed, as I outline below, during those discussions Stockhausen was arguably directly unhelpful.

As in the previous year, the problem was Boulez. Steinecke had written twice to Boulez, proposing his attendance at the 1958 courses.[8] Steinecke's later letter suggests that the very late dates of the 1958 courses – 2 to 13 September – had been chosen precisely to suit Boulez's own schedule: the aim was to make the courses as close as possible to the dates of the Donaueschingen festival in October, at which Boulez's *Poésie pour pouvoir* (1955–8) was to be premièred. It is hard to imagine Steinecke making such alterations to the courses for any other of the younger composers, and it is certainly testament to the importance he laid on Boulez's attendance. The details of Boulez's planned trip to Darmstadt in 1958 were hammered out in person when Boulez and Steinecke were together in Hamburg in mid January 1958. Though the specifics found themselves in flux until about May 1958 – one of Steinecke's proposals, dismissed by Boulez ('très mauvais!'), was ultimately replaced by Gilbert Amy's *Mouvements* (1958),[9] for instance – the principles remained consistent: the Domaine Musical was to give two concerts – the first on 6 September, the second on 11 September – while Boulez would be the principal member of composition staff, leading ten seminars on the theme of 'Sound and the Instrument'.

Since the broad sweep of Boulez's 1958 Darmstadt activities had been agreed so early (and since Steinecke doubtless felt to some degree that

[5] Tudor to Steinecke, 1 March 1958, IMD.
[6] See Misch and Bandur (eds.), *Karlheinz Stockhausen bei den Internationalen Ferienkursen*, 185.
[7] Stockhausen to Steinecke, 1 March 1958, in ibid., 194–6.
[8] Steinecke to Boulez, 15 and 23 December 1957, IMD.
[9] Boulez to Steinecke, 15 Feburary 1958, IMD.

Boulez really owed Darmstadt something, after his late cancellation in the previous year), it must have been something of a shock on 5 August, less than a month before the scheduled start of the courses, to receive notice from Boulez that he intended to cancel again. The problem, on this occasion, was (as Boulez described it) almost entirely out of his hands: it was, so he argued, a question of technical problems, which were simply taking far longer to resolve than he had anticipated. The upshot, however, was that he would either remain in Baden-Baden to complete the work for Donaueschingen or come to Darmstadt and leave the work unfinished at its première, a situation that he suggested would represent a 'catastrophe'. Boulez did provide details for all the musicians of the Domaine Musical to Steinecke, but said that he had been unable to think of a replacement for himself in terms of the composition courses, though he suggested that something might be achieved with Maderna leading a course, assisted by Nono and Pousseur.[10]

Both Shultis and Trudu propose that the suggestion that Cage take over some of the work of the absent Boulez came from Maderna.[11] This information appears, in both cases, to have come from the recollection of Wilhelm Schlüter, the former archivist of the Internationales Musikinstitut in Darmstadt, and is faulty, though it is certainly the case that one of the first people to whom Steinecke turned in this crisis was indeed Maderna, probably standing the cost of what would still have been an expensive international telephone call to Verona, where Maderna was at the time, in the hope that some quick solution could be found. Around 7 August Maderna had already written to Steinecke with some proposals for solutions, saying that he and Nono had spoken for a long time regarding what they could do 'to overcome Boulez's treachery'. The first was that Stockhausen would simply take over Boulez's seminars directly; the second was that Nono and Maderna would take over the seminars Boulez would have run and, in effect, divide them up between them in addition to the composition studio they were already running. Maderna also said that he could take over Boulez's conducting duties with the Domaine Musical directly.[12] The first mention of Cage is in Steinecke's reply of 10 August. First and foremost, Steinecke was effusive in his thanks to Maderna: 'You are a true friend and the saviour of Kranichstein.' At the same time, though, he observed that there was simply no way that Maderna would have time and energy to do everything, since this would

---

[10] Boulez to Steinecke, 5 August 1958, IMD.
[11] Shultis, 'Cage and Europe', 33; Antonio Trudu, La 'scuola' di Darmstadt (Milan: Unicopli, 1992), 125 n. 6.
[12] Maderna to Steinecke, undated but probably 7 August 1958, in Dalmonte (ed.), Bruno Maderna–Wolfgang Steinecke, 164–6.

mean that he was close to undertaking both his role and Boulez's. He had spoken to Stockhausen on the telephone to ask about Maderna and Nono's other suggestion, that Stockhausen himself take over Boulez's seminars. Steinecke was clearly unimpressed by Stockhausen's pithy response: 'I asked Stockhausen on the telephone whether he would help out. He refused! ("No time").' Thus it was that Steinecke had decided that he required an alternative, since neither of the two proposed by Maderna was viable: Stockhausen would not help, and it would be too much work for Maderna and Nono. As Steinecke wrote to Maderna: 'So I came to the idea that 5 totally unusual seminars by John Cage could be held, because he is here and has little to do.'[13] Cage, then, was coming to Darmstadt anyway; without the influence of anyone other than Tudor, he had, from the outset, been expected to speak about his work in a relatively informal setting. The idea that Cage should do more than this, though, was Steinecke's. Even though Stockhausen had proposed that Cage should have a course, in the wake of his direct refusal to help, it would go too far to claim, as Misch and Bandur do, that Cage was invited on Stockhausen's recommendation.[14] If Maderna had not agreed with Steinecke's idea, it would have been irrelevant: Steinecke's invitation to Cage had already been sent.[15] His answer came in the form of a brief telegram: 'YES SUBJECT COMPOSITION AS PROCESS = CAGE +'.[16] It is far from clear what Cage did in these five seminars. This is not least because the bulk of what seems to be remembered about his presence is concentrated on the three studio presentations with Tudor, under the general title 'Composition as Process'. It may even be that, in the end, he never gave these seminars and it did fall to Nono and Maderna to run them.

Steinecke seemed keen, as soon as he had a solution, to let the Boulez issue rest. He wrote to Nono on 10 August to advise him that, because of what had happened, Nono would have to take the first half of the composition studio alone to give Maderna time to rehearse with the Domaine Musical, opening his letter with: 'nothing on the subject of Boulez – there's no time for that because there is such an enormous amount to do in order to make Kranichstein 58 really good – together with you and Bruno'.[17] Steinecke had also enclosed a copy of his letter to Maderna, in which the idea of Cage was raised, and in his reply Nono seemed hugely positive about such a development:

---

[13] Steinecke to Maderna, 10 August 1958, in ibid., 168.
[14] Misch and Bandur (eds.), *Karlheinz Stockhausen bei den Internationalen Ferienkursen*, 184.
[15] Steinecke to Cage, 8 August 1958, IMD.   [16] Cage to Steinecke, 15 August 1958, IMD.
[17] Steinecke to Nono, 10 August 1958, ALN.

everything seems fine, according to your letters!
I'm in agreement with everything!
5 seminars with Bruno and 5 with Cage: very good!
Also: you see how it is always possible to arrange something else quickly, and how no-one can damage Darmstadt, when he cancels. (= Boulez)[18]

For Maderna, though, the subject of Boulez clearly still rankled. In a letter to Steinecke, dated 21 August 1958, he observed that, if Gilbert Amy's *Mouvements* were to be made part of the Domaine Musical concert which he would himself direct on 6 September 1958, it would be impossible for anyone 'to say that we have anything against Boulez (Amy is certainly a close friend of Boulez's)'.[19]

Concert

Three days before Cage's first lecture, Cage and Tudor presented an evening concert for two pianos, performing Cage's own *Music for Two Pianos* (a selection from the *Music for Piano* series of 1952–6), *Variations I* (1958), and *Winter Music* (1957), Brown's *Four Systems*, Feldman's *Two Pianos* (1957), and Wolff's *Duo for Pianists I* and *Duo for Pianists II* (1957 and 1958, respectively). All of these were European premières, as the pieces had been given their world premières in the United States, with the exception of Wolff's *Duo for Pianists II*, which was performed for the first time at Darmstadt. Reports in the *Darmstädter Echo* and the *Darmstädter Tagblatt* dealt with Cage and Tudor's performance before Cage had delivered his lectures, and are particularly intriguing for the ways in which they suggest a response to Cage *without* reference to what he had to say. However, the *Darmstädter Tagblatt*'s correspondent – on this occasion, unusually, not Wolf-Eberhard von Lewinski – had some preconceptions, having heard Cage and Tudor's Donaueschingen performance. Nevertheless, on the basis of the evidence of the recording of Cage's *Variations I*, the report of both the performance and the interplay between stage and audience is extremely accurate:

> Anyone who experienced the concert of 'music for prepared piano' at Donaueschingen a few years ago was prepared for a thing or two after reading the names of Cage and Tudor. It lived up to expectations: the new listeners horrified or amused, encouraged into a sadly not always witty heckling, but at least astonished. Not only are the keys of the piano used for the production of

[18] Nono to Steinecke, 12 August 1958, ALN.
[19] Maderna to Steinecke, 21 August 1958, in Dalmonte (ed.), *Bruno Maderna–Wolfgang Steinecke*, 178.

pitches, as is usual, but here one plucks the strings (with refinement) too; the poor instruments were struck, there was squeaking and bleating from small pipes, and, for a couple of seconds, the Armed Forces Network or some other channel was turned on on the radio.[20]

If anything, on the basis of the recordings of Cage and Tudor's performance, it seems that this may be a little kind to some members of the audience, who dissolved into fairly raucous hilarity at the entry of any event not comprising modes of attack to which they were already accustomed, with recognisable snatches of music from the radio attracting the greatest uproar. Both Feldman's *Two Pianos* and Cage's *Winter Music* attracted some praise but, in both cases, the *Darmstädter Tagblatt*'s reviewer felt they overstayed their welcome, in Cage's case suggesting that 'overlong pauses' tired the ear. Notably, though, there was, it seems, 'rich applause', even if it was 'mixed with irony'.[21]

For Gustav Adolf Trumpff, too, the events of the concert were not 'accessible' without further explanation. Vitally, he suggested it was not the means of sound-production which were difficult to comprehend but, rather, the 'seemingly abrupt switches between improvisation and organised composition'. Nevertheless, Trumpff was impressed both by the music of Feldman and by Wolff's *Duo for Pianists I*, suggesting that the space between events became in itself meaningful. As for Cage, Trumpff was largely dismissive or, at least, bewildered. The question of what was notated in Cage's music was a matter which Trumpff obviously regarded as significant, not least perhaps because of his suspicions that the pianists were, in large part, improvising: 'one could see, even from a distance, large, black sound surfaces on the manuscript [of *Winter Music*], while in the other two pieces by Cage [*Music for Two Pianos* and *Variations I*] an idiosyncratic notation based on other premises predominated.' If Trumpff's eyewitness account is accurate, it is notable that at least one of the performers, then, was not performing from a standard five-line score. This may seem unsurprising in the case of *Variations I* especially, but as I will go on to discuss below, the situation is far from being so simple, especially with regard to the question of just what Tudor was doing and what relationship it might have to improvisation. In any case, what might otherwise have been helpful in seeing the notation was, so Trumpff thought, merely confusing. He concluded: 'music should, first and foremost, be heard and not seen'. He suggested, too, that it would be helpful if Cage were, in spoken or written

---

[20] [jg.], 'Konzert mit vielen Fragezeichen: John Cage und David Tudor an zwei Klavieren', *Darmstädter Tagblatt*, 5 September 1958.
[21] Ibid..

form, to 'build bridges that might lead to a real understanding'.[22] One might have presumed, then, that Trumpff would have been anticipating Cage's lectures with keen interest.

Lectures

Cage delivered his first Darmstadt lecture, 'Changes', on 6 September. In comparison with the concert presentation and the two lectures which followed, 'Changes' was uncontroversial. In it, Cage discussed, reasonably clearly, the changes in his compositional procedures from 1948 to 1958, which is to say from the *Sonatas and Interludes for Prepared Piano* through to the *Concert for Piano and Orchestra*. In doing this, he outlined the proportional workings of the *Sonatas and Interludes* and the *First Construction (in Metal)*, and showed how those proportions continued to figure in the *Music of Changes*, as well as the way in which the proportional 'boxes' ceased to be filled with specifically chosen materials, but were filled with materials from a fixed gamut, determined in each case through chance operations. Cage explained the way in which decisions were made for the *Music for Piano* series: 'notes were determined by imperfections in the paper upon which the music was written. The number of imperfections was determined by chance.'[23] More pertinently, in the context of what followed, Cage described the way in which the materials for *Variations I* had been formed and, vitally, gave some indications as to what a performer was expected to do with them:

> Sounds, as we know, have frequency, amplitude, duration, timbre, and in a composition, an order of succession. Five lines representing these five characteristics may be drawn in India ink upon transparent black squares. Upon another such square a point may be inscribed. Placing the square with the lines over the square with the point, a determination may be made to the physical nature of a sound and its place with a determined program simply by dropping a perpendicular from the point to the line and measuring according to any method of measurement [...] This describes the situation obtaining in a recent composition, *Variations*, the composing means itself one of the eighty-four occurring in the part for piano of *Concert for Piano and Orchestra*.[24]

Cage could hardly have been clearer: measurements had to be taken, and it was scarcely conceivable that this could be done in the moment of performance. Yet what was not made explicit was that this work is handed to the

---

[22] Gustav Adolf Trumpff, 'Spiel auf zwei Flügeln: John Cage und David Tudor', *Darmstädter Echo*, 5 September 1958.
[23] John Cage, 'Changes' [1958], in *Silence*, 26.   [24] Ibid., 28.

performer; Cage did not carry out the measurements himself. Also, the above section of text was not assimilable as a whole, since it was punctured, twice, by Tudor's performance of part of the *Music of Changes*. The first occasion was a two-second snatch from bar 51 of the second book of *Music of Changes* (and, thus, only a minor-third B–D dyad was played), which interrupted the text after 'may be drawn' and before 'in India ink'. The second was rather more substantial, a twenty-second break in the text, filled in with music from the second book of *Music of Changes* from bar 53 onwards, between 'the situation obtaining' and 'in a recent composition'.[25] Nevertheless, the text is clear in the German translation (to which I return below), which was handed out to participants in advance of Cage's lecture. One can only imagine that such specifics were largely missed in the wake of the controversies which began to develop across Cage's time at Darmstadt. These were already at a peak in the concert performance; the interleaving of the text of 'Changes' with the *Music of Changes* doubtless did little to defuse tensions. Moreover, Cage's own mention that the sounds hoped for in the *Concert for Piano and Orchestra* 'invite[d] the timbres of jazz' certainly would not have helped diminish any impressions that some sort of improvisation was involved. Cage's second lecture, which contained (in part at least) an unmuted criticism of Stockhausen, can hardly have helped a clear understanding of what Cage sought either.[26]

This second lecture, 'Indeterminacy', delivered two days after the first, was probably the most conventional of the three. Though it had a confrontational edge that 'Changes' did not, and though it was densely constructed, it explained reasonably clearly what Cage meant by indeterminacy, at least that form of indeterminacy that might be found between composition and performance. As Cage said at the outset, he was speaking about 'composition which is indeterminate with respect to its performance'.[27] What Cage meant by this was hardly unclear: in the case of a piece which was indeterminate with respect to its performance, there was no reason for any or all aspects of the piece to remain consistent from performance to performance. Thus, his own *Music of Changes*, though composed via chance procedures, was not an example of an indeterminate piece since '[t]hough no two performances of the *Music of Changes* will be identical (each act is virgin, even the repeated one, to refer to René Char's thought), two performances

---

[25] Tudor's typescript of 'Changes' showing which sections of *Music of Changes* were performed and where is available as a part of the David Tudor Papers at GRI.

[26] It is worth bearing in mind, however, that another reaction, too, was total lack of interest. Berio related to Peyser that he was 'bored to death. But it was the best moment for Cage to some. With his simplicity he accomplished a great deal. He proved to be a strong catalyst.' Peyser, *Boulez*, 140.

[27] John Cage, 'Indeterminacy' [1958], in *Silence*, 35.

will resemble one another closely.'[28] Similarly, Earle Brown's *Indices*, fully notated as it is, did not constitute an example of an indeterminate piece. Indeed, Cage went further and suggested that the situation in *Indices* ought to be regarded, properly, as intolerable: 'this situation of the subservience of several to the directives of one [the conductor] who is himself controlled, not by another but by the work of another [the composer's fixed score]'.[29] Cage was clear that the sticking point was not really Brown's work at all but, rather, a continuing tradition in Western music, in which the performers become subservient to the desires and demands of the composer, a notion which would re-occur in transfigured form in his third lecture. Brown seemed – in the company of the composers of the canon of Western music – to be comparatively tolerable in Cage's eyes because the sounds of *Indices* were, generated through tables of random numbers, 'just sounds'. Curiously, Cage observed that the bias introduced by Brown into the selection of numbers made the piece *more* rather than less acceptable in this context because, intentionally or not, it prevented it from being interested in 'elements acting according to scientific theories of probability, elements acting in relationship due to the equal distribution of each one of those present – elements, that is to say, under the control of man'.[30] Cage saved his most savage criticism of determinate music for his own *Music of Changes*. His estimation of *Music of Changes* is, in point of fact, probably closest to Boulez's disparagement of *Structures* in 'Alea' (that strict serial, numerical strategies are 'purely mechanistic, automatic, fetishistic'[31]): 'The *Music of Changes* is an object more inhuman than human, since chance operations brought it into being. The fact that these things that constitute it, though only sounds, have come together to control a human being, the performer, gives the work the alarming aspect of a Frankenstein monster.' Again, Cage concluded that it was the Western tradition that represented the horrifying extreme case of this, 'the masterpieces of which are its most frightening examples, which when concerned with humane communication only move over from Frankenstein monster to Dictator'.[32]

Thus Cage argued that music that was 'tolerable' was necessarily that in which at least some aspect of its performance remained undecided in the materials provided to the performer. Cage was also clear that performance indeterminacy might occur only in some parameters, as his example of *The Art of Fugue* suggests, where

> structure, which is the division of the whole into parts; method, which is the note-to-note procedure; and form, which is the expressive content, the

---

[28] Ibid., 36. The reference to Char must in this context be seen as a reference to Boulez.
[29] Ibid., 37. [30] Ibid. [31] Boulez, 'Alea', 28. [32] Cage, 'Indeterminacy', in *Silence*, 36.

> morphology of the continuity, are all determined. Frequency and duration characteristics of the material are also determined. Timbre and amplitude characteristics of the material, by not being given, are indeterminate. This indeterminacy brings about the possibility of a unique overtone structure and decibel range for each performance of *The Art of Fugue*.[33]

Nevertheless, it was clear in what Cage had to say that some forms of indeterminacy were more fruitful than others. Given his judgement of Stockhausen's Klavierstück XI, one might presume that he would have argued that the indeterminate aspects of *The Art of Fugue* were 'ineffective. The work might as well have been written in all of its aspects determinately' because those aspects which *are* determined in *The Art of Fugue* leave the piece within 'the body of European musical conventions'. This, then, was precisely Cage's estimation of the failure of Klavierstück XI, at least in terms of its attempt to create something unexpected, flexible, and 'indeterminate' in the act of performance itself. Though the nineteen groups of Klavierstück XI could be performed in any order (with no requirement that all groups be performed in any single realisation, ensuring 'a unique morphology of the continuity, a unique expressive content, for each performance'), the conventional presence of both frequency and pulse (and, though Cage does not say so, timbre) would lead a performer 'to give the form aspects essentially conventional to European music'. The only thing that Klavierstück XI gained from its indeterminacy was 'being printed on an unusually large sheet of paper which, together with an attachment that may be snapped on at several points enabling one to stretch it out flat and place it on the music rack of a piano, is put in a cardboard tube suitable for safekeeping or distributing through the mails.'[34] For Cage, then, indeterminacy – if it was to be successful – had to go beyond relatively tokenistic gestures, such as those found in Klavierstück XI (or, for that matter, *The Art of Fugue*), and certainly had nothing to do with systematic procedures, whether those of chance or series. In Feldman's case, his *Intersection 3* was loosely determined in terms of frequency and duration, but the specifics were not contained within the score; similarly, certain aspects of the structure and form of *Intersection 3* were determined – the succession of events was to occur in a specific order – though the precise moment at which an event would happen remained indeterminate. Moreover, Feldman's use of graph paper seemed better suited to distancing the resulting sounds from the conventions of Western music than Stockhausen's staves.

Similarly, Brown's *Four Systems* fulfilled Cage's criteria. The score comprises, as the title suggests, four systems, but these are about all that binds *Four*

---

[33] Ibid., 35.   [34] Ibid., 35–6.

Systems to the Western tradition. Each of the systems contains various rectangles of a variety of heights and widths, which may indicate, according to the score, 'dynamics or clusters'. Though no specific indication of pitch is given, the top of each system represents the top note of the piano and the bottom of the system, the piano's lowest note. Tempo, too, is free and the page may be read either way up.[35] Thus, as in Feldman's *Intersection 3*, not everything is left indeterminate; it hardly could be. Nevertheless, a wide range of interpretative possibilities would remain in any realisation of the piece, and many of those possibilities would result in radically different-sounding results. Cage's note at the close of his discussion of *Four Systems* is intriguing, however, for what it suggests regarding the function of notation. He observed that '[t]o ensure indeterminacy with regard to its performance, a composition must be determinate of itself [which is to say] each element of the notation must have a single interpretation rather than a plurality of interpretations.'[36] Though this was surely difficult for a listener to take in during the lecture itself, it may have meant, in the case of *Four Systems*, say, that though the thickness of lines could in theory determine amplitude or denote clusters, it ought not, in any single performance, to denote both (and certainly ought not to switch between those things).

Cage's final example of a piece which might be regarded as fruitfully indeterminate was Wolff's *Duo for Pianists II*. As he observed, the situation is extreme:

> In the case of *Duo II for Pianists* [*sic*], structure, the division of the whole into parts is indeterminate. (No provision is given by the composer for ending the performance.) Method, the note-to-note procedure, is also indeterminate. All the characteristics of the materials (frequency, amplitude, timbre, duration) are indeterminate within gamut limitations provided by the composer. The form, the morphology of the continuity, is unpredictable. One of the pianists begins the performance: the other, noticing a particular sound or silence which is one of a gamut of cues, responds with an action of his own determination from among given possibilities within a given time bracket. Following this beginning, each panist [*sic*] responds to cues provided by the other, letting no silence fall between responses, though these responses themselves include silences.[37]

To be sure, Cage over-egged the radicality of *Duo for Pianists II* a little, but not all that much. The note-to-note procedure is not, truly, indeterminate (or, if it is, it is so only in limited ways). Although the pianists do decide

---

[35] Cage erroneously suggests that the page can be read in any direction, suggesting that he may, in fact, have been thinking of *December 1952*, rather than *Four Systems*, though the ideas are close enough that Cage's points hold in any case (ibid., 37).
[36] Ibid.   [37] Ibid., 38.

which notes from given aggregates they play, and can choose to repeat notes, the pitch aggregates that are available are certainly finite. This and the system of cues are probably what makes *Duo for Pianists II* still the 'same' piece across numerous performances, even though the specifics of the sounding result are, in many respects, wildly variable.

Vitally, a form of indeterminacy is introduced in *Duo for Pianists II* with which Cage had himself not really engaged. Because of the system of cues, the responses between the two players, the piece *ought* to become determined only in the moment of performance. Unlike Cage's music, it would be difficult to prepare one's response to the score in advance. Indeed, it is arguably the case that Wolff's music is rather closer to improvisation than Cage's (though what Wolff is asking for is closer to a rather complex but rule-based system than it is to improvisation). It was in 'Indeterminacy' that, if one had had the impression that what Cage was asking for was really improvisation, in opposition to the fixed score, this idea might have been compounded, since Cage directly compared the tradition of Western music to particular solos in traditional Indian musics which are 'not a performance of something written by another but an improvisation by the performer himself within certain limitations of structure, method, and material'.[38] Cage certainly did not suggest that improvisation was his aim, only that this parenthetical remark might highlight the case of Western music more clearly, but Tudor's performances of Klavierstück XI and Cage's *Variations I* might have heightened such misleading impressions.

The two recordings of Tudor performing Klavierstück XI during Cage's lecture reveal exactly what Cage suggested. The piece is radically different in each performance, but each is, too, very recognisably a piece of European piano music quite traditionally conceived. However, the aural impression is such that one would not necessarily immediately suggest that there was sufficient consistency between the two performances to be secure in an assertion that they were, indeed, the 'same' piece, even though they might well be two pieces by the same composer. In this sense, Klavierstück XI conforms to one characteristic of indeterminacy in Cage's terms: the formal indeterminacy brings about results which are surprising, but on a very limited plane. Even though the piece is consistently 'different' from performance to performance, in Cage's terms this does not prevent its being otherwise unsurprising: the pitch and durational materials are – in the terms of the post-war avant-garde – conventional. Moreover, Tudor did shape the piece into one which was, as Cage suggested, 'possessed of a climax or climaxes and in contrast a point or points of rest'.[39]

[38] Ibid., 37.   [39] Ibid., 36.

Tudor performed Klavierstück XI from the score. In contrast, as was his practice, he prepared in advance fully realised versions of Cage's *Variations I*, written up on five-line staves, having taken numerous readings, via careful measurement, from various versions of the *Variations I* performance materials.[40] It was from these fully notated scores that he performed.[41] In all Tudor's realisations before this point, he had prepared only a single version. Methodical to a remarkable degree, Tudor spent such time and effort on creating a realisation that he seems not to have had much desire to return to a piece for which he had already established a solution (moreover, since his interest seems to have been in the 'cracking' of a particular compositional puzzle, once he had done this, there was little to return to a previous piece for). In the case of *Variations I*, however, Tudor prepared three different readings of Cage's notations.

Only one of these, the first, was performed in the concert on 3 September; two others were given performances during Cage's lecture, with the longer, lasting around five minutes, performed twice. Unlike the concert version, on this occasion all that the audience heard was Tudor's performance; Cage did not perform during the lecture, at least not according to the testimony of the recording. During Cage's lecture, Tudor certainly played from his own exceptionally small realisation copies. The first version performed correlates with his realisation marked 'Variations 2'; the second and third versions were both drawn from his 'Variations 5' realisation and were, near enough, identical. While it is clear from the recordings that this should have been evident to a listener, there is little to indicate that anyone in the hall necessarily noticed this, although since recordings survive only of Tudor's performance and not of the lecture as a whole, it is impossible to tell how long Cage's delivery of his intervening text took and, thus, how far apart from one another the two realisations were performed.[42] During the first realisation played during Cage's lecture, the audience members were notably more attentive and less restless than they had been during the concert. There was certainly none of the laughter and catcalling that had characterised the concert performance. The first version Tudor performed was short – only a little longer than two minutes – but quite active, with most

---

[40] As was almost always Tudor's way, the number of preparatory notes and measurements made in preparation of his versions of *Variations I* massively outweighs the amount of musical material generated. His realisations could be reduced to six pages of manuscript in total, while his notes require twenty-three pages, and his readings of the score of *Variations I* take twenty-seven pages (GRI).

[41] See John Holzaepfel, 'David Tudor and the *Solo for Piano*', in David W. Bernstein and Christopher Hatch (eds.), *Writings through John Cage's Music, Poetry, and Art* (University of Chicago Press, 2001), 137–56, and John Holzaepfel, 'Cage and Tudor', in David Nicholls (ed.), *The Cambridge Companion to John Cage* (Cambridge University Press, 2002), 169–85.

[42] The longest version, the concert version, is marked 'Variations 9'. All three versions, as well as the sketch material for them, are available in the David Tudor Papers at GRI.

events taking the form of sharp attacks, either on the keyboard or within the body of the instrument. Tudor made no use of the various whistles which had seemingly been an additional cause of general hilarity during the concert performance. The second lecture version was for the most part a much more sedate affair than the first, and generally quieter (though not without occasional loud attacks), but also more seemingly 'shaped', with clusters of activity accreting as the performance moved on (though it contained some extremely long silences of up to about twenty seconds). Only with the persistent ringing of a (to the audience) unexpected alarm in the second realisation did such laughter occur. Broadly, the audience seemed significantly more attentive than they had been during the concert performance. The third performance was, as noted above, conspicuously similar to the second, being performed from the same realisation copy. Nevertheless, it felt slightly stiller than its earlier performance and, when the alarm clock went off again, it elicited no nervous laughter, which suggests that it was unfamiliarity that had led to this reaction.

It must have been recognisable to the participants that at least two of the realisations were appreciably different from one another, even though Tudor was also obviously working with many of the same core musical materials in each: sustained pitches on the keyboard as 'normal', but also many stopped notes, as well as pizzicati and sweeps within the instrument, and strikes on the body of the instrument to achieve resonance. In the identical second and third versions performed within the lecture, several whistles and the alarm mentioned above also featured. The performances were, though, radically different in the sense of space that they showed, even if this continuity of materials might have made it seem reasonable enough to describe them as the 'same' piece. What the performances of *Variations I* showed was that (in no small part because of the comparatively sparse amount of 'musical' material, and the relatively large amount of silence) in this example of Cage's music, there were no real points of climax or repose. There were major 'events', but these were not prepared for in any way that might have indicated a sense of logical direction towards and away from them.

Tudor might as well have played all three versions of *Variations I* in succession, without a break, as a single piece. The only difference it would have made to the performance would have been to make it longer. 'Event' here was, just as Cage suggested, in essence meaningless, which is to say 'purposeless', in the context of the whole piece. That said, for all that Cage suggested that the outcome was not 'foreseen', the gamut of musical materials at Tudor's command was consistent enough, as suggested above, that particular broad timbral characteristics certainly *could* be have been anticipated by an audience member after two realisations at least.[43] The score of *Variations I* makes no demands regarding consistency of timbral material; Tudor added this consistency to it. The timbral materials he made use of were recognisably 'Cage', being drawn from the stock of Cage's music which Tudor already knew, and knew well, not least the sound-worlds of Cage's fully notated *Music of Changes*, *Two Pastorales* (1952), *34′46.776″*, and the *Music for Piano* series. In Tudor's hands, Cage was still Cage. Yet there was no mention at any point of *how* Tudor did what he did, though doubtless he explained what he was doing in his private working sessions. From the perspective of the audience, he may well have appeared simply to sit at the piano and perform.

On 9 September, Cage delivered his final lecture, 'Communication', the most controversial of the three. The printed version of Cage's lectures in *Silence* is careful to give the impression that what he said in 'Communication' was little different from what he had presented earlier that year at Rutgers University, 'an excerpt from which was published in the *Village Voice*, New York City, in April 1958'.[44] Such an assertion is only partly true. The version published in the *Village Voice* is very close to the opening of the Darmstadt lecture, following the printed version with a small number of excisions and abbreviating the number of questions to forty-five. Notably, one question which might have been thought to pertain directly to Darmstadt and the newly established notion of the 'Darmstadt School' was already present in this earlier print version: 'Which is more musical, a truck passing by a factory or a truck passing by a music school?'[45] However, its pointed subsequent question '[d]o you know what I mean when I say inside the school?' is absent.[46] Much more tellingly, the 'original' Rutgers version was of a radically different nature. Formally, it operated in similar ways: it comprised a list of questions, with a small number of insertions which were not, themselves, questions. Those insertions were almost exclusively repetitions of the single notion '[n]o pause for music at Rutgers since music was being played there the whole time.'[47] Indeed, for the most part, the Rutgers lecture focussed on food. Twenty of Cage's questions at Rutgers are, more or less, food-related:

> Are about 8 of us really going to lunch with your Dean and Faculty?
> That lunch, what will it be?
> 12. Vegetarian?

---

[43] Cage, 'Indeterminacy', in *Silence*, 39.
[44] John Cage, 'Composition as Process' [1958], in *Silence*, 18.
[45] John Cage, '25 Years and 45 Questions', *Village Voice* (9 April 1958), 4.
[46] John Cage, 'Communication', in *Silence*, 41.
[47] John Cage, 'Rutgers Original', 1958 (unpublished), JCP.

The Cage shock

> Have they dropped meat?
> We wouldn't like it, would we, if they had dropped meat?
> Will there be anything to drink?
> Of course, it's the middle of the day, isn't it?
> But, to repeat, will there be anything to drink?
> [...]
> What happens after lunch?
> Music?
> Coming back to that lunch, what will they serve?
> Have I any right to ask?
> Something from the Grand Union?
> The A&P?
> What do you think about food in this country anyway?
> Is the bread any good?
> Have you ever tasted sea salt?
> Can you identify wild mushrooms?
> Have you no interest in food?
> Do you know how to cook?
> Do you realize wild rice grows in the Passaic, just there free for the gathering?
> Would it have been better for me to bring my own lunch (a few weeds would have filled the ticket)?[48]

In a presentation containing thirty-six questions or, in some cases, statements, the dominance of the question of food left little space for discussion of music. Nevertheless, another one of those passing comments which might have been thought to pertain directly to the Darmstadt audience – the throwaway mention of the number twelve, here wholly in passing, since it was not even the twelfth question – was already present at Rutgers (and, although it was in the print version in *Silence*, the number twelve was not uttered in this context by Cage in his lectures).

Cage's stress, in Darmstadt, on the ways in which the American avant-garde might be considered to be doing something rather more interesting than the Europeans was, however, mirrored almost literally inversely at Rutgers:

> Here's a little information you may find useful about the European Avant-Garde, the European Musical Avant-Garde: in France, it's Pierre Boulez. In Italy, Luciano Berio, Maderna and Nono. In Belgium, Henri Pousseur. Sweden, Bo Nilsson and Bengt Hambraeus. Germany, Karlheinz Stockhausen. You can read about it in magazines: La Domaine Musicale, Incontri Musicale, Die Reihe, The Score. Here, in America, there's nothing to read.[49]

[48] Ibid. [49] Ibid.

In this sense, if Cage was critical, he was at least even-handed, though it would have been impossible for either 'side' to be aware of his even-handedness. From the Rutgers presentation, only one statement and one question survived at Darmstadt, the first in modulated form: 'We're passing through time and space. It's glorious' and 'I repeat, is sound a blessing?'[50] The long and short of the matter is that, although certain ideas and, indeed, particular statements and questions were prefigured in both the Rutgers lecture and the *Village Voice* piece, the Darmstadt lectures were especially prepared for presentation there. Such an assertion seems doubly likely given a particular aspect of Cage's questioning, in which he contrasted the questions 'would you like to hear the very first performance of Christian Wolff's *For Piano with Preparations*?' and 'would you like to hear *Quantitäten* by Bo Nilsson whether it's performed for the first time or not?'[51] It is significant, in this context, that it was precisely this Wolff piece that Tudor had offered Steinecke in place of the première of Klavierstück XI and that the questions here, too, revolve around the importance, or otherwise, of first performances. Even so, the pointedness of this particular line of questioning may well have been understood only by Tudor, Steinecke, Stockhausen, and Cage himself, as the only ones apparently privy to the detailed specifics of Tudor's attempts to make good.

This is the general thrust of 'Communication' as a whole. Even if there had not been factors within the translation that made the critique yet sharper, it seems reasonable to surmise that an audience committed to avant-gardism as understood in the European frame would have found aspects of Cage's line of questioning uncomfortable. Even though aspects of the earlier part of the lecture had appeared in the *Village Voice*, it is hardly conceivable that very many (if any) of Cage's audience at Darmstadt would have encountered that text. Thus, by the time Cage reached his fourteenth question, one might have thought that the discussion had moved from a satirical reflection on what it might mean for a composer to stand up at Darmstadt and speak about his or her work to a blistering attack on the newly formed idea of the 'Darmstadt School':

> Which is more musical, a truck passing by a factory or a truck passing by a music school?
> Are the people inside the school musical and the ones outside unmusical?
> What if the ones inside can't hear very well, would that change my question?
> Do you know what I mean when I say inside the school?[52]

---

[50] Ibid.   [51] Ibid., 48, 52.   [52] Ibid., 41.

A question which might have appeared innocuous in the *Village Voice* must have taken on a stark significance in an environment in which listeners (especially Darmstadt 'regulars', who would have been well aware of Nono's recent formulation of that developing idea) would have been sure to know what *they* thought Cage meant when he said 'inside the school'. Whether Cage himself would have recognised the significance is debatable, but it is sure that this comment was inserted for the benefit of his Darmstadt audience. Even if Cage was not aware of the significance of what he was saying, his translators – Metzger not least – must have been all too fully aware of the meaning, and clearly did not prevent his saying it.

After a brief quotation on information theory, Cage moved from the generic to the specific. In the version printed in *Silence*, this phase of questioning is numbered, such that the count of questions reaches 'twelve' around the point at which Boulez specifically enters the discussion:

> Do you agree with Boulez when he says what he says?
> Are you getting hungry?
> Twelve. Why should you (you know more or less what you're going to get)?
> Will Boulez be there or did he go away when I wasn't looking?[53]

In Cage's presentation version at Darmstadt, however, there was no counting-off of numbers, nor does the count appear in the German translation prepared by Metzger. In the Darmstadt context, Cage appears to have been well aware that any notion of proceedings being dominated by a dodecaphonic hegemony was spurious. As he went on to say,

> Why do you suppose the number 12 was given up but the idea of the series wasn't?
> Or was it?
> And if not, why not?[54]

In any case, even without the presence of the counted number twelve, the participants can hardly have been mistaken as to Cage's meaning. They had been sent, in advance of the courses, a copy of Boulez's apology for absence, which Steinecke had demanded from him.[55] Moreover, the inference that following strict serial procedures 'you know more or less what you're going to get' was clear. There is, though, greater ambiguity here than one might expect. Perhaps informed by Metzger (since, as noted above, 'Communication' was clearly prepared *for* Darmstadt, and there is no reason necessarily to suspect that those preparations were complete by the

---

[53] Ibid., 48. [54] Ibid.
[55] Steinecke to Boulez, 15 August 1958, and Boulez to Steinecke, undated but before 23 August 1958, IMD.

time of Cage's arrival there), Cage signalled that, for some European composers, the idea of the series *might* already be an old one, at least in the sense that Metzger had proposed in 'Das Altern der Philosophie der Neuen Musik'. Similarly, in Cage's later self-quotation from what he had previously said to 'the Belgians' regarding the American avant-garde, it is clear that Cage shared the European distinction between dodecaphony and serial method:

> THE YOUNG STUDY WITH NEO-CLASSICISTS, SO THAT THE SPIRIT OF THE AVANT-GARDE, INFECTING THEM, INDUCES A CERTAIN DODECAPHONY. IN THIS SOCIAL DARKNESS, THEREFORE, THE WORK OF EARLE BROWN, MORTON FELDMAN, AND CHRISTIAN WOLFF CONTINUES TO PRESENT A BRILLIANT LIGHT, FOR THE REASON THAT AT THE SEVERAL POINTS OF NOTATION, PERFORMANCE, AND AUDITION, ACTION IS PROVOCATIVE. NONE OF THESE USES SERIAL METHOD.[56]

Indeed, Cage was direct in his observation that what seemed exciting, to an 'American avant-garde' ear, about European music was not compositional technique but, on the contrary, the fact that that technique necessitated a certain rejection of convention and, perhaps, habit, making the music, as he said, 'provocative':

> THE AMERICAN AVANT-GARDE, RECOGNIZING THE PROVOCATIVE CHARACTER OF CERTAIN EUROPEAN WORKS, OF PIERRE BOULEZ, KARLHEINZ STOCKHAUSEN, HENRI POUSSEUR, BO NILSSON, BENGT HAMBRAEUS, HAS IN ITS CONCERTS PRESENTED THEM IN PERFORMANCE, NOTABLY BY DAVID TUDOR, PIANIST. THAT THESE WORKS ARE SERIAL IN METHOD DIMINISHES SOMEWHAT THE INTEREST THEY ENJOIN. BUT THE THOROUGHNESS OF THE METHOD'S APPLICATION BRINGING A SITUATION REMOVED FROM CONVENTIONAL EXPECTATION FREQUENTLY OPENS THE EAR.[57]

The key difference between the Europeans and the Americans was one of listening experience. For the Europeans, the composer remained central (and, indeed, the figure of the composer was at the centre of the experience of the music); for the Americans, the aim was to place the listener at the heart of the experience, seeking a unique hearing on behalf of *each* listener and dissolving distinctions between listening in 'life' and in 'art'. While Cage seemed to a certain extent disdainful of the naïve judgements of difference between Europeans and Americans – that the Americans made greater use of silence, a distinction which would place his own music and Boulez's in opposition – he also opined that such simplistic constructions hid a profound distinction, which *was* important: 'WHEN SILENCE,

[56] Cage, 'Communication', 52. [57] Ibid., 53.

The Cage shock

GENERALLY SPEAKING, IS NOT IN EVIDENCE, THE WILL OF THE COMPOSER IS. INHERENT SILENCE IS EQUIVALENT TO DENIAL OF THE WILL [. . .] NEVERTHELESS, CONSTANT ACTIVITY MAY OCCUR HAVING NO DOMINANCE OF THE WILL IN IT. NEITHER AS SYNTAX NOR STRUCTURE, BUT ANALOGOUS TO THE SUM OF NATURE, IT WILL HAVE ARISEN PURPOSELESSLY.'[58] The fundamental distinction, then, was not between serial method and chance operations at all, but rather between Europeans, who wanted to *be* 'composers' through the operations of their wills and compositional desires, and Americans, who were willing to allow music to occur unpurposively.[59] Boulez had suggested in the previous year that chance and automatism led ultimately in the same direction; Cage's stance opposes this. Boulez was discussing ways to re-integrate compositional will, following the abrogation of such ways of thinking in the wake of the 'serial moment' which occurred, for him, around 1950–2. Cage's interest was in ensuring that these did not return. This was the centre of the debate in Cage's terms, rather than any opposition between serialism and indeterminacy.

Throughout the above proceedings, Tudor performed sections from *Music for Piano*, while Cage occasionally lit cigarettes, having added, as he said in the print version, 'by chance operations indications of when, in the course of performance, I am obliged to light a cigarette'.[60] Only relatively late in the lecture, it seems, did the various commentators decide that they should probably count the number of cigarettes being lit and ascribe significance to them. Hans Heinz Stuckenschmidt counted twelve, and suggested that this was a representation of twelve-tone music similarly 'going up in smoke', as Decroupet has it.[61] Wolfgang Widmaier counted nineteen, and equated them with the number of modules in Stockhausen's Klavierstück XI, which Tudor had, of course, performed in several versions the previous day.[62] In doing this, Stuckenschmidt and Widmaier showed that they had rather missed the point: in Cage's terms the *number* was hardly significant at all; this was only another purposeless action, although the presence directly behind Cage in the hall of a sign which read 'Rauchen verboten' certainly lent it a transgressive air. For all this, it was the translation of Cage into German that moved his third lecture from playfulness and gentle irony into full-frontal assault.

---

[58] Ibid.
[59] My own previous reading of Cage's Darmstadt lectures is no less guilty than those of other commentators of erroneously reinforcing such an impression. See particularly my commentary in 'Gained in Translation: Words about Cage in Late 1950s Germany', in Attinello, Fox, and Iddon (eds.), *Other Darmstadts*, 97.
[60] Cage, 'Communication', 41.
[61] Pascal Decroupet, 'Aleatorik und Indetermination – die Ferienkurse als Forum der europäischen Cage-Rezeption', in Borio and Danuser (eds.), *Im Zenit der Moderne*, vol. II, 240.
[62] Wolfgang Widmaier, 'Catch as Cage Can: Drei Studios in Kranichstein', *Darmstädter Echo*, 12 September 1958.

Translation

Tudor suggested Heinz-Klaus Metzger as the translator of Cage's lectures, on the grounds that there had been aesthetic misunderstandings on his last visit to Darmstadt when he had been translated into German by Alexander Goehr. Though Metzger and Tudor already knew one another from the 1956 courses, this was to be Metzger's first (and decisive) encounter with Cage.[63] Already at the point of this suggestion, in mid July 1958, it was clear that Cage and Tudor wished to avoid the interruptions that translation could cause, and Tudor suggested that, as well as the possibility of having Metzger translate, the translations could be undertaken in the United States by Christian Wolff, then brought to Germany and mimeographed in sufficient quantities that the participants could, if they did not speak English, read along while Cage spoke and Tudor performed.[64] Steinecke seemed to approve of the idea that the translation be undertaken in advance and then reproduced: he wrote that he would be grateful if Tudor could forward the translations that Christian Wolff had prepared as quickly as possible, and that Metzger would take on what remained.[65] Yet shortly after Cage's departure by boat for Europe, Tudor wrote to Steinecke that there had 'been some difficulty in the translation of the lecture' and that Cage would bring the translations with him.[66] It seems that, when Cage arrived, whatever problems there had been with the translation had not been rectified and, if anything, were presumably worse than Steinecke had expected, since he engaged not only Metzger but also Wolf Rosenberg and Hans G. Helms to undertake the translations.[67] Simply allowing Cage to speak in English appears never to have been an option; as Helms suggested to Shultis, 'the knowledge of English was not nearly as widespread in Germany and Latin countries as it is today, [so] I am pretty sure that the translations were necessary to fully understand John's ideas and his way of thinking.' Helms also observed that, for the most part, those who were at all active in new music within Europe and who attended Darmstadt would have had at least some knowledge of German before English in any case, since the major centres for new music were the courses themselves, as well as the Donaueschingen festival and the Westdeutscher Rundfunk in Cologne.[68] In such a situation the importance of the translations was high. Even if those who had a smattering of English (or, for that matter, a reasonable level of

---

[63] Heinz-Klaus Metzger, 'Fragment zum Thema "Komet"', in Stephan et al. (eds.), *Von Kranichstein zur Gegenwart*, 250.
[64] Tudor to Steinecke, 14 July 1958, IMD.   [65] Steinecke to Tudor, 8 August 1958, IMD.
[66] Tudor to Steinecke, 21 August 1958, IMD.   [67] See Shultis, 'Cage and Europe', 38.
[68] Ibid., 263 n. 17.

fluency in English) listened to Cage in the original language during the lectures, it was the translations that they took away with them as a substantive record of what had been said.

As Metzger would later recall, the sheer volume of text would have made it impossible for a single translator to complete the work. As it was, Helms, Metzger, and Rosenberg worked through the night, with coffee regularly provided by Khris Helms.[69] Cage sent a note to Stockhausen on the morning of his last lecture, making it clear that, to his mind, Metzger was the most significant of the translators:

7^{00} A.M.!

Dear Karlheinz,

Please write a note or speak to Steinecke about Metzger, Helms + Rosenberg. We worked 'till [sic] 7^{00}. Let Steinecke know that Metzger has worked beautifully. On the translations about 40 hours extra work by all 3 together have been spent. The thought is that a proper remuneration would be 100 DM for Helms + Rosenberg each + 50 DM supplement for Metzger.[70]

As Helms recounted later to Shultis, work on each of the three lectures was guided by a 'lead' translator in order to ease the load.[71] Though Helms was unable to recall who did what (and said that Metzger too could not recall), Helms sent a copy of his translation of 'Indeterminacy' to Cage in 1961.[72] Since he had copies of none of the other lectures, one might presume that he worked principally on this lecture. Given that the third lecture was, in terms of translation, the most complex, one might also presume that it was for this, 'Communication', that Metzger had primary responsibility, which would mean that 'Changes' was handled by Wolf Rosenberg. In any case, it hardly matters who carried out the translation of the first lecture, since it is, largely, irreproachable. Within 'Indeterminacy', there are some occasional oddities: the opening sentence, for instance ('This is a lecture on composition which is indeterminate with respect to its performance'), becomes, in German, 'Dies ist ein Vortrag über Komposition, deren Aufführung nicht festgelegt ist' ('This is a lecture on composition, the performance of which is not determined'), which is very close, to be sure, but is slightly different in nuance.

---

[69] Metzger, 'Fragment zum Thema "Komet"', 250.
[70] Cage to Stockhausen, undated but almost certainly 9 September 1959, in Misch and Bandur (eds.), *Karlheinz Stockhausen bei den Internationalen Ferienkurse*, 205.
[71] Shultis, 'Cage and Europe', 263 n. 16.   [72] Hans G. Helms to John Cage, 16 March 1961, JCC.

Nevertheless, Cage's piece descriptions are preserved intact, such that, if there were any ambiguity about the repeated refrain – 'This is a lecture on composition which is indeterminate with respect to its performance' – any such confusion ought to have been clarified in the course of reading. The case of the translation of 'Communication' is rather different. Certainly Cage was complicit in some of the changes made – as Helms recalled to Shultis, 'John thought – as did we – that at this point in time [. . .] "a direct personal attack" was necessary to wake up the sleeping minds' – but Cage's German was almost certainly not adequate to identify the degree of nuance that was being introduced into his text.

Nevertheless, some of the changes are obvious, and unambiguous. Where Cage's version reads '[a]re sounds just sounds or are they Beethoven?', the translation queries '[a]re sounds sounds or are they Webern?'[73] Webern was certainly more pertinent in the Darmstadt context than Beethoven (although arguably Beethoven was the paradigmatic example of the sort of composer of Western music that Cage had criticised in 'Indeterminacy'). Moreover, it is clear that Cage would have recognised such a change and must have approved it.

For the most part, small alterations are the norm. However, the cumulative effects skew Cage's meaning substantially. The second section of Cage's interrogation contains the following five questions:

> Would we ever be able to get so that we thought the ugly sounds were beautiful?
> If we drop beauty, what have we got?
> Have we got truth?
> Have we got religion?
> Do we have a mythology?[74]

The translation does not use the everyday German binary opposition between 'schön' and 'hässlich' for 'beautiful' and 'ugly', and instead proposes, rather unusually, 'widrig', which would ordinarily be translated as 'adverse', or slightly more loosely as 'unfavourable' or 'unfortunate'. In the questions that follow, the meaning is skewed yet further: they now read 'If we drop beauty, what have we received?', or even, slightly more strongly, 'What have we accepted?', since 'empfangen' can also mean welcoming or greeting something, in the sense of 'a reception'.[75] If Cage's original is playful, the translation is accusatory. Rather than asking 'what would happen *if* . . . ?', it instead asks 'what have we/you done?' and, moreover,

---

[73] Cage, 'Communication', 41; John Cage, 'Kommunikation' [1958], tr. Heinz-Klaus Metzger, Hans G. Helms, and Wolf Rosenberg, in Metzger and Riehn (eds.), *Darmstadt-Dokumente I*, 161.
[74] Cage, 'Communication', 42–3.   [75] Cage 'Kommunikation', 162.

The Cage shock

'are you/we prepared to accept it?' This becomes clearer when one reads a more literal translation back into English of the subsequent lines:

> Have we accepted truth?
> Have we accepted religion?
> Do we possess a mythology?[76]

In one of Cage's quotations from earlier lectures, where Cage is again gently ironic, the translation is direct and admonitory. Cage states: 'Masterpieces and geniuses go together and when by running from one to the other we make life safer than it actually is we're apt never to know the dangers of contemporary music or even to be able to drink a glass of water.'[77] The translation is faithful until 'than it actually is', but thereafter reads: 'We will never again be capable of knowing the dangers of contemporary music, we won't even once be in the situation where we can drink a glass of water.'[78]

From proposing it as being a problem that one might tend towards (and could therefore be fought against), the translation makes it clear that once one has begun running from the masterpiece of, for example, *Le Marteau sans maître* back to Boulez the damage is already done. From the perspective of his audience, the translation of Cage advises them that, simply by coming to Darmstadt to study with the 'geniuses' of the avant-garde, they were a complicit part of a problem and, moreover, that it was one of their own creation. The passage mentioned above, which focussed on Boulez's absence, also has a very slight emendation: where Cage's English version queries whether Boulez will be 'there', the translation asks: 'Will Boulez be *here*, or did he go out while I wasn't looking?'[79]

Consistently, the translation makes Cage's questions into an oppositional grilling, with the European avant-garde the subject under interrogation. Nowhere is this clearer than in the passage of questions already ably described by Shultis. It is such an extreme case, however, that it bears repeating. The passage of Cage's text reads as follows:

> Why is it so difficult for so many people to listen?
> Why do they start talking when there is something to hear?
> Do they have their eyes not on the sides of their heads but situated inside their
>   mouths so that when they hear something their first impulse is to start talking?
> The situation should be made more normal, don't you think?
> Why don't they keep their mouth shut and their ears open?
> Are they stupid?
> And, if so, why don't they try to hide their stupidity?[80]

---

[76] Ibid. [77] Cage, 'Communication', 46. [78] Cage, 'Kommunikation', 165.
[79] Cage, 'Communication', 48; Cage, 'Kommunikation', 167. [80] Cage, 'Communication', 48–9.

It is already perfectly obvious in Cage's original text, given the context of its delivery, that the audience he is discussing is the Darmstadt audience itself. However, the translation makes this the explicit point of this section of text. Where the typescript of the translation originally had 'sie' (with a lower-case 's') for 'they', a capitalised 'Sie', for 'you', is typed over and therefore substituted, thus becoming:

> Why don't you keep your mouth shut and your ears open?
> Are you stupid?
> And, if so, why don't you try to hide your stupidity?[81]

Shultis is over-cautious when he queries, 'one cannot help wondering if the Darmstadt audience [...] "took it personally."'[82] As the reactions show, what Cage had to say *was* taken personally by many of those who heard him speak. For the most part, they felt that they were under personal attack. Some of the audience, Metzger not least, though, took it personally in quite a different, positive manner. Whether Cage had set out to achieve anything or not, his presence almost immediately changed the nature of what was happening at Darmstadt, and amongst the European avant-garde more generally.

Reaction

Whatever else it resulted in, Cage's presence at Darmstadt led to a more thorough press coverage than any previous event had done, even if much of the commentary was starkly critical. After Cage's lectures had been delivered, Antoine Goléa was the first commentator to 'break cover'. His tone had none of the charitableness of the earlier concert reviews. The attack was devastating, though one suspects that Goléa may have had rather a depressing time of it in general at the 1958 courses, dismissing (before he began his savaging of Cage, 'new music's impudent clown') the courses' opening concert, a performance of Berg's chamber music, including the Chamber Concerto and the Lyric Suite, as 'trivial'. He also stated that he would not wish his readers to think that he was blaming David Tudor, though he observed: 'The reasons for which he wastes his great talent on the "manifestations" of Mr Cage are unknown to me, but in any case incomprehensible.' Brown, Feldman, and Wolff, too, were slightly rejected: 'Three pieces were by Cage himself, others by various American "composers", who attempt to mimic him. Cage is, though, inimitable, which in this case cannot be regarded as a compliment.' Even if, for Goléa, there

---

[81] Cage, 'Kommunikation', 168. [82] Shultis, 'Cage and Europe', 39.

seemed to be something promising in the idea of the prepared piano, when the pianists began to strike the body of the instrument, the joke was at an end. He suggested that the laughing and jeering of the crowd was precisely what Cage wanted: 'Cage has the soul and the visage of a tragic clown; he reminds one compellingly of Buster Keaton.' The notion that Cage was a deadpan comic ran through Goléa's report of his lectures:

> Today it's only thanks to chance that he continues to 'compose'. Nothing is meaningful. Only the current gag.
> Through these bagatelles, held in deep earnest, Cage attempts to show his seriousness and sincerity. He is, in everyday life, an extremely sympathetic individual. Personally, I think that he has every right to earn his living with his schtick. It's a job like any other. He just doesn't have the right to defraud music students.[83]

Hans Heinz Stuckenschmidt was barely kinder. After suggesting that the performances had the flavour of cabaret, he went on to observe: 'That Cage's music and his theory have any productive value for European composition, I doubt. It is – to give it a pseudo-philosophical embellishment – an echo of the Dadaism of 1916, but without its vital élan, without the power of its newness, and without its revolutionary breakthrough.'[84] Wolfgang Widmaier – writing under the siglum 'W.' – also felt that the relationship was less to physical comedy than to Dada. As well as making the opening reference to Hans Arp, given below, the reviewer later observed that 'Cage's prose style shows the distinct influence of Gertrude Stein.' Though not so shocking, the correspondent suggests, Cage's lectures were bewildering and amusing in just the same way as the story with which the piece opens: 'Once upon a time, Hans Arp was invited to read from his work for a large audience. He arrived, took a bow, drew a tiny flute from a case (which he had presumably borrowed from David Tudor), played a couple of notes (which he had presumably borrowed from John Cage), bowed once again, and vanished.' Similarly, in the case of Cage's lectures, the listeners only occasionally felt they had firm ground under their feet.

Anecdotes puncture the surface: 'during the courses one could, for example, often see him, sitting alone in a café, toss three coins into the air. From the results of these tosses (heads or tails) result rows of numbers, which represent new compositions *in nuce*. These compositions sound more different from one another than one might think.' The description

---

[83] Antonie Goléa, 'Die neue Musik hat ihren frechen Clown: John Cage bei den Kranichsteiner Ferienkursen', *Der Mittag*, 11 September 1958.
[84] Hans Heinz Stuckenschmidt, 'Der Heiligenberg der Neuen Musik: Lagebericht von den Darmstädter Ferienkursen', *Frankfurter Allgemeine Zeitung*, 13 September 1958.

of the way in which Cage allowed the lighting of cigarettes to interfere with his delivery of his text is wonderfully evocative of the time taken:

> Before his mention of Webern, for example, Cage made a pause, during which he rummaged around in his bag to find a packet of cigarettes; he opened it; he took a cigarette; this, he placed in his mouth; he took a match from a box of matches; he lit it; lit the cigarette; took a deep drag – and then he exhaled, after which he naturally had to put out the cigarette that he had lit.

His smoking, the reviewer emphasised, had nothing to do with stress: 'Cage is the very incarnation of calm. And he does not smoke out of nervousness or passion, but because he wants the pause and the effect.' The review attempts to give a flavour of Cage's lectures beyond what literal reportage could manage, even if this seems sometimes to drift into sarcasm. Nevertheless, the tone was more charitable than Goléa's: 'the listeners enjoyed themselves royally. For Cage's three lectures were devoted to the most witty cabaret. If what I have heard is right, the translations of Cage's lectures have already gone onto the Kranichstein black market.' The black market in Cage lectures, or more accurately their translations, may have had effects unanticipated by their author. Like Cage's own quotations in 'Communication', the review itself ends thus: 'To finish, a quotation from the third lecture: "Is what's clear to me clear to you?"'[85]

Heinz-Klaus Metzger, for one, seemed furious with the tone of the review, suggesting that perhaps the reason why the reviewer had failed to recognise the importance of Cage – the most significant Schoenberg pupil after Webern and Berg – was that he or she was on secondment from the sports department (adding that the review reflected an ambition to rise as far as the cabaret department) and had never before encountered a musico-theoretical debate. Not least, Metzger felt, the reviewer had misjudged the fact that Cage was in deadly earnest.[86] The response of the editor of the *Darmstädter Echo* was no less brutal. For the most part it consists of a direct quotation from Stuckenschmidt's response, observing that so expert a witness had failed to recognise the seriousness of Cage's contribution. Yet the response to Metzger's query regarding the capability of its reviewer's expertise is the most devastating: 'Widmaier, whose subject knowledge Metzger placed in doubt, lectures in music theory and music history at the Akademie für Tonkunst in Darmstadt, the same academy at which Metzger once studied and, under Widmaier's supervision, took an examination.'[87]

---

[85] Widmaier, 'Catch as Cage Can'.
[86] Heinz-Klaus Metzger, '"... geschultest und entfaltetst ...": Eine Erwiderung auf "Catch as Cage Can"', *Darmstädter Echo*, 16 September 1958.
[87] 'Statt einer Erwiderung: Kabarett oder "Ernstcharakter" bei Cage', *Darmstädter Echo*, 17 September 1958.

The Cage shock

Metzger later received another blow in Nils Kayser's rather vicious letter to the *Darmstädter Echo* which described him as a 'Cage apologist, one of those easy-to-catch fish who has fallen prey to the net of this American itinerant preacher at this year's Kranichsteiner Ferienkurse. Meek and unaware, he is caught with a raft of other composers in Cage's mesh.'[88] Kayser's verdict would find resonances in Nono's response to Cage and, more pertinently, the Cageian exegetes at the 1959 courses.

Indeed, few other German reviewers shared Metzger's sympathies, though Egon Vietta proclaimed Cage 'the event of the courses' precisely because of the 'pain in the ass' he appeared to have become.[89] Heinz Joachim pulled no punches in a torrent of negativity. Cage was for him, by turns, 'naïve', a 'dilettante', and a composer of 'cabaret'.[90] Claus-Henning Bachmann seems to have felt insulted for the most part, observing that Cage's cigarette smoking was pantomimic and adding that, in any case, as a reviewer he was hardly fit to judge the music since he, at least, had not yet reached the stage where 'Beethoven would be as acceptable to the ear as a cow bell'.[91] Bachmann, again, counselled against the wisdom of turning over to the performer the degree of freedom that he believed Cage had. Elsewhere, though, Bachmann made very clear that, regardless of his own feelings on the matter, he was certain that Cage's presence would be decisive: 'The pieces this year can be divided into those which were influenced by Cage – now they stem exclusively from American composers, but by 1959 that will already be quite different – and those which were written under the influence of Karlheinz Stockhausen's Klavierstück XI or Pierre Boulez's Third Piano Sonata [. . .]'.[92] Likewise, though the review is hardly positive, it is evident in a piece for the *Bonner Rundschau* that, by October, the one talking point of Darmstadt 1958 remained John Cage and, as the critic observes, the central question was: 'Is that still music?'[93] To find truly positive reviews, it is necessary to look further afield to the reports of two composers who would, in their own differing ways, leave their own imprints upon the new musical scene in West Germany: Mauricio Kagel and Nam June Paik.

[88] Nils Kayser, 'Kein Überblick aus dem Netz', *Darmstädter Echo*, 18 October 1958.
[89] Egon Vietta, 'Gespräch, Experiment und Ärgernis: Bei den Kranichsteiner Ferienkurse für Neue Musik', *Stuttgarter Nachrichten*, 18 September 1958.
[90] Heinz Joachim, 'Musikalische Avantgarde in der Sackgasse: Die Frage ist: wie soll es weitergehen? – Zu den Kranichsteiner Ferienkursen', *Die Welt* (Hamburg), 19 September 1958.
[91] Claus-Henning Bachmann, 'Der Zufall in der Musik und seine Folgen', *Rhein-Neckar-Zeitung*, 18 September 1958.
[92] Claus-Henning Bachmann, 'Meditation und Liebestod: Neue Musik in Darmstadt. Avantgarde ist kontemplativ', *Fränkisches Volksblatt*, 7 October 1959.
[93] [mr] 'Kiss me Cage – oder: Ist das Musik? Von den XIII. Internationalen Ferienkursen für Neue Musik in Darmstadt', *Bonner Rundschau*, 15 October 1958.

Kagel brooked no misunderstanding: 'Let there be no doubt that the American composer John Cage rightly brushed away most of the compositional-technical concepts which have been used until today amongst the young European composers.' In contradistinction to Bachmann's view, Kagel suggested that Klavierstück XI and Boulez's Third Piano Sonata could hardly be separated from Cage; they were, from Kagel's perspective, part of the same conceptual revolution and, moreover, Cage had beaten both European composers to the punch.[94] In a sense, if Bachmann had been right that what was presented at Darmstadt in 1958 came under the sign of either Cageian indeterminacy or open form as practised by Boulez or Stockhausen, then it would follow that Cage and those whom he had influenced were all there was to hear at the courses that year. Kagel certainly went too far – Nono was, in terms of music presented, still the star attraction – but perhaps it is not so far from the truth. By 1958, the various strands of indeterminacy and open form were ranged against those who continued to follow serial trajectories, and, arguably, the latter were increasingly in the minority.

Nam June Paik's review was hardly less effusive than Kagel's. He recalled discussions with Cage from a private meeting. After Cage had explained the process of composing *Music for Piano*, Paik reported that he was stunned by how simple it seemed: '"So one could write a good twenty pieces in a day. Which of them should be played, and which not?" Wearing a half-undone tie and turning a coin back and forth in his fingers [. . .] he answered: "It's all the same which."' Where other commentators were shaken by the deviation from 'normal' modes of sound-production on the piano, Paik's reaction was quite the contrary: 'How young the piano still is!'[95]

In any case, for all the criticism, in terms of sheer numbers, this was press coverage of a sort that Steinecke could only have dreamed of. Cage had, no doubt, struck a nerve. Many commentators noted that, although there was no need to go so far as Cage had in terms of the admission of chance into compositional working, a relaxation of the strictures of serial procedure was vital to avoid coming to a dead end. Surprisingly few seemed to recall that this was what Boulez himself had noted a year earlier, and what Metzger had claimed had *already happened* in the case of much so-called serial music. That being the case, there is surely some irony in the seemingly general agreement that the major new work presented at Darmstadt in 1958 was

---

[94] Mauricio Kagel, 'John Cage en Darmstadt 1958', *Buenos Aires musical*, 16 October 1958.
[95] Nam June Paik, '"Musik der Zufalls": Darmstädter Ferienkurse für Neue Musik', *Jayu Shinmun*, 6–7 January 1959.

The Cage shock

Luigi Nono's *Cori di Didone* (1958), a piece which seemed to show that Nono, at least, had no intent of backing down from his own serial route, even if his route to his own serial technique had had little to do with the approaches of Boulez or Stockhausen.[96] What was truly significant, though, was that the divisions were in no sense between Europe and the United States. On the contrary, in the ways described by Bachmann and Kagel, the division at Darmstadt was really between the rising star of Stockhausen and the established force of Nono. Arguably, Cage had already started to represent some sort of proxy through which their disagreement could be fought.

Remarkably, amongst all this, Werner Freytag, writing for the *Hannoversche Presse*, was able to declare that it was 'all quiet on the Darmstadt front', with no mention of Cage whatsoever and a claim that 'if there are perceptible ways out of the constructivism of the "Darmstadt School"' they could be found in Hermann Heiß's *Configuration I* (1956) or Boris Blacher's Orchestral Fantasy, op. 51 (1956).[97] Freytag was not entirely alone; Jiří Válek, too, observed that, in his opinion, 'the lectures from the course of the West German composer Boris Blacher, which concerned stage, radio, and television music, were the most valuable'.[98] Clearly not everyone had noticed the shockwaves that were already developing in Cage's wake.

Setting music free?

Heinz-Klaus Metzger had a further opportunity to express his personal response to Cage and what it was that Metzger thought was at stake only a little over a month later. A few days after the close of the courses, Cage and Tudor travelled to Cologne for the European première of the *Concert for Piano and Orchestra*, which took place on 19 September 1958. Metzger was invited to record some prefatory notes on Cage's theory and his practice for broadcast alongside the *Concert*, which he did on 30 October 1958, though the broadcast would not take place until almost a year later, on 30 July 1959,[99] by which point Metzger's contribution had already been published

---

[96] See, for instance: Bachmann, 'Der Zufall in der Musik und seine Folgen'; Goléa, 'Die neue Musik braucht Kranichstein'; Stuckenschmidt, 'Der Heiligenberg der Neuen Musik'; Wolf-Eberhard von Lewinski, 'Musik der Zeit – Musik der Zukunft: 50 Ur- und Erstaufführungen bei den Kranichsteiner Ferienkursen', *Süddeutscher Zeitung*, 10 September 1958; Werner Freytag, 'In Darmstadt nichts Neues', *Hannoversche Presse*, 16 September 1958;.

[97] Freytag, 'In Darmstadt nichts Neues'.

[98] Jiří Válek, 'Neue Musik: Des Zaubers des Neuen beraubt', originally published in *Hudebni Rozhledy*, vol. 11, no. 19 (October 1958); German translation (translator unknown) IMD.

[99] Decroupet, 'Aleatorik und Indetermination', 241.

as 'John Cage o della liberazione' in the third volume of *Incontri musicali*.[100] As Decroupet observes, the position Metzger gives to Cage here placed him in opposition both to what Boulez had had to say at Darmstadt in 1957 and to what Nono would say in 1959. Moreover, it points to a disparity between presentations of what was 'really' happening at Darmstadt. The actuality of compositional work suggests that, if the aesthetic clash was between approaches to open form and indeterminacy on the one hand and serial practice on the other, such a debate had Stockhausen and Nono at its head from the Darmstadt perspective. Metzger's presentation instead opposed Cage to the whole European tradition, including those who were sympathetic to Cage in Europe. According to Metzger,

> [i]t is a slap in the face of every traditional European aesthetic concept that the performance of Cage's work is a procedure largely constituted by accidents that are, strictly speaking, accidents of performance that cannot be related conclusively to notation. It is a further slap that during the performance the notations themselves refuse to generate a correlative sensuous appearance that would communicate meaning, since these notations are the results of mere chance operations in the technique of writing and in no way the formulations of a composing subject [...] That notes should stay exactly where they have fallen through blind chance, for example, or that performers should take those that first strike them accidentally and – God knows how – translate them into definite actions, cannot be reconciled with this idea.[101]

Not only did Metzger reproduce Cage's procedural thinking, but he also made this activity one which expressed a certain violence, a 'slap in the face'. He noted, too, that no relationship could be found between the appearance of the score and the sounding result of the music, which is certainly as Cage would have described it. Yet Metzger's 'God knows how' is telling. The performers, in the way in which he described it, were necessarily construed as responding immediately – taking the notations that 'first strike them accidentally' – and in unknown (perhaps unknowable) ways transforming these impulses into music. Such an activity – essentially guided improvisation – could hardly be more distant from the disciplined activities undertaken by Tudor. Either Metzger's 'God knows how' was genuine and he did not know how Tudor 'did it' until later and thought, like many others, that he was improvising, or this was wholly disingenuous. Metzger's then-partner, Sylvano Bussotti, certainly did know about Tudor's working methods by 1959 at the latest, since they appear clearly in his own *Pièces de chair*

---

[100] Heinz-Klaus Metzger, 'John Cage o della liberazione' [1958], tr. Sylvano Bussotti, *Incontri musicali*, vol. 3 (August 1959), 1–31.
[101] Heinz-Klaus Metzger, 'John Cage, or Liberated Music' [1958], tr. Ian Pepper, *October*, vol. 82 (Fall 1997), 54.

The Cage shock

II (1958–60), to which I return below in the context of Stockhausen's 'Musik und Graphik' lectures, and it seems highly unlikely that Metzger would not have been privy to such information.

The general impression is only reinforced by the way in which Metzger conceived of Cage's compositional work as being a proposal of 'social visions'. As Metzger viewed Cage's music and activity, the purpose was not a personal one – to free the music from the diktats of composerly taste – but instead an overtly political one. In essence, in Metzger's hands, Cage became a class fighter:

> Until now, musicians, even those trained to perform chamber music, only knew the law of coerced labor as specified in the musical text and the conductor's baton, invisible, virtual, reigning also over quartets and quintets. Cage set the musicians free, allowing them to do what they like in his works and giving them – although he is not always thanked for this at performances – the dignity of autonomous musical subjects: to act independently and to understand the significance of their work, just as in an emancipated society everyone will be permitted to realize his work without enforcement, watched only by the clock as a sign that even then morning would be followed by evening.[102]

This is some way distant from the Cage who would, some years later, assert clearly: 'Permission granted. But not to do whatever you want.'[103]

Metzger construed what Cage *signified* as a violent attack on the values of the capitalist, imperialist West: 'The idea of freedom is performed as a theatrical play – whereas outside it would be necessary to murder the conductor and tear to pieces that score according to which the world at large is performed'; he explicitly stated that Cage's music is political, in a tradition of engaged music which related to Schoenberg's *Survivor from Warsaw* and Nono's *Il canto sospeso*: 'Cage's disorganization of musical coherence, as of the performing ensemble that has nothing more to represent, may be understood as an attempt to place immanent musical material in accord with the bluntness of a political appeal.'[104] This comes from the same Metzger who, only a few years later, would dismiss Nono's effort, in the case of *Intolleranza 1960* especially, as 'serial Pfitzner', perhaps unintentionally recalling Goeyvaerts's judgement of Schoenberg in 1951, although as will become clear below, Metzger had strong reasons to think that the Nono he regarded as politically engaged was, by 1959, directly opposed to his new champion.[105]

In Metzger's terms, Cage had already trumped Stockhausen. In *Zeitmasse* and Klavierstück XI, 'commands that the performer perform specific

---

[102] Ibid., 54–5.
[103] John Cage, 'Seriously Comma' [1966], in *A Year from Monday* (London: Marion Boyars, 1985), 28.
[104] Metzger, 'John Cage, or Liberated Music', 55.
[105] Heinz-Klaus Metzger, 'Das Altern der jüngsten Musik' [1962], in *Musik wozu*, 121.

actions replace an intelligible text, and interpretation itself is actually eliminated; obedience takes its place, guaranteeing a result that has been precisely precalculated by the composer'. This, too, was far from the Stockhausen portrayed by Cage. Cage had gone little further than saying that, if Stockhausen wished to be surprised by the results of a piece, the notational strategies of Klavierstück XI fell short. In Metzger's description, Stockhausen was a dictator figure, contrasted with 'the composer of Cage-type music' who 'is no longer the figure of the leader'.[106]

In short, for Metzger, Cage's music, shorn of purpose or value in the sense that European music had inherited from nineteenth-century aesthetics, was fundamentally about an unveiling of social truths:

> Its truth consists in the fact that it proclaims a condition in which the hierarchy of purpose – without which the inherited idea of musical meaning itself would be unthinkable – and the law of value would no longer be assumed; its untruth lies in the fact that it undertakes this under social conditions that mock all of this. In this sense it is also experimental. It does not pretend to be something in fact already attained.[107]

Whoever this modeller of social truths may have been, this class fighter for freedom in a leftist European sense, it was certainly not Cage. In Metzger's version of him, Cage became a totem. This was far from the last time he would be so treated.

The impact of Metzger's introduction to Cage's *Concert for Piano and Orchestra* should not be underestimated. To have heard Cage at Darmstadt, naturally one had to have been there, even if the translations of his lectures were slowly circulating around the West German (or, perhaps better, the European German-speaking) avant-garde. Metzger's description of Cage was broadcast as a part of the Westdeutscher Rundfunk's 'Nachtprogramm' to which, anecdotally at least, everyone involved – or wishing to be involved – with the European avant-garde listened almost religiously. One might recall that, as far away as Hungary, György Ligeti listened to the Westdeutscher Rundfunk's broadcasts whenever they were not being jammed by the Hungarian or Soviet authorities and that it was the station's broadcast of Stockhausen's *Kontra-Punkte* and *Gesang der Jünglinge* in November 1956 that led Ligeti to aim for Cologne in the wake of the Soviet invasion and takeover of Hungary.[108] In short, anyone who was anyone was listening.

---

[106] Metzger, 'John Cage, or Liberated Music', 61.   [107] Ibid., 57.
[108] Custodis, *Die soziale Isolation der neuen Musik*, 80.

5 In Cage's wake

Cage, Nono, and the *Darmstädter Beiträge*

The *Darmstädter Beiträge*, which across nineteen volumes reprinted 'key' lectures from the most recent Darmstadt courses,[1] might be suspected to represent some sort of analogue to the publication of *Die Reihe*, which by the close of 1955 had already published its first two volumes, devoted to 'Electronic Music' and 'Anton Webern' respectively. Certainly, Eimert felt that the first volume of the *Beiträge* seemed to him like an edition of *Die Reihe* published by someone else, as well as feeling personally slighted that Stockhausen had contributed an essay to it which could just as well have appeared in his own publication.[2]

Steinecke appears to have put the first volume of the *Darmstädter Beiträge* together largely under his own steam, seeking contributions from those who seemed to him to represent the central parts of Darmstadt. The list of contributors to the first volume of the *Beiträge* probably gives a better indication than anything else of Steinecke's 'dream team': Schoenberg, Adorno, Krenek, Fortner, Nono, Pousseur, Boulez, Stockhausen, Henze, Kolisch, and Stuckenschmidt. Nevertheless, the work was clearly tiring, and before the first volume was published, Steinecke had written to Nono, suggesting that the two of them, perhaps with the assistance of Karl H. Wörner, might be able to turn the first volume into a regular series.[3] Nono was sceptical, not of the idea of the series – he was strongly in favour of the continuation of the *Beiträge* – but of anyone other than Steinecke being in charge of it, though he replied: 'I will help as much as I can. Doubtless Wörner too!'[4]

One must presume that Nono had his arm twisted a little by Steinecke during the 1958 courses since, only a little more than a month after their end, Nono had taken over the majority of the work on the second volume. The plan, in the aftermath of the 1958 courses, was to devote the whole volume to Cage, no doubt in recognition of the discussion his presence had fostered, though there is nothing in the correspondence between Nono and Steinecke to indicate whose idea this focus was. Nono advised Steinecke that

---

[1] Though technically the *Darmstädter Beiträge* run to twenty volumes, volume 7, which would have contained Boulez's 'Musikdenken 3', is absent, and seems most likely to remain so.
[2] Custodis, *Die soziale Isolation der neuen Musik*, 86–7.
[3] Steinecke to Nono, 13 February 1958, ALN.   [4] Nono to Steinecke, 15 February 1958, ALN.

he had already written to Cage and Brown to request essays, and that Stockhausen, Ligeti, and Tudor had agreed to contribute to the Nono-edited Cage volume, with Nono himself planning to contribute an essay. Nono said, too, 'naturally I'll write to Boulez (hopefully he's not still totally set on his "poesie pour pouvoir"/?!?!?!?!?) In which case, "no poetry".'[5] Nono estimated that the work on the volume would be completed, ready to be sent to Schott, by the end of December, and that he would like to reproduce a short piece by Cage in facsimile.[6] Yet Cage did not agree with Nono's selection of writers. Decroupet cites a letter from Cage to Nono, dated 11 November 1958, in which Cage proposed his own ideas: Christian Wolff would contribute an essay, as would Metzger ('who of all the critics has been the single one to have a conception of my work'), but Tudor would not.[7] An undated letter from Nono to Steinecke was presumably sent some time after this:

> Now: I wrote to Cage a long time ago about a Cage volume with him, with Browne [sic], with Stock, with me, with Ligeti: he answered totally differently, he wants it to be totally different, with Metzger etc.
>
> Because I don't want to go this way, the Cage volume is cancelled.
>
> Because: my idea was: a sort of discussion about Cage and his mentality, in order to clarify that here – thus a discussion about chance, indeterminacy etc., thus the compositional problem – as in 11 by Stockhausen/as with Pousseur/ and Boulez/and Cage should be confronted and discussed. (one can do that otherwise) with all this butchery [Metzgerei] it won't happen: I didn't want critics anyway, just composers.[8]

Instead, Nono proposed either compiling the most significant lectures of 1958 for the second volume of the *Darmstädter Beiträge* or carrying out a survey of new music according to national trends across the world.

Decroupet's account has it that this was where things ended, but as late as 11 July 1959, Nono assured Cage that his enthusiasm for the volume remained undimmed, though at present there was 'a bit of a chaos' and he had 'to clear things up with Steinecke and with Schott'.[9] Given that Cage visited Nono in February 1959 and, as I suggest below, seems to have got on amicably with both him and Nuria Nono, one might speculate that the confusions regarding who was to contribute what to the *Beiträge* were smoothed over. Yet two factors – regardless of what Nono was soon to say

---

[5] Ibid.   [6] Nono to Steinecke, 28 October 1958, ALN.
[7] Decroupet, 'Aleatorik und Indetermination', 244.
[8] Nono to Steinecke, undated but between November 1958 and February 1959, ALN.
[9] Nono to Cage, 11 July 1959, JCC.

about Cage at the 1959 courses – ensured that this volume came to nothing, even after Nono and Cage had, perhaps, reached agreement. First, as Decroupet rightly observes, the third volume of Berio's *Incontri musicali* is, to all intents and purposes, the version of the Cage volume, put together as Cage wanted it: alongside Cage's 'Lecture on Nothing' were an Italian translation of 'Alea', Metzger's 'John Cage o della liberazione', and essays by Pousseur and Umberto Eco. Given the publication of this volume in August 1959, one might wonder whether Nono's July letter was written in the full knowledge that the rival volume would be released very shortly if he did not persuade Cage otherwise (and certainly Nono felt there was a rivalry between himself and Berio, after Nono was shut out from the RAI studios in Milan, as he had mentioned to Steinecke by letter).[10] Second, if the Cage volume had happened it would clearly have represented something *different* from the reproduction of the major lectures from the previous year's courses. Steinecke wrote to Nono on 9 November 1959 that, after lengthy discussions with Schott, it had been decided that there would be no volumes produced between the ones devoted to the courses 'proper'. Thus, a little over a year after it was mooted, and after a version of the volume had, in effect, already appeared (albeit in Italy), the idea for a volume specifically devoted to Cage was dropped. The first composer to take over a whole volume would, ultimately, prove to be Boulez, with the publication of his 'Musikdenken heute' lectures in 1963.

Preparations for 'Musik und Graphik'

One of the attractions of the 1959 courses was Stockhausen's series of commentaries on new pieces, his 'Musik und Graphik' lectures, which considered Cornelius Cardew's *February Piece*, Cage's *Concert for Piano and Orchestra*, Sylvano Bussotti's *Pièces de chair II*, Mauricio Kagel's *Transición II* (1958–9), and Stockhausen's own *Zyklus* (1959). Though the lectures themselves are a central part of the – comparatively well-trodden – history of Darmstadt, examining the negotiations and preparations for them reveals that they might, ultimately, have taken a rather different shape and that their final form was very far from fixed until close to the beginning of the courses themselves.

Initially, it was foreseen that a part of Boulez's *Pli selon pli* (1957–62) would be the focus of one of Stockhausen's 'Musik und Graphik' lectures. Briefly – as proposed by Stockhausen to Steinecke by letter on 10 May 1959, and agreed by Steinecke on 24 May 1959 – the plan was to examine

[10] Nono to Steinecke, 15 February 1959, ALN.

'Improvisation III sur Mallarmé' (1959).[11] It seems clear from Steinecke's reply that at some point it had been intended that the Hessischer Rundfunk Symphony Orchestra would perform 'Improvisation III', presumably as a part of the first orchestral concert of the Frankfurt New Music Days on 2 September 1959, but that already this performance was unlikely to happen. This was in line with Stockhausen's general intent to comment on pieces which had actually been performed during the courses, wherever possible on the day following the concert.[12] A further letter from Stockhausen suggests that not only would 'Improvisation III' not be able to be performed within the ambit of the courses, but that it would not, in fact, be ready in time for its projected première in Tübingen either. Thus, no recording would be available to Stockhausen for his commentary. He suggested that Boulez would have to be considered either without a recording or, instead, through 'Improvisation II sur Mallarmé'.[13] Finally, Stockhausen gave up the idea of discussing Boulez at all, since 'Improvisation III' was unfinished, and it seemed to him foolish to look at 'Improvisation I' and 'Improvisation II'. They were replaced by the music of Sylvano Bussotti, to which I return below.[14]

It was not only Stockhausen's plans to examine Boulez's 'Improvisation III' that were frustrated. Though Cage's *Concert for Piano and Orchestra* remained central to his 'Musik und Graphik' commentaries, a projected performance of the piece did not come to pass. It seems that the idea of performing the concerto at Darmstadt was initially that of Tudor, who proposed to Stockhausen an extremely small-scale version using only two or three musicians.[15] The idea was enthusiastically taken up by Stockhausen, who put it to Steinecke within a few days of receiving Tudor's letter.[16] Steinecke's response was, in certain senses, positive. However, he advised Stockhausen that a performance would be impossible without Tudor, and that he had not heard from Tudor in two months. Moreover, though he certainly did not rule out a performance, Steinecke proposed to Stockhausen that any performance should follow the end of one of his seminars and could not form a part of the 'official' concert programme. Finally, for the sake of convenience (and given that no further monies could be made available to hire additional musicians), Steinecke and Stockhausen agreed that the performance forces of *Kreuzspiel*, which was already projected to have a performance during the courses, could be used,

---

[11] Stockhausen to Steinecke, 10 May 1959; Steinecke to Stockhausen, 24 May 1959, in Misch and Bandur (eds.), *Karlheinz Stockhausen bei den Internationalen Ferienkursen*, 236–8.
[12] Steinecke to Stockhausen, 24 May 1959, in ibid., 238.
[13] Stockhausen to Steinecke, 31 May 1959, in ibid., 242.
[14] Stockhausen to Steinecke, undated but *ca.* 25 July 1959, in ibid., 250.
[15] Tudor to Stockhausen, 1 May 1959, in ibid., 234.
[16] Stockhausen to Steinecke, 10 May 1959, in ibid., 237.

but no further performers could be procured.[17] The cautiousness of Steinecke's reply – along with the various conditions set upon such a performance – suggest that Stockhausen's words to Tudor on the matter may have been over-optimistic: 'I asked Steinecke many many times to make a performance of Cage's Concerto. Now he agreed!! Bravo! Hihuha.'[18] Though Stockhausen was clearly aware of the variable disposition of the ensemble in a performance of the *Concert for Piano and Orchestra*, he was not, it appears, in possession of a full knowledge of which orchestral parts existed. Amongst the instrumental parts for *Kreuzspiel* – an oboe, a bass clarinet, a piano, and three percussionists – the only overlap with the available parts for the concerto was the piano part itself, alongside a part for clarinet, rather than bass clarinet. Though Stockhausen seems to have had hopes for the performance of the concerto as late as the end of July 1959,[19] realistically it was never an option. A letter from Steinecke to Tudor of 25 July 1959 made the situation unambiguously clear: 'Unfortunately, it's financially impossible for me to engage the musicians for a successful performance of the Cage piano concerto.'[20] Ultimately Stockhausen would have no option but to rely upon the recording of the Cage concerto from the Cologne performance the previous year for the session of his lecture series devoted to it.

The performance of Kagel's *Transición II*, which would also feature centrally in Stockhausen's lecture series, was, in contradistinction, a relatively early part of Steinecke's plan for the performances at Darmstadt in 1959. When Steinecke took his own decision to programme it is hardly certain, but Kagel expressed disappointment that Steinecke had been unable to attend the most recent 'Music der Zeit' concert in Cologne, since it would have enabled him to play the tape of the first section of the piece to Steinecke. Kagel nevertheless provided a list of the necessary technical equipment and confirmed that the percussionist Christoph Caskel was ready and willing to perform in the piece, having already begun rehearsing it.[21]

A further letter from Steinecke to Kagel suggests that Kagel originally expected to perform the piano part of *Transición II* himself. While Kagel did take part in the three performances of *Transición II* at Darmstadt in 1959, ultimately the piano part was performed by David Tudor; Kagel took over direction of the sound and tape part,[22] and expressed his pleasure at

---

[17] Steinecke to Stockhausen, 24 May 1959, in ibid., 238–40.
[18] Stockhausen to Tudor, 30 May 1959, in ibid., 241.
[19] As expressed in a letter from Stockhausen to Steinecke, *ca.* 25 July 1959, in ibid., 249.
[20] Steinecke to Tudor, 25 July 1959, GRI.
[21] Mauricio Kagel to Steinecke, 17 March 1959, in Björn Heile and Martin Iddon (eds.), *Mauricio Kagel bei Internationalen Ferienkursen für Neue Musik in Darmstadt* (Hofheim: Wolke, 2009), 33–4.
[22] Steinecke to Kagel, 25 May 1959, in ibid., 35.

Tudor's involvement, while remaining concerned regarding the paucity of rehearsal time.[23]

It is plausible, as is suggested by Stockhausen's letter to Steinecke, that it was Steinecke himself who proposed *Transición II* to Stockhausen for consideration as a part of his analytical commentaries. Certainly, this letter represents Stockhausen's first mention of it to Steinecke as a part of the series and also contains Stockhausen's responses to the scores by other composers which Steinecke had supplied to him. With one exception, these do not seem to have met with any interest. That exception was the score of Bussotti's *Pièces de chair II*. Though Stockhausen observed that it was practically impossible to offer much in the way of critical commentary without the benefit of seeing the performance directions, he had 'rarely taken so much pleasure from *reading* a score'. His suggestion to Steinecke was that the best plan – and this only as an experiment – would be to ensure Bussotti's presence at Darmstadt, to place a singer and a pianist at his disposal, and to ensure that Bussotti was, himself, made responsible for rehearsing the piece, so that an adequate performance could be achieved.[24] Though, in the end, it would prove to be only the *Five Piano Pieces for David Tudor* (1959) that were featured at Darmstadt (and of those only the second, third, and fifth), a letter from Tudor to Stockhausen certainly implies that Steinecke had made some attempts to secure exactly this arrangement. Bussotti had suggested William Pearson and Cathy Berberian as his preferred singers, which Tudor said would please him too, since 'clowns are better when there're more of them'.[25] However, the selection from the *Five Piano Pieces* was finally performed only as a part of the Stockhausen lectures, and not in the main run of concerts. The sticking point, as Stockhausen explained to Tudor in a letter only a few days later,[26] consisted of the words, which, as Attinello describes them, are 'largely based on overtly homosexual texts. Many of those texts are somewhat paedophiliac, and they inevitably emphasize bodies as erotic objects to be enjoyed or dominated, rather than any kind of emotional content; some idealize desire itself, as an operating force for which bodies are merely the tools'.[27] Whether it was the homosexuality, the paedophilia, or the treatment of bodies that was ultimately the problem, the upshot was that 'nobody wanted to put it in a program'.[28]

[23] Kagel to Tudor, 18 June 1959, GRI.
[24] Stockhausen to Steinecke, 10 May 1959, in Misch and Bandur (eds.), *Karlheinz Stockhausen bei den Internationalen Ferienkursen*, 236–7.
[25] Tudor to Stockhausen, 7 July 1959, in ibid., 246.
[26] Stockhausen to Tudor, 12 July 1959, in ibid., 247.
[27] David Osmond-Smith and Paul Attinello, 'Gay Darmstadt: Flamboyance and Rigour at the Summer Courses for New Music', in Attinello, Fox, and Iddon (eds.), *Other Darmstadts*, 112.
[28] Stockhausen to Tudor, 12 July 1959, in Misch and Bandur (eds.), *Karlheinz Stockhausen bei den Internationalen Ferienkursen*, 247.

Aside from Bussotti, of the scores provided to Stockhausen by Steinecke, Górecki was despatched perfunctorily: 'Górecki is *nothing*', Isang Yun's work was regarded as 'wholly academic in technique and form', and a now entirely forgotten composer, Tartani, hardly met with a better response: 'The whole thing is decoration. Apart from that I see no difference in this score from Nono's.' Given the comparison with Nono, perhaps Stockhausen's reaction to Nono's more recent music might also have been that it 'gets on the nerves, because it has nothing to say, and only wants to shake things up'.[29] In this context, it is surprising that, at the earliest stages of planning the lectures, Stockhausen also considered examining Nono's *Cori di Didone* (1958). In Steinecke's first detailed letter asking for specifics regarding his 1959 courses, he suggested that Stockhausen had previously proposed this.[30] Stockhausen's reply had nothing to say on the matter, although his theme at this stage was merely 'analysis' rather than any sort of examination of new notational practices. He did, however, respond extremely positively to Steinecke's query regarding the quality of Cardew's *Two Books of Study for Pianists* (1958), recommending the work for performance.[31] Nono was relatively swiftly dropped; regardless of any aesthetic considerations, as the idea to discuss notation developed, it ceased to be relevant to the theme, *Cori di Didone* being wholly conventional in its notational practice. Nevertheless, it is worth noting that, regardless of how matters turned out, during the planning stages Boulez, Nono, and Cage were composers who remained very much a part of Stockhausen's considerations.

A further indication of the rising status of Stockhausen within the new music scene more generally and at Darmstadt specifically may be seen in the fact that his *Zyklus* (1959), for solo percussionist, was not only commissioned for Darmstadt, and premièred by Christoph Caskel as a part of the opening concert on 25 August, but was also the selected obligatory piece for performance for competitors for the Kranichsteiner Musikpreis in that year, alongside two freely selected pieces. As well as the première of *Zyklus*, the opening concert in 1959 featured performances by other members of the performance faculty of obligatory pieces for their categories: Varèse's *Density 21.5* performed by Severino Gazzelloni, and Boulez's First Piano Sonata (1946) in a performance given by David Tudor. *Zyklus* would be the Stockhausen piece central to the 'Musik und Graphik' lecture series.

---

[29] Stockhausen to Steinecke, 10 May 1959, in ibid., 236–7.
[30] Steinecke to Stockhausen, 13 March 1959, in ibid., 229.
[31] Stockhausen to Steinecke, undated but *ca.* 14 March 1959, in ibid., 230–1.

'Musik und Graphik'

The situation in the hall in which Stockhausen presented his 'Musik und Graphik' lectures is ably captured by Ernst Thomas in his review for the *Frankfurter Allgemeine Zeitung*:

> The hall is in half-darkness. The roller blinds only partially keep out the bright, hot August sun. Heat radiates through the walls and ceiling, but the rows of chairs are packed with diligent listeners and note-takers. The silence they keep as they attend to the presentation is as oppressive as the heat which continues to rise throughout the course of each hour-and-a-half lecture.[32]

The text of 'Musik und Graphik' published in the *Darmstädter Beiträge* is a version of Stockhausen's first lecture, a transcription made by Gottfried Michael Koenig based on the spoken presentation, but sharpened through Koenig's access to Stockhausen's original script. In this respect, the mode of presentation is very close to that which Stockhausen employed in 'Musik und Sprache', which is to say that in the live version he extemporised more detailed explanations for many of the points he made, presumably in order to slow down the pace of delivery. Since these extemporisations barely alter the sense of Stockhausen's presentation, I rely here principally on the published version, although I turn to archival recordings in the case of Stockhausen's later lectures.

Stockhausen opened by both making clear and confusing what was at stake. In arguing that a historical division had long existed between the position of the composer ('who writes') and the interpreter ('who plays'), Stockhausen observed that when a performer operated without a text to determine his or her actions, then it was what one might term improvisation and that, from Stockhausen's perspective, little 'spontaneous invention' was likely to be found there. On the contrary, what could be expected was 'the reproduction of learned clichés'.[33] What Stockhausen was looking for, then, was just the sort of spontaneity that the seeming freedoms of jazz did *not* give to performers. Though he did not say so, it is not difficult to see how a listener might have thought that he was discussing ways to introduce a certain form of improvisation into scored music, thus 'solving' the problems of spontaneity in both written and unwritten musics. Yet even if such an idea can be found to underpin certain aspects of Stockhausen's thought, the main purpose of his introductory lecture to the series was to show that the

---

[32] Ernst Thomas, 'Klänge für das Auge? Gefährliche Doktrinen auf den Darmstädter Ferienkursen', *Frankfurter Allgemeine Zeitung*, 1 September 1959.

[33] Karlheinz Stockhausen, 'Musik und Graphik' [1959], *Darmstädter Beiträge zur neuen Musik*, vol. 3 (1960), 5.

written traces of music had never exhibited literal relationships to the sounding results and that close proximities between the two had occurred only within a relatively brief historical time span. What this would mean, then, was that there was necessarily some degree of space between the written and aural manifestations of music, and that this space was necessarily indeterminate. A composer could play on that distinction, and it was here that a certain sort of freedom (or spontaneity) might be found. Stockhausen was clear, too, that recognition of this space could result in a wide variety of different practices, with Cage and Bussotti at the most extreme end and, though he did not explicitly say so, Cardew at the least extreme.

Throughout his presentations Stockhausen insisted that what was at stake in the pieces under examination was *Vieldeutigkeit*, which is to say 'ambiguity' as the usual translation of the word would have it, but also that the pieces under discussion were capable of expressing multiple, perhaps contradictory, meanings. The relationship between the notation of the scores and the sounding result is such that multiple different versions of the pieces are conceivable, to be sure, and that, too, the sounding results of the pieces are not necessarily predictable from their written traces. Stockhausen noted that one of the 'benefits', if it could be seen that way, was that the new notational devices allowed the composer to move between *Eindeutigkeit* (clarity, but also, thus, a singularity of meaning) and absolute *Vieldeutigkeit*. Arguably, the graphical strategies of Stockhausen's title were really only a focus through which he examined indeterminacy, though it should become evident that his understanding of that idea cannot wholly be reconciled with the way in which Cage seems to have understood it.

Stockhausen began with examples drawn from his own *Zyklus*, the focus of his second lecture on 27 August, in one of which several fully determined lines were provided to the performer. The performer was to select only one, the others remaining unheard in an individual performance. Stockhausen went on to show the total gamut of nine different degrees of determination used across the piece's seventeen periods, ranging from the almost fully determined to sections where significant degrees of decision-making are demanded of the performer.[34] However, he made no suggestion within his presentation that a percussionist need do more than read the piece from the

---

[34] A re-worked version of this lecture may be found within Karlheinz Stockhausen, 'Nr. 9: Zyklus für einen Schlagzeuger (1959)' [1959], in *Texte*, vol. II, 73–100, which also contains a description of the structural cycle (p. 93). This suggests strongly that, from Stockhausen's own perspective, *Zyklus* still represents 'aleatoric' music in the sense in which Meyer-Eppler had described it, which was to say that the larger form was pre-determined, even though the smaller parts were not. The distinction, of course, was that in Stockhausen's earlier music, even though the smaller units were not *pre*-determined, they were determined, which is to say fixed in the score.

given score, and indeed the physically circular nature of the piece's set-up in live performance strongly suggests that Stockhausen *aimed* at performance without concrete realisation into other notation of a particular instantiation of *Zyklus*. Nevertheless, Fox's note on performing *Plus-Minus* (1963) – 'I took it away to prepare more carefully and quickly realised that one could not expect to play spontaneously from the seven pages of graphic symbols and seven pages of pitch materials' – surely holds true in the case of *Zyklus* too.[35] John Evarts's later discussion of such approaches retains the idea that what is aimed at in the sorts of music Stockhausen discussed was improvisation as a live reaction to graphical stimulus. Evarts queried: 'Shall we in the future be reading that the Boris Blatherwick Ensemble gave a superb joint improvisation on Picasso's *Guernica*?'[36] That confusion remained regarding precisely what was being expected of a performer will be seen in the press reception described below, and it may be strikingly seen in the juxtaposition of two comments by Roger Smalley. With reference to *Zyklus*, Smalley observes that '[t]he performer of *Zyklus* can start at the beginning of any of the work's sixteen pages. The score can also be turned upside down and played backwards, so that there are actually 32 possible starting points. After deciding where to begin the performer must play through the score in the normal way, ending with the sound he began with.' This is, albeit in some very specific ways, at odds with Smalley's subsequent statement (here in the case of indetermined graphic scores more generally) that

> [i]n most cases the freedom of the performer ceases to exist long before the performance begins. These scores are so complex that it is necessary for the performer to decide upon a particular ordering and distribution of all the elements before commencing rehearsal [. . .] What is eventually heard is therefore in fact a fixed version prepared by one particular player, or a group of players.[37]

Smalley is quite correct that a performance of *Zyklus* would be a fixed, predetermined one, perhaps different each time but with the materials for a specific performance determined in advance by the performer. Where his statement is almost certainly erroneous is in its assertion that the score is played 'in the normal way'. An accurate performance of *Zyklus* relies upon the performer making rather more specific determinations, even if not necessarily going so far as Tudor's practice of transcribing performance

---

[35] Christopher Fox, 'Written in Sand: Stockhausen's *Plus-Minus*, More or Less', *Musical Times*, vol. 141, no. 1871 (Summer 2000), 16. Fox is reminiscing in particular here regarding working with students on graphic scores, predominantly dating from the 1960s, in the late 1970s.

[36] John Evarts, 'The New Musical Notation: A Graphic Art?', *Leonardo*, vol. 1, no. 4 (October 1968), 412.

[37] Roger Smalley, 'Some Aspects of the Changing Relationship between Composer and Performer in Contemporary Music', *Proceedings of the Royal Musical Association*, vol. 96 (1969–70), 79–80.

materials onto five-line staves. Though Stockhausen gave little indication that this was what a performer would *have* to do, that it *is*, nevertheless, a necessary requirement for a performance of *Zyklus* suggests strongly that he was aware of what Tudor's practices would have been in the case of Cage's indeterminate music and that what Tudor was doing did not involve improvisation.

It was to Cage that Stockhausen turned in his third lecture, held on 28 August, though Cage was buffered, as it were, by Stockhausen's assistant, Cornelius Cardew. The piece by Cardew about which Stockhausen spoke is described in the print version of 'Musik und Graphik' in the *Darmstädter Beiträge* as *Piano Piece 1960*, and this also provides a brief example of the score.[38] Borio and Danuser's tabulation of performances at the 1959 Ferienkurse suggests, instead, that *Piano Piece 1959* was featured in this session.[39] These were almost certainly not the same pieces as one another. The extract printed in the *Darmstädter Beiträge* is clearly from the piece which would later be re-titled *February Piece III* (1960), while the piece Cardew himself played an extract from during the lecture was certainly what became *February Piece I* (1959).[40] That unusual (and seemingly needless) change notwithstanding, what is particularly striking about Stockhausen's description of the piece is that what he said was almost identical to Cardew's own later description. Indeed, Tudor would later compliment Stockhausen for the degree to which he had not imposed his own aesthetic judgement on the music he was describing. In his later essay 'Notation–Interpretation, *etc.*', Cardew stated:

> One feature of the piece [*February Piece I*] is the method used for controlling the length of tones: a tone is struck at a particular dynamic, and is released when it has reached another. So for example, the length of a tone is the time taken by this particular tone to make the diminuendo from *mf* to *pp*. Such tones are sometimes accompanied by a sign meaning *e.g.* 'relatively long', and it becomes clear that our interpretation of the signs *mf* and *pp* will also have to be relative, and we come up against the question: 'are the dynamics controlling the durations, or are the durations controlling the dynamics?' Neither, for the player controls both, that is he controls their interaction. This is the real meaning of such signs as 'long', 'loud', *etc.*: their function is to put the player in a position where he is conscious of himself, of his own experiences of 'long', 'loud', *etc.* He is conscious of what he is doing and of the capacities of the instrument at which he sits. The function of such signs is to bring the pianist to life.[41]

---

[38] Stockhausen, 'Musik und Graphik', 14–17.
[39] Borio and Danuser (eds.), *Im Zenit der Moderne*, vol. III, 597.
[40] *February Piece III* was not, in fact, finished until 1960, and could not, therefore have formed a part of this lecture.
[41] Cornelius Cardew, 'Notation–Interpretation, *etc.*', *Tempo*, no. 58 (1961), 27.

Regardless of whether or not Cardew may have, after the fact, mimicked Stockhausen's formulation, this was the sum of what Stockhausen had to say about *February Piece I*, down to the question of what was controlling what (or whom). It may well be worth noting, too, that, although there was certainly strong applause following Cardew's performance of *February Piece I* during the lecture, there was also a considerable amount of booing. Similarly, during Stockhausen's description of the performances of Cage's *Concert for Piano and Orchestra* in the same lecture, it was clear that some audience members expected there to be jokes: the first peal of laughter came when Stockhausen described the New York première as having taken place at a 'cabaret'. Stockhausen was quick to silence the laughter, pointing out that not only was the cabaret a 'proper' concert hall in the evening, but that many prominent New York artists had turned out to support the performance. Even so, as Stockhausen further described the difficulties of the Cologne performance of the piece, more widespread laughter suggested that many of the audience supported those performers who had taken the freedoms granted them by Cage to mean that they were at liberty to, for instance, quote from the canonic repertoire during the performance, activities that Hans G. Helms had suggested were a scandal, not least because of the insult they offered to Tudor's performance.[42] The audience may well have taken Tudor rather more seriously than they took Cage, though, since there was no laughter during or following any of his performances of fragments from the *Solo for Piano* (which is to say the solo piano part of *Concert for Piano and Orchestra*), not even when they featured the duck whistle, an instrument which had seemed to occasion great hilarity both at Donaueschingen and Darmstadt in the past.

The commentary on Cage which followed was, rather disappointingly, one of the least interesting sections of what Stockhausen had to say, even if it was clear that he felt that Cage's work operated on a level with his own and with that of Bussotti, Cardew, and Kagel. Most of what he had to say, though, re-hashed Cage's own lectures in the previous year, with Stockhausen repeatedly stressing the idea that one should, according to Cage's position, let tones be tones, and nothing more. His recollection of a conversation with Tudor in this context, however, is intriguing. Stockhausen had, it seemed, tried to suggest that Cage's music was spiritual (*geistliche*) music. Tudor countered, after a long pause, that Augustine had suggested that if a truly *geistliche* music were possible, there would be no

---

[42] See, for instance, Michael Struck-Schloen, 'Wie ein Bad in kochendem Wasser – die WDR-Klangkörper als "Instrumente" Neuer Musik', in Frank Hilberg and Harry Vogt (eds.), *Musik der Zeit 1951–2001: 50 Jahre Neue Musik im WDR* (Hofheim: Wolke, 2002), 117.

need for humans to make it; indeed, no-one ever would have made music at all. This becomes of real significance only in Stockhausen's note, immediately following this comment in the lecture, that Tudor had also proposed that the performers of the *Concert for Piano and Orchestra* should play without any 'passion'. That Stockhausen specifically chose the German word *Passion*, rather than *Leidenschaft*, which would have been a perhaps more natural choice, suggests that he may have been pursuing the Augustinian direction, given that Augustine was concerned in *De musica* to discuss how *passiones* (the 'affects' of musical sound) affect the soul (which is to say, here, the *Geist*).[43] The performers ought, according to Stockhausen's understanding of Tudor's position, to play their instruments to the best of their abilities, but without attaching any particular significance to or opinion regarding the sounding music that would result, thus mirroring what Cage himself had done in the process of writing the piece. Without saying so in so many words, Stockhausen seemed to be pointing to the question of whether Cage really was the liberating spirit that one might think, or was setting his own position up in a mode which allied his own activities with divine utterances in ways which might be regarded as problematic.

For the most part, though, Stockhausen simply described the *Solo for Piano* via examinations of a small number of the notational devices used, which he named 'structures', following his own terminology in describing *Zyklus*. Yet he was vague in explaining the gap between the score and the sounding result, observing only that there was a codex at the head of the score which explained how the symbols were to be realised. This is certainly true, but that codex hardly gives all the information a performer would need. In particular, it gives no indication of the sort of strategies a performer might be expected to undertake in the process of realising the score, which is to say whether the performer would be expected to make his or her own realisation copy of the score in fresh notation, according to the model of Tudor.[44] Though Tudor played fragments from what he had done with the various structures, no indication was given of the *process* of realisation or, indeed, even of the fact that there was much of a process to carry out at all. One might even wonder whether Stockhausen himself quite knew what had

---

[43] See Brian Brennan, 'Augustine's *De musica*', *Vigiliae Christianae: A Review of Early Christian Life and Language*, vol. 42, no. 3 (September 1988), 267–81.

[44] John Holzaepfel provides a comprehensive examination of the second of Tudor's two realisations of the *Solo for Piano* in 'David Tudor and the *Solo for Piano*'. The particular performance on which Stockhausen relied was Tudor's first, which he used for the première of the piece at Town Hall in New York and in Cologne. By 1959, Tudor was already at work on his second realisation. The reasons for his dissatisfaction with the first are unknown. In any case, after 1959, he used only the second version.

to be done in order to perform *the Concert for Piano and Orchestra* were it not for passing comments. For instance he noted that the proportional notational strategies of structure 'CC' meant that its duration was precisely delineated (and Stockhausen stressed the precision of Cage's score on multiple occasions, even if he stressed too that what Tudor played was wholly independent of what Cage had written), and this precise duration could hardly be determined in performance without careful preparatory work. In this sense, Stockhausen ensured that Cage's work fell within his broad understanding of the compositional world: it was necessarily a balance between the precisely determined and the indeterminate. Again, from Stockhausen's perspective, if *Zyklus* remained an aleatoric piece in the sense that Meyer-Eppler had described it, so too did the *Concert for Piano and Orchestra*. Nevertheless, in connection with the 'CE' structure, one might feel that Stockhausen's insistence on a complete differentiation between what Cage notated and what Tudor played was disingenuous, since it was clear that Tudor simply fixed what was left ambiguous in Cage's notation: here, for instance, reading each of the uncleffed staves as if they were in the treble clef. The relationship may not have been a precise or deterministic one, but it was surely clear that a relationship *existed* between the two modes of presentation. Indeed, Stockhausen stated in this precise case that what was at stake was not *Vieldeutigkeit* but *Doppeldeutigkeit* (a double meaning, rather than a multiplicity of meanings).

Yet Stockhausen's stress, throughout these descriptions, was on what Cage *wanted*. In short, he returned repeatedly to the desires of the composer, in contradistinction to what he had suggested were Cage's ends. Underlying Stockhausen's rather didactic description of the score was, one might think, an insistence, first and foremost, that Cage did have compositional desires and that these were precisely expressed, even if when Tudor played the piece it was impossible to hear the relationship between the written and sounding traces of the music. In short, Stockhausen might well have been saying: look, he is just like the rest of us; Cage is a composer, after all.

Unlike the rest of what Stockhausen presented (and operating in a curious relationship to Stockhausen's complaint regarding the snobbish attitude of people who bought the new graphic scores to frame and hang as art),[45] the fourth of Bussotti's *Five Piano Pieces for David Tudor* was, Stockhausen suggested at the beginning of his fourth session, not initially intended for performance at all. The printed version of the score gives the

---

[45] Stockhausen, 'Musik und Graphik', 6.

same indication, suggesting that Bussotti, who had drawn the image which underpins the score as early as 1949, had initially intended it simply to be understood as an image. It was ten years later, on 27 March 1959, that he turned his artwork into a piano piece by adding indications for the meaning of the piece's various parameters at the left-hand side of the score. Perhaps it was in view of this, in particular, that Evarts would later wonder whether one might simply 'interpret' Picasso's *Guernica* as if it were a score. In any case, the slight disturbance in the hall following Stockhausen's description of Bussotti's lowest stave – where the parameter descriptor shows an A in the middle of the treble clef, though the stave of the piece itself has an alto clef and is intersected only once by a jagged line and once by a point at the very top of the stave – suggests that those watching and listening had little idea of how to come immediately to terms with Bussotti's notation and were unconvinced that it should be taken *too* seriously. What interested Stockhausen in particular was the *Doppeldeutigkeit* (just as he had seen it in the *Solo for Piano*) of the space *between* the staves, which ought not, according to Bussotti, to be regarded as a continuous motion between parameters (almost inconceivable in any case, since what a motion between a muted sound on the case of the instrument and a 'sequence' would be is hard to imagine, those ideas surely overlapping with one another if they are conceived of as distinct parameters). Rather, what was meant was that those spaces could refer to *either* the upper or the lower stave.

Tudor had, according to Stockhausen's account, asked Bussotti whether he was expected to perform the whole of the fourth piano piece. Bussotti's response was that only a small section need be used in a single performance, small details being sufficient for an adequate realisation of the piece, such that it could be repeatedly interpreted in 'new' fashions. In truth, Tudor played the Bussotti piano pieces only very occasionally, with a marked preference for the second, third, and fifth. Of these, the second and fifth, it should be noted, are in more or less fixed notation and thus performable from the score, although Tudor made five-line stave realisations of the first, third, and fourth pieces, all of which are graphically notated.

It was after Tudor's performance, in Stockhausen's lecture, of the third of the *Five Piano Pieces for David Tudor* that a participant queried whether Tudor was capable of repeating his performance. Not only *could* Tudor have repeated his performance (indeed, he could probably *only* have repeated his performance, since he was performing from his own realisation copy), but it is also important that the score of *Pièces de chair II*, from which the *Five Piano Pieces for David Tudor* are an extractable part, actually shows realisation in practice, giving three different, fully notated realisations of the short movement 'J.H-K.S.' Stockhausen certainly could have shown matter like this, making absolutely clear that what Bussotti, like Cage, expected was that the graphical notations were transcribed into readable (and traditional) notation.[46] He did not, though, preferring that this, too, remained 'ambiguous'.[47] It is probably worth noting, too, that though the applause for Bussotti's music was relatively muted, there was, in the case of this performance, no booing.

One of the issues that is particularly notable in the 'Musik und Graphik' presentations is that, in contrast to previous presentations, Stockhausen made no obvious attempt to suggest that his own music 'solved' any of the difficulties which an 'ambiguous' approach to notation threw up. Even structurally, he dealt with his own *Zyklus* first, not giving it 'pride of place', but rather simply placing it amongst the other scores as one example of a range of approaches. Indeed, in his commentary on Cardew's *February Piece I*, Stockhausen specifically noted that Cardew's work on it had begun at a point when he and Stockhausen had not discussed any of the ideas that Stockhausen was outlining in 'Musik und Graphik'. Stockhausen thus insisted that his and Cardew's conceptions of the possibilities of such

---

[46] Erik Ulman identifies the three realisations for what they are, but asks: 'Which, one may ask, is the authentic text? What relations exist between the realizations and the score, since they are not necessarily apparent?' (Erik Ulman, 'The Music of Sylvano Bussotti', *Perspectives of New Music*, vol. 34, no. 2 (Summer 1996), 190). With the advantage of knowing what Tudor's procedures were, it becomes obvious that this is clearly not the point. What Bussotti's score shows in the case of 'J.H-K.S.' (the initials standing for John Cage, Heinz-Klaus Metzger, and Bussotti himself) is that the music can and should be realised into traditional (or at least performable) notation. The three realisations given simply demonstrate the possible degree of variations, not that there is any reason to privilege these particular realisations over any others. It is not likely to be coincidental either that 'J.H-K.S' is the first piece in *Pièces de chair II* with indeterminate graphic notation: it is the most obvious place to demonstrate the ways in which realisation might function in this context, and none of the other indeterminate pieces in the cycle contain sample realisations.

[47] The degree to which this could have been made explicit and was not, despite the very large number of ideal opportunities so to do, might make one wonder whether there was, for reasons which are not wholly explicable, some sort of post-war analogue to Lowinsky's 'secret chromatic art' taking place (Edward E. Lowinsky, *Secret Chromatic Art in the Netherlands Motet* (New York: Columbia University Press, 1946)). The idea that Tudor's activities were being intentionally concealed for some reason may be seen at perhaps its zenith in Heinz-Klaus Metzger's remark, quoted above, that 'performers should take those that first strike them accidentally and – God knows how – translate them into definite actions' (Metzger, 'John Cage, or Liberated Music', 54). While it is just about possible that Metzger did not know precisely what Tudor was doing in 1958, it seems relatively unlikely. Much more likely is that he was aware of Tudor's activities and felt that it was important that some sense of mystery or ambiguity be maintained. It is difficult, however, to speculate upon the motivations for this, other than to say that, with a knowledge of quite the degree of work Tudor undertook to realise certain scores, the impression may have been given that it was he who was doing the 'real' compositional work. The composers would be, in this sense, providing little more than conceptual models for compositional work. Plausibly the difference was between those who knew both Cage and Tudor and those who knew only Tudor, since, as Cage would tell Retallack, even after Tudor had turned to composition, 'how he composes is unknown, because he loves keeping secrets. He doesn't want people to know what he's doing. He said once – even as a performer – I want to have an instrument that no one else knows how to play' (John Cage and Joan Retallack, 'July 30, 1992' [1992], in *Musiccage: Cage Muses on Words, Art, Music* (Hanover, NH: Wesleyan University Press, 1996), 298).

notational strategies were reached independently. Perhaps this is not so surprising, since *Zyklus* was Stockhausen's first graphically notated score. A more cynical response might have it, though, that it would prove advantageous to Stockhausen to show that the ideas he was presenting *could* have been conceived without direct reference to, for instance, Cage. Thus it would not be implausible that Stockhausen, too, might have reached *Zyklus* shortly after experiencing Cage's *Concert for Piano and Orchestra* by happy coincidence. Another, similarly cynical, response might observe that while Cage and Bussotti, on the one hand, and Cardew, on the other, represented the extreme poles of indeterminate graphical practice, Stockhausen's *Zyklus* made use of the whole gamut, from more-or-less fully determined sections to almost wholly indeterminate material. One might conclude from this that, while other composers were hidebound by particular ideas regarding graphic notation, Stockhausen sought to synthesise the whole range of modes of operation into a single, fully articulated mode of working. Such cynicism is only partly undermined by the sense given in Stockhausen's final lecture, on 31 August, that Kagel's *Transición II*, too, exhibits approaches very similar to Stockhausen's own exemplar of graphic notation, moving between wholly determined and wholly indeterminate 'structures'. *Transición II* has, like Stockhausen's own *Zyklus*, a particular way of arranging the structures into a larger form, selecting only a particular number of the structures, which ensures that the piece lasts at least ten minutes. Perhaps it helped that many of Kagel's notational strategies so closely recalled Stockhausen's own.

Critical response to 'Musik und Graphik'

Writing to M. C. Richards after the event, David Tudor felt that Stockhausen's sessions had been almost wholly lacking in critical analysis, a positive aspect as far as Tudor was concerned; he suggested that Stockhausen was, in essence, simply presenting the pieces 'in themselves':

> It's been an interesting session, K.-H. gave a class mostly devoted to graphics & a series of lectures in which scores of new works with graphic tendencies were explained and presented (sometimes with performance), quite dispassionately & without analysis (Cage, Bussotti, Cardew, Stockhausen, Kagel), also without criticism of any sort. You can imagine that this was not very well understood by most, they prefer opinions.[48]

---

[48] Tudor (Cologne) to M. C. Richards, 8 September 1959, GRI.

In contradistinction to Tudor's report – as will become clearer in the discussion of Nono's 1959 presentation – many did not 'prefer opinions'. This is not to say, though, that Tudor was mistaken in his assertion that many did not understand the detail of what Stockhausen had to say. As has already been noted, one of the repeated tropes of Cage's reception in the European scene is a misunderstanding of what he was attempting to do and the methods he was using to achieve those ends. What is seen in the responses to Stockhausen's presentation is that, even to the degree that he was seen to be discussing a single idea, what that idea represented was hardly clearly defined in the minds of his journalistic observers. Moreover, whether Stockhausen was acting in a manner that might be regarded as non-partisan is debatable; the work selected for presentation clearly suggested that Stockhausen ascribed to those pieces a certain significance and importance. Ernst Thomas's report assessed Stockhausen's 'Musik und Graphik' sessions in precisely this respect.

Stockhausen's own *Zyklus* functions as something of a hinge to get towards Thomas's main concern, which has much more to do with Cage than with Stockhausen. His opening gambit reads like pure reportage (though the tone of what had preceded it, and the title of Thomas's piece 'Sounds for the Eye? Dangerous Doctrines at the Darmstadt Ferienkurse', should have alerted any reader that what was to follow would not be positive):

> The principle according to which this piece [*Zyklus*] was composed touches on the idea that the ambiguity of a serial structure should be recognisable in a singular realisation, at a single listening. Stockhausen juxtaposes free and fixed structures such that 'at critical points of contact, the extreme point of one changes unnoticeably into the other'. He wants 'to show the static in the dynamic, the aimless in the goal-directed – not eliminate the one or the other, nor to destroy either, nor even to search after a third idea through a synthesis of the two'.[49]

So far, so seemingly typical of the sorts of pronouncements for which the post-war avant-garde is regularly lampooned. Yet for Thomas this was clearly a posture too far. He dubbed precisely this description 'a largely muddle-headed philosophy' and stated that it was derived, unmediatedly, from Cage, citing the following passage from Cage's 'History of Experimental Music in the United States' as evidence:

> [M]ore essential than composing by means of chance operations, it seems to me now, is composing in such a way that what one does is indeterminate of its

---

[49] Thomas, 'Klänge für das Auge?'

performance [...] I take a sheet of paper and place points on it. Next I make parallel lines on a transparency, say five parallel lines. I establish five categories of sound for the five lines, but I do not say which line is which category. The transparency may be placed on the sheet with points in any position and readings of the points may be taken with regard to all the characteristics one wishes to distinguish. Another transparency may be used for further measurements, even altering the succession of sounds in time.[50]

It is difficult to see any close correlation between Stockhausen's statement above and the quotation from Cage cited by Thomas. This is not to say that Thomas is wrong to suggest a link, even a causal link, between Cage's thinking and *Zyklus*. Fritz Muggler, writing in *Musikalische Jugend*, effects a very similar juxtaposition, without any particularly compelling evidence for the connection: 'After Cage held some lectures at the Darmstadt courses last year, a whole group of young composers have surprisingly fallen under his influence. Stockhausen's example (Klavierstück XI) has exercised a poor influence here.'[51]

The links that Thomas (or Muggler) drew are hardly as precise as one might infer from the juxtaposition of texts he made. His concern was much more with what Stockhausen – now, as Thomas had it, 'on Cage's side' – was suggesting must be removed from musical experience. His contempt for the idea that it might be impossible to imagine, in the mind's ear, what a piece might sound like from its score pervades his report: 'The "notes" become pictures [...] such that the inner ear, with which one is accustomed to read a score, becomes redundant.' Thomas distinguished between the sorts of 'good' chance present in Stockhausen's own Klavierstück XI and Boulez's Third Piano Sonata, where the sonic results can still be predicted with greater or lesser accuracy from the printed page, and the sort of 'bad' chance which he saw in the work of Cage and Bussotti (and in Stockhausen's *Zyklus*). The distinction became one between pieces which *can* be realised from the page and those which must be realised into another form of notation if performance is to take place without improvisation.[52]

---

[50] John Cage, 'History of Experimental Music in the United States' [1959], in *Silence*, 69. The version Thomas quotes from is actually Heinz-Klaus Metzger's translation, printed as 'Zur Geschichte der experimentellen Musik in den Vereinigten Staaten', *Darmstädter Beiträge zur neuen Musik*, vol. 3 (1959), 46–53.

[51] Fritz Muggler, 'Der Zufall und die Musik: Notizen von den Darmstädter Ferienkurse für Neue Musik', *Musikalische Jugend*, October 1959. Not the least of the problems with this is the implication that Stockhausen's Klavierstück XI had something to do with Cage's Darmstadt visit. That the piece exhibits links with Cage (and with Feldman and Brown too) is certainly clear from the score, but having been completed in 1956, it can hardly be held to have had any direct causal relationship with Cage's presence at Darmstadt two years later.

[52] Thomas, 'Klänge für das Auge'.

In his discussion of Tudor's performance of the third of Bussotti's *Five Piano Pieces for David Tudor*, the score for which was reprinted at the head of Thomas's review, it was again clear that precisely what the European actors in the new music scene expected of an indeterminate score was hardly precise at all. As Thomas reported it, Tudor had the idea of performing the third Bussotti piano piece via glissandi on the strings of the piano, with Bussotti's agreement that this was a valid interpretation. What is rather more significant is the way in which Thomas read Bussotti's relationship to the score, however: 'He wants to avoid providing the performer with rules and regulations, but rather to free his sonic imagination. Is that the acme of freedom, for both? Or grounds for conflict? It's all the same to Bussotti whether all the symbols drawn on his page are realised or not, whether it's all played.'[53] On the one hand, this is simply erroneous. Although Bussotti's performance instructions for the *Five Piano Pieces for David Tudor* are not publicly available, and do not form any part of the published performance materials for either that separable set or for the complete cycle of *Pièces de chair II*, they certainly exist, and existed in the hands of David Tudor. That only Tudor had a copy of the 'rules and regulations' that would make a performance of the piano pieces possible *without* resorting to some form of improvisation is wholly in keeping with Bussotti's oft-repeated remark that 'the element "for David Tudor" in the title is not a dedication, but rather an indication of instrumentation'. On the other hand, however, it reveals the degree to which confusion reigned regarding notations of this sort. While for some it was precisely the degree to which a 'new' version of the piece (that was nevertheless still the same piece) could be performed on each occasion that was important, for others the expectation was that it should be possible for a performer – if the score really *meant* anything as a score – to create essentially the same sounding impression on multiple occasions. It is clear from Thomas's comments that a central part of musical experience for him included the ability to come to terms with a score's immanent sounding presence through the aural imagination of score reading. Indeterminacy on this level was, thus, wholly unacceptable. As Thomas described the issue:

> The pianist David Tudor interpreted this image [i.e. Bussotti's *Five Piano Pieces for David Tudor*, No. 3], since these 'notes' are for a piano piece. One listener wanted to hear this interpretation a second time; he wanted to be sure that Tudor was really able, following such notation, to play the same thing a second time. Stockhausen refused: the curious listener could meet with Tudor [...] not much store is set by the clear, repeatable presentation of music any more.[54]

[53] Ibid. [54] Ibid.

That Stockhausen refused, and that the listener (and Thomas) remained unclear on this matter, suggests that the way in which Tudor worked on preparing indeterminate scores for performance was not known to everybody in the new music community, and may have been known only to those who were closely associated with Cage. It is difficult to square the many and variable responses to Cage's music with regard to its repeatability without this being the case. The vital link between the possibility of music itself and the possibility of hearing it in the presence of only the score copy could not be clearer, in Thomas's mind: 'Here ends both an aesthetic of music, and an aesthetic of listening.'[55] Thomas's final judgement on Cage is damning: 'It is for these things that John Cage's primitive philosophy stands [...] If the oppositions between spirit and nature, between construction and "what happens" in the process of writing are neutralised, composition becomes trivial. Cage believes it, the imitators revel in it. There is a word for this, as ambiguous as it is unequivocal: dilettantism.'[56] For all his personal antipathy to the content of Stockhausen's lectures, Thomas was doubtless overestimating the likelihood of any real dissent from the participants regarding what Stockhausen presented when he described a moment at which there was, seemingly, a raspberry blown from the floor of the room: '[T]he speaker span around. "Is that directed at me?" he demanded. No answer from the hall, the protest is stifled.'[57] This one event seems unlikely to have anything to do with any 'protest' which might actually have developed into anything more serious, but there could be no reader of Thomas's review who missed his general verdict upon what he regarded as the true context of Stockhausen's presentation. What was really being discussed was, as far as Thomas was concerned, no more than 'the short head by which one composer can be said to lead another'. In a situation where this was the main focus, talk of 'conceptions, possibilities, evolutions' was questionable at best.[58]

Nevertheless, with the notable exception of Thomas's assessment, Stockhausen's presentations were generally viewed as relatively fair and reasonable representations of the work of the composers he was examining. Gustav Adolf Trumpff, Ernst Thomas's successor as the main music reporter for the *Darmstädter Echo*, praised Stockhausen's objectivity.[59] Likewise, Otto Tomek, in a broadcast for the Westdeutscher Rundfunk, suggested that Stockhausen was able to introduce a variety of new notational paradigms 'without necessarily wholly identifying with them all as a composer'.[60]

---

[55] Ibid. [56] Ibid. [57] Ibid. [58] Ibid.
[59] Gustav Adolf Trumpff, 'Das Crescendo der Ferienkurse: Drei Wochen "Neue Musik" im Rückspiegel', *Darmstädter Echo*, 9 September 1959.
[60] Otto Tomek, 'Darmstädter Ferienkurse 1959', broadcast, Westdeutscher Rundfunk, 26 October 1959, transcript IMD.

Nevertheless, Trumpff suggested that Stockhausen's courses represented the 'after-effects of John Cage's courses in the previous year: the play with chance, with Far Eastern philosophy'.[61] Not only that, but while Trumpff defended the possibilities that Stockhausen's notation for *Zyklus* created, for him it was Bussotti who represented the sticking point: 'whether the notation has to encroach so far into the realm of the image, as it does in the case of Bussotti, seems to me to be questionable, if the composer does not wish to give chance too much room to dictate meaning'.[62]

Wolf-Eberhard von Lewinski's response, written a couple of days after Thomas's, appears to take direct issue with Thomas's reading, even though it does not name him. Lewinski suggested that, although one very often had the feeling that a speaker chose the examples he or she relied upon in a particular presentation because of some sort of personal identification with them, 'Stockhausen distanced himself wholly from these works, reporting only what the composers themselves had attempted or what the performer thought about them.' That this observation was pointedly directed at Ernst Thomas, as well as anyone who had taken Thomas's version of events as gospel, became even more evident in Lewinski's somewhat catty comment that '[i]t was only attentive listeners who were able to work out [. . .] to what degree Stockhausen was suppressing his own opinions; in any case, he is certainly no apologist for Cage, as some people have said.'[63] It should not be taken from Lewinski's defence of Stockhausen, however, that he had a similarly positive view of the music presented, in opposition to Thomas's pessimism of the direction it represented. Lewinski's broad view of what Stockhausen had presented was briefly summarised: '[T]he newest music has, at least, become more interesting to look at.'[64] In this, his first report from the courses of 1959, however, Lewinski endeavoured, at least in part, to reserve judgement on the sonic results of the new notation, suggesting that he would want to hear the music performed in concert, rather than as a part of a series of lectures, before confirming his instinctive opinion that the performance of such music was 'acoustically absurd, visually amusing'.[65] Any doubts he may have had were thoroughly cemented by the time of a second report, written for *Der Kurier* only a little over a week later. The byline gives the flavour of what Lewinski had concluded well enough: 'Meagre modern music: it's only interesting to *look* at'.[66]

---

[61] Trumpff, 'Das Crescendo der Ferienkurse'. [62] Ibid.
[63] Wolf-Eberhard von Lewinski, 'Von der Verantwortung der Komponisten: Nonos aggressiver Vortrag/Ergebnisse der ersten Kranichsteiner Woche', *Darmstädter Tagblatt*, 3 September 1959.
[64] Ibid. [65] Ibid.
[66] Wolf-Eberhard von Lewinski, 'Magere moderne Musik – nur optisch reizvoll', *Der Kurier*, 11 September 1959 (my italics).

The response to Bussotti was not wholly negative. Otto Tomek apologised for not being able to play for his listeners a recording of one of Bussotti's piano pieces, but assured them that he, along with David Behrman, had made the strongest impression of all the participants in the 1959 Darmstadt composition studios. As for notation, Tomek took a slightly different view: these new notational paradigms were certainly worth discussing, but 'more interesting than such personal solutions were the works themselves'; Kagel's *Transición II* and Stockhausen's *Zyklus* were the major pieces. Given the degree to which Cage figures in discussions of what Stockhausen had to say, it is perhaps surprising how little the presentation devoted to his *Concert for Piano and Orchestra* was discussed in the journalistic commentary. It featured prominently only in Metzger's discussion of 'Musik und Graphik', in which it was, unsurprisingly, one of his highlights (alongside *Transición II* and *Zyklus*). Metzger hoped that Stockhausen's presentation of it would rehabilitate the work from its portrayal after its performance in Cologne in the previous year as something of a 'jamboree'.[67]

In Stockhausen's composition course, described in the course plan as 'practical composition exercises', a young American composer, by the name of La Monte Young, would later say that he had discovered not Stockhausen, but Cage. As Young would observe in 1966, '[i]n those days, there was no Cage on the West Coast, except on records. Dennis Johnson had played the recording of the *Sonatas and Interludes for Prepared Piano* for me maybe once, and Terry Jennings had a record of the String Quartet which we used to listen to, but I had to go to Europe to really discover Cage.'[68] For all Young's discovery, his *Study III* (1959) seemed to elicit little European interest, though, according to Potter's account, it, just like Goeyvaerts's Sonata for Two Pianos, is based throughout on the number seven. The piece was supposed to have been given a performance by David Tudor during the studio concert section of Stockhausen's course, but the score was mysteriously mislaid until it was too late for Tudor to prepare it adequately.[69]

As for the discovery being that of Cage, Peyser's account makes clear that Cage regarded his 'ownership' of the ideas as dubious in any case. Peyser observes that 'Stockhausen, in fact, embraced Cage with such fervor that by absorption he all but annihilated him from the musical scene. Appropriating Cage's interest in Eastern mysticism as well as his notions of performer involvement and chance, Stockhausen continued to pour out work after

---

[67] Heinz-Klaus Metzger, 'Kranichsteiner Musiktreffen beendet: Rückblick auf die Internationalen Ferienkurse für Neue Musik in Darmstadt', *Der Mittag*, 11 September 1959.
[68] La Monte Young, quoted in Keith Potter, *Four Musical Minimalists: La Monte Young, Terry Riley, Steve Reich, Philip Glass* (Cambridge University Press, 2004 [1996]), 44.
[69] Ibid.

work.' Yet Peyser continues by quoting Cage's own view that 'none of these ideas belonged to me personally'.[70] Nevertheless, her interview with Henze gives an indication of how some might have viewed Stockhausen's appropriations: 'He describes how Stockhausen "embraced" Cage. Henze extends his arms in a wide circle, then brings them together as though to caress a friend, and finally crushes them tightly against his chest.'[71]

Boulez and the Third Piano Sonata

The pieces which formed a part of Stockhausen's lectures were not the only ones performed at Darmstadt in 1959 to bear the stamp of 'indeterminacy'. Boulez, too, was present to discuss and perform his (then, as now, uncompleted) Third Piano Sonata. Yet the performance during Boulez's lecture on 30 August (which comprised an extended commentary on the piece) was not undertaken either by Tudor or by Paul Jacobs (who had performed Stockhausen's Klavierstück XI in Tudor's absence in 1957), but by Boulez himself.

Boulez's presentation of the piece was divided into two main parts: the first introduced the territory on which the Third Piano Sonata stood, both literary and aesthetic; the second reiterated what he had suggested in 'Alea', with the distinction that, on this occasion, he made direct references to the sections in the Third Piano Sonata which had only been implied in the earlier presentation. As Decroupet observes, any listener who had expected to hear from Boulez a direct response to Cage's presentations in 1958 would have been rather disappointed.[72] Cage did not feature at all, although Boulez mentioned that he, as a Westerner, had been shocked to discover the absence of 'masterworks' in non-Western musics.[73] Instead, Boulez suggested outright that 'literary affiliations' were the source of that which might be found in the Third Piano Sonata, specifically Joyce and Mallarmé, and also Kafka's 'The Burrow'. The ideas taken were: first, that the musical work ought to be a 'work-in-progress'; second, that the work ought not to be a journey starting at one point and ending at another, but instead a single object; third, that the word ought to be self-reflexive, which is to say, it ought to reveal itself *as* a musical work; fourth, if the work were an object, that object was to become a maze or labyrinth. In the light of the sort of openness that Boulez discussed, and given Cage's and Tudor's activities in 1958, it is intriguing that, though Boulez had initially promised to perform the Third Piano Sonata twice, in the event only one performance was forthcoming

---

[70] Peyser, *Boulez*, 140.   [71] Ibid., 141.   [72] Decroupet, 'Aleatorik und Indetermination', 257.
[73] Pierre Boulez, 'Kommentar zur 3. Klaviersonate', recital-lecture, 30 August 1959, recording IMD.

and, in Metzger's lapidary comment as translator, 'not *only* on grounds of laziness'.[74] As a careful examination of 'Constellation–Miroir' shows, the number of plausible routes through it is very limited, though perhaps not so limited as Jacobs's comment on the piece might imply: 'The piece works in one particular order, that is the one published and played. No omission or repetition is permissible.'[75] Boulez would nevertheless later acknowledge that 'a few privileged pathways become established since some routes are perceived to be more satisfactory than others'.[76] Likewise, for Tudor, the form was essentially dialectical (and hardly indeterminate): 'With Boulez the form is completely external. In the big section, there's a breathtaking sound that is just like glass. With one of us younger cats the sound itself would have dictated the form of the whole work, whereas that section is just a minor insertion in a great big dialectical piece.'[77]

An explanation for this might be found in Boulez's insistence that one of the things the work *must* do is to point to itself *as* a work: the work must reveal that it is a constructed, manufactured object. In this sense, the labyrinth was only the form; the *content* of the piece was this very self-reflexivity. Viewed from this perspective, it becomes not really a question of indeterminacy at all, but rather the *idea* of indeterminacy is one which helps reveal the artifice of the musical work. That the piece *appears* to be indeterminate is vital, since that is what performatively enacts the unveiling of the Third Piano Sonata's constructedness (the scattering of fragments across the page, mirroring Mallarmé's 'Un coup de dés', too, achieves this end).[78] Whether it actually exhibited indeterminate characteristics was hardly the point. Indeed, given that Mallarmé's poetry could indeed be read in radically different directions, the similarities to Boulez's score were only superficial, since although it *could* be read in a (very few) different ways, it could not be heard so, though Boulez would observe that his aim was to investigate 'permanent revolution [...] rather than simply to rebaptize the reader's ear into still another state of grace'.[79]

Regardless of Cage's assertions of a prior claim to 'chance', in broad terms, the reception of Boulez's Third Piano Sonata seems to suggest that

---

[74] Ibid..   [75] Peyser, *Boulez*, 128.
[76] Pierre Boulez, quoted in Campbell, *Boulez, Music and Philosophy*, 203.
[77] Peyser, *Boulez*, 128.
[78] Boulez referred specifically to the typography of this poem as compositional material during his commentary, and Metzger, providing simultaneous translation, showed an example from 'Un coup de dés' (Boulez, 'Kommentar zur 3. Klaviersonate').
[79] Pierre Boulez, 'Sonate, que me veux-tu?', in *Orientations*, tr. Martin Cooper, ed. Jean-Jacques Nattiez (London: Faber, 1986 [1959]), 143. I draw here on the later, published version of this lecture, because the very beginning of the recording is rather muffled and, though the exact phraseology is certainly tightened in the print version, the content remains fundamentally unchanged.

the critics certainly did not see so starkly the relationships between Boulez's work and Cage's that appeared clear on the other side of the Atlantic. If, as Cage said, '[n]ow Boulez was promoting chance, only it had to be *his* kind of chance',[80] in the Darmstadt frame at least, Boulez's references to Mallarmé seemed distinct enough to ground his activity, without any reference to Cage. Lewinski, at least, took Boulez at his word, stating that the formal procedures with which Boulez was working in the Third Piano Sonata were drawn from his engagement with Joyce and, above all, Mallarmé.[81] Though Lewinski was glowing in his praise for Boulez and for his Third Piano Sonata – regarding it as the first high-point of the 1959 courses and stating, moreover, that it could be seen as the 'most important and significant landmark for the development of the newest music' – he was not above passing faint criticism. While Boulez may have been, for him, 'one of the most brilliant, but also the most imaginative and lively on the musical avant-garde', Lewinski also reminded his readers that one of the reasons to be pleased by Boulez's attendance in 1959 was that he 'had disappointed earlier Ferienkurse participants through sudden cancellations'.[82]

Trumpff enthusiastically reported exactly the same literary sources, although the linking term 'ebenso' ('by the same token') between his discussion of Boulez and the 'after-effects of John Cage's course in the previous year' on Stockhausen suggests that Trumpff had wondered whether stronger links between Boulez and Cage could be drawn. For Ernst Thomas, the new formal principles seemed to have been inspired exclusively by the poetry of Mallarmé.[83] Moreover, the distinction between Boulez and Stockhausen was utterly clear in Thomas's mind: 'It is absolutely correct, as Stockhausen's French colleague Pierre Boulez believes, that the ambiguity of a musical structure derived via chance procedures should be perceived rather through reading than through listening.'[84] In Otto Tomek's annual broadcast for the Westdeutscher Rundfunk, he made clear that, from his perspective, there were stark and unarguable distinctions to be made between chance in the hands of Cage and in the hands of Boulez:

> Naturally some weighty voices have been raised against the adoption of uncontrolled chance as a compositional element. I am not thinking here of those critics who take a development still in progress as if it were a completed

[80] Peyser, *Boulez*, 129.
[81] Wolf-Eberhard von Lewinski, 'Auf der Suche nach der neuen Form: Pierre Boulez erläuterte und spielte seine dritte Klaviersonate', *Darmstädter Tagblatt*, 1 September 1959.
[82] Ibid.
[83] Ernst Thomas, 'Kontroverse und Konzert: Darmstädter Ferienkurse und Hessischer Rundfunk', *Frankfurter Allgemeine Zeitung*, 8 September 1959.
[84] Thomas, 'Klänge für das Auge?'

result, isolate it, generalise it, and finally end up coming to a false judgement. Rather, I am thinking of those critics who themselves come from the group of composers itself. I have already alluded to the *Darmstädter Beiträge*, that publication of the most important lectures from the courses. Here already, last year, Pierre Boulez drew a clear line, and also counted out the possibilities, which might allow a sensible introduction of change into composition. Interpretative 'chance', which must however be implicit in the musical text, or 'conducted' chance, represents today for Boulez a wholly legitimate, irreproachable place within the range of compositional means, without which the composer must abrogate some aspect of his decision-making process. Seen from this perspective, chance here has a wholly different function from that in the works of the American John Cage, who is regularly cited as an exemplar.[85]

Without question, Tomek was right to conclude that indeterminate form in the case of Boulez (or, though he did not say so, Stockhausen) was quite different from that in the hands of Cage. A simplistic distinction might be made in that Stockhausen's Klavierstück XI could be, and was, performed from the score, as could Boulez's Third Piano Sonata (for the sections for which a score actually existed, at any rate) after a relatively brief period of preparatory work to ensure that the route taken through 'Constellation–Miroir' would indeed allow the performance of each section only once. With Cage's music, unless one was to improvise, substantial preparatory work was necessary.

Nono

As far as the planning for the 1959 courses was concerned, Nono's session had never been expected to be a formal lecture. It was planned that it would be, on the contrary, a studio concert in which Nono would discuss student work, followed by workshop performances. By July 1959, however, it had already been decided that Nono would actually offer a presentation, at that time under the speculative title 'The Responsibility of the Composer Today'. In the official course booklet this title was changed to, in Italian, 'Presenza storica nella musica oggi' ('The Presence of History in the Music of Today') or, in German, 'Geschichte und Gegenwart in der Musik von heute' ('History and the Present in the Music of Today'). Nono's presentation represents the most strident negative response of a major Darmstadt figure to what Cage had brought to the courses and, in a sense, to the European avant-garde more broadly conceived.

---

[85] Tomek, 'Darmstädter Ferienkurse 1959'.

Nono's targets were, at first glance, two-fold: the thinking of 'two men of American culture, Joseph Schillinger (actually of Russian origin) and John Cage', the latter of whom had, according to Nono, 'exerted an influence, directly and indirectly, in the past few years, which determines a particular musical situation in Europe, in increasingly confusing ways'.[86] As will become clearer below, whether the superficial objects of Nono's discontent truly represented his aims is debatable. However, in terms of the immediate content of what he had to say, there was little avoiding the impression that his discussion was pointed directly at Cage.

On one level, Nono's interest was in considerations of what it might mean to be 'free' and what it might mean to write music which was truly 'new', though these ideas were intertwined with other, more technical, thoughts regarding the principles of collage and improvisation. The specific notion of newness against which Nono railed is one which he neatly summarised in the words of Antonin Artaud:

> I, Antonin Artaud, I am my son,
> > my father, my mother,
> > and me;
> leveller of the imbecilic periplus in which
> > engendering is caught up
> > the periplus papa-mama,
> > the child[87]

This rejection of the possibility of prior influence, Nono suggested, represented the 'manifesto of those who fancy that they can, *ex abrupto*, open up a new era in such ways, one in which everything must be programmatically "new", and want [...] to position themselves as the beginning and the end, as gospel'.[88] This sort of stance was one which Nono argued operated according to the 'fiction of a *tabula rasa*'. For Nono the self-proclaimed 'new' music, which rejected the conditioning of history, was, at best, self-deluding. It would not be difficult, either, to regard the beginning of Nono's essay as a sly, if anonymous, dig at Boulez, whose filiation to Artaud was well known and long-standing.

Nono's strike against Schillinger was brief, but pointed. In the passage from Schillinger's *The Mathematical Basis of the Arts* that he quoted, it was the sentence 'no artist is truly free' which Nono picked on specifically, and notions of what 'freedom' might mean in an artistic sense pervaded his

---

[86] Luigi Nono, 'Geschichte und Gegenwart in der Musik von heute' [1959], in Jürg Stenzl (ed.), *Luigi Nono: Texte, Studien zu seiner Musik* (Zürich: Atlantis, 1975), 34–5.

[87] Ibid., 34. English translation drawn from Paule Thévenin, 'A Letter on Artaud', *Tulane Drama Review*, vol. 9, no. 3 (Spring 1965), 100.

[88] Nono, 'Geschichte und Gegenwart', in Stenzl (ed.), *Luigi Nono*, 34..

discussion. Schillinger might be regarded as representing an opposing pole to Artaud in this sense, since his argument against true artistic freedom rested on the notion that artists are historically, culturally, and geographically conditioned. If they were not, so suggested Schillinger, it would be plausible for an artist born in Paris spontaneously to begin expressing himself in the language of fourth-century China. One might expect that Nono would have had some sympathy for such a position, which demanded that an artist's historico-cultural background determined, at least in part, his or her artistic language. Yet it was Schillinger's notion that it would be *desirable* to be freed from such modes of conditioning that Nono found it most important to condemn, not least because of the method proposed by Schillinger: 'The key to true freedom and emancipation from geographical dependency is the scientific method.'[89] From Nono's perspective this would barely have represented freedom at all. Indeed, as Nono saw it, if Schillinger's dictum 'no artist is truly free' were really the case, then art would never have existed at all, 'because art and freedom are synonymous on every occasion when a person expresses his consciousness, his knowledge, his definitive decision at a particular moment of a structural, historical process, and every time he consciously and resolutely intervenes in the process of liberation, which is taking place *in history*'.[90] In any case, Nono claimed, 'adherence to a schematic principle, be it of a scientific or mathematical nature, has never breathed life into an artwork; only the dialectical synthesis between a principle and its implementation in history achieves this, which is to say its individuation in a particular moment, neither earlier, nor later'.[91] Any systematic procedure, such as serialism, was *on its own* useless; what was important was the way in which a composer might interact with such procedural principles and make decisions according to the possibilities thrown up by them. Simultaneously, the very act of seeking validity for compositional actions in a recourse to scientific principles or mathematical relations – avoiding careful, *responsible* consideration of what it might mean to be doing such things and making, through such grounding of activity, a claim to universality – was already a rather typical product of its own epoch.[92] In short, claims to 'timeless' validity on the basis of scientistic arguments like Schillinger's were themselves uniquely modern. In the Darmstadt context, it was hardly Schillinger's thought that was presented as a justification of the scientific basis of composition. As the composer most concerned with showing the scientifically justified auditory 'reality' of

---

[89] Joseph Schillinger, quoted in ibid., 35.
[90] Nono, 'Geschichte und Gegenwart', in Stenzl (ed.), *Luigi Nono*, 35.   [91] Ibid., 35–6.
[92] Ibid., 35.

sound, Stockhausen was hardly likely to have been fooled by Schillinger's name being given in place of his.

The question of compositional responsibility to material was fundamental to Nono, and in this aspect of his presentation Cage was central. Nono reminded his audience of one of Cage's questions, from the previous year's 'Communication': 'Are sounds just sounds or are they Webern?' From Nono's perspective one might as well have asked: 'Are people just people, or are they heads, feet, hands, stomachs; limbs aren't people, are they?' The analogy was clear: there exist structural relations between elements, which are meaningful and should not be cast aside lightly. From an attitude such as Cage's, in which material was freely available for use (whether or not it was Webern or, for that matter, as in Cage's English-language version, Beethoven), this led to a situation in which what happened on the level of musical material would become collage, in which historically sedimented materials could be spirited away from their cultural origins and placed alongside elements from other cultures without the composer feeling a responsibility to show the link between the two. The problem as Nono expressed it was not technical but, rather, ethical: 'the collage method originates from colonial thinking'.[93] What Cage had, to Nono's mind, effectively proposed allowed a composer to appropriate music at will from another culture, without needing to be concerned about what that meant about one's relationship with that culture. There was, Nono suggested, 'no functional difference between using an Indian temple drum as a rubbish bin in a modern European household and the orientalism which serves in Western culture to make aesthetic material more attractive'.[94]

For Nono, the philosophical foundations upon which Cage proceeded were also suspect. Nono suggested that what was attractive about the way in which Cageian thought had been presented at Darmstadt – what gave it its particular 'spice' – was that it focussed on ideas of 'spontaneity' and 'freedom'. The latter of these was certainly of concern to Nono, even though the sorts of seeming freedom created by spontaneous action appeared to him to be no closer to any genuine freedom than that offered by Schillinger's rigorous method. Yet it was in the combination of 'spontaneity' and 'freedom' that Nono found greater problems since, as far as he was able to see, that combination meant nothing more, ultimately, than the practice of improvisation. Nono suggested further that, historically speaking, improvisation in ancient China was based on a particular, limited range of materials which could be freely used in most parameters, while one – that of pitch – was fixed. Nono also insisted that, in such contexts, the purpose of

[93] Ibid., 38.   [94] Ibid.

improvisation was cultic, that it 'always concerned a higher being, which is to say a god'.[95]

Returning to the position with which he opened, Nono proposed that improvisatory practice, as carried out (as he seems to have seen it) by performers such as Gazzelloni and Tudor in the presentation of indeterminate music, 'today still occurs in the spirit of oriental cultic improvisation. There it serves as the adjuration of a god, such that today it is one's own ego which is conjured up.'[96] From Nono's perspective, any recourse to ideas of 'freedom' and 'spontaneity' in the ways in which Cage had presented them – denuded of any dialectical relationship with order and system – was a false promise. Those notions served only self-reflexively to return to the self, having no relationship with history, and, since 'freedom' meant the suppression of the *Geist* of the age by mere momentary instinct, 'their freedom is spritual suicide'. Near the end of his essay Nono summed up his core position with regard to all of the results of chance: 'To replace one's own decisions with chance and its acoustic results as if it will bring *insight* can only be the method of one who is afraid to make his or her own decisions, who is afraid when faced with the freedom of the spirit.'[97] In very simple terms, Nono's points should be clear: neither the absolute restriction of compositional system nor the freedom of spontaneous improvisation could lead to artistic freedom. Any freedom worth the name would come about through the dialectical interplay of the two. Similarly, a rigid insistence that all materials must be remorselessly 'new', and thus extracted from their relationship to history, was just as problematic as an attitude which suggested that any and all materials may be utilised at any point, without any concern for their historical specificity. Finally, one's responsibility as a composer was not first and foremost to oneself and one's own aggrandisement, but rather to the *Geist*, seemingly understood by Nono, in a broadly Hegelian sense, to suggest that one was obliged to carry out the work which was appropriate and vital for the teleological thrust of one's own age.[98]

Significant in many respects though Nono's broad points were, it is what they expose about Nono's knowledge which might be taken to be most vital in the immediate context. To propose that Tudor was improvising suggests that Nono was one of those unaware of Tudor's working practices. This implies, in turn, that Nono either did not fully follow up, or simply did not

---

[95] Ibid.   [96] Ibid., 39.   [97] Ibid., 40.
[98] As Zagorski observes, in comparison with his 'Die Entwicklung der Reihentechnik', here 'Nono's Hegelian *Geschichtsphilosophie* seems even more pronounced: the "only" proper activity of a responsible composer is described as a mutually penetrating recognition of matter through spirit and the knowledge of spirit through matter' (Zagorski, 'Material and History in the Aesthetics of "Serielle Musik"', 282 n. 27).

fully follow, the suggestion made to him by Earle Brown. Brown had written to Nono in advance of the 1959 courses, suggesting Nono examine Brown's 'December 1952':

> ((you might ask Metzger about the piece I wrote, called 'for David Tudor, Dec. 1952'.... he is the only one, besides myself, who has played this piece 'spontaneously' ... (that I know of) ... but neither of us played it in public and neither of us is a performer, in the strict sense of the word.)) [...] By 'spontaneous', in this particular score, I mean that the performers should not write out, or compose-in-advance, their freedom. As I imagine it, (and this to me is practical) the performers will play through these implicit areas in rehearsal, but not 'set' them ... so that in effect what they do in each rehearsal and each performance will be similar (if they play from the same score-part each time) but different.[99]

From what Brown had to say, a plausible reading would be that, in the past, performers had failed to do what Brown wanted – which *was* to perform spontaneously, to improvise – and that he had been working on ways to make that more possible, which is to say, to avoid the need to prepare parts from the score in advance. Perhaps, if Nono extrapolated general principles from this, he could have come to the conclusion that the music of the Americans was moving increasingly towards improvisation. It is just about conceivable that Nono knew of the ways in which Tudor went about realising Cage's own music – there is indeed some evidence to suggest that Nono intended little argument with Cage himself, a point I will return to below – but in order to claim that improvisation occurred in Tudor's performances, he cannot have known the painstaking lengths to which Tudor went to *avoid* improvisation, and must presumably have been equating Brown's aims with Cage's. What precisely Nono meant by the content of 'Geschichte und Gegenwart in der Musik von heute' ultimately hinges on just this point.

Earle Brown and *Hodograph I*

Nono's lecture was framed by two performances of Earle Brown's new piece, *Hodograph I* (1959), for flute, piano, celesta, bells, and marimba. Given that Earle Brown was, of the so-called New York School composers who passed through Darmstadt towards the end of the 1950s, the one most closely associated with the thought of Joseph Schillinger, it might have been easy for those 'in the know' to have construed Nono's presentation as critiquing Brown's practice at least as sternly as it did Cage's. It might be seen as ironic,

---

[99] Brown to Nono, 26 August 1959, Earle Brown Foundation, New York.

then, that the performance of Brown's music in this year was almost a direct result of the ministrations of Nono's close friend Bruno Maderna. Already in early March, Maderna had proposed Brown's *Indices* as an alternative to Henry Brant's *Galaxy II* (1954), which was also under consideration for performance at the same concert as Maderna's own Piano Concerto, which he was writing for David Tudor.[100] That concert took place on 2 September 1959, and also included the première of Nono's *Composizione per orchestra n. 2: Diario polacco '58*. It included, however, music by neither Brown nor Brant. Although Maderna had suggested specifically that this version of *Indices* was for ballet, and noted that it required Carolyn Brown to dance Cunningham's *Springweather and People* with it, by the time Steinecke contacted Brown – after a visit by Maderna to Darmstadt in May 1959 – dance had seemingly been forgotten. Steinecke's letter to Brown suggested that he would be interested in Tudor performing the piano reduction of *Indices*, since Maderna had been so impressed by the Merce Cunningham Dance Company's performance of *Springweather and People* in Brussels earlier that year.[101] Brown's response to this proposal was wholly negative:

> I greatly appreciate Bruno's interest and his desire to have my work represented but I must state that this particular proposal is completely unacceptable to me [...] The reduction of *Indices* was made after the piece was composed for orchestra and is intended only to be used in conjunction with the dance; *Indices* is originally for a ballet and the reduction is for rehearsal and an occasional dance performance when an orchestra is unavailable. The reduction is not a self-sufficient piano work and cannot of course express the orchestral structure of the original scoring.

Nevertheless, Brown was ready with a counter-proposal, which was to write a new piece for Tudor, Gazzelloni, and Caskel. There can be little doubt, in fact, that Tudor had already proposed this to Brown, especially given the hardly coincidental fact that the piece was designed specifically for that year's instrumental faculty members. Not that this need suggest that there was any conniving at play. Brown was hardly ambiguous when he said: 'David seems very interested in this and if it meets with your approval I will be very happy to do it.....as a matter of fact, I am doing it now.'[102] In any case, the idea was certainly acceptable to Steinecke, who advised Brown that the new piece would receive its première directly before Nono's presentation, with a second performance directly after the lecture.[103]

---

[100] Maderna to Steinecke, undated but between 5 and 17 March 1959, in Dalmonte (ed.), *Bruno Maderna–Wolfgang Steinecke*, 184.
[101] Steinecke to Brown, 25 May 1959, IMD.   [102] Brown to Steinecke, 15 June 1959, IMD.
[103] Steinecke to Brown, 25 July 1959, IMD.

Tudor brought the performance materials for *Hodograph I* with him to Darmstadt, making it possible for rehearsals to begin on the piece only after Gazzelloni, Caskel, and Tudor himself had arrived in Darmstadt on 16 August; the performances took place, as planned, on 1 September. When Brown requested, in early 1960, that Steinecke might be able to make available to him the recordings of the two performances he noted that 'David Tudor said that the performances were not very good because of having had very little rehearsal but I am very anxious to hear the results in any case.'[104]

Responses to Nono

That Nono should have set out to launch a personal attack on Cage – which is to say an attack which went beyond what might be considered a musical disagreement – seems to have come out of the blue. In 1959, at least before Nono's presentation, there was no rancour between them. Indeed, the small amount of correspondence suggests that relations were friendly.

Nuria Nono wrote to Cage in late February, informing him of Nono's current work – on the piece that was to become *Composizione per orchestra n. 2: Diario polacco '58* – and of Nono's attempts to find out further information for Cage regarding a potential performance of Cage's work at the Biennale: 'If there is any information that you need or anything we can do for you please don't hesitate to write us. It was very nice having you here for lunch the other day + you are always welcome to sleep, eat etc. at Giudecca 882.'[105] Similarly, in a postcard to his parents from Venice, Cage mentioned his visit to the Nonos, and seemed to think of both with respect and, in Nuria Nono's case, affection: 'Also visited Nono, very fine composer, who is married to Schoenberg's daughter, Nuria, whom I saw in L.A. when she was still carried around in arms. Now she is herself about to have a baby.'[106]

In a letter later that year – much closer to Nono's presentation at Darmstadt – Nono wrote to Cage discussing his hopes that it would be possible to realise plans for a project in Rome, which he and Cage had discussed during Cage's stay in Venice during the winter of 1958–9, involving Merce Cunningham, the artists Alberto Burri and Emilio Vedova, and Luciano Berio, alongside Nono and Cage. Not only that, but Nono had received a commission from the Library of Congress's Coolidge Foundation

---

[104] Brown to Steinecke, 11 January 1960, IMD.
[105] Nuria Nono to Cage, 25 February 1959, JCC.
[106] Cage (Venice) to Crete and John Milton Cage Sr, 18 February 1959, JCC.

for the piece that was to develop into *Sarà dolce tacere* (1960). Nono had hoped to spend six months working in the United States in advance of the première (plans which ultimately failed to develop) and expressed a desire to work directly with Cage and Cunningham in New York, if it were possible to arrange such a long-term residency in the United States. Finally, as a part of Nono's course at the Dartington International Summer School on the development of singing from Schoenberg to the present, he had hoped to cover Cage's work, alongside Schoenberg, Webern, Dallapiccola, Boulez, Maderna, Stockhausen, and his own music. None of this has the ring of someone who was preparing a devastating critique against Cage, even if Nono had been less than effusive regarding Cage in the aborted preparations for the volume of the *Darmstädter Beiträge* which was to have been devoted to him.[107]

In a letter to Nono after the courses, asking whether a version of Nono's presentation might be printed in *Melos*, Steinecke was cautious regarding who might be thought of as the 'subject' of Nono's critique. He suggested that adaptations might be considered for a print version:

> shouldn't one express the polemic, which takes aim at 'unknowns' (and is thus directed at the young composers who write poor scores for Tudor and Gazzelloni), better? Precisely because the polemic has precise aims at its beginning (Schillinger, Cage), naturally everyone believes that specific people are meant here, who aren't named (these people can, within this context, only be seen as: Stockhausen, perhaps Boulez, Brown, Bussotti).[108]

Steinecke tempered this statement, suggesting that he was well aware that Nono's thoughts turned to subjects which were not in the nature of a personal attack: 'You mean the general danger of a particular tendency, and you have said this too, in your discussion with Stockhausen.' Yet this 'addition' to the essay was, so Steinecke thought, absent from the text itself, and that, along with the specific political comparisons made, was dangerous for Nono's own position. In closing, Steinecke warned Nono: 'Think it over!'[109]

If it was these matters that were truly of most concern to Steinecke, others were the ones which surfaced most strongly in the press. The precise format of Nono's presentation was a concern to some; the quality of his music – or, to be more precise, a sense that the music would have to feel more advanced, somehow 'better', if Nono were to launch an attack of this kind – was uppermost in the minds of others.

One of Nono's sternest critics was Lewinski. One might be surprised by this, since Lewinski was some way from sympathising with Cage. Indeed, in

---

[107] Nono to Cage, 11 July 1959, JCC. [108] Steinecke to Nono, 9 November 1959, ALN.
[109] Ibid.

stating his conviction that Nono's discussion was not only of Cage but also of those more latterly influenced by him, Lewinski argued that those 'epigones of Cage [...] have emerged in alarming number'.[110] Lewinski's concern was actually quite close to one plausible interpretation of what lay at the heart of Nono's discussion; the worry was not necessarily to do with Cage's music itself (which as Lewinski puts it 'is so finely tailored to Cage himself') but more that, as a music and a mode of thought, Cage could not simply be transplanted into someone else's compositional approach without becoming 'mystical mumbo-jumbo'.[111] It was not because of a perceived attack on Cage or those who were utilising ideas drawn from his work that Lewinski felt Nono had been foolish; instead the precise mode of his critique and the forum in which it took place seemed the main problem. Lewinski's words are wholly clear regarding his estimation of what had taken place:

> If some musicians want to found a sect of super-serialists, well and good, but not at Kranichstein, not during the Ferienkurse. The idea of 'Kranichstein' was sabotaged with this presentation. It must remain the case that everything finds a forum there: the ponderers and the serious, the speculators and the enquirers. And it has to be that way, so that information is provided without ideology, so that no-one disputes anyone else's right to be there, no-one puts themselves in the leading position, becomes doctrinaire, and abuses the others in front of the public.[112]

Lewinski was definitive in his claim that the problem was not necessarily what Nono had said, but that it went against the spirit of collegiality that Lewinski felt was central to Darmstadt as a powerful force. This, too, according to Hugh Wood's report, was the sum of a stand-up argument between Stockhausen and Nono a few days after Nono's presentation:

> Stockhhausen blamed Nono for intolerance, for betraying the principles of Kranichstein i.e. that it should be an absolutely open forum for all kinds of music however experimental, for holding Cage responsible for his followers, and for imparting an unwelcome tone of moral disapproval to a purely artistic question. Their discussion, which was heated, showed signs of a considerable rift, and it will be interesting to see how this divergence affects their mutual relations to Darmstadt in the future.[113]

Not all felt that Nono had overstepped a line. Speaking more generally about the work undertaken in 1959, Trumpff suggested that all happened *sine ira et studio* (with neither anger nor affection), recalling Stockhausen's observation that 'Darmstadt is a place where manifold opinions and views clash,

---

[110] Lewinski, 'Von der Verantwortung der Komponisten'.   [111] Ibid.   [112] Ibid.
[113] Hugh Wood, 'Darmstadt 1959' (unpublished report). I am grateful to Ed Venn for drawing my attention to this source.

without it resulting in hostility'.[114] Arguably, Nono felt this too, and was simply trying to show that others had adopted Cage's ideas in a doctrinaire way. Ernst Thomas's review of these events suggests that what Nono had done was precisely that: to have discussed pressing issues without the dogmatic approach Thomas saw in Stockhausen's promotion of Cage. Thomas suggested that Nono had brought to the surface controversies which Stockhausen's 'dictatorial gestures' had wanted to prevent being discussed in such terms: 'Let us hope it continues next year in just this vein, as unmediated and undoctrinaire as possible, without dialectical tattle-telling.'[115] Such a position cannot be seen, however, in Lewinski's report. As noted above, many of the newspaper critics were impressed by the way in which Stockhausen managed to appear non-partisan, showing what other composers were doing and explaining some of the detail of their reasoning. This, for Lewinski, was exactly the 'proper' role of a composer at Darmstadt, while Thomas – though doubtless speaking from a position already suffused with anti-Cage sentiment – felt that Stockhausen was simply playing the role of the unbiased observer while simultaneously promoting one particular vision of the composition of new music, without ever saying what he was doing. For Lewinski, critique ought to have come from the critics: '[i]t would have been more congenial if it had not been a composer who had given this lecture, but instead someone impartial, such as a critic.'[116] The reason why Lewinski suggested this, though, is important: the lecture contained 'so much truth and so many liberating formulations' that for them to be diffused through accusations of compositional one-upmanship on Nono's part was deeply unfortunate. Lewinski felt that Nono was unfortunate, too, in being followed by the performance of Brown's *Hodograph I*, though not because it showed the positive results of the sorts of ideas associated with Cage; on the contrary, it was because it 'moves in exactly the sorts of murky waters which Cage navigates'. For Lewinski, Brown's music 'makes use of an artistic naïvety, feigning simple primitivism, as if a Neanderthal flute or piano had come to hand'.[117]

Tomek also reminded his listeners that 'naturally not everything turns to gold in Darmstadt'. Yet he was cautious in apportioning blame for what he saw as the failure of *Composizione per orchestra n. 2: Diario polacco '58*: a programme of the breadth and scale presented at Darmstadt was likely to lead to fatigue not only for the audience, but also for the performers. Nevertheless, he added that it was a commonplace that a new stylistic

[114] Trumpff, 'Das Crescendo der Ferienkurse'. Trumpff's classical allusion is to Tacitus's famous statement of his own impartiality at the head of his *Annals*.
[115] Thomas, 'Kontroverse und Konzert'.
[116] Lewinski, 'Von der Verantwortung der Komponisten'.   [117] Ibid.

direction would rapidly turn into mere imitation, the implication being that Nono was doing little more than mimicking the more innovative efforts either of his own earlier writing or of Stockhausen, Boulez, and others. Despite the absence of names, though, the juxtaposition of the title of Nono's latest piece and the following closing statement could hardly be clearer: 'one shouldn't rant about the incidental chaff, when there is, so to speak, wheat to harvest'.[118] Similarly, Lewinski found himself unimpressed by what Nono had, musically speaking, to offer. His verdict was blunt: '*Diario polacco '58* for a monster-orchestra [is] expensive but musically unconvincing'.[119]

It was the *New York Times* which provided the strongest support for Nono. While Peter Gradenwitz was impressed by the seriousness and rigour with which composers who, following Cage's example, dealt with the changed paradigm of composition, he suggested that

> one can only agree with Nono's verdict that the newly won freedom often leads to 'spiritual suicide' – freedom 'like that of a madman in an asylum who believes he is a weasel'. John Cage (who lectured in Darmstadt last year) takes refuge in remote times and Far-Eastern philosophy, said Nono, in the same spirit of indecision, escapism and false naiveté as the composers who for lack of courage and direction leave the final act of composition to the virtuoso who will make their work successful even where they have failed themselves.[120]

Gradenwitz is biting in his passing comment that 'a prominent visitor ventured to say that the only real composer this year was Tudor, who built complete edifices of music out of sparse lines of notation or drawing'.[121] Even if Nono was right in his criticism, then, it hardly saved him from the observation that what was most exciting to listen to at Darmstadt was the performance of David Tudor. Nono was defended in the *Frankfurter Allgemeine Zeitung* by Ernst Thomas, who regarded *Composizione per orchestra n. 2: Diario polacco '58* as 'large-scale music, in which introverted meditations are shattered by sonic blasts'.[122] Thomas also made it more than clear with whom his sympathies lay in terms of any opposition between Nono and Cage, describing Nono's presentation as 'a blazing protest against both Schillinger's scientific theory of artistic production and Cage's childish belief in the products of chance'.[123] In light of all of the above, it is rather surprising to read Trumpff's comment that 'one might regret the fact that in this year, unlike previous years at the Ferienkurse,

---

[118] Tomek, 'Darmstädter Ferienkurse 1959'. [119] Lewinski, 'Magere moderne Musik'.
[120] Peter Gradenwitz, 'Darmstadt Debates: German City Host to a Festival that Discussed as well as Played Music', *New York Times*, 21 September 1959.
[121] Ibid. [122] Thomas, 'Kontroverse und Konzert'. [123] Ibid.

opinions have not clashed so much'.[124] Yet it is significant that he, at least, had not seen what had happened in such stark relief as many other commentators, because it reveals that, while the debates that occurred may have been central for certain participants, for others they were largely irrelevant. Trumpff, perhaps without meaning to, explained that, apart from anything else, a strong international dimension meant that, linguistically speaking, the participants were unable to enter into discussions at the sort of broadly philosophical level at which it was taking place. Without access to the language of debate, the debate might as well not have happened.[125]

Regardless of the criticism he had received in the German press, Nono seems to have had little intention of retracting any part of what he had written, and dismissed journalistic critical responses. After Steinecke's warnings to him, Nono remained intransigent, though it is clear that he was concerned that, in some sense, Steinecke had betrayed him, since Düsseldorf's *Der Mittag*, of which Steinecke was the music editor, had published a response to Nono's presentation, from the pen of Heinz-Klaus Metzger.

Metzger agreed with what seems to have been a general opinion that not only was Nono's *Composizione per orchestra n. 2: Diario polacco '58* a comparatively weak piece, but it was one in which Nono had made little attempt to develop any further on a technical level. To Metzger's mind, the techniques used were, if anything, retrogressive: 'the composer seems to want rigidly to retain only those things which in 1952 were an important stage in the development of composition, particularly with respect to the treatment of rhythm, but also in the erroneous serial procedures, which can no longer be taken seriously, if one really wants to talk about "serial" music'.[126] Yet Metzger went significantly further than any of Nono's previous critics, at least with regard to this particular piece, in opining that Nono's misunderstanding of serial technique was one in which predetermination became nothing like determination at all. What resulted was, truly, a piece of chance music.

This was little more than a prelude for the contempt Metzger reserved for Nono's presentation. Evidently, the rhetoric of setting Nono up as the composer who was, in reality, the one pursuing chance operations was vital, since it allowed Metzger to move to his opening salvo: 'Perhaps this explains the petulance with which Nono accused his colleagues of his own failings, to project those failings at the same time onto others.'[127] Metzger did not stop there, seizing on the notion of what it would mean to be 'responsible' as a composer in the post-war world, and reversing Nono's position against him: 'He gave an

---

[124] Trumpff, 'Das Crescendo der Ferienkurse'.   [125] Ibid.
[126] Metzger, 'Kranichsteiner Musiktreffen beendet'.   [127] Ibid.

irresponsible lecture, in which the talk was mainly of the composer's responsibility: one understood that he was thinking only of himself.'[128] If this were not bad enough, Metzger's only explanation for how Nono might have been capable of coming to the conclusions that he did, a mirror of the accusations he had earlier ranged against Adorno, was that he could not have known enough about the music under discussion. Metzger's review closed by observing that '[i]t was particularly embarrassing that he polemicised against those absent by name and against those present anonymously.'[129]

Clearly, between receiving Steinecke's letter of 9 November and his reply on 22 December 1959, Nono had heard of – though, it seems, not seen a copy of – Metzger's review. Nono anxiously sought assurances from Steinecke:

> Someone has told me that, after the Ferienkurse, a wild attack on me (by Metzger) was published in *Der Mittag*. I would like to know: is it true? If so, was it printed there with your agreement? (Are you not the music editor of *Der Mittag*?) If all this is the case: what is your opinion about it: why? To what end?

In any case, Nono's responses seem to suggest that he was simply incapable of seeing that he might have done something which might endanger his standing within Germany: 'for me, what he or other such similar indigents say: the world is large, there's space for everyone, even pigs. What I mean is: one must always question and discuss everything DIRECTLY, and one is obliged always to express these things clearly.' Nono had little appreciation that there might be any difficulty with the publication of his text: 'One thing is unclear to me: why should my essay not be published in the 1960 *Darmstädter Beiträge*? WHO DOES NOT WANT THAT? Or IS THAT NOT ALLOWED?' That Nono placed great stock on personal loyalty – regardless of any practical considerations – is clear from the close of his letter: 'Please Wolfgang, write to me in the way that we have always spoken between ourselves: clearly, without diplomacy, because I trust that our relationship is founded on pure friendship – everything else is nothing.'[130]

In the end, Nono did make some adaptations to the print version for the 1960 volume of the *Darmstädter Beiträge*, though these were marginal. These changes, too, found their way into the version of the essay printed in *Melos* under the title 'Prison Bars in the Heaven of Freedom', which is identical to the Darmstadt publication,[131] though an abridged version, drawing directly on the script from Nono's spoken version in Darmstadt,

---

[128] Ibid. [129] Ibid. [130] Nono to Steinecke, 22 December 1959, ALN.
[131] Luigi Nono, 'Geschichte und Gegenwart in der Musik von heute' [1959], *Darmstädter Beiträge zur neuen Musik*, vol. 3 (1960) (Mainz: Schott), 41–7; Luigi Nono, 'Gitterstäbe am Himmel der Freiheit', *Melos*, vol. 27 (1960 [1959]), 69–75.

had been published in early October by the *Kölner Stadt-Anzeiger*, using yet another title: 'Fear of Freedom'.[132]

Many of the changes to the later, complete print versions are of a grammatical nature, but one important section of the original presentation is excised almost *in toto*. This section is precisely that in which Severino Gazzelloni and David Tudor are discussed by name, precisely the moment at which Nono stated clearly that '[t]he performance of the worst music by these two players will always exercise a sonic fascination, for which the high level of performance technique alone can be thanked.' In the 'live' presentation, Nono had gone further, opining that 'now, naturally, scores for flute and for piano sprout up like mushrooms from the ground, pieces in which the composers allow nothing more to happen than more or less subtle methods of notation, in order to conjure improvisation from the virtuoso Gazzelloni and the virtuoso Tudor, from the quality of whose performance they hope to gain their own prestige.' This situation, suggested Nono, had exchanged speculation for composition, and any young composer who pursued such a trajectory ought to be warned that 'we are not all idiots, and are quite capable of distinguishing between instrumental mastery and compositional poverty'.[133]

A second, much smaller but no less potent, change was made to Nono's discussion of the sorts of political comparisons that might be made with musical systems. In the version Nono presented at Darmstadt he stated clearly: 'The attempt to bring a thoroughly organised musical structure into association with either existing or prior totalitarian political systems is, in all its spitefulness, nothing more than a pathetic attempt to gag the spirit which, by the word "freedom", understands something quite other than the exercising of one's own will.'[134] In many respects, the *content* of this statement remained, but in a much more muted form: 'Attempts to compare "through-organised" composing with the state of political systems are, in their crudeness, a pathetic paternalism of the intellect, which, by the word "freedom", understands something quite other than the exercising of one's own will.'[135] Thus a critique which in the original many must surely have thought to be directed against Adorno was modulated by the removal of the word 'totalitarian', a word which had made the initial attack virtually unambiguous. In other respects, though, the later version was sharpened by the accusation that what was at play was 'paternalism'. This latter adaptation may well have come too late. As noted above, an abbreviated version of Nono's presentation had been printed in the *Kölner Stadt-Anzeiger*

---

[132] Luigi Nono, 'Die Angst vor der Freiheit', *Kölner Stadt-Anzeiger*, 4 October 1959.
[133] Nono, 'Geschichte und Gegenwart', in Stenzl (ed.), *Luigi Nono*, 39. [134] Ibid.
[135] Nono, 'Geschichte und Gegenwart', *Darmstädter Beiträge zur neuen Musik*, vol. 3 (1960), 46.

on 4 October 1959. Despite the incendiary nature of the debate in the immediate aftermath of the session at Darmstadt, the editorial stance of the *Kölner Stadt-Anzeiger*, indicated in a short preface to its publication of Nono's presentation, is quite different: 'The intense discussion which his [Nono's] statements aroused demonstrates what burning questions regarding "music-making today" Nono has touched upon.'[136]

While the section which concerned Tudor and Gazzelloni had clearly proved too specific to the new music scene to be of interest to a more general readership, a comparison between serial thinking and totalitarianism was certainly news fit to print. Even though Nono was arguing quite the contrary – which is to say that a comparison between serial organisation and Nazist modes of statism was crude, at best – in the context of the Germany of the late 1950s, a composer discussing the relationship between music and politics remained largely unpalatable. Nono's situation here was doubtless not helped by his membership of the Italian Communist Party, in a country where the national communist party had only recently been banned.[137]

Nono's presentation certainly had an impact on the composers who were associated in European minds with Cage. After *The Score* had printed an English-language version of Nono's essay in 1960,[138] the Los Angeles-based music critic Peter Yates wrote to Cage, describing it as 'Nono's silly attack on you'.[139] Christian Wolff, then stationed at Fort Sam Houston in Texas, wrote to David Tudor on 18 October 1959: 'Too bad about Nono's lecture – talk about music seems inevitably to include polemics'.[140] One presumes that what Tudor had communicated to Wolff regarding the content of Nono's presentation was not wholly dissimilar from what he wrote to his partner, the poet and potter M. C. Richards, on 7 September 1959:

> Nono came and gave a short talk, rather pathological in tendency, denouncing everything new & all the efforts of the young composers, & John in particular. Applause, cheers, etc. At the same time espousing Earle as the only one on the right path & performing his piece twice altho [sic] in contradiction with all stated premises obviously. Very bad atmosphere. Lots of political ramifications & I'm sure the press is going to have a field day.[141]

If one had access only to the printed versions of 'Geschichte und Gegenwart in der Musik von heute', the suggestion that Nono might have praised

---

[136] Nono, 'Die Angst vor der Freiheit'.
[137] See Patrick Major, *The Death of the KPD: Communism and Anti-Communism in West Germany, 1945–1956* (Oxford: Clarendon Press, 1997).
[138] Luigi Nono, 'The Historical Reality of Music Today', *The Score*, vol. 27 (1960 [1959]), 41–5.
[139] Peter Yates to Cage, 21 August 1961, JCC.
[140] Christian Wolff to Tudor, 18 October 1959, GRI.
[141] Tudor (Cologne) to M. C. Richards, 7 September 1959, GRI.

In Cage's wake

Brown would be confusing. What are not retained in any printing of the essay are Nono's introductory words to the performance of *Hodograph I*, which are, indeed, very positive regarding the music.[142]

Tudor wrote to Cage regarding what had happened:

> Fontana Mix was great success in Darmstadt! Cathy was perfectly incredible (in purple) & entertained royally. This in spite of Nono's outburst, which everyone knew was directed against Karlheinz, except critics, there in force. K. was very active, lectures & comp. class all based on new graphic tendencies (his own, yours, Kagel, Cardew, Bussotti, Boulez, Brown), & works written as a result, which were performed by Severino Caskel & self. Beside this Nono was just a shadow in the corner & hoped to gain everything with violence; most of what he said was without names, but he used your (& Schillinger's) like a 'symbol'. It was all quite obvious, unfortunate, & disgusting. For instance: 'you see that pieces for flute & pno. are growing like mushrooms, because they hope that they will be performed by Gazzelloni and Tudor; they see that they only have to spit on the paper & these artists will make something beautiful' etc., & worse. It's rather pathological; the next evening he came to Karlheinz because 'he heard that he was angry & couldn't understand why'.[143]

It is surely not insignificant that the specific section of Nono's presentation which Tudor regarded as 'obvious, unfortunate, & disgusting' was just that section removed by Nono to mollify the text as a whole. It is striking, too, that Nono's failure to understand that one could have taken the presentation as being in any way aggressive, rather than as simply a heartfelt, honest contribution to the debate, was recognised by Tudor.

As well as this, at the time it was very far from clear just who the subject of Nono's lecture really was. On the one hand, Cage and Schillinger were named. The discussion of mushrooms sprouting could hardly be taken as holding any ambiguity, especially not for an Italian, given Cage's recent high-profile appearances on the Italian game-show *Lascia o raddoppia* ('Double or Quits') answering questions on fungi. Elsewhere, Tudor suggested that, really, this was a disguised strike against Stockhausen (and it certainly seems from Tudor's letter to Cage on the matter that Stockhausen

---

[142] It is worth noting that there is ongoing debate regarding the degree to which Helmut Lachenmann, ostensibly Nono's translator, may have gone rather further in formulating the text of 'Geschichte und Gegenwart in der Musik von heute'. My reading of the archival sources suggests to me that Lachenmann wrote, and did not simply translate, large portions of the essay, which may account in part for the degree to which the argumentative strategy is so intertwined with a more obviously Germanic philosophy of history. Nevertheless, Nono never repudiated the essay; on the contrary, he defended it strongly in private, as his correspondence with Steinecke shows. Such conflicts of authorship may account for Nono's seemingly inconsistent position regarding Brown, for instance, but they do not materially alter the fact that what he said in 'Geschichte und Gegenwart' was what he meant, even if he did not write most of the text.

[143] Tudor to Cage, 8 October 1959, JCC.

thought this too). The press was broadly divided regarding just who it was that Nono wished to censure, though even amongst those who agreed with his point in general terms, there was strong feeling that both the mode of discourse employed and the forum in which it had been presented were wholly inappropriate. At the same time, there seems to have been little recognition that Adorno received a few barbed words along the way, although this was a section of the presentation that was amended before its wider circulation in print. There may well have been a great deal of truth in the saw that while a great many of those involved in the European new music scene of the 1950s had purchased a copy of Adorno's *Philosophie der neuen Musik*, very few had actually gone so far as to read it.

The question of whether Nono's attack was truly directed against Cage or against the growing proliferation of Cageian exegetes in Europe ultimately rests on a simple question: was Nono aware that what Cage was asking of his performers was *not* improvisation? In short, if he believed that Tudor was improvising when he performed a Cage score, then Cage too was implicated in the attack; if Nono knew that that had nothing to do with Tudor's practices then, on the contrary, what he was concerned with was composers who had *misunderstood* Cage. In this latter case, far from being an attack on Cage, 'Geschichte und Gegenwart in der Musik von heute' might be held to represent a *defence* of Cage against those who would use his starting point to take an 'easy' route. In the end, the question is probably moot, though Nono could have chosen – and did not choose – to make such a position unambiguous. What is much more significant in the context of the history of Cage's reception in Europe, and within the Darmstadtian arena specifically, is the way in which Nono's remarks actually functioned, separately from anything he may have intended by them. Nevertheless, it is clear that, just as there was no general agreement on (or indeed, truly, knowledge of) what serialism 'was' or represented, there was also a great divergence of awareness amongst the various Darmstadt participants (including the leading figures) of just what it was that Cage's music *did*, let alone what it might be held to represent.

Whatever the specifics, these events marked the beginning of the end for Nono's involvement at Darmstadt. He would return in 1960 with another presentation, 'Text–Musik–Gesang', but was thereafter not present at the courses, though his music was occasionally performed: *Polifonica–Monodia–Ritmica* was performed in the opening concert of the 1961 Ferienkurse, alongside Boulez's *Livre pour quatuor*, Berio's *Sequenza I* (1958), and Stockhausen's Klavierstück XI, and in 1962 *Cori di Didone* and *Ha venido – canciones para Silvia* (1960) were presented by the choir and orchestra of the Bayerischer Rundfunk. In what might seem almost a symbolic reduction of Nono's 'actual' presence, he was represented in 1963 only by a recording of *Composizione per orchestra n. 2: Diario polacco '58*. Then it would not be until 1980, the last year in which the second director of the courses, Ernst Thomas, presided, that Nono's music would be represented, by Bernhard Wambach's performance of ... *sofferte onde serene*... (1976).

On 19 February, Nono wrote to Ernst Thomas that he planned to speak about 'Music Theatre Today' during the 1962 Ferienkurse, taking *Intolleranza 1960* as a starting point. His worries about a continuing involvement, though, were already clear in this letter. His core concern was that his own presence, along with that of Boulez, Maderna, and Stockhausen, would detract from the opportunities available to young composers, for he stated: 'From my side, I always remain ready to give up a place for my music – if it isn't new, which is to say if it isn't a première – in favour of unknown youngsters', adding, '[n]aturally also *with* us, but please not a festival *of* us!!!!!!'[144] Doubtless the performance of a piece as old as *Polifonica–Monodia–Ritmica* in the previous year was part of the spur in this case. Yet these concerns proved of little relevance, since Nono cancelled his attendance in a very brief telegram to Thomas ('Sadly impossible to come, best, Nono') on 12 July 1962.[145] Thomas invited Nono to attend again in 1963, in a letter of 2 November 1962, but seems to have received no reply. Further attempts to woo Nono back, in letters of 2 December 1963, 11 December 1963, 16 January 1964, and, later, 7 January 1966 (this last another attempt to bring Nono to Darmstadt to speak regarding *Intolleranza 1960*, as a part of the sessions looking at new music theatre), also came to nothing: Nono declined an attendance in 1964 as a result of the pressures of completing *Da un diario italiano* (1964) for the Venice Biennale and seems not to have replied to Thomas's final letter to him.[146] Nevertheless, a slightly earlier letter from Nono to Thomas suggests strongly that Nono believed that his participation at Darmstadt had become a matter of historical fact: 'My bond with Darmstadt doesn't need any particular sign. I think that that is already fixed in "history".'[147] When Nono did not return to Darmstadt after 1960, this put the seal on matters. Whatever Darmstadt *had* been, it now had to become something else. As Nono himself would later put it: 'There are now so many "Darmstadts" in the world that the real

---

[144] Nono to Ernst Thomas, 19 February 1962, ALN.
[145] Nono to Thomas, 12 July 1962, ALN.
[146] Nono's rejection of the 1964 invitation was again in the form of a short telegram: 'New work for the Biennale takes all my time, must sadly decline invitations from Darmstadt and the Mozarteum' (telegram from Nono to Thomas, 28 January 1964, ALN).
[147] Nono to Thomas, 13 April 1965, ALN.

Darmstadt needs to become something really *different*. Is that possible? Or is it true that "after the revolution, almost always comes the restoration?"'[148]

Leaving 1959: three snapshots

Three other snapshots of the 1959 courses are worth giving, though they remain very much that: the performances of Stockhausen's *Kreuzspiel* on 3 September, Cage's *Aria* with *Fontana Mix* (both 1958) on 4 September, and Fortner's *Chant de naissance* (1958) in the closing concert on 5 September.

Though Stockhausen's 'Musik und Graphik' lectures were central to press coverage of the 1959 courses, the performance of his earlier music, in the form of *Kreuzspiel*, attracted less attention. What description there was is notable, though, for the disparity between recollections of its initial impact at its 1952 première and its impact now, at the end of the decade. Ernst Thomas made passing reference to the performance, saying, 'last not least Stockhausen's *Kreuzspiel*, from 1951, today makes just as great an impression as it did eight years ago'.[149] Thomas's memory is faulty here, since it had been premièred only seven years earlier (even if *written* in 1951), and while perhaps he was correct that it made the same volume of impression, the nature of that impression was quite different: in the intervening seven years, *Kreuzspiel* had moved from being a curious (perhaps outrageous) outlier to a central piece of the post-war canon. In this sense, Otto Tomek's recollection was keener: 'It was interesting to encounter once again an experiment from the year 1951, the première of which ended in scandal [...] Eight years have sufficed to make this revolutionary language into one spoken by young composers all over the world and one understandable by the public.'[150]

Similarly, though Cage was very much the subject of discussion, it is notable that his music, represented in live performance at Darmstadt in 1959 by the German premières of both *Aria* and *Fontana Mix* (performed simultaneously, the former by Cathy Berberian), was almost wholly ignored, despite Tudor's assertion, mentioned above, of the success of the performance. While the excitements and temptations of notation seemed to be central to the press reception, Heinz-Klaus Metzger was one of the few to mention Berberian's performance. Even in his hands, the report seems to exhibit only scholarly dispassion, though. The concert on which he was focussing was devoted to music for tape and instrumental resources, and

---

[148] Ibid.
[149] Thomas, 'Kontroverse und Konzert'. 'Last not least' is in English in Thomas's review.
[150] Tomek, 'Darmstädter Ferienkurse 1959'.

Metzger contrasted the attempts to fuse the electronic and the acoustic in Roman Haubenstock-Ramati's *Interpolations* (1959) and Maderna's revised version of *Musica su due dimensioni* (1957–8) with Cage's *Aria* with *Fontana Mix* which 'represented the opposite pole of this tendency [...] creating total discontinuity, and not fusion'.[151]

1959 was the last occasion on which one of the courses' founding figures would be present. Wolfgang Fortner led a course devoted to 'New Sonic and Structural Questions', and was represented in the final orchestral concert by a performance of his *Chant de naissance*, in which he himself directed the symphony orchestra of the Hessischer Rundfunk. The performance was, it seems, hardly a happy one with which to end Fortner's association with the courses. Ernst Thomas's review came to its close with dispirited remarks: 'in this piece a continuity shows itself, without which the Darmstadt Ferienkurse could not have become the unique, artistic institution of new music which they represent today. The young hecklers, mixed in with the applause, ought to think of that. This was no place for controversy.'[152]

Certainly the discord surrounding the events of 1959, properly understood as the concrete results of Cage's physical presence in Darmstadt in 1958, hardly seem to have affected every composer present, and the majority kept their thoughts on the matter out of their correspondence with the Internationales Musikinstitut in the wake of that year's course. Kagel's letters to Steinecke were concerned with the possibility of arranging a performance of *Anagrama* (1957–8) with the Rheinsche Kammerorchester at the 1960 courses.[153] Similarly, Maderna had no direct correspondence with Steinecke until the new year, and then only to discuss the conducting course he would lead in 1960.[154] One important shift in the dynamic of the course can, however, be seen in Stockhausen's altered relationship with Steinecke. Steinecke's final letter to Stockhausen before the 1959 courses used formal terms of address;[155] in their first correspondence after the courses, an undated letter from Stockhausen to Steinecke, the form of address had entirely changed: Herr Steinecke had become Wolfgang and, in Steinecke's next letter, Herr Stockhausen had become Karlheinz.[156] Indeed, Steinecke's tone was wholly different: 'I send you and your family my most heartfelt best wishes for

---

[151] Metzger, 'Kranichsteiner Musiktreffen beendet'.   [152] Thomas, 'Kontroverse und Konzert'.
[153] Kagel to Steinecke, 10 October 1959 and 2 December 1959, in Heile and Iddon (eds.), *Mauricio Kagel bei Internationalen Ferienkursen*, 39.
[154] Maderna to Steinecke, 1 January 1960; Maderna to Steinecke, undated but after 17 January 1960; Steinecke to Maderna, undated but between 1 January and 16 January 1960, in Dalmonte (ed.), *Bruno Maderna-Wolfgang Steinecke*, 194–7.
[155] Steinecke to Stockhausen, 2 August 1959, in Misch and Bandur (eds.), *Karlheinz Stockhausen bei den Internationalen Ferienkursen*, 252.
[156] Stockhausen to Steinecke, undated but after 5 September 1959; Steinecke to Stockhausen, 28 December 1959, in ibid., 259–60.

the new year, in grateful memory of our happy collaboration in 1959, which I hope renews our friendship often and from year to year. Perhaps that sounds a little solemn, but it's meant quite simply and seriously.'[157]

'Vieldeutige Form' ('Ambiguous Form'), 1960

In the context of Stockhausen's writings, his 1960 Darmstadt presentation, 'Vieldeutige Form', is certainly exceptional. Delivered on the evening of 13 July, in Stockhausen's absence by the omnipresent Heinz-Klaus Metzger, it certainly confused his audience. The text is, to be sure, *un*ambiguously Cageian. Indeed, it is closer to a performance piece than it is to any sort of conventional lecture.

Stockhausen had initially expected to be able to come to Darmstadt in 1960, though only for a couple of days, since his work on *Monophonie*, it was evident, had to take precedence.[158] He was also in the process of completing a print version of his 'Musik und Graphik' lectures from the 1959 courses for publication in the *Darmstädter Beiträge*, and one might perhaps account for the relative brevity of this contribution, in comparison with the scope of the lectures themselves, by the fact that Stockhausen's time was spent almost wholly with his new orchestral piece in time for its première at Donaueschingen. In the end, Stockhausen's absence from Darmstadt in order to complete *Monophonie* was to prove to be entirely pointless. Hans Rosbaud, who was to have conducted it, fell out with Heinrich Strobel, and the piece was never completed.[159] Nevertheless, ideas from *Monophonie* would occur in his 1960 presentation in ways which help to inform how Stockhausen conceived of his procedural modes of composition at the time (and how distant they were from any stereotypical conception of serial practice).

Stockhausen delivered his text to Steinecke on 5 July 1960, but he made clear that it was, really, only a *part* of the text. Throughout the text there were points at which Metzger – whom Stockhausen had nominated to read the essay in his absence – was requested to provide commentary on what Stockhausen had said.[160] On the same day, Stockhausen wrote to Metzger with instructions for the delivery of the text, and, in order to see what was expected from it (and the degree to which it represents not only a

---

[157] Steinecke to Stockhausen, 28 December 1959, in ibid., 260.
[158] Stockhausen to Steinecke, undated but *ca.* beginning of March 1960, in ibid., 270.
[159] Kurtz, *Stockhausen*, 106–7.
[160] Stockhausen to Steinecke, 5 July 1960, in Misch and Bandur (eds.), *Karlheinz Stockhausen bei den Internationalen Ferienkursen*, 271.

In Cage's wake

performance rather than a lecture but, moreover, a Cageian one), it is probably simplest to quote from his letter at length:

> I promised Steinecke a text on ambiguous form. In order to keep my promise, I have transcribed recordings. I would like to turn over the performance of this text to you. If you want and are happy to do it, I would be very happy. If you don't want to do it, then that would be fine with me too. What I do not want, though, is that anyone else perform it this year.
>
> For a performance I would make the following suggestions:
> 1. Read everything that I have written, which is to say also parts of the text like 'commentary – or' etc. and 'strike high cymbal' etc.
> 2. The reading speed is variable, but free.
> 3. When an indication of the sort of commentary is given through the word 'or', each time just one of the options should be selected.
> 4. The order of succession of the eleven one-page, two-page, and three-page sheets (double and triple pages are stapled together) is free. A sheet that has already been read can only be repeated if the commentary on this sheet is a fresh one and if a new way of reading it is chosen.
> 5. The total duration of the performance is indeterminate. You would be best to decide in consultation with Dr Steinecke.
> 6. The duration of the total commentary – not the individual ones – is related to the total duration of the performance.
>   (You could therefore also read for as long as it takes until the last audience member has, of their own volition, left the hall, and begin before any audience members have come into the hall. This depends upon the time you have available to prepare your commentaries.)
> 7. You will need: a tamtam, a gong, a low cymbal (which will not be struck), a mid-range cymbal, and a high cymbal. The type of beater used is up to you.
>
> I would recommend that you photocopy my text and staple it together in the order you choose to perform it. The examples that you use in the performance may be ripped up at the end.[161]

Metzger was required in the first place to read fragments of Stockhausen's text (in any order), which had been transcribed – so Stockhausen claimed – from recordings of things he had said, inserting his own commentary wherever it was marked. Stockhausen gave directions for the *sort* of commentary that was expected, such as, to take a few examples, '*incomprehensibly* or *scientifically* or *poetically*', '*musicologically*', or '*in extreme disagreement* or *restrictively* or *optimistically* or *medically*'. Metzger was not necessarily expected to produce commentary coterminous with what

---

[161] Stockhausen to Metzger, 5 July 1960, in ibid., 272.

he actually thought. At any rate, one commentary, and only one, has the instruction that it be undertaken 'à la Metzger'.

Although Stockhausen would later change his mind – 'Vieldeutige Form' was published in the second volume of his *Texte* – at this point he regarded its performance by Metzger as necessarily unique.[162] Ernst Thomas, having taken over as director of the Darmstadt courses by this stage, wrote to him on 12 March 1962 to suggest that, since there was a print-ready copy of the manuscript held at Darmstadt, it might be suitable for publication in the *Darmstädter Beiträge*.[163] Stockhausen was horrified: 'The 1960 text survives against my will! [. . .] I made the text for a one-off reading and asked that my written examples be torn up after the lecture. What Steinecke was thinking to act against my wishes … Anyway: the text is absolutely, in no way suitable for print.'[164] Whatever Stockhausen may ultimately have thought about the text, and it is possible that he was stung by some of the reaction to it, in 1960 it represented his own direct commentary on the events of the past few years at Darmstadt. Boulez, Cage, Metzger, Nono, and Tudor are all clearly present in the text.

That the formal characteristics of 'Vieldeutige Form' may be held to be Cageian (even if, perhaps, satirically so) can be seen from the following brief passage, which not only recalled the format of 'Communication' but also used Metzger's commentary to puncture the text in the same way as *Music of Changes* had been used in 'Changes':

> Can I, anytime I like,
>   *Commentary – quizzically* or *negatively*: To this end, I am not in the position to be outdone by people, since nature can quickly become scared.
>   come to a finish? *Gratia finalis*! Is God nearby? Distant? Is He a skater? On the way back from Lourdes – according to Janka's report – the border police came into the compartment, opened a bottle of Lourdes water, cried: 'That is pure cognac!' The owner: 'GodJesusMaryJoseph: another miracle!'
> Predetermined forms, in which one invents,
>   *Commentary – political* or *technical* or *hostile* or *questioning*: I would like here to reject only the question of whether God is nearby or distant. Catholics and atheists alike ought to know that he can't be either. It would be the same with either his omnipresence or his non-existence. Except, one could fancy, as Bloch says that Christians imagine Him themselves: as a gasiform vertebrate.
>   are crutches for those with impaired mobility. Find forms, not 'give form to'![165]

---

[162] Karlheinz Stockhausen, 'Vieldeutige Form' [1960], in *Texte*, vol. II, 245–61. Metzger's commentaries were, however, excised from this print version. I rely here instead on Metzger's later version, containing both parts.
[163] Thomas to Stockhausen, 12 March 1962, in Misch and Bandur (eds.), *Karlheinz Stockhausen bei den Internationalen Ferienkursen*, 324.
[164] Stockhausen to Thomas, 15 March 1962, in ibid.
[165] Stockhausen and Metzger, 'Vieldeutige Form', 194.

In Cage's wake 279

For all the potential levity of the presentation – the wit, too, lifted from Cage – there was certainly a serious side to proceedings. One might even think that the mode of delivery Stockhausen used was much like the way in which Cage had *become* accusatory in German, through Metzger's translation: some of the playfulness survived, but turned into interrogation.

It was Nono's remarks on David Tudor which were first to face the inquisitor: 'A year ago Nono said in Darmstadt that there are so many scores written trusting that a performer like Tudor will make something brilliant out of them: what a wealth of suspicion directed against Tudor, as if he could not resist the temptation to make bread from stones!'[166] Metzger's commentary on this (*apologetic, it doesn't matter to whom* or *partisan*), too, is instructive:

> I regard David Tudor, who is sadly not with us this year, as the finest performer. He knows all about the interpretation of scores and knows how to use the instrument with which he works to its best advantage. Other people can do both of these things, but with them it is often separately, rare that they are the same thing [. . .] In this respect almost all other performers together do not need defending against Nono.[167]

Stockhausen was, without question, attacking Nono's views here, even if in the context of Metzger's observation that it was, in truth, *only* Tudor who was in need of any defence against Nono. Thus it feels somewhat mischievous that he immediately moved to ask: 'Have musicians once again moved into a polemical arena? Soon it will become "official" – Herr Nono, Herr Cage; Herr Boulez, Herr Cage and Herr Nono; Herr Berio, Herr Nono, and who else I hardly know.' As Stockhausen observed, though, from a certain perspective this had become inevitable: 'It really seems as Cardew has put it: "One cannot say anything any more without rejecting something else."'[168] This would hardly stop Stockhausen from making his later lapidary observation: 'It cannot be that one can cry "Hail Boulez, down with Cage", and the others "Hail the aristocrat Nono, down with the other plebeians." Cage wrote in the *Darmstädter Beiträge*: "We are all one body."' Thus, even at the point where Stockhausen was on the one hand suggesting that new music ought to abandon its 'star cult', in which one composer was held to be right and thus, by necessity, all the others wrong, on the other he retained the sideswipe that the Marxist revolutionary Nono was, by birth at least, an aristocrat.[169] The religious implications of 'we are all one body' were hardly disguised.

Nor was Metzger, even in the act of reading Stockhausen's text, above criticism. Stockhausen noted that he had recently been termed a 'cornerstone'

---

[166] Ibid., 187.   [167] Ibid.   [168] Ibid.   [169] Ibid., 193.

of new music in an essay by Metzger. First Stockhausen was catty: 'Being counted in this category makes me feel like one of those cigarettes which also bears the name "cornerstone" until it is, a moment later, blown out into the air.'[170] Second, he was clear that, if there were questions of priority of invention at stake, Metzger was erroneous in his assertion that Boulez's *Polyphonie X* was the first piece in which all parameters (pitch, duration, dynamic, and, to a certain degree, timbre) were given pre-compositional arrangement, observing that Messiaen's *Mode de valeurs et d'intensités* assuredly had the prior claim in that respect and that, moreover, in the case of *Structures*, he and Boulez had discussed the piece in January 1952, during Stockhausen's time in Paris, looking at the earlier efforts of Goeyvaerts and Fano, as well as Stockhausen's own *Kreuzspiel*. Nor did Stockhausen fail to observe that a case could be made for the earlier significance of *Music of Changes* in this regard. Even in 1960, he would say, 'if the discussion is one about "historical priority in Europe", then the Belgian Goeyvaerts must be credited next to Messiaen', though his trailing 'but . . .' suggests strongly that, as far as Stockhausen was concerned, 'historical priority' was something of a red herring.[171]

Stockhausen also recalled his discussion with Boulez, following Tudor's working group sessions in 1956, in which Boulez had decried Stockhausen's disavowal of compositional responsibility in Klavierstück XI, before sending him, later that year, sketches of the Third Piano Sonata. If Stockhausen were sceptical regarding the importance of historical priority, he nevertheless reminded his audience that, in the case of a European piece of formally indeterminate music, he had been ahead of Boulez. Yet Stockhausen went rather further in exposing – as he seemed to see it – what Boulez was about:

> When I was in Paris at the beginning of 1957, I asked him [Boulez] why he had to write articles like 'Alea' when, if he wanted to score points against Cage or me or sought to show how it could be done better, he could simply communicate this to us directly. He opined: 'I want to circumvent misuse, since people like Cage are dangerous.'[172]

Plausibly, from Stockhausen's point of view, if Boulez was willing to speak publicly in this way, there was no reason for him to hold back either. Cage, though, was not met with the same attack. As far as Stockhausen was concerned, it was uplifting to have discovered that Cage had come to similar conclusions to the ones that he himself had reached through information theory via 'oriental modes of thought', insisting upon the independence of

---

[170] Ibid., 189. Eckstein ('cornerstone') is a German cigarette brand, dating back to the mid nineteenth century.
[171] Ibid.   [172] Ibid., 190.

In Cage's wake

the origin of his own trajectory from Cage's, even if the conclusions were closely related. As Stockhausen put it, Cage was 'less an inventor – as people are apt to describe him – than a discoverer'.[173] Nevertheless, a hint of Nono's critique may be found in an only slightly later description of Cage (though Stockhausen is clearly reporting the speech of others here, and perhaps intentionally echoes Nono in this respect, rather than giving his own opinion): 'For Cage everything is apparently equal, from which one takes it that he has no scruples, no conscience.'[174] Later, Stockhausen also took Metzger to task for having compared 'us old-fashioned European composers with the most "extreme" of all, Cage', querying whether Cage was really so extreme after all. Stockhausen here leaned on the well-worn cliché of an America without a tradition: 'Cage has absolutely no distance from any music. He flies in a space without gravity, nothing holds him back: he is the first American to make no secret of his lack of tradition.' This is, though, only a backhanded compliment, if it is a compliment at all, since Stockhausen suggested that Schoenberg was already more extreme than Cage; it had cost Schoenberg so much more to come to the ideas he had, whereas 'for Cage everything costs only a smile'.[175] Clearly this, too, as Misch and Bandur observe, recalled Nono's criticism of Cage's lack of historical sense.[176]

Stockhausen's frustration with a widespread misapprehension regarding serial music, in his conception of it, was clear too in the section of 'Vieldeutige Form' which considered his unfinished *Monophonie*:

> I am writing a piece with just one note [...] All is to become one, and yet remain itself (individuality of timbre). Transformations within the note, instead of transformations *of* the note [...] The piece will be a monotone, and endless. That it must be endless, I have known since the performance of *Kontakte*. One note from eternity to eternity – and everyone can listen for as long as they wish. I no longer have any reasons to make an end – or indeed a start: *every* end will be a start [...] Perhaps people will now stop asking me whether I have used a twelve-tone row, and if so, which [...] Even if there is not a single series that can be measured by numbers or the clock, the piece is still a serial composition.[177]

Stockhausen suggested that, surely, it would now only be Peter Stadlen who would continue to insist upon the question of which twelve-tone row was at play in Stockhausen's music. Stockhausen had insisted often enough, he

---

[173] Ibid., [174] Ibid., 191. [175] Ibid., 200.
[176] Misch and Bandur (eds.), *Karlheinz Stockhausen bei den Internationalen Ferienkursen*, 265.
[177] Kurtz, *Stockhausen*, 107. The original quotations amongst which Kurtz's extract may be found are in Stockhausen and Metzger, 'Vieldeutige Form', 193 and 196.

thought, that what was fundamental to serial method was the independent treatment of parameter, as revealed to him through Meyer-Eppler's communication theory, and not the transformation of a series which might be spelled out in numerical terms.[178] Indeed what made serialism 'serialism' for Stockhausen was just this independence of parameters.

The situation must have taken on comic proportions, however, when Stockhausen's discussion turned to Metzger's 'Cologne Manifesto'. When Metzger's historiography was questioned earlier in the presentation, Metzger had been given little commentary space for a 'right to reply'. In the discussion of the 'Cologne Manifesto', however, Metzger seemingly alternated between 'being' Stockhausen and being himself. Stockhausen began this section of 'Vieldeutige Form' thus: 'Metzger said in his manifesto in some context or other that the "Holy Ghost of Stockhausen" cannot help any more either (this was probably the same point at which he swept all the functions of music off the table).' Metzger's commentary (*arbitrary* or *ironic*) countered with a direct quotation from the 'Cologne Manifesto':

> By the by, even Stockhausen has not wholly resisted this mood and published an essay, 'Musik in Funktion', in the course of which music to some extent readies itself to wait on spiritual function, as though it, if it has nothing more to do on earth except to concern itself *with* itself, is able to receive binding instructions from the Holy Ghost.[179]

The quotation made clear that what Metzger was concerned to suggest with the reference was hardly that Stockhausen was setting himself up as some sort of spiritual guru, nor that he felt himself to be receiving direct instruction as a composer from the ether, but rather than at certain points he was prepared to accept the old-fashioned Germanic separation of *Kultur* and *Zivilisation*, as if music somehow enjoyed an autonomous existence outside the everyday or political spheres. Metzger's explanation of what he *had* said, as opposed to what Stockhausen had taken him to have said, made Stockhausen's subsequent commentary seem a little shallow: 'the Holy Ghost is quite simply the human creative spirit, and everybody knows that there is such a thing'.[180] As Martin Bernheimer recalled the moment, writing in the *New York Herald Tribune*, 'Metzger himself was called upon to read the lecture in Stockhausen's absence. Metzger interpolated words of self-defense, and punctuated the speech with unrelated gong-blows dictated by the script. The final result suggested a witty, jargonish squabble; the

---

[178] Stockhausen and Metzger, 'Vieldeutige Form', 196.
[179] Ibid., 199. The original citation may be found in Heinz-Klaus Metzger, 'Kölner Manifest' [1960], in *Musik wozu*, 11.
[180] Stockhausen and Metzger, 'Vieldeutige Form', 199.

Darmstadt public was generally amused. A few listeners, however, left asking the age-old musical question: who is fooling who?'[181] The press reports in Germany seem to have ranged from confusion to amusement to outrage. The *Darmstädter Tagblatt*'s reporter noted that 'many were attacked; even Metzger was not spared, which he took with cool equanimity and, in part, answered pointedly or clinically, in his commentaries'. Yet it was clear that from the perspective of this reporter at least, there was less interest in hearing Stockhausen's concerns that the Darmstadt composers might have built an ivory tower for themselves than there was in Metzger's comment that he was interested 'only in sexuality and gastronomy, the spirit is spineless volatility'.[182] Widmaier, writing in the *Darmstädter Echo*, presented only fragmentary excerpts from, presumably, the notes he had made during the presentation. The briefest of quotations is probably enough to make clear that he had hardly taken the proceedings too seriously: 'We have not built an ivory tower, but we have been placed in one nevertheless Goonnnnnnnnnnnggg - - - g forte, g piano, g high, g low, g behind, g in front, go right, go left'.[183] His opening description of events is written almost as if it were the credits of a stage play:

> Category: Large panopticon; half cabaret, half ritual; half rhymed, half unrhymed, whereby the unrhymed turns out actually to be rhymed, when one unwraps the Cageian packaging.
>
> Subject: Ambiguous Form
>
> Author: Karlheinz Stockhausen (*in absentia*)
>
> Commentator: Heinz-Klaus Metzger (*in praesentia*)
>
> Actor: Heinz-Klaus Metzger (in a double role)
>
> Stage music: Karlheinz Stockhausen (composer), Heinz-Klaus Metzger (interpreter)
>
> Configuration of the stage: left, a lectern; next to it a magic altar, with percussion of various sorts; behind, a stand with gongs and cymbals.[184]

If Widmaier was amused, Lewinski most assuredly was not. He suggested that the lecture moved between 'seemingly serious passages' and 'passages

---

[181] Martin Bernheimer, 'Darmstadt Festival Baffling', *New York Herald Tribune*, 24 July 1960, 5.
[182] [ig], 'Ein vieldeutiger Vortrag: Referat von Stockhausen, von Metzger gelesen und kommentiert', *Darmstädter Tagblatt*, 15 July 1960.
[183] Wolfgang Widmaier, '"Das größte Maul": Auch das gibt es bei den Kranichsteiner Ferienkursen', *Darmstädter Echo*, 15 July 1960.
[184] Ibid.

intended to be amusing which were, nevertheless, wholly lacking in jokes'. As far as Lewinski was concerned this presentation (though not only this one) was a total disappointment because composers 'from whom one would hardly have expected such a frivolous attitude have swung into line with the forced absurdity. This evil began with John Cage.'[185]

Though the commentators in general appear to have regarded Metzger as being under direct, if curious, attack in 'Vieldeutige Form', Metzger's own perspective was quite different. He seemed not to have taken to heart in the slightest any criticism Stockhausen might have made and, on the contrary, enjoyed the whole affair royally. A long letter from him to Stockhausen described in great detail the circumstances surrounding the lectures. Metzger insisted that he had read the text as accurately as he was able ('to be sure I fluffed a couple of times, but corrected myself'), yet nevertheless it seems that Gottfried Michael Koenig and Josef Häusler of the Südwestfunk had certainly misunderstood. Häusler had, as Metzger reported it, spoken to Metzger at the closing concert to tell him that he had heard that the presentation had contained 'wildly polemical passages against the German radio institutions as well as against Nono and Boulez'. Metzger had retorted, he relayed, that if there were any question regarding the quality of radio personnel it had been directed against only one Dr Heck, and not against the radio stations in general. He claimed, too, that the polemics against Nono and Boulez had stemmed from his own commentaries and not from Stockhausen's original text, while Stockhausen's own polemics railed against polemics themselves.[186] This was hardly true, as the examples given above suggest, even if Metzger's opposition to Boulez and Nono was more overt.

Adorno, at least, seemed to have understood what had gone on. He wrote to Stockhausen: 'I enjoyed Metzger's intervention, which certainly wasn't carried out without your approval.'[187] Yet, if Stockhausen's relationship with Metzger as expressed in 'Vieldeutige Form' was partly misunderstood, Nono's already precarious stance *vis-à-vis* Stockhausen could not have been regarded as ambiguous. In his final presentation, 'Text–Musik–Gesang', a few days before Stockhausen's presentation (and again formulated in German by Lachenmann), Nono closed with a retort to the question that Stockhausen had asked three years earlier in 'Musik und Sprache'. Stockhausen had then queried, on the subject of the texts used in *Il canto sospeso*, '[w]hy, then, texts at all, and why

---

[185] Wolf-Eberhard von Lewinski, 'Magere Bilanz der neuen Musik', *Süddeutsche Zeitung*, 21 July 1960.
[186] Metzger to Stockhausen, 10 August 1960, in Misch and Bandur (eds.), *Karlheinz Stockhausen bei den Internationalen Ferienkursen*, 277.
[187] Adorno to Stockhausen, 21 July 1960, in ibid., 274.

In Cage's wake

these in particular?'[188] In the version of his essay printed in *Die Reihe*, Stockhausen had added a note to the effect that Nono regarded his interpretation of *Il canto sospeso* as fundamentally incorrect and that '[t]he reader must therefore not take my reflections and analyses as being demonstrations of Nono's composition, but rather of my own – demonstrated on the work of another composer.'[189] In any case, such apology as this might have constituted obviously went nowhere near far enough for Nono. Having quoted from Stockhausen's 1957 presentation, Nono commented:

> The legacy of these letters becomes, expressively, my composition. And all of my later choral compositions can be understood through this relationship between the word as a phonetic-semantic totality and music as the composed expression of words. And it is totally senseless to conclude from an analytical handling of the sounding form of the text that the semantic content is thus cast out. The question of why I used just these texts and no other is no more intelligent than the question why one, in order to enunciate the word 'stupid', uses just the letters s–t–u–p–i–d.[190]

Nono concluded, having made direct reference to the history of text setting, that

> The principle of text setting, as it has developed in *Cori di Didone* into the fragmentation of consonants and vowels, has not cast out the meaning of the text, but has rather turned the phonetic-semantic structure into musical expression. Composition with the phonetic elements of a text serves today, just as earlier, as the transposition of semantic meaning into the musical language of the composers.[191]

Lothar Knessl suggests that the response to Nono was, unsurprisingly, far from positive. Where, in the previous year, his disdain for Cageian thinking had, despite its controversy, won many plaudits *during* the lecture itself, here Knessl was right to conclude that 'Nono's lecture aroused much anger amongst the Cageians who were present. But they got a chance to have their say – one must be fair – and demonstrated their presence both visually and aurally.'[192] Knessl explained further what had occurred in a later description:

> Nono expands his continually developing technique. The structures of the work are the results of his particular decisions (and not the results of a serial mechanism). For him, text which is transposed into music must always

---

[188] Stockhausen, 'Sprache und Musik', 67.
[189] Karlheinz Stockhausen, 'Music and Speech', tr. Ruth Koenig, *Die Reihe*, vol. 6 (1964 [1960]), 49.
[190] Nono, 'Text–Musik–Gesang', 60.   [191] Ibid.
[192] Lothar Knessl, 'Darmstadt – Sommerresidenz der Musikavantgarde', *Neues Österreich*, 12 July 1960.

remain comprehensible, even when that text concerns human problems. Nono has, of late, been faced with attacks because of his 'antiquated' attitude. He feels himself pushed back into a defensive position, but he must not defend his works – they are too valuable. In any case, they assert their own musical value.[193]

If Knessl felt this, his was probably a minority voice. For Lewinski, Nono, along with Kagel, Pousseur, and Wolpe, had served up thinking that was 'either boring or silly, half-baked or contorted verbiage'.[194] The title of Knessl's piece for the *Salzburger Nachrichten* – 'Are the Paths Diverging?' – was close to the mark. In the few brief years between the formulation of the 'Darmstadt School' idea, its central two figures, Nono himself and Stockhausen, had found themselves increasingly at loggerheads. Little surprise that, following Nono's unambiguous declaration that the questions Stockhausen was asking were 'stupid', it would be, as Kurtz says, 'years before they spoke to one another again'.[195] Not only that, but Maderna was increasingly seen as a conductor who composed, rather than the other way round. Boulez's and Stockhausen's positions were strongly opposed, if communicated through the totem of Cage. In short, by 1960 any sense of collegiality had gone. By 1960, Darmstadt, in its mythical sense, was over. It is hardly possible to say that Cage was the root cause of this, though his name was used as a token or a proxy in many of the debates which followed his arrival on the Darmstadt stage. The divisions between Stockhausen and Nono in particular could already be felt before this. Yet Cage's arrival clearly had a catalytic effect, bringing those tensions to the surface and making discussion of them seemingly unavoidable.

As for Stockhausen, though he had defended Cage before, it was clear by this stage that he saw him as only a rival. He wrote to Adorno:

> Your great strength is evident in the number of your opponents; your great weakness is that your opponents are no real opponents. It is the same for me with my numerous pseudo-opponents. In reality I have two opponents: Boulez and Cage – or Cage and Boulez. Boulez counters with the technique of getting through my guard and lopping off limbs, Cage with the technique of silence and cutting loose. My technique is one of surprise attacks, and taking a stand. When I read your books or your articles, I know that I am truly an opponent of yours, though we may not even suspect this when we meet. Now and then I discover a sentence of yours that sends shudders through my spine. And I

---

[193] Lothar Knessl, 'Gehen die Wege auseinander? Ferienkurse für Neue Musik in Darmstadt – logische Konstruktionen, Vieldeutigkeiten und Regressionen – nur das der Gegenwart entsprechende Klangbild bleibt unverändert', *Salzburger Nachrichten*, 18 July 1960.
[194] Wolf-Eberhard von Lewinski, 'Neue Musik in Darmstadt 1960', broadcast, Sender Freies Berlin, 16 August 1960, transcript IMD.
[195] Kurtz, *Stockhausen*, 98.

strike back, if I have not already done so, with weapons that are sinister and sharp. In my music, things have happened lately that are so much at odds with your thinking that you will surely be astonished if you discover them one day. You will be struck just as I know I was struck; but this time, secretly and dangerously.[196]

Perhaps Stockhausen did not regard attacks by Nono as having any great relevance, sensing that Nono's star was very much on the wane in Germany; his commitment to an outlawed political ideology – as noted above, the German Communist Party was banned in 1956 – made his position difficult, even if his music and outspoken position regarding Cage had not done so. In any case, Stockhausen clearly understood the whole situation as a confrontational one: a struggle for dominance. It is notable, too, that Stockhausen was evidently disdainful of Metzger; he was 'no real opponent' for Adorno. It is in the light of this letter, not least, that it is worth re-considering the content of Adorno's 'Vers une musique informelle', as well as Metzger's final direct riposte to Adorno (and the whole generation of Darmstadt composers: Boulez, Nono, and Stockhausen not least), 'Das Altern der jüngsten Musik'.

'Vers une musique informelle'

'Vers une musique informelle' was delivered by Adorno across two sessions, on the afternoons of 4 and 5 September 1961. Its opening statements suggested strongly that Adorno had markedly softened his thinking, and was now at least prepared to countenance the idea that it was really his fault that he had failed to come to terms adequately with the music that Boulez and Stockhausen had produced (seemingly Maderna and Nono still fell outside the bracket of the 'Darmstadt School' in Adorno's conception of it, though Pousseur and Cage were mentioned in other sections of his presentation). Nevertheless, the self-deprecating nature of the opening still suggested that he felt that systematic thinking prevailed in much new music and remained dangerous:

> Anyone of my age and experience who is both a musician and who thinks about music finds himself in a difficult quandary. One side of it consists in the attitude 'so far and no further'. In other words, it consists in clinging to one's youth as if modernity were one's own private monopoly. This means resisting at all costs everything which remains inaccessible to one's own experience or at least one's primary, basic reactions [...] Sometimes, of course, my narcissism, which asserts itself even though I can see through it, has a hard task persuading itself that the

[196] Ibid., 98.

> countless composers of music that can only be understood with the aid of diagrams and whose musical inspiration remains wholly invisible to me can really all be so much more musical, intelligent and progressive than myself. I frequently find myself unable to repress the thought that their system-driven music is not so very different from the false notes arbitrarily introduced into the neo-Classical concertos and wind ensembles of thirty or forty years ago. Musicians are usually truants from maths classes; it would be a terrible fate for them to end up in the hands of the maths teacher after all.[197]

The self-deprecation continued in Adorno's suggestion that he 'would not wish to claim that my membership in Schoenberg's Viennese school confers any particular authority on me or to assert that as an initiate I had easy answers'.[198] Even if Zagorski rightly suggests that such modesty was belied by Adorno's self-identification as an 'initiate',[199] what is probably more striking is the admission that much of the music that had found an audience in Darmstadt was a reflection of the historical *Geist* (even if Zagorski is right, too, that his insistence on the historical succession from Schoenberg to the Darmstadt composers may compound a sense that his humility was not wholly sincere): 'What we have to contend with in the development of music since 1945 did not simply appear from a clear blue sky. It can be seen to have been haunting everything that is included nowadays under the rather suspect title of "classical" twelve-tone technique.' He stated quite directly that he had 'been very favourably impressed by works of the Kranichstein or Darmstadt School such as Stockhausen's *Zeitmaße*, *Gruppen*, *Kontakte*, and *Carré*, as well as Boulez's *Marteau sans maître*, his Second and Third Piano Sonatas, and his Sonatina for Flute' and that he 'was also deeply moved by a single hearing of Cage's Piano Concerto played on Cologne Radio', even if he 'would be hard put to define the effect with any precision. Even at the best of times precise definition is anything but straightforward with works of this kind.'[200] Not only that, but Adorno recalled, yet again, his first encounter with the new post-war music, in the form of Goeyvaerts's Sonata for Two Pianos in 1951:

> In Kranichstein I once accused a composition, which in intention at least had managed to unify all possible parameters, of vagueness in its musical language. Where, I asked, was the antecedent, and where the consequent? This criticism

---

[197] Theodor W. Adorno, 'Vers une musique informelle', tr. Rodney Livingstone, in *Quasi una fantasia: Essays on Modern Music* (London: Verso, 1998 [1961]), 269. Adorno's original text may be found as 'Vers une musique informelle' in 'Quasi una fantasia', *Gesammelte Schriften*, ed. Rolf Tiedemann, vol. XVI: Musikalische Schriften I–III (Frankfurt am Main: Suhrkamp, 1978 [1961]), 493–540.
[198] Adorno, 'Vers une musique informelle', 270.
[199] Zagorski, '"Nach dem Weltuntergang"', 687.
[200] Adorno, 'Vers une musique informelle', 270.

In Cage's wake

> has to be modified. Contemporary music cannot be forced into such apparently universal categories as 'antecedent' and 'consequent', as if they were unalterable. It is nowhere laid down that modern music must a priori contain such elements of the tradition as tension and resolution, continuation, development, contrast, and reassertion; all the less since memories of all that are the frequent cause of crude inconsistencies in the new material and the need to correct these is itself a motive force in modern music.[201]

This is quite a retraction since, as Zagorski, a little cruelly, but entirely accurately, points out, 'It *was* in fact "laid down that modern music must a priori contain such elements of the tradition." And indeed, it was laid down only a few years earlier by Adorno himself in "Das Altern der Neuen Musik" – using precisely the same traditional categories that are here disavowed.'[202]

These new touchstones of 'acceptable' practice both include and go beyond the 'pointers' that Metzger had given to Adorno. Adorno was willing to use Metzger's term 'a-serial' as an analogue for his own preferred description of the 'ideal' music of the future: *musique informelle*. The closest Adorno came to describing what he meant by a *musique informelle* occurred early on in his presentation:

> What is meant is a kind of music which has discarded all forms which are external or abstract or which confront it in an inflexible way. At the same time, although such music should be completely free of anything irreducibly alien to itself or superimposed on it, it should nevertheless constitute itself in an objectively compelling way, in the musical substance itself, and not in terms of external laws.[203]

It is most notable that most of the parameters under which such an informal music would function are precisely those which Stockhausen, Boulez, and Nono had already staked out. Paddison accurately notes that, in part at least, the idea might be regarded as '"informal music" in the sense of "formless music", more accurately form which negates the received formal norms and which emerges from the demands of the material.' Yet he is, arguably, rather too swift to agree with Zenck's conclusion that 'its influence on the compositional praxis of the "New Music" was considerable, particularly on composers like Boulez, Stockhausen, and Ligeti'.[204] This idea that pre-given, historically determined forms should be abandoned in favour of what was suggested in the working-through of material was already almost fully present in what Boulez had had to say on the occasion of the Webern

---

[201] Ibid., 282. [202] Zagorski, '"Nach dem Weltuntergang"', 696.
[203] Adorno, 'Vers une musique informelle', 272.
[204] Paddison, *Adorno's Aesthetics of Music*, 182.

evening in 1953: 'Thus with Webern the first elements of a musical thought [...] which does not lead back to traditional fundamental schemes burst in.'[205] In truth, the notion of *musique informelle* may well have influenced Ligeti's output after 1961, but if it did, that only went to suggest that he had, perhaps, rather misunderstood the degree to which *Structure Ia* might represent any sort of paradigm for serial praxis.

To be slightly more accurate, then, Adorno's *musique informelle* represented a sort of halfway house, described by Paddison as

> the refusal to fall either into what Adorno sees as the positivism and false totality of multiple serialism or back into the 'bad universality' of pre-given, handed-down forms. It is 'informal' in that its form arises out of a denial of pre-determined or pre-existing form, while at the same time developing the equivalent to the old formal categories (which in themselves cannot be restored) according to the needs of the new materials.[206]

Yet, despite the fact that Paddison continues to say that '[t]he concept of *musique informelle* was doubtless put forward more as an ideal than as an existing reality', a compositional praxis which operated in just this way already existed, and had done since (at the latest) the freedoms introduced to deterministic procedures by Stockhausen in, for example, Klavierstück III or by Boulez in *Le Marteau sans maître*. Arguably, this was the way in which Nono had composed all along, both in earlier pieces like *Polifonica–Monodia–Ritmica*, where the results of the permutation of materials were then freely composed with, and in later pieces such as *Il canto sospeso*, which undermined any false positivistic view of the material through the seemingly paradoxical use of series-controlling series according to the 'tecnica degli spostamenti'.

If 'Vers une musique informelle' made much impact upon the compositional decisions of the young composers at Darmstadt, it can only have been to spur them down paths similar to those which the members of the putative 'Darmstadt School' had already taken. In truth, Adorno was probably well aware of this, given those whom he took as his authority in saying that

> [t]he idea, still widely prevalent among young composers, that the basic givens of a single note could determine the totality of a piece of music come into the category of what Stockhausen has scornfully called *Quanteln*. Such an idea forgets something which is incapable of further reduction, namely relationships. This is the fact that music consists not just of notes, but of the relations between them and that the one cannot exist without the other.[207]

---

[205] Pierre Boulez in Eimert, 'Junge Komponisten', 60.
[206] Paddison, *Adorno's Aesthetics of Music*, 182.
[207] Adorno, 'Vers une musique informelle', 299.

As well as noting the 'quantising' implied by Stockhausen's 'Quanteln', Adorno also deployed the same criticism that Nono (or Lachenmann) had raised against the use of material in Cage's music. Later in 'Vers une musique informelle', Adorno relied directly on Boulez's notion of 'so-called parentheses', presumably of the sort used in the Third Piano Sonata, as an example of what he meant when he said that 'sections should no longer just be juxtaposed, as is commonly done nowadays to the point of monotony; they must be placed in a dynamic relationship, comparable to the relationship of subordinate clauses and main clause in grammar'.[208]

If the sorts of already 'informal' serial practice that Boulez and Stockhausen had undertaken were acceptable, and if even Goeyvaerts's attempt was now seen as reflecting some sort of – albeit underdeveloped – historical necessity, another former sparring partner was hardly allowed to escape so lightly. Eimert – whom Adorno clearly still saw as a fundamental part of the 'problem' – is painted as one who, unlike the younger composers, had failed to move on from the idea that 'all musical dimensions of the entire piece of music should be deducible from the properties of individual notes'.[209] Behind Adorno's descriptions there remained a subtle attack on Eimert; Adorno later returned to criticism of a 'virtually total organisation, in which every feature serves the whole and the whole on its side is constituted as the sum of its parts, [which] points to an ideal which cannot be that of a work of art – that is to say, the ideal of a self-contained thing in itself'.[210] Stockhausen had, from Adorno's perspective, gone some way beyond his former mentor since, as he had said in '... wie die Zeit vergeht ...', from which Adorno quoted in this context, 'it frequently appears more fruitful to start from a contradiction'.[211]

In this sense, far from being a programme for the future, as it has sometimes been taken to be, 'Vers une musique informelle' represents a recognition that, at least in the case of the composers who had come to prominence at Darmstadt in the early 1950s (and those like Boulez who had been unwillingly co-opted into it), Adorno had misunderstood, if not in the way that Metzger had claimed he had. While Adorno now had, it seemed, a positive image of what a post-war composer ought to do, albeit almost ten years after the fact, and could point to Boulez and Stockhausen (and, to a lesser extent, Pousseur) as examples of how one might operate in historically responsible ways which the altered material conditions of new music, he also had newer compositional issues to worry about, in the guise of 'Cage and his school', the aspirations of whom

---

[208] Ibid.. [209] Ibid., 286. [210] Ibid., 306. [211] Ibid., 288.

have eradicated all topoi, without going into mourning for a subjective, organic ideal in which they suspect the topoi of maintaining an after-life. This is why to dismiss anti-art as pretentious cabaret and humour would be as great an error as to celebrate it. But such aspirations do not yet amount to a *musique informelle*. As a joke they hurl culture into people's faces, a fate which both culture and people richly deserve. They do not do this as a barbaric gesture, but to demonstrate what they have made of each other. The joke only turns sour when it appeals to an exotic, arty-crafty metaphysics and ends up with an exaggerated version of the very positivism which it set out to denounce. This helps to explain why the joke, which I respect, has been neutralized in contemporary society. The latter defends itself ideologically by swallowing everything. A *musique informelle* should also take good care to protect itself against revivals of *Die Aktion* and Dadaism, against Alexandrian anarchy.[212]

Thus, as an 'abstract negation' of any societal belief in the absolute power of 'truth' to be revealed in 'art', what Cage was doing was, as Adorno saw it, perfectly reasonable, even useful in and of itself. The difficulty came – and perhaps here Adorno tilted once more at Metzger – when someone took precisely this abstract negation up *as* art, as if it too would unveil some sort of metaphysical truth. Like Nono, perhaps, Adorno seemed to have some time for Cage's own work, as an 'intervention' at least, but was concerned at the idea that young European composers might attempt to generalise, which is to say reify, 'indeterminacy' into a guarantor of musical or artistic success.

Gertrud Meyer-Denkmann, for one, thought that he had misunderstood Cage, in a way clearly analogous to his reading of Goeyvaerts in 1951. He was in need of getting to know rather more music by not just Cage, but also Brown, Feldman, and Wolff before suggesting that what they were doing was in any way intended as a pointed joke or having much to do with Dada, even if that was just how Strobel had characterised it in 1954. She recollected that 'David Tudor and I played compositions by John Cage and Christian Wolff in a seminar in 1961 – Adorno sat silently in the first row – no comment.'[213]

Metzger, 'Das Altern der jüngsten Musik'

If Adorno had finally come to terms with music that had seemed so incomprehensible to him in 1951, and even music a little later than that, it was not long afterwards that Heinz-Klaus Metzger seemingly took his leave of Darmstadt and the composers that had been associated with it, with the

---

[212] Ibid., 314.
[213] Gertrud Meyer-Denkmann, *Zeitschnitte meines Lebens mit neuer Musik und Musikpädogogik 1950–2005* (Hofheim: Wolke, 2007), 33.

In Cage's wake

exception of Cage, in what might be regarded as his final contribution to the 'ageing' debate: 'Das Altern der jüngsten Musik' ('The Ageing of the Most Recent Music'). Though the text was written in 1962, it was not until 13 May 1963 that it was broadcast on the Bayerischer Rundfunk, and almost another year until it was published in *Collage*, in March 1964. In it, Boulez, Nono, and Stockhausen are, one by one, pointedly despatched. Metzger, too, softened his earlier criticism of Adorno: he dedicated the essay to him and suggested that if, at the time of 'Das Altern der Neuen Musik', Adorno's 'prophecies of doom' were impossible to verify, it had turned out in the end that Adorno had had a point, precisely in his concerns that new music might begin to show signs of 'false satisfaction'.[214] For Metzger it was in the way serial composition had become the everyday argot of musical festivals, conferences, composition competitions, and academies that the 'danger of the dangerless', which was to say 'the stabilisation of music', as Adorno had put it, could be seen.[215]

For Metzger, the worst culprit was probably Boulez: 'more than a decade ago, Boulez was the only clear representative of musical progress; more, he was the only composer of any relevance'. Yet Boulez's music, as early as *Le Marteau sans maître*, was music suitable only for 'music festivals', which endeavoured to try to reconcile the new music with what the public wanted to hear. After *Polyphonie X*, 'the regression of musical language is evident'.[216] It was for *Pli selon pli* (1957–62) that Metzger reserved his sternest critique. This was, in Metzger's view, a 'masterwork', but he did not mean the term kindly; 'masterpieces', the products of the bourgeois European cultures of the nineteenth century, ought to have lost the right to see the light of day as long ago as Mahler's era:[217] 'Whatever Boulez took from his theoretical knowledge of Debussy is artfully cashed in on here to make a hit, worthy of the avant-garde. The work stands under the sign of a new suaveness, smearing a sort of sweet glaze over the ears of the listeners [...] The work has a bad conscience.'[218] In the context of the essay as a whole, however, Boulez is hardly as strongly assaulted as Nono. Suggesting that every epoch requires a triumvirate of great composers – Haydn, Mozart, and Beethoven, or Schoenberg, Berg, and Webern – Metzger noted that he found it curious that Nono would be named alongside Boulez and Stockhausen as a great. There were, he proposed, no achievements in terms of either compositional technique or musical language that could be ascribed to Nono. Though he confessed that both the *Variazioni canoniche* and *Polifonica–Monodia–Ritmica* were immaculately

---

[214] Metzger, 'Das Altern der jüngsten Musik', 113.   [215] Ibid., 114.   [216] Ibid., 116.
[217] Ibid., 114.   [218] Ibid, 116.

orchestrated, these were exceptional (and, in any case, stemmed from his lessons with Maderna). Following this period, Nono's political commitments led to an immediate rejection of progressive compositional means: 'in one of the García Lorca epitaphs, he juxtaposes folkloric Spanish rhythms, Gregorian chant – or Ambrosian: I'm no specialist – tonal harmonies and the most primitive of speaking choruses in a sort of collage, which he wants to be understood as socialist realism'.[219] *Il canto sospeso* was, then, at best opportunistic, at worst offensive: '[I]t is no longer possible for a partisan fighting against reactionary violence to write a final letter home to his mother, before he is liquidated, without a composer making a masterwork out of it'.[220] *Intolleranza 1960* was perhaps the worst case from Metzger's perspective, since 'the war in Algeria wasn't even over before Nono got himself ready to process the cries of those tortured there musically, with the requisite twelve notes, in order to place them before the applause of the enraptured bourgeoisie, at the next major festival at the latest'.[221]

Nor was Stockhausen, with whom Metzger had had good relations at least as late as 1961, spared the bile and vitriol. Metzger initially, though, damned with faint praise:

> In technical fields, Stockhausen is just as good as everyone thinks. He was the first to recognise and elaborate effective relationships between parameters; the spatial location of sound was emancipated by him, thus allowing spatial composition, the most valuable examples of which still remain his *Gesang der Jünglinge*, his *Gruppen*, his *Kontakte*, and to go the whole hog he turned primitive experience with elementary rows into the serial communication of qualities.[222]

Yet, if *Gruppen* (1955–7) was remarkable, so *Carré* (1959–60) was the first expression of artistic bankruptcy.[223] It was in *Momente* (1962–9), though, that Metzger noted that Stockhausen's 'debasement seems to reach its critical extreme'.[224] As far as Metzger was concerned, what Stockhausen thought was 'timelessness' (the idea which was to have reached its apotheosis in *Monophonie*) seemed to him – though as he confessed, 'I'm no mystic' – to be just space;[225] any more profound conceptualisation of it than that was simply 'fannying about'.[226] Perhaps more significantly, though, as Metzger saw it, *real* moment form had already been a feature of Cage's music long before Stockhausen conceptualised such a thing: 'the late semi-Cageisms of Stockhausen are then entirely the expression of helplessness; he wants to make his composition "up to date" with them'.[227]

---

[219] Ibid., 118. [220] Ibid., 120. [221] Ibid. [222] Ibid., 121. [223] Ibid., 124. [224] Ibid., 126.
[225] Ibid., 124. [226] Ibid., 126. [227] Ibid., 127.

For all the bluff and bluster of 'Das Altern der jüngsten Musik', it had negligible impact. Even if Metzger *were* right that the Darmstadt composers had abandoned promising avant-garde beginnings in a Faustian pact with fame, no-one really seemed to be listening to him any more. The same Darmstadt against which Metzger railed here was, ironically, the one which had made his words count for something. As it faded into mythology, so too did Metzger's ability to critique it.

Steinecke's death

Although there can be little doubt from what has preceded that, in the wake of Cage's Darmstadt visit, tensions which were already implicit in, for example, Stockhausen's 'Musik und Sprache' exploded into open warfare between the Darmstadt composers, a symbolic, and tragic, end to Darmstadt's 'golden age' occurred on 23 December 1961. Steinecke was, in December 1961, still heavily involved with preparations for the following year's courses, writing to David Tudor on 15 December that it would, again, be hugely important for the courses that Tudor attended and, on this occasion, perform Stockhausen's Klavierstück X (1961). Yet on 23 December, Steinecke was involved in a hit-and-run incident on the streets of Darmstadt, and he died from his injuries on the same day. Emmy Zedler, the secretary of the Internationales Musikinsitut Darmstadt, wrote to Earle Brown:

> Mrs. Steinecke requested me to tell you the unhappy sudden death of Dr. Wolfgang Steinecke. He died on December 23th [*sic*] in consequence of the injuries he has to suffer from a terrible street accident in which he was involved without any fault on his own part. You may imagine how very much we are mourning.[228]

Hella Steinecke's letter to Brown of 18 January 1962 mentioned her husband only with the brief note, 'You know of the terrible disaster that has happened.'[229] With rather less sensitivity, Heinz-Winfried Sabais, who would become mayor of Darmstadt by the close of the 1960s, wrote to David Tudor:

> You will know that Dr. Steinecke died so sudden [*sic*] in consequence of a terrible street accident. With this letter we should like you to know that the 'Ferienkurse' will take place at any rate from July 8th to 20th, and that we must know as soon as ever possible, if we can count with you and your presence in the planned courses and concerts as we have written you on 15th of December.

---

[228] Emmy Zedler to Brown, 7 January 1962, IMD.
[229] Hella Steinecke to Brown, 18 January 1962, IMD.

> We are starting now the dispositions to succeed in fixing immediately the program, and to be able to publish the prospectus of our 'Ferienkurse'.[230]

There was no shortage of tributes. When his 'Musikdenken heute' lectures were published in the *Darmstädter Beiträge* in 1963, Boulez dedicated the volume to Steinecke. He also reprinted as a preface the words that he had spoken at Steinecke's funeral. The tribute juxtaposes affectionate reminiscence of Steinecke's gentle presence with a commitment to 'go on':

> a silhouette rises behind a screen of white paper – wobbles, finally breaks through the paper of the screen and appears with a very gentle laugh. Then this dialogue develops between shadows, both shaking with the same gentle laughter:
>
> 'so!'
> 'good, good!'
> 'unbelievable!'
> 'yes, yes!'
> 'and there's so much going on!'
> 'and why not? there has to be some fun'
> 'true ... but nevertheless ... who'd have thought it?'
> [...]
>
> let us wrest from unfortunate chance the presence in us of our friend, to whom life gave only an aggressive, insolent farewell: we owe him this vengance on the blindness of 'fate', which abuses its right to interrupt and cut short.[231]

Another tribute by Boulez, published in *Melos* in February 1962, promised to Steinecke that things would continue, as he, presumably, would have wanted: 'the lectures and rehearsals still go on; the discussions are as lively as ever, everyone contributes something, some new interest, some new passion. new arrivals cannot wait to make their first contacts; old hands go straight on to talk shop. groups form and scatter.'[232] In the same issue of

---

[230] Heinz-Winfried Sabais to Tudor, 19 January 1962, IMD.
[231] Pierre Boulez, 'Wolfgang Steinecke in memoriam', tr. Josef Häusler and Pierre Stoll, *Darmstädter Beiträge zur neuen Musik*, vol. 5 (1963), 6. The opening passage of Boulez's eulogy is a parody of the fifteenth scene of Jean Genet's final play, *Les Paravants* (*The Screens*). In Genet's play it is Kadidja who breaks through the white paper 'screen of the dead' to claim: 'You people don't seem to realize what I did for them down there. I organized the rebellion, drew the men into it, and died for freedom.' Though the parallels Boulez thus implicitly draws with revolutionary struggle in Algeria are perhaps a little crass, it is nevertheless clear that it was Steinecke, in this context, who 'organized the rebellion' and 'drew the men' into it. Jean Genet, *The Screens*, tr. Bernard Frechtman (London: Faber, 2009 [1963]), 126–7.
[232] Pierre Boulez, 'From the Distance', in *Orientations*, tr. Martin Cooper, ed. Jean-Jacques Nattiez (London: Faber, 1986 [1962]), 496; originally published as 'Dans la distance', *Melos*, vol. 29, no. 2 (February 1962), 55–6.

Melos there was also a tribute from Stockhausen. It, likewise, contained a promise to continue Steinecke's work: 'The first question Hella Steinecke put to me after the night he died: do you all want to carry on? I didn't think about it and just speaking for myself said: Yes.'[233] Just as Boulez had, even in his funeral oration, insisted that it was blind chance that had taken Steinecke from them, Stockhausen too took the opportunity (though not without affection one feels, here) to prod his former colleagues:

> I have always said that there would be no new music in heaven. But I know Wolfgang Steinecke well enough to realise that he will now be trying, with an irresistible smile, to change that. He won't lay off his gentle appeals until he has got so much on St Cecilia's nerves that she has provided him with a 'chamber ensemble of angels' and '20 more beds' for the celestial course participants. And he will make sure that heaven is open to participants of all countries, races, religions; that some unbelievers are awarded full scholarships; that Boulez, Cage and Nono must sit together for 14 days in *one* waiting room in Limbo.[234]

Adorno's tribute, published in the *Darmstädter Echo* on 31 July 1962, which is to say shortly after the close of that year's new music courses, concluded that 'the memory of the great organiser is of one who was an equal of the famous composers, not simply because he advocated them and supported them, but because what he did is just as important for the new production process as what they write'.[235]

It was arguably not really the case that Steinecke's death, as Attinello puts it, 'left the balance of power undecided, and the field was open for a rather embarrassing public struggle amongst the three [Boulez, Nono, and Stockhausen]'.[236] As what has preceded should have made clear, by the time of Steinecke's death, the public struggle had already taken place. The upshot of that was parlous for Darmstadt. Nono's later letters to Steinecke show that he felt himself to be unwanted at the courses and, although a presentation on *Intolleranza 1960* was advertised for the 1962 courses, Nono did not ultimately attend. Nor would he ever do so again. Ironically, given Nono's well-documented complaints regarding late cancellations on behalf of Boulez, his own telegram communicating his absence in 1962 was sent only on 12 July 1962, four days *after* the courses had begun. This might be considered surprising, since Nono and the new director of

---

[233] Karlheinz Stockhausen, 'Steineckes Tod' [1962], in *Texte*, vol. II, 243; originally published in Wolfgang Fortner, Pierre Boulez, Bruno Maderna, Luigi Nono, and Karlheinz Stockhausen, 'Wolfgang Steinecke in memoriam', *Melos*, vol. 29, no. 2 (February 1962), 56–7.
[234] Stockhausen, 'Steineckes Tod', in *Texte*, vol. II, 244.
[235] Theodor W. Adorno, 'Gedenkreder auf Wolfgang Steinecke', *Darmstädter Echo*, 31 July 1962.
[236] Paul Attinello, 'Postmodern or Modern: A Different Approach to Darmstadt', in Attinello, Fox, and Iddon (eds.), *Other Darmstadts*, 27.

Darmsatdt, Ernst Thomas, formerly music correspondent for the *Frankfurter Allgemeine Zeitung*, were of one mind regarding the irresponsibility of indeterminacy *à la* Cage. Thomas's words in his review of Stockhausen's presentation on Cage's work in 1959 are, in this context, worth quoting a second time: 'composition becomes trivial. Cage believes it, the imitators revel in it. There is a word for this, as ambiguous as it is unequivocal: dilettantism.'[237] Cage was not likely to meet with a warm welcome in Thomas's Darmstadt, even if it would be an exaggeration to say that Thomas was against American experimental music *in toto*.

As for Stockhausen, his interests had turned to Cologne, where he was able to set up the Cologne New Music Courses, after Hugo Wolfram Schmidt took over direction of the Rheinische Musikschule in 1962. It seemed reasonably clear that, in Cologne, Stockhausen saw the opportunity to run courses *like* those at Darmstadt, but organised wholly according to the directions which seemed most important to him. As early as 26 June 1962, Stockhausen had already written to Tudor that he wanted him to form a part of the new developments in Cologne and that '[n]aturally I shall try to get also John [Cage], and I thought that Pousseur, Kagel (?) (I hope that you tell me what you think about every person according to the necessity of a good collaboration in a team), Ligeti (?), Merce [Cunningham] (!) (if possible to include dance), Caskel, could be together with us.'[238] Tudor did not play a part in Stockhausen's courses, not least, one might presume, because it was around this point that Tudor had begun to cease thinking of himself primarily as a performer of the music of other composers and more as a composer in his own right, his first sole-authored piece, *Fluorescent Sound*, being premièred at the Moderna Museet in Stockholm on 13 September 1964.

For his part, Stockhausen was close to refusing to return to Darmstadt in 1963, writing to Ernst Thomas on 11 November 1962 that

> what I felt at Darmstadt this year was confirmed by your subsequent attitude and through your letter, for which I thank you.
>
> A new form of the Ferienkurse begins with your direction. In this sense, it is quite natural that your personal preferences for people and works determine this form. It does not suit me, though, that they establish a hierarchy, which Steinecke could have avoided. For that reason I can no longer accept your invitation for 1963.[239]

---

[237] Thomas, 'Klänge für das Auge?'
[238] Stockhausen to Tudor, in Misch and Bandur (eds.), *Karlheinz Stockhausen bei den Internationalen Ferienkursen*, 328.
[239] Misch and Bandur (eds.), *Karlheinz Stockhausen bei den Internationalen Ferienkursen*, 333.

Whatever hierarchies it may have been that concerned Stockhausen, he seemed to put them aside (and seems never to have sent the above letter), following a suggestion from Thomas that he might offer lectures in 1963 on *Gruppen* as well as take part in a general discussion with the composition lecturers, who were to be Boulez, Pousseur, Berio, and Stockhausen himself. Nevertheless, with the success of the Cologne New Music Courses, for a time Stockhausen took little interest in a further return to Darmstadt. He was not present in either 1964 or 1965.

Whether Thomas had intended to create hierarchies or not, they developed in the wake of Steinecke's death. While Nono and Stockhausen gradually distanced themselves from Darmstadt, under the new regime Boulez took centre stage in 1962, 1963, and 1965. Indeed, one might suspect that it was just this hierarchy – the centrality of Boulez – which had driven Stockhausen away. For all that Boulez may have opined that the one good thing about Cage's visit was that 'it cleaned out the academics',[240] under Boulez's charge the Ferienkurse became dusty indeed, being dominated by a sequence of rather dry (and, indeed, academic) congresses: 'Notation of New Music' in 1964, 'Form in New Music' in 1965, and 'New Music, New Stages', on music theatre, in 1966, though in truth the fault doubtless lay more squarely with Thomas than with Boulez. After the first one of these, Cardew commented that 'the Darmstadt Summer School has become an excellent Academy, and problems like Notation and Electronic Sound are competently handled in a rather academic way'. What had been a forum for presentation of that which was newest had entered a 'nostalgic' and rather retrospective phase.[241] The 'action' was, by now, happening elsewhere. It would be a long time before Darmstadt would recover.

Boulez, for whom Darmstadt had only ever been peripheral, no matter what attempts were made to bring him into the fold of the 'Darmstadt School', abandoned Darmstadt entirely after 1965, leaving a compositional vacuum at the head of the courses. Stockhausen was clearly pleased to return and assume almost total leadership of the courses, until his own unceremonious dethroning in 1974. It was, truly, in 1965 that Stockhausen's Darmstadt began – the hierarchy seemingly acceptable when he was at the head of it – but the story of that fresh beginning, after the fallow years following Steinecke's death, falls outside the scope of what is outlined here.

---

[240] Peyser, *Boulez*, 140.
[241] Cornelius Cardew, 'New Music has Found its Feet', *Financial Times*, 31 July 1964.

Conclusion

A stranger in paradise?

'All societies produce strangers', Zygmunt Bauman claims, 'but each kind of society produces its own kind of strangers, and produces them in its own inimitable way.'[1] The image Bauman paints recalls very closely the impact Cage had upon the European avant-garde, or at least on that aspect of it that regularly attended the courses at Darmstadt:

> If the strangers are the people who do not fit the cognitive, moral, or aesthetic map of the world – one of these maps, two or all three; if they, therefore, by their sheer presence, make obscure what ought to be transparent, confuse what ought to be a straightforward recipe for action, and/or prevent the satisfaction from being fully satisfying; if they pollute the joy with anxiety while making the forbidden fruit alluring; if, in other words, they befog and eclipse the boundary lines which ought to be clearly seen; if, having done all this, they gestate uncertainty, which in its turn breeds the discomfort of feeling lost – then each society produces such strangers.[2]

It would be hard to imagine a more accurate description of Cage's effect in Darmstadt. As Dahlhaus put it, Cage's appearance 'swept across the European avant-garde like a natural disaster'.[3] Though this does not hold absolutely, it is certainly the case that in the years after Cage's Darmstadt attendance, a composer was defined in part by his or her relationship to Cage. It is significant, though, that Cage had this impact in 1958 at Darmstadt, and not in 1954 at Donaueschingen. In 1954, Cage and Tudor were largely dismissed as a pair of comedians; in 1958, the sense that what they were doing might be regarded as a joke remained, but even those who took it that way suggested that it might well be a gag with a point. Many more participants in the European new music scene took Cage and Tudor seriously this time. Something must have changed in the intervening period.

It is vital to reiterate that the order that Cage ruptured could not have been that of multiple serialism. As Part I of this book showed in detail, the idea that multiple serialism was any sort of single entity is difficult to

---

[1] Bauman, *Postmodernism and its Discontents*, 17.   [2] Ibid.
[3] Carl Dahlhaus, 'Form: Introduction', in Ruth Katz and Carl Dahlhaus (eds.), *Contemplating Music: Source Readings in the Aesthetics of Music*, vol. III: *Essence* (New York: Pendragon, 1992), 777.

sustain. Not only that, but it was only in the very rarest of cases that serial music was truly 'ordered', in the Darmstadt context at any rate. In 1955, Meyer-Eppler had suggested that an aleatoric approach to composition would be one which is 'determined in general but depends on chance in detail'.[4] Yet the example of Stockhausen's Klavierstück III suggests that, even before his studies with Meyer-Eppler, he was already writing what Meyer-Eppler would have termed aleatoric music. This distinction is much like the one which Boulez made in 'Alea', and one can see the particular fluidities of Boulez's Third Piano Sonata as following a logical trajectory away from *Le Marteau sans maître*, in the realm of generally determined direction with local improvisation. Stockhausen's move from the first four Klavierstücke to Klavierstück XI operates similarly, even though there were more intermediary steps in his case. In Nono's first Lorca epitaph, one might argue that he, too, had determined the broad direction of the piece through his preparatory work, with the 'chance in detail' being a function of his gradual excision of various pre-determined elements. Yet this is something of a stretch: Nono's trajectory (and Maderna's too) overlapped with those of Boulez and Stockhausen, but diverged from them relatively quickly, and well before Nono came to try to unify the approaches of all four in written form. In the musical sense, there was no single thing for Cage to undermine. The order that Cage truly ruptured was hardly musical but social, even if the way in which reactions to him were articulated in Europe largely crystallised around the question of whether or not 'indeterminacy' *à la* Cage meant that Tudor was being called upon to improvise. What Cage ruptured, through words rather than music, was the centrality of an *idea* of order – the order that might be symbolically represented by the term 'Darmstadt School' – even if that idea did not exist in any musically precise way. In 1958 there was a more-or-less stable picture of what Darmstadt might be. It was this 'map of the world' that Cage was a stranger to, hardly the 'world' itself. This is to say that it was not significant in this context that the 'Darmstadt School' was in no small part an invention of Eimert's, though it was enthusiastically taken up by the press, which he surreptitiously used to strike against Adorno.

That Cage might most fruitfully be considered a stranger in the European context in Bauman's sense is suggested by the way in which, Bauman proposes, those *of* the world of the 'Darmstadt School' might be expected to react. As Bauman puts it:

---

[4] Meyer-Eppler, 'Statistische und psychologische Klangprobleme', 22.

> [T]wo alternative, but also complementary, strategies were intermittently deployed. One was *anthropophagic*: annihilating the strangers by *devouring* them and then metabolically transforming into a tissue indistinguishable from one's own. This was the strategy of *assimilation* ... The other strategy was *anthropoemic*: *vomiting* the strangers, banishing them from the limits of the orderly wall and barring them from all communication with those inside. This was the strategy of *exclusion*.[5]

The former approach might be seen most clearly in the responses of Stockhausen and of Heinz-Klaus Metzger. In Stockhausen's case, Cageian modes of writing rapidly became a part of Stockhausen's own compositional and rhetorical arsenal. This was prefigured in his discussion of notational strategies in 'Musik und Graphik', in which the ground was levelled between Cage's work and that of various Europeans, especially (but not only) Stockhausen's own. His literal adaptation of Cage's rhetoric in 'Vieldeutige Form' was a yet more explicit way of absorbing Cage's linguistic tissue into his own. Similarly, Metzger's translations of Cage into German and, perhaps more pertinently, in his own 'John Cage, or Liberated Music' transformed Cage into a class fighter whose opposition to societal and compositional norms mirrored Metzger's own.

Similarly, the latter stance might be most obviously exhibited by Ernst Thomas, who, having regarded Cage and Tudor's work at Darmstadt as a product of dilettantism, later stated, according to Reinhard Oehlschlägel, that 'this charlatan will never again come across the threshold of this house while I am in charge'.[6] Thomas was largely true to his word: under his direction, Cage's music was not performed at Darmstadt until 1974, even if Earle Brown was a regular, and welcome, guest there in the 1960s. Nono's response made clear that what Cage had to say, or the way in which it had been interpreted at least, had no place in the sort of struggle for musical (and social) freedom that Nono felt should be at the heart of the Darmstadt project.

Yet, after Cage, there was no 'Darmstadt project' any more, if there ever had been in the first place, and Nono quickly recognised that. Given Stockhausen's clear signal of intent in 1957 that he regarded his individual path as different from both Boulez's and Nono's, that dispersal would doubtless have happened sooner or later in any case. Yet it was Cage who became the totem around which the various position-takings were made. After Steinecke's death, there was no remnant of personal loyalty to the man who had 'made it all happen', and the long shadow of the collapse of

---

[5] Bauman, *Postmodernity and its Discontents*, 18.
[6] Reinhard Oehlschlägel, interviewed in Amy C. Beal, 'Patronage and Reception History of American Experimental Music in West Germany 1945–1986' (PhD dissertation, University of Michigan, 1999), 166.

the 'Darmstadt School' would dog Darmstadt almost throughout the tenure of Ernst Thomas.[7] It would not be until 1990, already midway through the tenure of Darmstadt's third director, Friedrich Hommel, that Cage would return to Darmstadt, still perhaps a stranger, but this time a postmodern one: 'joyfully or grudgingly, but by common consent or resignation, here to stay'.[8]

---

[7] For a specific discussion of this issue, see Martin Iddon, 'Trying to Speak: Between Politics and Aesthetics, Darmstadt 1970–72', *twentieth-century music*, vol. 3, no. 2 (2006), 255–75.

[8] Bauman, *Postmodernity and its Discontents*, 30.

Bibliography

Adorno, Theodor W., 'Ideen zur Musiksoziologie', *Schweizer Monatshefte*, vol. 38, no. 8 (November 1958), 679–91
'Gedenkreder auf Wolfgang Steinecke', *Darmstädter Echo*, 31 July 1962
'Das Altern der Neuen Musik' [1956], in *Gesammelte Schriften*, ed. Rolf Tiedemann, vol. XIV: *Dissonanzen: Einleitung in die Musiksoziologie* (Frankfurt am Main: Suhrkamp, 1973), 143–67
'Kriterien der neuen Musik' [1957], in 'Klangfiguren', *Gesammelte Schriften*, ed. Rolf Tiedemann, vol. XVI: *Musikalische Schriften I–III* (Frankfurt am Main: Suhrkamp, 1978), 170–228
'Vers une musique informelle' [1961], in 'Quasi una fantasia', *Gesammelte Schriften*, ed. Rolf Tiedemann, vol. XVI: *Musikalische Schriften I–III* (Frankfurt am Main: Suhrkamp, 1978), 493–540
'Music, Language, and Composition' [1956], tr. Susan Gillespie, *Musical Quarterly*, vol. 77, no. 3 (1993), 401–14
'Vers une musique informelle' [1961], tr. Rodney Livingstone, in *Quasi una fantasia: Essays on Modern Music* (London: Verso, 1998), 269–322
Aesthetic Theory, tr. Robert Hullot-Kentor (London: Athlone, 1999 [1970])
'Criteria of New Music' [1957], in *Sound Figures*, tr. Rodney Livingstone (Stanford University Press, 1999), 145–96
'Anton von Webern' [1959], in *Sound Figures*, tr. Rodney Livingstone (Stanford University Press, 1999 [1959]), 91–105
'The Aging of the New Music' [1954, rev. 1955], tr. Robert Hullot-Kentor and Frederic Will, in *Essays on Music*, ed. Richard Leppert (Berkeley, CA: University of California Press, 2002), 181–202
'Cultural Criticism and Society' [1949], tr. Samuel Weber and Shierry Weber Nicholsen, in Rolf Tiedemann (ed.), *Can One Live after Auschwitz? A Philosophical Reader* (Stanford University Press, 2003), 146–62
Philosophy of New Music, tr. Robert Hullot-Kentor (Minneapolis, MN: Minnesota University Press, 2006 [1949])
'Atonal Intermezzo' [1929], in *Night Music: Essays on Music 1928–1962*, ed. Rolf Tiedemann, tr. Wieland Hoban (Calcutta: Seagull, 2009), 322–38
'New Music Today' [1955], in *Night Music: Essays on Music 1928–1962*, ed. Rolf Tiedemann, tr. Wieland Hoban (Calcutta: Seagull, 2009), 384–400
Adorno, Theodor W., and Heinz-Klaus Metzger, 'Disput zwischen Theodor W. Adorno und Heinz-Klaus Metzger' [1957], in Heinz-Klaus Metzger,

Musik wozu: Literatur zu Noten, ed. Rainer Riehn (Frankfurt am Main: Suhrkamp, 1980), 90–104
Attinello, Paul, 'Postmodern or Modern: A Different Approach to Darmstadt', in Paul Attinello, Christopher Fox, and Martin Iddon (eds.), *Other Darmstadts* (*Contemporary Music Review*, vol. 26, no. 1 (2007)), 25–37
Attinello, Paul, Christopher Fox, and Martin Iddon (eds.), *Other Darmstadts* (*Contemporary Music Review*, vol. 26, no.1 (2007))
Bachmann, Claus-Henning, 'Zwischen Kult und Elektronenröhre: Darmstadts Rechenschaftsbericht über die neuen Musik', *Schwäbische Landeszeitung*, 22 June 1955
  'Sie suchen Rückhalt bei Mozart. Neue Musik in Darmstadt: Handwerk mit Phantasie', *Westdeutsche Allgemeine*, 3 August 1956
  'Ende der Mechanisierung: Eindrücke von den Tagen Neuer Musik in Darmstadt', *Stuttgarter Zeitung*, 1 August 1957
  'Der Zufall in der Musik und seine Folgen', *Rhein-Neckar-Zeitung*, 18 September 1958
  'Meditation und Liebestod: Neue Musik in Darmstadt: Avantgarde ist kontemplativ', *Fränkisches Volksblatt*, 7 October 1959
Bailey, Kathryn, *The Twelve-Note Music of Anton Webern: Old Forms in a New Language* (Cambridge University Press, 1991)
  '"Work in Progress": Analysing Nono's *Il canto sospeso*', *Music Analysis*, vol. 11, nos. 2–3 (1992), 279–334
Bandur, Markus, *Aesthetics of Total Serialism* (Basle: Birkhäuser, 2001)
Bauman, Zygmunt, *Postmodernity and its Discontents* (Cambridge: Polity, 1997)
Beal, Amy C., 'Patronage and Reception History of American Experimental Music in West Germany 1945–1986' (PhD dissertation, University of Michigan, 1999)
  'Negotiating Cultural Allies: American Music in Darmstadt, 1946–1956', *Journal of the American Musicological Society*, vol. 53, no. 1 (2000), 105–40
  'The Army, the Airwaves, and the Avant-Garde: American Classical Music in Postwar West Germany', *American Music*, vol. 21, no. 4 (Winter 2003), 474–513
  New Music, New Allies: American Experimental Music in West Germany from the Zero Hour to Reunification (Berkeley, CA: University of California Press, 2006)
  'David Tudor in Darmstadt', in Paul Attinello, Christopher Fox, and Martin Iddon (eds.), *Other Darmstadts* (*Contemporary Music Review*, vol. 26, no. 1 (2007)), 77–8
Bernheimer, Martin, 'Darmstadt Festival Baffling', *New York Herald Tribune*, 24 July 1960, 5
Biddiscombe, Perry, *The Denazification of Germany: A History 1945–1950* (Stroud: Tempus, 2007)
Bielwiese, Fritz, 'Im Grenzgebiet der musikalischen Wirkungen', *Kölner Stadt-Anzeiger*, 4 August 1953
Blüggel, Christian, *E. = Ethik + Ästhetik: Zur Musikkritik Herbert Eimerts* (Saarbrücken: Pfau, 2002)

Blume, Friedrich, 'Musik und Rasse: Grundfragen einer musikalischen Rassenforschung', *Die Musik*, vol. 30, no. 11 (August 1938), 736–48
  Das Rasseproblem in der Musik (Wolfenbüttel: Kallmeyer, 1944)
Blumröder, Christoph von, *Die Grundlegung der Musik Karlheinz Stockhausens* (Stuttgart: Franz Steiner, 1993)
  'Orientation to Hermann Hesse', tr. Jerome Kohl, *Perspectives of New Music*, vol. 36, no. 1 (Winter 1998), 65–96
Borio, Gianmario, 'Kontinuität der Moderne?', in Gianmario Borio and Hermann Danuser (eds.), *Im Zenit der Moderne* (Freiburg im Breisgau: Rombach, 1997), vol. I, 141–283
  'Wege des ästhetischen Diskurs', in Gianmario Borio and Hermann Danuser (eds.), *Im Zenit der Moderne* (Freiburg im Breisgau: Rombach, 1997), vol. I, 427–69
  'Tempo e ritmo nelle composizioni seriali: 1952-1956', in Gianmario Borio, Giovanni Morelli, and Veniero Rizzardi (eds.), *Le musiche degli anni cinquanta* (Florence: Leo S. Olschki, 2004), 61–115
  'Work Structure and Musical Represenation: Reflections on Adorno's Analyses for Interpretation', in Paul Attinello, Christopher Fox, and Martin Iddon (eds.), *Other Darmstadts* (*Contemporary Music Review*, vol. 26, no. 1 (2007)), 53–75
Borio, Gianmario, and Hermann Danuser (eds.), *Im Zenit der Moderne*, 4 vols. (Freiburg im Breisgau: Rombach, 1997)
Born, Georgina, *Rationalizing Culture: IRCAM, Boulez, and the Institutionalization of the Musical Avant-Garde* (Berkeley, CA: University of California Press, 1995)
Bösche, Thomas, 'Auf der Suche nach dem Unbekannten oder Zur Deuxième Sonate (1946-1948) von Pierre Boulez und der Frage nach der seriellen Musik', in Orm Finnenhahl (ed.), *Die Anfänge der seriellen Musik* (Berlin: Wolke, 1999), 37–96
Botting, Douglas, *In the Ruins of the Reich* (London: Methuen, 2005 [1985])
Boucourechliev, André, 'Darmstadt 1957', *Nouvelle revue français*, vol. 5, no. 59 (1957), 972
Boulez, Pierre, 'Kommentar zur 3. Klaviersonate', recital-lecture, 30 August 1959, recording IMD
  'Dans la distance', *Melos*, vol. 29, no. 2 (February 1962), 55–6
  'Wolfgang Steinecke in memoriam', tr. Josef Häusler and Pierre Stoll, *Darmstädter Beiträge zur neuen Musik*, vol. 5 (1963), 6
  Relevés d'apprenti, ed. Paule Thévenin (Paris: Éditions du Seuil, 1966)
  Conversations with Célestin Deliège (London: Eulenburg, 1976)
  'Sonate, que me veux-tu?' [1959], in *Orientations*, tr. Martin Cooper, ed. Jean-Jacques Nattiez (London: Faber, 1986), 143–54
  'From the Distance' [1962], in *Orientations*, tr. Martin Cooper, ed. Jean-Jacques Nattiez (London: Faber, 1986), 496
  'Proposals' [1948], in *Stocktakings from an Apprenticeship*, tr. Stephen Walsh (Oxford University Press, 1991), 47–54

'Schoenberg is Dead' [1952], in *Stocktakings from an Apprenticeship*, tr. Stephen Walsh (Oxford University Press, 1991), 209–14

'Corruption in the Censers' [1956], in *Stocktakings from an Apprenticeship*, tr. Stephen Walsh (Oxford University Press, 1991), 20–5

'Alea' [1957], in *Stocktakings from an Apprenticeship*, tr. Stephen Walsh (Oxford University Press, 1991), 26–38

'Claude Debussy et Anton Webern' [1955], tr. Heinz-Klaus Metzger, in Heinz-Klaus Metzger and Rainer Riehn (eds.), *Darmstadt-Dokumente I* (Munich: text +kritik, 1999), 72–9

'Erinnerung', in Frank Hilberg and Harry Vogt (eds.), *Musik der Zeit 1951–2001* (Hofheim: Wolke, 2002), 52–3

Brasch, Alfred, 'Neue Musik bei der Selbstkritik: Zum zehnten Male "Internationale Ferienkurse" in Darmstadt', *Aachener Volkszeitung*, 8 June 1955

Brennan, Brian, 'Augustine's *De musica*', *Vigiliae Christianae: A Review of Early Christian Life and Language*, vol. 42, no. 3 (September 1988), 267–81

Cage, John, '25 Years and 45 Questions', *Village Voice* (9 April 1958), 4

'Rutgers Original', 1958 (unpublished), JCP

'Zur Geschichte der experimentelle Musik in den Vereinigten Staaten', tr. Heinz-Klaus Metzger, *Darmstädter Beiträge zur neuen Musik*, vol. 3 (1959), 46–53

'Indeterminacy' [1959], tr. Hans G. Helms, *Die Reihe*, vol. 5 (1961), 83–120

'45′ for a Speaker' [1954], in *Silence* (London: Marion Boyars, 1968), 146–93

'Changes' [1958], in *Silence* (London: Marion Boyars, 1968), 18–34

'Communication' [1958], in *Silence* (London: Marion Boyars, 1968), 41–56

'Composition as Process' [1958], in *Silence* (London: Marion Boyars, 1968), 18

'Indeterminacy' [1958], in *Silence* (London: Marion Boyars, 1968), 35–40

'History of Experimental Music in the United States' [1959], in *Silence* (London: Marion Boyars, 1968), 67–75

'Indeterminacy' [1959], in *Silence* (London: Marion Boyars, 1968), 260–73

Silence (London: Marion Boyars, 1968)

'Seriously Comma' [1966], in *A Year from Monday* (London: Marion Boyars, 1985), 26–9

'Kommunikation' [1958], tr. Heinz-Klaus Metzger, Hans G. Helms, and Wolf Rosenberg, in Heinz-Klaus Metzger and Rainer Riehn (eds.), *Darmstadt-Dokumente I* (Munich: text+kritik, 1999), 161–74

Cage, John, and Joan Retallack, 'July 30, 1992' [1992], in *Musiccage: Cage Muses on Words, Art, Music* (Hanover, NH: Wesleyan University Press, 1996), 291–312

Cahn, Peter, 'Wolfgang Fortners Kompositionskursse in Darmstadt (1946–51)', in Rudolf Stephan, Lothar Knessl, Otto Tomek, Klaus Trapp, and Christopher Fox (eds.), *Von Kranichstein zur Gegenwart* (Stuttgart: DACO, 1996), 36–43

Campbell, Edward, *Boulez, Music and Philosophy* (Cambridge University Press, 2010)

Cardew, Cornelius, 'Notation–Interpretation, etc.', *Tempo*, no. 58 (1961), 21–33

'New Music has Found its Feet', *Financial Times*, 31 July 1964

Carvalho, Mário Vieira de, 'Towards Dialectical Listening: Quotation and *Montage* in the Work of Luigi Nono', in Stephen Davismoon (ed.), *Luigi Nono: Fragments and Silence (Contemporary Music Review*, vol. 18, no. 2 (1999)), 37–85.

Christiaens, Jan, '"Absolute Purity Projected into Sound": Goeyvaerts, Heidegger and Early Serialism', *Perspectives of New Music*, vol. 41, no. 1 (Winter 2003), 168–78

Clark, Mark W., *Beyond Catastrophe: German Intellectuals and Cultural Renewal after World War II, 1945–1955* (Lanham, MD: Lexington, 2006)

Claussen, Detlev, *Theodor W. Adorno: One Last Genius* (Cambridge, MA: Harvard University Press, 2008 [2003])

Cook, Nicholas, *A Guide to Musical Analysis* (Oxford University Press, 1994 [1987])

Curjel, Hans, 'Cage oder das wohlpräparierte Klavier', *Melos*, vol. 22, no. 4 (April 1955), 97–100

Custodis, Michael, *Die soziale Isolation der neuen Musik: Zum Kölner Musikleben nach 1945* (Stuttgart: Franz Steiner, 2004)

  '"Unter Auswertung meiner Erfahrungen aktiv mitgestaltend": Zum Wirken von Wolfgang Steinecke bis 1950', in Albrecht Riethmüller (ed.), *Deutsche Leitkultur Musik? Zur Musikgeschichte nach dem Holocaust* (Stuttgart: Franz Steiner, 2006), 145–62

  Tradition – Koalitionen – Visionen: Wolfgang Steinecke und die Internationalen Ferienkurse in Darmstadt (Saarbrücken: Pfau, 2010)

Dahlhaus, Carl, 'Form: Introduction', in Ruth Katz and Carl Dahlhaus (eds.), *Contemplating Music: Source Readings in the Aesthetics of Music*, vol. III: *Essence* (New York: Pendragon, 1992), 777–9

Dalmonte, Rossana (ed.), *Bruno Maderna–Wolfgang Steinecke: Carteggio/Briefwechsel* (Lucca: LIM, 2001)

Decroupet, Pascal, 'Boulez: Schlüssige Kompositionssysteme. Dem flexiblen Musikdenken Vorrang eingeräumt', in Rudolf Stephan, Lothar Knessl, Otto Tomek, Klaus Trapp, and Christopher Fox (eds.), *Von Kranichstein zur Gegenwart* (Stuttgart: DACO, 1996), 225–9

  'Aleatorik und Indetermination – die Ferienkurse als Forum der europäischen Cage-Rezeption', in Gianmario Borio and Hermann Danuser (eds.), *Im Zenit der Moderne* (Freiburg im Breisgau: Rombach, 1997), vol. II, 189–275

Decroupet, Pascal, and Elena Ungeheuer, 'Through the Sensory Looking Glass: The Aesthetic and Serial Foundations of *Gesang der Jünglinge*', tr. Jerome Kohl, *Perspectives of New Music*, vol. 36, no. 1 (Winter 1998), 97–142

Delaere, Mark, 'Auf der Such nach serieller Stimmigkeit: Goeyvaerts' Weg zur Komposition Nr. 2 (1951)', in Orm Finnendahl (ed.), *Die Anfänge der seriellen Musik* (Berlin: Wolke, 1999), 13–36

Dibelius, Ulrich, *Moderne Musik nach 1945* (Munich: Piper, 1977 [1966])

Drew, David, 'The Darmstadt Summer School of New Music, 1954', *The Score and IMA Magazine*, no. 10 (December 1954), 77–81

Durazzi, Bruce, 'Luigi Nono's *Canti di vita e d'amore*: Musical Dialectics and the Opposition of Present and Future', *Journal of Musicology*, vol. 26, no. 4 (Fall 2009), 451–80

Eimert, Herbert, *Lehrbuch der Zwölftontechnik* (Wiesbaden: Breitkopf & Härtel, 1950)
   'Uraufführung von Nono's *Canto sospeso* in Köln', *Melos*, vol. 23 (1956), 354
   'Junge Komponisten bekennen sich zu Anton Webern' [1953], in Gianmario Borio and Hermann Danuser (eds.), *Im Zenit der Moderne* (Freiburg im Breisgau: Rombach, 1997), vol. III, 58–65
Eimert, Herbert [?], 'Intermezzo II' [1958], *Die Reihe*, vol. 4 (1960), 81–4
Engler, Günter, 'Musik der jungen Generation? Experiment und Manier bei den "Ferienkursen"', *Neue Zeitung*, 23 July 1952
Enke, Heinz, 'Gestörtes Konzert', *Frankfurter Rundschau*, 9 July 1951
   'Anton von Weberns Geist über Kranichstein: Die junge Generation bei den Internationalen Ferienkursen', *Allgemeine Zeitung*, 26 July 1952
   'Im Zeichen Schönbergs und Weberns: Die Internationalen Ferienkurse in Darmstadt', *Allgemeine Zeitung*, 5 August 1953
   'Die Historie von Kranichstein: Beginn der 13. Internationalen Ferienkurse für Neue Musik', *Frankfurter Rundschau*, 5 September 1958
Evans, Richard J., *In Hitler's Shadow: West German Historians and the Attempt to Escape from the Nazi Past* (London: I. B. Tauris, 1989)
   The Third Reich in Power (London: Penguin, 2006 [2005])
Evarts, John, 'The New Musical Notation: A Graphic Art?', *Leonardo*, vol. 1, no. 4 (October 1968), 405–12
Fearn, Raymond, *Bruno Maderna* (Chur: Harwood, 1990)
Fox, Christopher, 'Luigi Nono and the Darmstadt School: Form and Meaning in the Early Works (1950–1959)', in Stephen Davismoon (ed.), *Luigi Nono: Fragments and Silence* (*Contemporary Music Review*, vol. 18, no. 2 (1999)), 111–30
   'Written in Sand: Stockhausen's Plus-Minus, More or Less', *Musical Times*, vol. 141, no. 1871 (Summer 2000), 16–24
   'Music after Zero Hour', in Paul Attinello, Christopher Fox, and Martin Iddon (eds.), *Other Darmstadts* (*Contemporary Music Review*, vol. 26, no.1 (2007)), 5–24
Freedman, Guy, 'An Interview with John Cage', December 1976, publication details unknown, JCC
Freytag, Werner, 'In Darmstadt nichts Neues', *Hannoversche Presse*, 16 September 1958
Friedländer, Walther, 'An den Grenzen der Hörbarkeit: Internationale Ferienkurse für Neue Musik in Darmstadt', *Der Standpunkt*, 8 August 1952
   '"Kranichstein" muß sich entscheiden: Zu den zehnten "Internationalen Ferienkursen für Neue Musik"', *Frankfurter Allgemeine Zeitung*, 14 June 1955
Genet, Jean, *The Screens*, tr. Bernard Frechtman (London: Faber, 2009 [1963])
Gerberding, Elke, 'Darmstädter Kulturpolitk der Nachkriegszeit', in Rudolf Stephan, Lothar Knessl, Otto Tomek, Klaus Trapp, and Christopher Fox (eds.), *Von Kranichstein zur Gegenwart* (Stuttgart: DACO, 1996), 29–35
   Darmstädter Kulturpolitik in der Nachkriegszeit 1945–1949 (Darmstadt: Justus von Liebig, 1996)
Goeyvaerts, Karel, 'Evolution eines Komponisten: Olivier Messiaen – 1952 gesehen', *Darmstädter Echo*, 22 July 1952

'Paris – Darmstadt 1947–1956: Excerpt from the Autobiographical Portrait', *Revue belge de musicologie*, vol. 48 (1994), 35–54

Goléa, Antoine, 'Die Klangwelt der elektronischen Musik', *Der Mittag*, 29 August 1950

'Die Musik der jungen Generation: Fünf Studiokonzerte der Darmstädter Ferienkurse', *Der Mittag*, 17 July 1951

'Ausklang in Kranichstein: Problematik und Meisterstil', *Der Mittag*, 29 July 1952

Musik unserer Zeit, tr. Antoine Goléa and Willi Reich (Munich: C. H. Beck, 1955 [1954])

'Die neue Musik hat ihren frechen Clown: John Cage bei den Kranichsteiner Ferienkursen', *Der Mittag*, 11 September 1958

'Die neue Musik braucht Kranichstein ... aber es müßte gründlicher geprobt werden – trotzdem gab es herrliche Aufführungen von Nono und Boulez', *Der Mittag*, 17 September 1958

Göttig, Willy Werner, 'Hermann Scherchen rügte Pfeifkonzert in Darmstadt', *Abendpost*, 10 July 1951

Gradenwitz, Peter, 'Darmsatdt Debates: German City Host to a Festival that Discussed as well as Played Music', *New York Times*, 21 September 1959

Grant, M. J., *Serial Music, Serial Aesthetics* (Cambridge University Press, 2001)

Grassl, Markus, and Reinhard Kapp (eds.), *Darmstadt-Gespräche* (Vienna: Böhlau, 1996)

Gräter, Manfred, 'Darmstädter Ferienkurse 1957' (unpublished report), IMD

Griffiths, Paul, *Modern Music: A Concise History* (London: Thames & Hudson, 1994)

Guerrero, Jeannie Ma., 'The Presence of Hindemith in Nono's Sketches: A New Context for Nono's Music', *Journal of Musicology*, vol. 26, no. 4 (Fall 2009), 481–511

Harth, Walther, 'Musik-Olympiade der Jüngsten', *Der Kurier*, 8 September 1950

Harvey, Jonathan, *The Music of Stockhausen: An Introduction* (Berkeley, CA: University of California Press, 1975)

Hayse, Michael R., *Recasting West German Elites: Higher Civil Servants, Business Leaders and Physicians in Hesse between Nazism and Democracy, 1945–1955* (New York: Berghahn, 2003)

Heile, Björn, 'Darmstadt as Other: British and American Responses to Musical Modernism', *twentieth-century music*, vol. 1, no. 2 (2004), 161–78

The Music of Mauricio Kagel (Aldershot: Ashgate, 2006)

Heile, Björn, and Martin Iddon (eds.), *Mauricio Kagel bei Internationalen Ferienkursen fur Neue Musik in Darmstadt* (Hofheim: Wolke, 2009)

Heiß, Hermann, 'Zwei Wege der Zwölftonmusik', *Darmstädter Echo*, 3 July 1951

Helm, Everett, 'Darmstadt, Baden-Baden, and Twelve-Tone Music', *Saturday Review* (30 July 1955), 33–5, 46

Henck, Herbert, *Hermann Heiß: Nachträge einer Biografie* (Deinstadt: Kompost, 2009)

Henius, Carla, 'Genie-Blitze in der Waschküche: Erinnerung an Hermann Heiß', in Rudolf Stephan, Lothar Knessl, Otto Tomek, Klaus Trapp, and Christopher Fox (eds.), *Von Kranichstein zur Gegenwart* (Stuttgart: DACO, 1996), 44–8

Bibliography

Henze, Hans Werner, 'German Music in the 1940s and 1950s', tr. Peter Labanyi, in *Music and Politics: Collected Writings, 1953–81* (London: Faber, 1982), 27–56

Bohemian Fifths, tr. Stewart Spencer (London: Faber, 1998 [1996]

Herchenröder, G. N., 'Darmstädter Ferienkurse: Musik-Klänge der Maschinen-Zeit', *Abendpost*, 1 August 1953

'Musik an der Grenze des Schweigens', *Abendpost*, 8 June 1955

Hermann, Wilhelm, 'Die jüngste Komponistengeneration: Internationaler Wettstreit bei den Darmstädter Ferienkursen', *Badisches Tagblatt*, 4 September 1950

'Internationale Ferienkurse für Neue Musik: Kritischer Rückblik [sic] auf das Darmstädter Treffen', *Rhein-Neckar-Zeitung*, 1 August 1952

Hicks, Michael, 'John Cage's Studies with Schoenberg', *American Music*, vol. 8, no. 2 (Summer 1990), 125–40

Hill, Peter, 'Messiaen Recorded: The *Quatre études de rythme*', in Christopher Dingle and Nigel Simeone (eds.), *Olivier Messiaen: Music, Art and Literature* (Aldershot: Ashgate, 2007), 79–90

Hill, Peter, and Nigel Simeone, *Olivier Messiaen: Oiseaux exotiques* (Aldershot: Ashgate, 2007)

Hindemith, Paul, *A Composer's World: Horizons and Limitations. The Charles Eliot Norton Lectures 1949–1950* (Cambridge, MA: Harvard University Press, 1952)

Holzaepfel, John, 'David Tudor and the Performance of American Experimental Music, 1950–1959' (unpublished PhD dissertation, City University of New York, 1994)

'David Tudor and the *Solo for Piano*', in David W. Bernstein and Christopher Hatch (eds.), *Writings through John Cage's Music, Poetry, and Art* (University of Chicago Press, 2001), 137–56

'Cage and Tudor', in David Nicholls (ed.), *The Cambridge Companion to John Cage* (Cambridge University Press, 2002), 169–85

'Painting by Numbers: The *Intersections* of Morton Feldman and David Tudor', in Steven Johnson (ed.), *The New York School of Music and Visual Arts* (London: Routledge, 2002), 159–72

Iddon, Martin, 'Trying to Speak: Between Politics and Aesthetics, Darmstadt 1970–72', *twentieth-century music*, vol. 3, no. 2 (2006), 255–75

'Gained in Translation: Words about Cage in Late 1950s Germany', in Paul Attinello, Christopher Fox, and Martin Iddon (eds.), *Other Darmstadts* (*Contemporary Music Review*, vol. 26, no.1 (2007)), 89–104

'Pamphlets and Protests: The End of Stockhausen's Darmstadt', in Beate Kutschke (ed.), *Musikkulturen in der Revolte: Studien zu Rock, Avantgarde und Klassik im Umfeld von '1968'* (Stuttgart: Franz Steiner, 2008), 55–63

'Serial Canon(s): Nono's Variations and Boulez's Structures', in Lisa Colton and Martin Iddon (eds.), *Recycling and Innovation in Contemporary Music* (*Contemporary Music Review*, vol. 29, no. 3 (2010)), 265–75

Jarausch, Konrad H., *After Hitler: Recivilizing Germans, 1945–1995* (Oxford University Press, 2006)

Joachim, Heinz, 'Musikalische Avantgarde in der Sackgasse: Die Frage ist: wie soll es weitergehen? – Zu den Kranichsteiner Ferienkursen', *Die Welt* (Hamburg), 19 September 1958

Kagel, Mauricio, 'John Cage en Darmstadt 1958', *Buenos Aires musical*, 16 October 1958

Kapp, Reinhard, 'René Leibowitz in Darmstadt', in Rudolf Stephan, Lothar Knessl, Otto Tomek, Klaus Trapp, and Christopher Fox (eds.), *Von Kranichstein zur Gegenwart* (Stuttgart: DACO, 1996), 76–85

Kater, Michael, *The Twisted Muse: Musicians and their Music in the Third Reich* (Oxford University Press, 1997)

Composers of the Nazi Era: Eight Portraits (Oxford University Press, 2000)

Kayser, Nils, 'Kein Überblick aus dem Netz', *Darmstädter Echo*, 18 October 1958.

Király, Susanne, *Ludwig Metzger: Politiker aus christliche Verantwortung* (Darmstadt: Hessische Historische Kommission Darmstadt and Historische Kommission für Hessen, 2004)

Knessl, Lothar, 'Darmstadt – Sommerresidenz der Musikavantgarde', *Neues Österreich*, 12 July 1960

'Gehen die Wege auseinander? Ferienkurse für Neue Musik in Darmstadt – logische Konstruktionen, Vieldeutigkeiten und Regressionen – nur das der Gegenwart entsprechende Klangbild bleibt unverändert', *Salzburger Nachrichten*, 18 July 1960

'Das Dezennium des großen Aufbruchs: Rückblick-Notizen – ohne (?) Verklärung', in Rudolf Stephan, Lothar Knessl, Otto Tomek, Klaus Trapp, and Christopher Fox (eds.), *Von Kranichstein zur Gegenwart* (Stuttgart: DACO, 1996), 139–45

Koblyakov, Lev, *Pierre Boulez: A World of Harmony* (Chur: Harwood, 1990)

Kovács, Inge, 'Webern zwischen gestern und morgen: Die Rezeption seiner Musik bei den Ferienkursen der fünfziger Jahre', in Rudolf Stephan, Lothar Knessl, Otto Tomek, Klaus Trapp, and Christopher Fox (eds.), *Von Kranichstein zur Gegenwart* (Stuttgart: DACO, 1996), 181–7

'Die Institution – Entstehung und Struktur', in Gianmario Borio and Hermann Danuser (eds.), *Im Zenit der Moderne* (Freiburg im Breisgau: Rombach, 1997), vol. I, 59–139

'Neue Musik abseits der Avantgarde? Zwei Fallbeispiele', in Gianmario Borio and Hermann Danuser (eds.), *Im Zenit der Moderne* (Freiburg im Breisgau: Rombach, 1997), vol. II, 13–61

Kowalke, Kim H., 'Music Publishing and the Nazis: Schott, Universal Edition, and their Composers', in Michael H. Kater and Albrecht Riethmüller (eds.), *Music and Nazism: Art under Tyranny, 1933–1945* (Laaber, 2003), 170–218

Kurtz, Michael, *Stockhausen: A Biography*, tr. Richard Toop (London: Faber, 1992 [1988])

Lepenies, Wolf, *The Seduction of Culture in German History* (Princeton University Press, 2006)

Leukert, Bernd, 'Musik aus Trümmern, Darmstadt um 1949', *Musik-Texte: Zeitschrift für neue Musik*, no. 45 (July 1992), 20–8

Lewinski, Wolf-Eberhard von, 'Musik der jungen Generation: Ein Studio- und ein Kammerkonzert', *Darmstädter Tagblatt*, 10 July 1951

'Musik der jungen Generation: Die letzten Kammer- und Orchesterkonzerte', *Darmstädter Tagblatt*, 12 July 1951

'Geräuschrhythmik und Dodekaphonie: Die 7. Internationalen Ferienkurse für Neue Musik in Darmstadt', *Wiesbadener Tagblatt*, 31 July 1952

'Die neue Musik am Scheidwege: Aufschlußreiche Ergebnisse der Kranichsteiner Ferienkurse 1953', *Düsseldorfer Nachrichten*, 3 August 1953

'Amerikanische Musiker und das Experiment: Ein Vortragsabend mit Klangbeispielen bei den Ferienkurse', *Darmstädter Tagblatt*, 16 August 1954

'Junge Komponisten in Kranichstein: Bericht über die Kranichsteiner Ferienkurse 1954', broadcast, Bayerischer Rundfunk, Munich, date unknown, transcript IMD

'Prominenz der jungen Komponisten: Uraufführungen bei den Kranichsteiner Ferienkursen', *Bremer Nachrichten*, 3 June 1955

'Debussy – Webern – Boulez: Yvonne Loriod und H. A. Kaul spielten auf der Marienhöhe', *Darmstädter Tagblatt*, 4 June 1955

'Stockhausen – Maderna – Boulez: Zum dritten Studio Konzert der Kranichsteiner Ferienkurse', *Darmstädter Tagblatt*, 20 July 1956

'Neue und nicht mehr neue Musik aus Amerika: Ein Vortrag von Stefan Wolpe auf der Marienhöhe', *Darmstädter Tagblatt*, 21 July 1956

'Blick in Kranichsteins Komponisten-Atelier', broadcast, Radio Bremen, August 1956 (exact date unknown), transcript IMD

'Absage an das Idol des Musik-Ingenieurs: Mit den Kranichsteiner Ferienkursen 1957 begann eine neue Phase', *Darmstädter Tagblatt*, 3 August 1957

'Der musikalische Roboter tritt an: Die modernste Musik zwischen Mensch und Maschine', *Christ und Welt*, 15 August 1957

'Kranichstein 1957: Grundsätzliche Gedanken zu den 12. Internationalen Ferienkursen für Neue Musik in Darmstadt', broadcast, Westdeutscher Rundfunk, 25 September 1957, transcript IMD

'Die neueste Musik von Kranichstein: Bericht von den Internationalen Kranichsteiner Ferienkursen für Neue Musik Darmstadt, Juli 1957', broadcast, Radio Audizioni Italiane, date unknown, transcript IMD

'Musik der Zeit – Musik der Zukunft: 50 Ur- und Erstaufführungen bei den Kranichsteiner Ferienkursen', *Süddeutscher Zeitung*, 10 September 1958

'Kranichstein nur alle zwei Jahre? Zum Vorschlag des Stadtverordneten Brust: Eine schöpferische Pause für junge Komponisten', *Darmstädter Tagblatt*, 30 September 1958

'Themen und Thesen der Kranichsteiner Ferienkurse 1958', broadcast, Westdeutscher Rundfunk, date unknown, transcript IMD

'Auf der Suche nach der neuen Form: Pierre Boulez erläuterte und spielte seine dritte Klaviersonate', *Darmstädter Tagblatt*, 1 September 1959

'Von der Verantwortung der Komponisten: Nonos aggressiver Vortrag/Ergebnisse der ersten Kranichsteiner Woche', *Darmstädter Tagblatt*, 3 September 1959

'Magere moderne Musik – nur optisch reizvoll', *Der Kurier*, 11 September 1959

'Magere Bilanz der neuen Musik', *Süddeutsche Zeitung*, 21 July 1960

'Neue Musik in Darmstadt 1960', broadcast, Sender Freies Berlin, 16 August 1960, transcript IMD

Ligeti, György, 'Pierre Boulez: Entscheidung und Automatik in der *Struktur Ia*', *Die Reihe*, vol. 4 (1958), 38–63

Lowinsky, Edward E., *Secret Chromatic Art in the Netherlands Motet* (New York: Columbia University Press, 1946)

Lucchesi, Joachim, 'Um in ihnen mehr Klarheit zu schaffen: Hermann Scherchen in Darmstadt', in Rudolf Stephan, Lothar Knessl, Otto Tomek, Klaus Trapp, and Christopher Fox (eds.), *Von Kranichstein zur Gegenwart* (Stuttgart: DACO, 1996), 60–4

Maconie, Robin, *The Works of Karlheinz Stockhausen* (London: Oxford University Press, 1976)

Other Planets: The Music of Karlheinz Stockhausen (Lanham, MD: Scarecrow, 2005)

Major, Patrick, *The Death of the KPD: Communism and Anti-Communism in West Germany, 1945–1956* (Oxford: Clarendon Press, 1997)

Malina, Judith, *The Diaries of Judith Malina 1947–1957* (New York: Grove, 1984)

Mann, Thomas *Doctor Faustus: The Life of the German Composer Adrian Leverkühn as Told by a Friend*, tr. John E. Woods (New York: Vintage, 1999 [1947])

Mauser, Siegfried, 'Emigranten bei den Ferienkursen in Darmstadt (1946–1951)', in Horst Weber (ed.), *Musik in der Emigration 1933–1945* (Stuttgart: J. B. Metzler, 1994), 241–8

Mayer, Hans, 'Beton und Krach: Amerikanismus in einer westdeutschen Stadt', *Freies Volk*, 11 September 1951

'Kulturkrise und neue Musik' [1948], in Heinz-Klaus Metzger and Rainer Riehn (eds.), *Darmstadt-Dokumente I* (Munich: text+kritik, 1999), 17–25

McClelland, Grigor, *Embers of War: Letters from a Quaker Relief Worker in War-Torn Germany* (London: British Academic, 1997 [1945])

Meinecke, Friedrich, *The German Catastrophe*, tr. Sidney B. Fay (Cambridge, MA: Harvard University Press, 1950 [1946])

Mendius, Helmut, 'Aus der Sicht der Orchestermusikers', in Rudolf Stephan, Lothar Knessl, Otto Tomek, Klaus Trapp, and Christopher Fox (eds.), *Von Kranichstein zur Gegenwart* (Stuttgart: DACO, 1996), 58–9

Metzger, Heinz-Klaus, '"... geschultest und entfaltetst ...": Eine Erwiderung auf "Catch as Cage Can"', *Darmstädter Echo*, 16 September 1958

'Intermezzo I: Das Altern der Philosophie der Neuen Musik', *Die Reihe*, vol. 4 (1958), 64–80

'John Cage o della liberazione' [1958], tr. Sylvano Bussotti, *Incontri musicali*, vol. 3 (August 1959), 1–31

'Kranichsteiner Musiktreffen beendet: Rückblick auf die Internationalen Ferienkurse für Neue Musik in Darmstadt', *Der Mittag*, 11 September 1959

'Just Who is Growing Old?', tr. Leo Black, *Die Reihe*, vol. 4 (1960), 63–80

'Verhältnis zur Historie' [1957], in *Musik wozu: Literatur zu Noten*, ed. Rainer Riehn (Frankfurt am Main: Suhrkamp, 1980), 20–6

'Das Altern der Philosophie der Neuen Musik' [1957], in *Musik wozu: Literatur zu Noten*, ed. Rainer Riehn (Frankfurt am Main: Suhrkamp, 1980), 61–89

'Zur Verdeutlichung einer Polemik und ihres Gegestandes' [ca. 1958], in *Musik wozu: Literatur zu Noten*, ed. Rainer Riehn (Frankfurt am Main: Suhrkamp, 1980), 105–12

'Kölner Manifest' [1960], in *Musik wozu: Literatur zu Noten*, ed. Rainer Riehn (Frankfurt am Main: Suhrkamp, 1980), 9–14

'Das Altern der jüngsten Musik' [1962], in *Musik wozu: Literatur zu Noten*, ed. Rainer Riehn (Frankfurt am Main: Suhrkamp, 1980), 113–28

'Musikalische Qualität als Verinnerlichung von Gebrauchs- und Tauschwert' [1973], in *Musik wozu: Literatur zu Noten*, ed. Rainer Riehn (Frankfurt am Main: Suhrkamp, 1980), 244–62

Musik wozu: Literatur zu Noten, ed. Rainer Riehn (Frankfurt am Main: Suhrkamp, 1980)

'Fragment zum Thema "Komet"', in Rudolf Stephan, Lothar Knessl, Otto Tomek, Klaus Trapp, and Christopher Fox (eds.), *Von Kranichstein zur Gegenwart* (Stuttgart: DACO, 1996), 250–1

'John Cage, or Liberated Music' [1958], tr. Ian Pepper, *October*, vol. 82 (Fall 1997), 49–61

Metzger, Heinz-Klaus, and Rainer Riehn (eds.), *Darmstadt-Dokumente I* (Munich: text+kritik, 1999)

Metzger, Ludwig, *In guten und in schlechten Tagen: Berichte, Gedanken und Erkenntnisse aus der politischen Arbeit eines aktiven Christen und Sozialisten* (Darmstadt: Reba, 1980)

Meyer-Denkmann, Gertrud, *Zeitschnitte meines Lebens mit neuer Musik und Musikpädogogik 1950–2005* (Hofheim: Wolke, 2007)

Meyer-Eppler, Werner, 'Statistische und psychologische Klangprobleme', *Die Reihe*, vol. 1 (1955), 22–8

'Möglichkeiten der elektronischen Klangerzeugung' [1951], in Gianmario Borio and Hermann Danuser (eds.), *Im Zenit der Moderne* (Freiburg im Breisgau: Rombach, 1997), vol. III, 102–4

Misch, Imke, and Markus Bandur (eds.), *Karlheinz Stockhausen bei den Internationalen Ferienkursen für Neue Musik in Darmstadt 1951–1996: Dokumente und Briefe* (Kürten: Stockhausen, 2001)

Moldenhauer, Hille, '"Punktuelle" Musik und Filzpantoffeln: Eindrücke von den Internationalen Ferienkursen für Neue Musik', *Hamburger Echo*, 26 July 1952

Monod, David, *Settling Scores: German Music, Denazification, and the Americans, 1945–1953* (Chapel Hill, NC: University of North Carolina Press, 2005)

Muggler, Fritz, 'Der Zufall und die Musik: Notizen von den Darmstädter Ferienkurse für Neue Musik', *Musikalische Jugend*, October 1959

Müller, Paul, 'Schmelztiegel der Neuen Musik: Abschluß der Kranichsteiner Tage', *Rheinische Post*, 30 July 1952

Nattiez, Jean-Jacques, 'Cage and Boulez: A Chapter of Music History' [1990], in Jean-Jacques Nattiez (ed.), *The Boulez–Cage Correspondence*, tr. Robert Samuels (Cambridge University Press, 1993), 3–24

Nattiez, Jean-Jacques (ed.), *The Boulez–Cage Correspondence*, tr. Robert Samuels (Cambridge University Press, 1994 [1993])

Nauck, Gisela, *Risiko des kühnen Experiments: Der Rundfunk als Impulsgeber und Mäzen* (Saarbrücken: Pfau, 2004)

Neidhöfer, Christoph, 'Bruno Maderna's Serial Arrays', *Music Theory Online*, vol. 13, no. 1 (March 2007), www.mtosmt.org/issues/mto.07.13.1/mto.07.13.1.neidhofer.html (accessed 25 April 2011)

Nicholls, David, *John Cage* (Chicago, IL: University of Illinois Press, 2007)

Nielinger, Carola, '"The Song Unsung": Luigi Nono's *Il canto sospeso*', *Journal of the Royal Musical Association*, vol. 131, no. 1 (2006), 83–150

Nono, Luigi, 'Die Entwicklung der Reihentechnik', tr. Willi Reich, *Darmstädter Beiträge zur neuen Musik*, vol. 1 (1958), 25–37

'Die Angst vor der Freiheit', *Kölner Stadt-Anzeiger*, 4 October 1959

'Geschichte und Gegenwart in der Musik von heute' [1959], *Darmstädter Beiträge zur neuen Musik*, vol. 3 (1960), 41–7

'Gitterstäbe am Himmel der Freiheit' [1959], *Melos*, vol. 27 (1960), 69–75

'The Historical Reality of Music Today' [1959], *The Score*, vol. 27 (1960), 41–5

'Geschichte und Gegenwart in der Musik von heute' [1959], in Jürg Stenzl (ed.), *Luigi Nono: Texte, Studien zu seiner Musik* (Zürich: Atlantis, 1975), 34–40

'Text–Musik–Gesang' [1960], in Jürg Stenzl (ed.), *Luigi Nono: Texte, Studien zu seiner Musik* (Zürich: Atlantis, 1975), 41–60

'Luigi Dallapiccola e i *Sex carmina Alcaei*' [*ca.* 1948], in *Scritti e colloqui*, ed. Angela Ida De Benedictis and Veniero Rizzardi (Lucca: Ricordi, 2001), vol. I, 3–5

'Presenza storica nella musica d'oggi' [1959], in *Scritti e colloqui*, ed. Angela Ida De Benedictis and Veniero Rizzardi (Lucca: Ricordi, 2001), vol. I, 46–56

'Colloquio con Luigi Nono su musica e impegno politico' [1969], in *Scritti e colloqui*, ed. Angela Ida De Benedictis and Veniero Rizzardi (Lucca, Ricordi, 2001), vol. II, 42–75

'Intervista di Renato Garavaglia' [1979–80], in *Scritti e colloqui*, ed. Angela Ida De Benedictis and Veniero Rizzardi (Lucca: Ricordi, 2001), vol. II, 235–48

'Intervista di Philippe Albèra' [1987], in *Scritti e colloqui*, ed. Angela Ida De Benedictis and Veniero Rizzardi (Lucca: Ricordi, 2001), vol. II, 415–29

'Un'autobiografia dell'autore raccontata da Enzo Restagno' [1987], in *Scritti e colloqui*, ed. Angela Ida De Benedictis and Veniero Rizzardi (Lucca: Ricordi, 2001), vol. II, 477–563

'Ein Autobiographie des Komponisten Enzo Restagno mitgeteilt' [1987], in *Luigi Nono: Dokumente, Materielen*, ed. Andreas Wagner (Saarbrücken: Pfau, 2003), 34–138

Incontri: Luigi Nono im Gespräch mit Enzo Restagno, ed. Matteo Nanni and Rainer Schmusch (Hofheim: Wolke, 2004 [1987])

Oehlmann, Werner, 'Die junge Generation in Darmstadt: Instrumentale und elektronische Musik', *Der Tagespiegel*, 10 June 1955

Osmond-Smith, David, and Paul Attinello, 'Gay Darmstadt: Flamboyance and Rigour at the Summer Courses for New Music', in Paul Attinello, Christopher Fox, and Martin Iddon (eds.), *Other Darmstadts* (*Contemporary Music Review*, vol. 26, no. 1 (2007)), 105–14

Paddison, Max, *Adorno's Aesthetics of Music* (Cambridge University Press, 1997 [1993])

   Adorno, Modernism and Mass Culture (London: Kahn & Averill, 2004 [1996])

Paik, Nam June, '"Musik der Zufalls": Darmstädter Ferienkurse für Neue Musik', *Jayu Shinmun*, 6–7 January 1959

Patterson, David W., 'Cage and Asia: History and Sources', in David Nicholls (ed.), *The Cambridge Companion to John Cage* (Cambridge University Press, 2002), 41–59

Peyser, Joan, *Boulez: Composer, Conductor, Enigma* (London: Cassell, 1977 [1976])

Potter, Keith, 'Earle Brown in Context', *Musical Times*, vol. 127, no. 1726 (December 1986), 679, 681–3

   Four Musical Minimalists: La Monte Young, Terry Riley, Steve Reich, Philip Glass (Cambridge University Press, 2004 [1996]

Prieberg, Fred K., *Handbuch Deutsche Musiker 1933–1945* (Auprès des Zombry: self-published, 2004)

Pringsheim, Heinz, 'Kranichsteiner Ferienkurse', broadcast, Bayerischer Rundfunk, 3 June 1955, transcript IMD

Pritchett, James, 'David Tudor as Composer/Performer in Cage's *Variations II*', *Leonardo Music Journal*, vol. 14 (December 2004), 11–16

Raposo Martín, Juan José, *Luigi Nono: Epitafios Lorquianos. Estudio musicológico y analítico* (La Palma del Condado: Hergué, 2009)

Razumovsky, Andreas, 'Webern und die junge Generation: Die Darmstädter Ferienkurse 1957', *Frankfurter Allgemeine Zeitung*, 5 August 1957

Rebner, Wolfgang, 'Veteran im Vorfeld der Neuen Musik', *Darmstädter Echo*, 14 August 1954

  'Amerikanische Experimentalmusik' [1954], in Gianmario Borio and Hermann Danuser (eds.), *Im Zenit der Moderne* (Freiburg im Breisgau: Rombach, 1997), vol. III, 178–89

  'American Experimental Music', in Amy C. Beal, 'Negotiating Cultural Allies: American Music in Darmstadt, 1946–1956', *Journal of the American Musicological Society*, vol. 53, no. 1 (Spring 2000), 128–35

Rehmann, Ruth, 'Insel der Unseligen: Zu den Darmstädter Musiktagen', *Rheinische Merkur*, 20 July 1951

Revill, David, *The Roaring Silence: John Cage: A Life* (New York: Arcade, 1992)

Rittel, Ernst, 'Nachtstudio', broadcast, Südwestfunk, 30 August 1955, transcript IMD

Rizzardi, Veniero, 'La "nuova scuolo veneziana": 1948–1951', in Gianmario Borio, Giovanni Morelli, and Veniero Rizzardi (eds.), *Le musiche degli anni cinquanta* (Florence: Leo S. Olschki, 2004), 1–59

Rodemann, Albert, 'Musik der jungen Generation: Musikalische Jugend aus aller Welt in Darmstadt', *Allgemeine Zeitung*, 17 July 1951
  'Ein Tag des Experimentes: Zwei Veranstaltungen in den Kranichsteiner Ferienkursen', *Darmstädter Tagblatt*, 23 July 1952
  'Ein Unbekannter bildet Schule: Anton-Webern-Gedächtnis-Konzert im Seminar Marienhöhe', *Darmstädter Tagblatt*, 25–6 July 1953
  'Musik der jungen Generation III: Bandaufnahmen und Diskussions-Quartett im Radio Frankfurt', *Darmstädter Tagblatt*, 27 July 1953
  'Neue Musik in Darmstadt: Resumee der Internationalen Ferienkurse', *Allgemeine Zeitung*, 31 August 1954
  'Konkrete Ziel und abstraktes Ideal: Das Kammerorchester der Nordwestdeutschen Musik-Akademie Detmold', *Darmstädter Tagblatt*, 4 June 1955
Roderick, Peter, 'Rebulding a Culture: Studies in Italian Music after Fascism, 1943–1953' (unpublished PhD dissertation, University of York, 2010)
Ross, Alex, *The Rest is Noise: Listening to the Twentieth Century* (London: Harper Perennial, 2007)
Roth, Matthias, *Ein Rangierbahnhof der Moderne: Der Komponist Wolfgang Fortner und sein Schülerkries 1931–1986. Erinnerungen, Dokumente, Hintergründe, Porträts* (Freiburg im Breisgau: Rombach, 2008)
Rufer, Josef, 'Darmstädter Thema mit Variationen', *Der Mittag*, 7 September 1950
Rülke, Volker, 'Eduard Steuermann', in Rudolf Stephan, Lothar Knessl, Otto Tomek, Klaus Trapp, and Christopher Fox (eds.), *Von Kranichstein zur Gegenwart* (Stuttgart: DACO, 1996), 113–19
Runge, Gertrud, 'Gefahren der neuen Musik', *Welt am Sonntag*, 8 July 1951
  'Überorganisierte Tonkunst: Eindrücke von den Darmstädter Ferienkursen', *Die Zeit*, 7 August 1952
  'Ergebnis der Darmstädter Ferienkurse: Anschluß an die Weltmusik endlich wiedergewonnen', *Welt am Sonntag*, 2 August 1953
Sabbe, Herman, *Karlheinz Stockhausen: ... wie die Zeit verging ...*, ed. Heinz-Klaus Metzger and Rainer Riehn, Musik-Konzepte, vol. XIX (Munich: text +kritik, 1981)
Saunders, Frances Stonor, *Who Paid the Piper? The CIA and the Cultural Cold War* (London: Granta, 1999)
Schäfer, Thomas, 'Zwischen Schönberg und Stockhausen: Rudolf Kolisch bei den Internationalen Ferienkursen', in Rudolf Stephan, Lothar Knessl, Otto Tomek, Klaus Trapp, and Christopher Fox (eds.), *Von Kranichstein zur Gegenwart* (Stuttgart: DACO, 1996) 104–11
Schaller, Erika, *Klang und Zahl: Luigi Nono, serielles Komponieren zwischen 1955 und 1959* (Saarbrücken: Pfau, 1997)
Schibler, Armin, 'Rundschreiben', in Gianmario Borio and Hermann Danuser (eds.), *Im Zenit der Moderne* (Freiburg im Breisgau: Rombach, 1997), vol. III, 66–8
Schiffer, Brigitte, 'The Citadel of the Avant-Garde', *World of Music*, vol. 11, no. 3 (1969), 32–43

Schlösser, Inge, 'Zu neuen Interpretationsweisen: Einblick in ein Seminar: Der Klavierkurs David Tudors', *Darmstädter Echo*, 19 July 1956

   'Der neue Instrumentalstil: Darmstädter Aufführung der "Zeit-Maße" von Karlheinz Stockhausen', *Darmstädter Echo*, 25 July 1957

Schoenberg, Arnold, 'Hauer's Theories' [1923], in *Style and Idea*, ed. Leonard Stein, tr. Leo Black (London: Faber, 1975), 209–13

Schonberg, Harold C., 'U.S. Role Abroad: Varèse Says our Influence must be Cultural Too', *New York Times*, 8 October 1950

Schubert, Giselher, 'Musik gleich Wahrheit? Theodor W. Adornos Einfluß auf die Musikentwicklung in unserem Jahrhundert', in Hanspeter Krellmann (ed.), *Oper aktuell: Die Bayerische Staatsoper 1999/2000* (Munich: Bruckmann, 1999), 105–12

Searle, Humphrey, 'Young Composers at Darmstadt', *Halle: Magazine for the Music Lover* (October 1950), 7–9

   'Frankfurt ISCM – Darmstadt Summer School', *Monthly Musical Record* (September 1951), 185–6

Sebald, W. G., *The Natural History of Destruction*, tr. Anthea Bell (New York: Random House, 2003 [2001])

   Luftkrieg und Literatur (Frankfurt: Fischer, 2005 [2001])

Shultis, Christopher, 'Cage and Europe', in David Nicholls (ed.), *The Cambridge Companion to John Cage* (Cambridge University Press, 2002), 20–40

Smalley, Roger, 'Some Aspects of the Changing Relationship between Composer and Performer in Contemporary Music', *Proceedings of the Royal Musical Association*, vol. 96 (1969–70), 73–84

Spotts, Frederic, *Hitler and the Power of Aesthetics* (London: Pimlico, 2003 [2002])

Steinecke, Wolfgang, '2. Vortrage. Darmstadt', broadcast, Radio Basel, date unknown but presumably late 1950, transcript IMD

   'Positionen der neuen Musik heute', broadcast, Hessischer Rundfunk, 18 September 1953, transcript IMD

   'Internationale Ferienkurse für Neue Musik, Darmstadt 1956, III', broadcast, Hessischer Rundfunk, 20 September 1956, transcript IMD

   'Webern und die junge Generation', broadcast, Hessischer Rundfunk, 24 October 1957, transcript IMD

   '1. Bericht über die XII. Internationalen Ferienkurse für Neue Musik in Darmstadt 1957', broadcast, Bayerischer Rundfunk, 5 November 1957, transcript IMD

   'Neue Musik in Darmstadt 1946–1958', *Darmstädter Beiträge zur neuen Musik*, vol. 2 (1959), 75–94

   'Kranichstein – Geschichte, Idee, Ergebnisse', *Darmstädter Beiträge zur neuen Musik*, vol. 4 (1962), 9–24

Stenzl, Jürg, *Luigi Nono* (Reinbek bei Hamburg: Rowohlt, 1998)

Stephan, Rudolf, Lothar Knessl, Otto Tomek, Klaus Trapp, and Christopher Fox (eds.), *Von Kranichstein zur Gegenwart* (Stuttgart: DACO, 1996)

Stockhausen, Karlheinz, 'Weberns Konzert für 9 Instrumente op. 24: Analyse des ersten Satzes', *Melos*, vol. 20, no. 12 (December 1953), 343–8

'... wie die Zeit vergeht ...', *Die Reihe*, vol. 3 (1957), 13–42

'Sprache und Musik' [1957], *Darmstädter Beiträge zur neuen Musik*, vol. 1 (1958), 57–81

'Musik und Raum' [1958], *Darmstädter Beiträge zur neuen Musik*, vol. 2 (1959), 30–5

'Musik und Graphik' [1959], *Darmstädter Beiträge zur neuen Musik*, vol. 3 (1960), 5–25

'Steineckes Tod', in Wolfgang Fortner, Pierre Boulez, Bruno Maderna, Luigi Nono, and Karlheinz Stockhausen, 'Wolfgang Steinecke in memoriam', *Melos*, vol. 29, no. 2 (February 1962), 56–7

'Weberns Konzert für 9 Instrumente op. 24: Analyse des ersten Satzes' [1953], in *Texte*, ed. Dieter Schnebel, vol. I (Cologne: DuMont, 1963), 24–31

'... wie die Zeit vergeht ...' [1957], in *Texte*, ed. Dieter Schnebel, vol. I (Cologne: DuMont, 1963), 99–139

Texte, ed. Dieter Schnebel, 3 vols. (Cologne: DuMont, 1963, 1964, 1971)

'Komposition 1953 Nr. 2: Studie I, Analyse' [1954], in *Texte*, ed. Dieter Schnebel, vol. II (Cologne: DuMont, 1964), 23–36

'Klavierstück XI' [1956], in *Texte*, ed. Dieter Schnebel, vol. II (Cologne: DuMont, 1964), 69

'Musik und Sprache III' [1957], in *Texte*, ed. Dieter Schnebel, vol. II (Cologne: DuMont, 1964), 58–60

'Nr. 9: Zyklus für einen Schlagzeuger (1959)' [1959], in *Texte*, ed. Dieter Schnebel, vol. II (Cologne: DuMont, 1964), 73–100

'Vieldeutige Form' [1960], in *Texte*, ed. Dieter Schnebel, vol. II (Cologne: DuMont, 1964), 245–61

'Music and Speech' [1960], tr. Ruth Koenig, *Die Reihe*, vol. 6 (1964), 40–64

'Steineckes Tod' [1962], in *Texte*, ed. Dieter Schnebel, vol. II (Cologne: DuMont, 1964), 243–44

'Kölner Kurse für Neue Musik', in *Texte*, ed. Dieter Schnebel, vol. III (Cologne: DuMont, 1971), 196–211

'Intuitive Music' [1971], in *Stockhausen on Music: Lectures & Interviews*, ed. Robin Maconie (London: Marion Boyars, 1989), 112–25

Stockhausen, Karlheinz, and Heinz-Klaus Metzger, 'Vieldeutige Form' [1960], in Heinz-Klaus Metzger and Rainer Riehn (eds.), *Darmstadt-Dokumente I* (Munich: text+kritik, 1999), 184–207

Struck-Schloen, Michael, 'Wie ein Bad in kochendem Wasser – die WDR-Klangkörper als "Instrumente" Neuer Musik', in Frank Hilberg and Harry Vogt (eds.), *Musik der Zeit 1951–2001: 50 Jahre Neue Musik im WDR* (Hofheim: Wolke, 2002), 117–24

Stuckenschmidt, Hans Heinz, 'Apokalyptische Gespräche und Klänge: Nachwort zum Sommer der Neuen Musik in Darmstadt', *Neue Zeitung*, 7 August 1949

'Spielerei, Pathos und Verinnerlichung: Abschluß der Darmstädter Konzertreihe', *Neue Zeitung*, 30 August 1950

'Leidenschaftlich suchen Komponisten nach neuen Ordnungen und Formen der Musik', *Die Welt*, 8 June 1955

'Drei Generation Neuer Musik in Darmstadt', *Berichte und Information*, 17 June 1955

'Das Laboratorium der Neutöner: Zehn Jahre Darmstädter Ferienkurse', *Deutsche Zeitung*, 25 July 1956

'Der Heiligenberg der Neuen Musik: Lagebericht von den Darmstädter Ferienkursen', *Frankfurter Allgemeine Zeitung*, 13 September 1958

Taruskin, Richard, *Music in the Late Twentieth Century*, The Oxford History of Western Music, vol. V (Oxford University Press, 2010 [2005])

Thacker, Toby, *Music after Hitler, 1945-1955* (Farnham: Ashgate, 2007)

Thévenin, Paule, 'A Letter on Artaud', *Tulane Drama Review*, vol. 9, no. 3 (Spring 1965), 99–117

Thomas, Ernst, 'Die Situation des "kaputt"', *Darmstädter Echo*, 27 July 1953

'Werkstatt für Neue Musik: Die Darmstädter Ferienkurse im Jubiläumsjahr', *Düsseldorfer Nachrichten*, 9 June 1955

'Klänge für das Auge? Gefährliche Doktrinen auf den Darmstädter Ferienkursen', *Frankfurter Allgemeine Zeitung*, 1 September 1959

'Kontroverse und Konzert: Darmstädter Ferienkurse und Hessischer Rundfunk', *Frankfurter Allgemeine Zeitung*, 8 September 1959

'Darmstadt: Internationale Ferienkurse für Neue Musik', in German Section of the International Society for New Music (eds.), *Neue Musik in der Bundesrepublik Deutschland: Dokumentation 1958/59* (Mainz: Schott, 1959), 25–9

'Luigi Nono, Intolleranza', in *Der Neue Musikbericht: Eine Auswahl aus 100 Sendungen des Westdeutschen Rundfunks 1961-1966* (Cologne: Westdeutscher Rundfunk, 1967 [1961]), 11–16

Tomek, Otto, 'Darmstädter Ferienkurse 1959', broadcast, Westdeutscher Rundfunk, 26 October 1959, transcript IMD

Trudu, Antonio, *La 'scuola' di Darmstadt* (Milan: Unicopli, 1992)

Trumpff, Gustav Adolf, 'Das Wort dominierte', *Darmstädter Echo*, 7 July 1951

'Es geht um eine neue Musikästhetik: Versuche mit elektronische Musik – Karl Heinz [sic] Stockhausen's *Kreuzspiel*', *Darmstädter Echo*, 24 July 1952

'Musik der jungen Generation: Eindrücke von den Darmstädter Ferienkursen', *Göttinger Presse*, 30 July 1953

'Atelier für autonome Musik: Zwei Studioveranstaltungen auf der Marienhöhe', *Darmstädter Echo*, 20 July 1956

'Spiel auf zwei Flügeln: John Cage und David Tudor', *Darmstädter Echo*, 5 September 1958

'Das Crescendo der Ferienkurse: Drei Wochen "Neue Musik" im Rückspiegel', *Darmstädter Echo*, 9 September 1959

Ulman, Erik, 'The Music of Sylvano Bussotti', *Perspectives of New Music*, vol. 34, no. 2 (Summer 1996), 186–201

Ulmer, Judith S., *Gescichte des Georg-Büchner-Preises: Soziologie eines Rituals* (Berlin: Walter de Gruyter, 2006)

Ungeheuer, Elena, *Wie die elektronische Musik 'erfunden' wurde ... : Quellenstudie zu Werner Meyer-Epplers Entwurf zwischen 1949 und 1953* (Mainz: Schott, 1992)

 'In den Klang und in die Welt – elektronisches Komponieren in Nordrhein-Westfalen', in Heike Stumpf and Matthias Pannes (eds.), *Zeitklänge: Zur Neuen Musik in NRW 1946–1996* (Cologne: Studio, 1996), 45–53

Válek, Jiří, 'Neue Musik: Des Zaubers des Neuen beraubt', originally published in *Hudebni Rozhledy*, vol. 11, no. 19 (October 1958); German translation (translator unknown) IMD

Vietta, Egon, 'Gespräch, Experiment und Ärgernis: Bei den Kranichsteiner Ferienkurse für Neue Musik', *Stuttgarter Nachrichten*, 18 September 1958

Wagner, Andreas 'Jenseits von Humanität und Autonomie: Anmerkungen zu Luigi Nono', *Luigi Nono: Dokumente, Materielen*, ed. Andreas Wagner (Saarbrücken: Pfau, 2003), 168–77

Wehagen, Walther, 'Neue Musik in der Sackgasse', *Wiesbadener Kurier*, 20 July 1951

 'Vor-Ort neuer Musik: Darmstadt hat Schule gemacht', *Das blaue Blatt*, 1 September 1956

Whittall, Arnold, *Serialism* (Cambridge University Press, 2008)

Widmaier, Wolfgang, 'Catch as Cage Can: Drei Studios in Kranichstein', *Darmstädter Echo*, 12 September 1958

 '"Das größte Maul": Auch das gibt es bei den Kranichsteiner Ferienkursen', *Darmstädter Echo*, 15 July 1960

Williams, Alastair, *New Music and the Claims of Modernity* (Aldershot: Ashgate, 1997)

 'New Music, Late Style: Adorno's "Form in the New Music"', *Music Analysis*, vol. 27, nos. 2–3 (2008), 193–9

Willnauer, Franz, 'Heute: Die "Darmstädter Schule"', *Die Furche*, 7 September 1957

Wolpe, Stefan, 'On New (and Not-So-New) Music in America', tr. Austin Clarkson, *Journal of Music Theory*, vol. 28, no. 1 (Spring 1984), 1–45

Wood, Hugh, 'Darmstadt 1959' (unpublished report)

Wörner, Karl H., 'Jugend diskutiert über sich selbst: Die sechsten Kranichsteiner Internationalen Ferienkurse', *Mannheimer Morgen*, 13 July 1951

Xenakis, Iannis, 'La Crise de la musique serielle', *Gravesaner Blätter*, no. 1 (1955), 2–4

Zagorski, Marcus, '"Nach dem Weltuntergang": Adorno's Engagement with Postwar Music', *Journal of Musicology*, vol. 22, no. 4 (Fall 2005), 680–701

 'Material and History in the Aesthetics of "Serielle Musik"', *Journal of the Royal Musical Association*, vol. 134, no. 2 (November 2009), 271–317

Zenck, Claudia Maurer, 'Und dann ins Eck gestellt: Ernst Krenek als vermittlungswillige (und verschmähte) Vaterfigur', in Rudolf Stephan, Lothar Knessl, Otto Tomek, Klaus Trapp, and Christopher Fox (eds.), *Von Kranichstein zur Gegenwart* (Stuttgart: DACO, 1996), 156–63

Zenck, Martin, 'Auswirkung einer "musique informelle" auf die Neue Musik: Zu Theodor W. Adornos Formvorstellung', *International Review of the Aesthetics and Sociology of Music*, vol. 10, no. 2 (December 1979), 137–65

Unsigned newspaper articles by date

'Protest nach zwei Seiten: "Musik der jungen Generation" in Darmstadt', *Frankfurter Allgemeine Zeitung*, 30 August 1950

[K.], 'Musik der jungen Generation: Studienkonzert für Alban Berg und Ernst Krenek – das Ende der Experimente in Kranichstein', *Aachener Nachrichten*, 5 September 1950

[ski], 'Schoenberg, Webern, Berg: Die Vorträge zum Internationalen Zwölftonkongress', *Darmstädter Tagblatt*, 5 July 1951

[GE], 'Darmstädter Musikkurse werfen Probleme auf: Bloße Beherrschung des "Materials". Zwölftonkongreß: Nichts Neues', *Bochumer Anzeiger*, 18 July 1951.

[S.], 'Neue Musik in Kranichstein: Zwölftonkongreß –Woche der jungen Generation', *Kölner Stadt-Anzeiger*, 18 July 1951

[Kemp.], 'Die "Neue Musik" und die Gesellschaft: Für wen denn eigentlich schaffen unsere Jüngsten?', *Aachener Nachrichten*, 25 July 1952

[N.], 'Die Jugend der Neuen Musik in gefährdendem Zwielicht', *Abendpost*, 28 July 1952

[Gallus.], 'Mit Musik nichts zu tun: Schlußkonzert der Internationalen Ferienkurse für Neue Musik in Darmstadt', *Sozialistische Volkszeitung*, 3 August 1953

[hkr.], 'Nur noch routinierte Zwölftonerei: Die Darmstädter Ferienkurse für Neue Musik bald Sektiererei', *Pfälzische Volkszeitung*, 8 June 1955

[ski], 'Die Diskussion der Kritiker: Stuckenschmidt, Rostand und Rognoni zur neuen Musik', *Darmstädter Tagblatt*, 8 June 1955

[jg.], 'Konzert mit vielen Fragezeichen: John Cage und David Tudor an zwei Klavieren', *Darmstädter Tagblatt*, 5 September 1958

'Statt einer Erwiderung: Kabarett oder "Ernstcharakter" bei Cage', *Darmstädter Echo*, 17 September 1958

[mr] 'Kiss me Cage – oder: Ist das Musik? Von den XIII. Internationalen Ferienkursen für Neue Musik in Darmstadt', *Bonner Rundschau*, 15 October 1958

[ig], 'Ein vieldeutiger Vortrag: Referat von Stockhausen, von Metzger gelesen und kommentiert', *Darmstädter Tagblatt*, 15 July 1960

Index

Adorno, Theodor W. 3, 41, 45, 50–51, 53, 55, 62, 84, 85, 92–93, 110–116, 117, 118, 127–128, 129–141, 167, 175, 184, 189, 192–193, 229, 268–269, 272, 286–293, 297, 301
Amy, Gilbert, *Mouvements* (1958) 197, 200
Andriessen, Juriaan
   Hommage à Milhaud (1948) 103
Antheil, George 167
Arendt, Hannah 3
Arp, Hans 221
Artaud, Antonin 256–257
Augustine 240–241

Babbitt, Milton, Second String Quartet (1954) 174
Bach, Johann Sebastian 14
   The Art of Fugue 26, 204–205
Banks, Don, Violin Sonata (1953) 103
Barraqué, Jean 183
Bartók, Béla 16, 26, 28, 29, 126, 147, 181
   Suite for Piano (1916) 178
   Two Rumanian Dances (1909–10) 25
Bauman, Zygmunt 300–302
Baumann, Max, *Concerto grosso* (1950) 63
Beethoven, Ludwig van 14, 113, 218, 258, 293
Bennett, Richard Rodney 179
Berberian, Cathy 234, 274
Berg, Alban 10, 25, 26, 28, 93–94, 126, 130, 220–221, 222, 293
   Piano Sonata (1907–8, rev. 1920) 178
Bergson, Henri 132
Bergsträsser, Ludwig 13
Berio, Luciano 122, 135, 211, 231, 262, 279, 299
   Sequenza I (1958) 272
Beyer, Robert 64–66
Bitter, John 4
Bischoff, Friedrich 161
Blacher, Boris 29, 196, 225
   Orchestral Fantasy (1956) 225
Blume, Friedrich 10–11
Borries, Fritz von, *Magnus Fahlander* (1937) 10
Boulez, Pierre 58, 61, 69–70, 72, 84, 85, 89, 90, 92, 93–94, 95, 97, 98–100, 102, 104, 106, 107–109, 110, 112, 113, 115–120, 124, 125–128, 129, 131, 133, 138, 139–140, 141, 144, 145, 146–148, 154, 156, 157, 162, 167, 174, 180–181, 184–193, 195, 196–197, 211, 213–215, 219, 223–224, 229–231, 235, 252–255, 263, 271, 278–280, 284, 286–287, 289, 291, 293, 296–297, 299, 301–302

Deux études concrètes (1952) 69
First Piano Sonata (1946) 235
Flute Sonatine (1946) 178, 183, 288
Le Marteau sans maître (1953–5) 118, 135, 140, 147, 148, 149, 153, 154, 288, 290, 293, 301
Livre pour quatuor (1948–9) 140, 272
Pli selon pli (1957–62) 231, 293
Poésie pour pouvoir (1955–8) 197, 230
Polyphonie X (1951) 89, 140, 280, 293
Second Piano Sonata (1947–8) 68, 69, 140, 159, 288
Le Soleil des eaux (1948) 108
Structures (1952) 61, 69, 82–83, 107, 114, 119, 132, 140, 141, 144, 147, 152, 187, 189, 204, 280, 290
Third Piano Sonata (1955–7) 181, 189–193, 196, 247, 252–255, 280, 288, 291, 301
Le Visage nuptial (1946) 107–109
Brahms, Johannes 32
Brant, Henry, *Galaxy II* (1954) 261
Braunmühl, Hans Joachim von 64
Briehm, Tilla 50
Britten, Benjamin 29
   Lachrymae (1950) 103
Brown, Carolyn 160, 195, 261
Brown, Earle 132, 139, 140, 158–162, 173, 175–176, 194–195, 196, 214, 220, 230, 260, 263, 271, 292, 295, 302
   'December 1952' 132, 260
   Four Systems (1954) 132, 161, 200, 205–206
   Hodograph I (1959) 260–262, 265, 271
   Indices (1954, rev. 1957) 194–195, 204, 261
   Music for Cello and Piano (1955) 182, 183, 193–195
   Octet (1952–3) 133, 161
   Pentathis (1958) 195
   Perspectives (1952) 162, 179, 194
Brown, Netty 175
Bruckner, Anton 32
Burns, Ralph 21–22
Burri, Alberto 262
Buxtehude, Dieterich 14
Busoni, Ferruccio 65
Bussotti, Sylvano 107, 226, 232, 234–235, 237, 243–245, 247–248, 250–251, 263, 271
   Pièces de chair II (1958–60) 226, 231, 234, 240, 242–244, 248

Index

Cage, John 52, 69, 108, 119, 131–132, 140, 155, 156–164, 167–170, 171–177, 184, 186, 195, 196–228, 229–231, 235, 237, 239–242, 245–247, 249–256, 258–260, 266, 270–272, 274–275, 278–281, 284, 287, 291–292, 293, 295, 297–299, 300
   31'57.9864" (1954) 161, 162, 163
   34'46.776" (1954) 161, 162, 163, 210
   Aria (1958) 275
   A Book of Music (1944) 108, 156, 167
   Concert for Piano and Orchestra (1957–8) 197, 202, 225, 228, 231, 231, 240–243, 251, 288
   First Construction (in Metal) (1939) 108–109, 156, 202
   Fontana Mix (1958) 271, 275
   Imaginary Landscape No. 4 (1951) 168
   Music for Piano (1952–6) 202, 210, 215, 224
   Music of Changes (1951) 156, 159, 179–182, 187, 196, 202–204, 210, 280
   Second Construction (1940) 156
   Sonatas and Interludes (1946–8) 52, 202, 251
   String Quartet in Four Parts (1950) 251
   Two Pastorales (1952) 210
   Variations I (1958) 200, 201, 202–203, 207–210
   Williams Mix (1952) 161
   Winter Music (1957) 200, 201
Calonne, Jacques, *Trois bagatelles* (1956) 128
Cardew, Cornelius 179, 237, 239–240, 244–245, 271, 299
   February Piece I (1959) 231, 239–240
   Two Books of Study for Pianists (1958) 235
Carter, Elliott 20–21
Casella, Alfredo 26
Caskel, Christoph 233, 261–262, 298
Castigliono, Niccolò 179
Cerha, Friedrich 179
Char, René 203
Clay, Lucius 13
Copland, Aaron 50
Cowell, Henry 162, 167–168, 170, 173
Cunningham, Merce 157, 160, 195, 262–263, 298
   Springweather and People (1955) 261

Dahlhaus, Carl 300
dall'Oglio, Renzo, *Cinque espressioni* (1952) 86
Dallapiccola, Luigi 263
   Quaderno musicale di Annalibera (1952) 103
Dammert, Udo 19
Debussy, Claude 26, 118–119, 126–127, 181, 293
   Douze études (1915) 119
   Lindraja (1901) 103
Degen, Helmut 19, 24, 28
Deutsch, Max 129
Distler, Hugo 19, 24, 28
Dubensky, William 19, 20–21

Eco, Umberto 231
Egk, Werner 130

Eimert, Herbert 52–53, 62, 67, 70–71, 72, 85, 89–90, 92–93, 98, 100, 110–111, 112, 118, 129, 138, 150, 155, 156–157, 159, 162–163, 229, 291, 301
   Étude über Tongemische (1953–4) 162
   Glockenspiel (1953) 162
Eklund, Hans, *Kleine Serenade* (1954) 103
Engel, Ludwig 6, 8
Engelmann, Hans Ulrich 68
Erbse, Heimo, Piano Trio (1953) 103
Evarts, John 49, 238, 243

Faith, Walter, *Sinfonietta* (1950) 64
Falla, Manuel de 26, 29
Fano, Michel 107, 280
   Sonata for Two Pianos (1952) 104
Feldman, Morton 132, 139, 140, 158–162, 172–173, 175–176, 196, 214, 220, 292
   Intersection 3 (1953) 161, 162, 179, 205–206
   Three Pieces (1954) 179
   Two Pianos (1957) 200, 201
Ferrari, Luc, *ELYB* (1954) 128
Finkbeiner, Reinhold
   Ciacona (1954) 171
   Second String Quartet (1955) 128
Fortner, Wolfgang 13, 15, 17–19, 22, 23, 27, 28, 48, 51, 147, 229
   Chant de naissance (1958) 274–275
Frank, Maurits 48
Fricker, Peter Racine, Three Movements for Viola Solo (1955) 126
Furtwängler, Wilhelm 32

Gazzelloni, Severino 70, 171, 178, 235, 259, 261–262, 263, 269–270
Gerster, Ottmar 25
Gertler, André 67
Gesualdo, Carlo 150
Glanville-Hicks, Peggy 164, 167
Glock, William 32
Goehr, Alexander 102
   Piano Sonata (1951–2) 103
Goeyvaerts, Karel 51–52, 63, 67–68, 71, 72–73, 88, 89, 90, 91, 92, 94, 104, 106, 110, 115, 120, 129, 131, 133, 134, 136, 145, 153, 227, 280, 291, 292
   Komposition Nr. 5 (1953) 162
   Music for Violin, Contralto, and Piano (1948) 52, 58
   Opus 2 for 13 Instruments (1951) 67
   Opus 3 with Bowed and Struck Tones (1952) 68
   Second Violin Concerto (1951) 67–68
   Sonata for Two Pianos (1951) 40, 52–58, 66, 68, 73, 114, 175, 251, 288
Goléa, Antoine 45, 58–59, 65–66, 85, 89, 90, 220, 222
Górecki, Henryk 235
Göttig, Willy Werner 30, 63
Grano, Romolo 86

Gredinger, Paul
  Formanten I (1954) 162
  Formanten II (1954) 162
Grimaud, Yvette 63, 69

Hagen, Holger E. 22, 25
Hambraeus, Bengt 211, 214
  Gacelas y casidas de Federico García Lorca (1953) 103–104, 171
  Music for Trumpet, Violin and Piano (1949) 47
Hamel, Fred 25, 116
Hartmann, Karl Amadeus 29, 35, 126
Haubenstock-Ramati, Roman, *Interpolations* (1959) 275
Hauer, Josef Matthias 10, 16, 61, 92–93, 133
Häusler, Josef 284
Haydn, Joseph 293
Heiß, Hermann 2, 14–17, 22, 25, 27, 28, 51, 61, 90, 147, 159–160
  Blumenlieder (1936-7) 16
  Configuration I (1956) 225
  Jagdfliegermarsch (1940) 17
  Das Jahresrad (1931-2) 16
  Symphonisches Konzert (1944) 14
  Wir sind des Reiches leibhaftige Adler: Eine Fliegerkantate (1940) 17
Helm, Everett 20–21, 22, 49, 50, 124–125
  Eight Minutes for Two Pianos (1943) 171
Helms, Hans G. 216–218, 240
Helms, Khris 217
Henry, Pierre, and Pierre Schaefer
  Orphée 51 (1951) 66
  Symphonie pour un home seul (1949-50) 66
Henze, Hans Werner 68, 72, 108–109, 126, 146, 229, 252
  Boulevard Solitude (1952) 72
  Ode an den Westwind (1953) 103
  Quattro poemi (1955) 124
Hermann, Hugo 18, 24–25
Hesse, Hermann, *The Glass Bead Game* 58
Hindemith, Paul 10, 24, 25, 26, 27, 28–29, 32, 126
  Cello Concerto (1940) 29
  Die junge Magd (1922) 25
  Lehrstück (1929) 25
  Ludus tonalis (1942) 14, 25
  Das Marienleben (1922-3, rev. 1936-48) 25, 29
  Meditation (1938) 25
  Sixth String Quartet (1945) 29
  String Quartet in E flat (1943) 25
  Viola Sonata (1922) 29
  When Lilacs Last in the Door-Yard Bloom'd (1946) 29
Hinnenberg-Lefèbre, Margot 48
Höffer, Paul 19, 24, 28
Hofferberth, Willi 7
Hölderlin, Friedrich 14
Holl, Karl 26
Hommel, Friedrich 31, 303

Honegger, Arthur 24, 26, 29
  Fifth Symphony (1950) 59
Hovhaness, Alan 173
Hovhaness, Serafina 173
Husa, Karel, Second String Quartet (1953) 103

Ives, Charles 167–168

Jacobs, Paul 183, 252
Jaspers, Karl 3
Jemnitz, Sándor 147
Jennings, Terry 251
Johnson, Dennis 251
Jolivet, André, Piano Concerto (1949-50) 59
Joyce, James 252

Kafka, Franz 252
Kagel, Mauricio 107, 223–225, 233, 240, 245, 271, 286, 298
  Anagrama (1957-8) 275
  Transición II (1958-9) 231, 233–234, 245, 251
Kästner, Erich 2–3
Katunda, Eunice 43–44
Kaul, Hans Alexander 119
Kelting, Karl-Heinz 17
Klebe, Giselher 146
  Rhapsody (1953) 103
Knorr, Ernst-Lothar von 18
Kodály, Zoltán 29
Koenig, Gottfried Michael 83, 129–141, 179, 236, 284
  Horae (1950) 63
  Klangfiguren II (1955-6) 133, 140
Kolisch, Rudolf 125, 129, 167, 195, 229
Kontarsky, Alfons 194
Kotschenreuther, Hellmut 138
Kraus, Else C. 16, 50
Krenek, Ernst 24, 28, 147, 167, 195, 196, 197, 229
  Dark Waters (1950-1) 171
  Fourth Symphony (1947) 42
  Medea (1951-2) 103
Kruttge, Eigel 159–160, 163
Kuhlmann, Georg 25
Kuhnert, Rolf 178
Kulemann, Alfred 6

Lachenmann, Helmut 284, 290
Lange, Carl Mathieu 19
Lechner, Leonhard 14
Leibowitz, René 22, 27, 48, 102, 147
Lewinski, Wolf-Eberhard 99, 119, 124, 154–155, 168, 170–171, 174, 178, 192–193, 250, 254, 263–266, 286
Liebermann, Rolf 27, 48, 157
Ligeti, György 107, 228, 230, 298
Loriod, Yvonne 31, 67, 68, 69, 119

Index

Machaut, Guillaume de 150
Maderna, Bruno 35–37, 70, 71–72, 82–84, 86–87, 90, 106, 108–109, 115, 125–129, 131, 141, 143, 145, 146, 154, 180, 196, 198–200, 211, 261, 263, 275, 286, 287, 301
  Composizione (1948) 35
  Composizione II (1950) 36, 38–39
  Double Piano Concerto (1947–8) 35
  Fantasia and Fugue (1948) 35–36
  Musica su due dimensioni (1952) 48, 66–67, 68, 69, 70, 78–82, 84, 154
  Musica su due dimensioni (1957–8) 275
  Piano Concerto (1959) 261
  Quartetto per archi in due tempi (1955) 121–124, 127, 142, 144
  Tre liriche greche (1948) 35
Mahler, Gustav 41
Malina, Judith 173
Mallarmé, Stéphane 252–254
Mann, Thomas 3, 41
  Doktor Faustus 57
Manzoni, Giacomo 179
Maxfield, Richard 179
Mayer, Hans 26
Mayzumi, Toshiro 179
McClure, Robert A. 22
Meinecke, Friedrich 3
Mercenier, Marcelle 120, 164
Messiaen, Olivier 29, 31–32, 52, 58, 60, 65, 67, 71, 73, 89, 90, 117–118, 126, 280
  Canéyojdjayâ (1949) 103
  Île de feu II (1950) 178
  Le Merle noir (1951) 178
  Quatre études de rythme (1949–50) 31–32, 59–60, 73, 119, 132, 189, 280
    Mode de valeurs et d'intensités (1949) 178
  Quatuor pour la fin du temps (1940–1)
  Visions de l'amen (1943) 31
Metzger, Heinz-Klaus 43, 110, 115, 119, 129–135, 137–141, 184–186, 193, 213–214, 216, 222–228, 231, 251, 260, 267–268, 274–275, 276–284, 287, 289, 291–292, 295, 302
Metzger, Ludwig 2, 6–9, 12–14, 20, 29–30, 49
Meyer-Denkmann, Gertrud 292
Meyer-Eppler, Werner 48, 64–67, 81–82, 85, 96, 106, 169, 301
Michel, Günther 29
Michel, Wilhelm 7
Milhaud, Darius 24, 26, 126
Mozart, Wolfgang Amadeus 169, 293
Müller, Willy 17

Nedden, Otto zur 18
Nilsson, Bo 140, 211, 214
  VIII. Schlagfiguren (1956) 183
  Frekvenser (1955–6) 128
  Quantitäten (1958) 212
Noack, Friedrich 25
Nono, Luigi 35, 37, 43–45, 60, 67, 70, 71–72, 82–84, 89–90, 91–92, 95–101, 102, 106, 107, 112, 115, 116–118, 125–128, 129, 138, 140–146, 147, 149–151, 152, 162, 174, 180, 192, 196, 200, 211, 223, 224–225, 226, 229–231, 233, 235, 246, 255–261, 274, 278–279, 284, 287, 290, 291, 292, 293–294, 297, 301–302
  Canti per 13 (1955) 143, 150, 152
  Il canto sospeso (1955–6) 87, 143, 147, 148, 149–150, 153, 154, 155, 227, 294
  Composizione per orchestra n. 2: Diario polacco '58 (1958–9) 261, 262, 265–267, 273
  Cori di Didone (1958) 225, 235, 272
  Da un diario italiano (1964) 273
  España en el corazón (1952) 44, 68, 69, 78, 87–88, 99, 301
  Ha venido – canciones para Silvia (1960) 272
  Incontri (1955) 124–125, 142, 143, 145
  Intolleranza 1960 (1960) 125, 227, 273, 294
  Liebeslied (1954) 140
  Polifonica–Monodia–Ritmica (1951) 43, 45, 66, 76, 77–78, 143, 153, 272–273, 290, 293
  Sarà dolce tacere (1960) 263
  . . . sofferte onde serene . . . (1976) 273
  Variazioni canoniche (1950) 37–40, 44, 45, 76, 78, 140, 143, 293
  La Victoire de Guernica (1954) 103
  Y su sangre ya viene cantando (1952) 89, 99
Nordenstrom, Gladys, *Rondo* (1948) 178

Oehlschlägel, Reinhard 302
Orff, Carl 18
  Der Mond (1937–8) 26

Paik, Nam June 223–224
Pearson, William 234
Pepping, Ernst 19, 24, 28
Piston, Walter 29
Pfarrer, Georg 29–31
Pfitzner, Hans 41, 92, 227
Plum, Karl Otto 178
Pousseur, Henri 107–108, 132, 139, 145, 147, 211, 214, 229, 231, 286, 287, 291, 298–299
  Prospection (1953) 107
  Quintette à la mémoire de Webern (1955) 140
  Seismogramme (1955) 162
  Trois chants sacrés (1951) 103, 107, 171
  Variations I (1956) 183
Prokofiev, Sergei 24, 29

Radigan, Harold P. 20
Rathaus, Karol 10
Ravel, Maurice 26
  Frontispiece (1918) 103
Rebner, Wolfgang 108, 156, 159, 167–171, 176, 181
Reiber, Julius 5
Reich, Willi 48, 141
Reutter, Hermann 10, 18

Index

Richards, M.C. 160, 245, 270
Robinson, Keith 175
Rognoni, Luigi 116–117
Rosbaud, Hans 194, 276
Rosenberg, Wolf 216–217
Rostand, Claude 116–117
Rufer, Josef 38, 48, 49

Sabais, Heinz-Winfried 295
San, Herman Van 140
Schaeffer, Pierre 163
Schäfer, Kurt, *Divertimento* (1950) 64
Scherchen, Hermann 15, 19, 26, 35, 36, 50, 63–64, 108, 127, 134, 147
Schibler, Armin 97–98
Schiller, Friedrich, *Mary Stuart* 25
Schillinger, Joseph 256–258, 260, 271
Schlüter, Wilhelm 198
Schmidt, Hugo Wolfram 298
Schnabel, Gottfried
  Sinfonie (1950) 64
Schnebel, Dieter 43, 107
Schoenberg, Arnold 10, 16, 24, 25, 26, 28, 29, 48–51, 52, 61, 65, 93–94, 99, 111–112, 117–118, 126, 127, 130–133, 138, 142, 143, 145, 147, 162, 168, 181, 227, 229, 262–263, 288, 293
  Drei Klavierstücke (1909) 178
  Erwartung (1909) 132
  Five Orchestral Pieces (1909) 50
  Gurrelieder (1900–11) 50
  Moses und Aron (1930–2) 51, 62–63
  Piano Concerto (1942) 103
  String Trio (1946) 50
  A Survivor from Warsaw (1947) 42, 50, 227
  Variations (1926–8) 50, 141
  Violin Concerto (1934–6) 50
Schoenberg-Nono, Nuria 230, 262
Schröter, Heinz 71
Schuller, Gunter 174, 175
  Dramatic Overture (1951) 103
Seeman, Carl 36
Sessions, Roger 174
Shostakovich, Dmitri 24
Singer, Gerhard 14–15
Smetana, Bedřich 11
Stadlen, Peter 29, 36, 48, 64, 281
Stein, Gertrude 221
Steinecke, Hella 31, 295, 297
Steinecke, Wolfgang 6, 8–12, 14, 20, 23–24, 27–28, 29–31, 32, 37, 48–51, 59, 65, 69, 70, 71, 89–90, 100–101, 107–109, 116, 120, 127, 129, 141, 152, 158–159, 161, 162, 170, 172, 179, 181–185, 193, 194–195, 196–200, 212, 216, 224, 229–232, 261, 263, 267–268, 275–276, 276–278, 295–297, 302
Steuermann, Eduard 115, 167
Stockhausen, Karlheinz 43, 51, 52–53, 55–61, 63, 66, 67, 68, 70–75, 82–83, 89, 91, 92, 95, 96–101, 104–106, 108–109, 110, 114, 116–118, 119–120, 121, 125–128, 129, 131, 132–133, 135, 138–140, 141, 142, 145–152, 153, 155, 156, 159, 160, 162–164, 169, 173–174, 178–179, 184, 187, 192, 197–199, 211–212, 214, 217, 224–228, 230, 231–235, 236–245, 245–247, 249–252, 258, 263–266, 274, 276–287, 289–290, 293–294, 295, 299
  Carré (1959–60) 288, 294
  Gesang der Jünglinge (1955–6) 133, 140, 146, 147, 148, 151, 228, 294
  Gruppen (1955–7) 288
  Klavierstücke 104, 107, 120, 127, 132, 140, 163–164, 171, 178, 179
  Klavierstück III (1952–3) 74, 104–106, 115, 290, 301
  Klavierstück VI (1954–5) 188, 190
  Klavierstück X (1961) 295
  Klavierstück XI (1956) 146, 147, 164, 181, 182, 184, 192, 195, 196, 205, 207–208, 212, 215, 223–224, 227–228, 252, 255, 272, 280, 301
  Kontakte (1959–60) 288, 294
  Kontra-Punkte (1952–3) 89, 98–99, 140, 228
  Kreuzspiel (1951) 60, 68, 69, 75, 84–88, 232–233, 274–275, 280
  Momente (1962–9) 294
  Monophonie (uncompleted) 276, 281, 294
  Plus-Minus (1963) 238
  Studie I (1953) 140, 142, 145, 162
  Studie II (1954) 66, 140, 142, 162
  Telemusik (1966) 44
  Three Lieder (1950) 52
  Zeitmasse (1955–6) 132, 135, 140, 142, 145, 146, 147, 151, 187, 227, 288
  Zyklus (1959) 231, 235, 237–239, 241–242, 244–245, 246–247, 250–251
Strauss, Richard 1, 18, 41
  Der Rosenkavalier (1911) 1, 63
Stravinsky, Igor 10, 24, 26, 28, 29, 50, 85, 126
  Capriccio (1928–9) 103
  Duo concertant (1931–2) 25
  Serenade en la (1925) 25
Strecker, Ludwig 28
Strecker, Willy 26, 27–28
Strobel, Heinrich 15, 25, 26, 48, 85, 116, 127, 156–158, 160, 194, 276
Stuckenschmidt, Hans Heinz 15, 26, 36, 37–38, 48, 50, 116–117, 119, 120, 121, 127–128, 215, 221, 229
Stürmer, Bruno 19

Taube, Werner 194
Thesing, Paul 7
Thomas, Dylan 173
Thomas, Ernst 24, 98, 100, 127, 236, 246–250, 254, 265–266, 273, 274–275, 278, 298–299
Tiessen, Heinz 18
Toch, Ernst 10

Index

Togni, Camillo
   Flute Sonata (1953) 103, 171
   Omaggio a Bach (1952) 68, 69
Tomek, Otto 179, 197, 249, 251, 254–255, 265, 274
Tudor, David 126, 127, 128, 140, 146, 155, 158–164, 171, 181, 184, 187, 193, 195, 196–197, 199–201, 207–210, 214, 215, 220–221, 226, 230, 232–234, 238–243, 245–246, 248–249, 251, 252–253, 259–260, 261–262, 263, 266, 269–272, 274, 278–280, 295, 298, 300–302

Válek, Jiří 225
Varèse, Edgard 21, 40–43, 64–65, 129, 167–168, 194
   Density 21.5 (1936) 235
   Déserts (1950) 48
   Ionisation (1929–31) 42
Varga, Tibor 48, 50
Vedova, Emilio 262
Verdi, Giuseppe 63
Vogel, Wladimir 157
Voss, Friedrich, Wind Trio (1956) 128
Vriesen, Hellmuth 30
Vuataz, Roger 26

Wagner, Richard 136
Wambach, Bernhard 273
Webern, Anton von 25, 29, 39, 40, 52, 62, 88, 89–101, 107, 110–113, 115–116, 117–118, 119, 121, 124–125, 126–127, 128, 130–132, 141, 145, 147, 156–157, 162, 168, 173, 178, 218, 222, 229, 258, 263, 293
   Concerto (1934) 91, 96, 99–100
   Five Movements (1909) 90
   Four Pieces (1910–14) 90
   Six Bagatelles (1911–13) 90
   Symphony (1928) 126
   Three Lieder (1933–4) 90
   Three Short Pieces (1914) 90
   Variations (1940) 142–143
Weill, Kurt 10, 24, 28
Weinberger, Wilhelm 7
Weinheber, Josef 16
Widmaier, Wolfgang 179, 215, 221, 222, 283
Wildberger, Jacques
   Quartet for flute, clarinet, violin, and violoncello (1952) 68, 69
   Trio for oboe, clarinet, and bassoon (1952) 103, 108
Wilder, William 196
Wildgans, Friedrich 86
Williver, Wilson W. 13
Wolff, Christian 140, 158–162, 168, 170, 173, 175–176, 182, 196, 214, 216, 220, 230, 270, 292
   Duo for Pianists I (1957) 200, 201
   Duo for Pianists II (1958) 200, 206–207
   For Piano II (1953) 161
   For Piano with Preparations (1955) 183, 212
   For Prepared Piano (1951) 162
   Suite (1954) 179
Wolpe, Irma 172
Wolpe, Stefan 172–181, 194, 286
   Battle Piece (1943–7) 172, 179
   Passacaglia (1936) 177
   Two Studies 179
Wood, Hugh 264
Wörner, Karl H. 14, 25, 62, 229

Yates, Peter 270
Young, La Monte 251
   Study III (1959) 251
Yun, Isang 235

Zedler, Emmy 295
Ziegler, Hans Severus 18
Zillig, Winfried 50
Zimmerman, Bernd Alois 179
Zuckmayer, Eduard 48
Zulueta, Jorge 178

CPSIA information can be obtained at www.ICGtesting.com
Printed in the USA
LVOW02*0606180614

390404LV00003B/4/P